How do I get **Enhanced InSite**?

For Students

- If a printed access card is packaged with this text, log on to **Enhanced InSite** by using the pin code printed on the card.*
- If a printed access card is not packaged with this text, check your local college store, or purchase instant access to **Enhanced InSite** at **www.ichapters.com**, our preferred online store.*

ichapters.com

* You will also need a class ID and password from your instructor in order to gain access to the appropriate class.

24/7 Service and Support

Twenty-four hours a day, seven days a week, you have access to downloadable support documentation and our customer support team. Ask any question and get an immediate response!

Take a Virtual Tour at **www.cengage.com/insite**.

TECHNIQUES FOR COLLEGE WRITING: THE THESIS STATEMENT AND BEYOND

TECHNIQUES FOR COLLEGE WRITING: THE THESIS STATEMENT AND BEYOND

Kathleen Muller Moore
University of California, Riverside

....

Susie Lan Cassel
California State University, San Marcos

WADSWORTH
CENGAGE Learning™

Australia • Brazil • Japan • Korea • Mexico • Singapore • Spain • United Kingdom • United States

Techniques for College Writing: The Thesis Statement and Beyond

Kathleen Muller Moore

Susie Lan Cassel

Publisher: Lyn Uhl

Acquisitions Editor: Margaret Leslie

Assistant Editor: Amy Haines

Editorial Assistant: Elizabeth Ramsey

Media Editor: Amy Gibbons

Marketing Manager: Jennifer Zourdos

Marketing Coordinator: Ryan Ahern

Marketing Communications Manager: Stacey Purviance

Content Project Manager: Aimee Chevrette Bear

Art Director: Jill Ort

Print Buyer: Betsy Donaghey

Permissions Editor: Bob Kauser

Production Services: S4Carlisle Publishing Services

Text Designer: Gary Ragaglia

Photo Manager: Kelly Franz

Cover Designer: Gary Ragaglia

Compositor: S4Carlisle Publishing Services

For product information and technology assistance, contact us at **Cengage Learning Customer & Sales Support, 1-800-354-9706**

For permission to use material from this text or product, submit all requests online at **www.cengage.com/permissions**

Further permissions questions can be e-mailed to **permissionrequest@cengage.com**

Library of Congress Control Number: 2009933294

ISBN-13: 978-1-4130-3343-4
ISBN-10: 1-4130-3343-1

Wadsworth
20 Channel Center Street
Boston, MA 02210
USA

Cengage Learning is a leading provider of customized learning solutions with office locations around the globe, including Singapore, the United Kingdom, Australia, Mexico, Brazil, and Japan. Locate your local office at **international.cengage.com/region.**

Cengage Learning products are represented in Canada by Nelson Education, Ltd.

For your course and learning solutions, visit **www.cengage.com.**

Purchase any of our products at your local college store or at our preferred online store **www.ichapters.com.**

Printed in the United States of America
1 2 3 4 5 6 7 13 12 11 10 09

TECHNIQUES FOR COLLEGE WRITING: THE THESIS STATEMENT AND BEYOND

Table of Contents

PART II: Thinking Through Your Writing Assignment

PART III: Writing Beyond the Composition Classroom

About This Book

Techniques for College Writing: The Thesis Statement and Beyond draws warranted attention to the thesis statement in a way that has not been previously done. We realize that students at all levels of writing are probably already familiar with the concept of the thesis statement. However, when we asked our students to describe the purpose of the thesis statement and the characteristics of a good thesis statement, few could respond confidently. More importantly, their writing revealed only a fundamental understanding of this single, most important aspect of formal writing.

We believe that the thesis is the key to developing, organizing, and writing a successful paper. However, in our discussions with students, we learned that many approach writing by thinking they have little control over the success of their essays; far too often, the evaluation process is a mystery to them. They don't understand the criteria for their grade and often attribute it to the whims of the instructor. Sometimes they believe the grade should reflect the number of hours invested, the number of revisions completed or the amount of emotion exhibited for the subject matter. Some students believe that to get a good grade, they must write what they think the instructor wants to hear. The underlying problem is that many do not understand the objective criteria for evaluating formal papers. The first step toward empowering students as writers is to uncover these criteria, the most fundamental of which is a precise and well-focused thesis statement. In other words, writing an essay that is grammatically sound and contains an introduction, a set of body paragraphs, and a conclusion does not necessarily guarantee success. The thesis statement does the most work to unify these components and give them significance. In this sense, the thesis statement is the key to the mystery behind successful writing.

Once we recognized the benefits of thesis-focused workshops to critical thinking, reading, and writing, we went to college and commercial bookstores in search of a skill-building book we and our students could use to fine-tune the thesis-centered essay. We found that textbooks on writing often devote small sections to the thesis statement, but they never seemed to go far enough, especially for struggling students. With that in mind, we began developing activities in our classes to help students understand the role of the thesis and to perfect their own. This book describes the techniques that were successful. We have deliberately presented them in a form we hope is accessible to students working on their own as well as to instructors who might use this book, whole or in part, in class.

Preface

To Students

We have tried to demonstrate the book's concepts using examples drawn from a broad range of topics in the hope that all students, no matter their particular coursework or major, would find at least some of the examples to be relevant to their current studies. As you read through the examples in this book, you may find that some of the novels or subjects referred to are unfamiliar to you. Therefore, we've provided **Did You Know . . .** boxes to fill in some of the background and help make the examples meaningful. We hope you will be able to master the techniques being illustrated and that you won't be distracted by the materials being used to illustrate them. Try to see the point we are getting at in each example and how it can apply to your current writing assignment.

To Instructors

Some may argue that *Techniques for College Writing* is overly traditional in its approach to writing. They may see our writing strategies as too rigid in an arena where they believe the expression of ideas is hampered rather than helped by the constraints of a stringent thesis. We believe that working with the techniques in this book provides a strong foundation for good writing. Students benefit from clear prescriptions to guide their development as writers. Without this kind of guidance, developing writers are left floundering and discouraged. The conventions and strategies that are a central part of *Techniques'* approach are like a safety net for an acrobat—something that, when well placed, can always be relied on. It is important, however, that instructors and students use them with flexibility. Without flexibility, guidelines become constraints that inhibit, rather than promote, the thinking and writing process. Like most basic steps, the strategies and conventions in this book are meant to serve as tools to enable their users. As writers gain confidence, they will be able to incorporate these techniques into their personal styles in effective and creative ways.

How to Use This Book

This book is divided into three parts that build on one another. **Part One (Thinking Through the Thesis Statement)** introduces the basics for writing a paper—from thinking about the audience and format to developing a thesis statement and concluding well. **Part Two (Thinking Through Your Writing Assignment)** moves to the next stage of the writing process by looking more closely at the writing prompt and its requirements to plan a response that is relevant and appropriate. **Part Three (Writing Beyond the Composition Classroom)** looks beyond the composition classroom to more specialized writing, such as writing for a scientific paper, an informative paper, and literature reviews.

More specifically, **Chapter One** overviews the academic essay, including the thesis statement and its basic and fundamental role in the essay. **Chapter Two** describes the components of effective thesis statements. **Chapter Three** presents several techniques for developing and writing a working thesis. **Chapter Four** shows how the thesis relates to and determines the rest of the paper through its burdens of proof. **Chapter Five** provides techniques for drafting and revising the essay through the lens of the thesis statement. **Chapters Six** and **Seven** examine several types of writing assignments and strategies for responding to them successfully. **Chapter Eight** looks at college writing across the disciplines and presents two additional essay formats—the informative essay and the scientific essay—as well as two stand-alone pre-essay formats—the lab report and the field notebook. **Chapter Nine** shows how to write about literature, and **Chapter Ten** explains how to write a paper that includes research information.

Within the chapters, we have many useful features. Each chapter, after a brief introduction, opens with a **What's Ahead** box that glosses the contents of that chapter for easy reference and review. The most important techniques are often listed as steps that are carefully discussed and thoroughly illustrated, often with several different examples. When we use examples that might benefit from a little background information, we add a **Did You Know . . .** box. We try to appeal to different kinds of learners by including graphs, charts, and visual images when possible, both in the text and the exercises. With particularly difficult or important concepts, **For Practice** exercises are inserted immediately into the text, as well as added to the end-of-chapter exercises. A wide range of essays by journalists, students, and well-known authors are included for broad audience appeal. **Thinking Through a Reading** questions precede each essay and are designed for active reading and in-class discussion. Often, checklists are included at the end of sections, such as those for following the academic essay format or for peer review, to help reinforce techniques that were covered. Each chapter concludes with **applications** that ask students to apply the techniques introduced, as well as **exercises** that aim to broaden writing skills. At the end of each part are **revision tools** and **writing assignments** that seek to reinforce the skills covered in each section of the book. Finally, **three appendices** are designed as reference tools that can be used at any time. They take some of the book's concepts to a more advanced level. For instance, they examine the "common pitfalls" of the thesis statement and identify some logical patterns of argument in the thesis statement. Appendix C identifies important grammar, style, and citation issues. Together, the writing and critical thinking techniques contained in this book can help you approach any writing assignment successfully.

Let us be clear that in advocating these techniques for thesis development, we are not arguing that this approach should replace the prewriting and revision that writers are doing now. Rather, we are suggesting that placing the priority on the thesis statement (like we do here) will empower students by giving them objective tools that add more structure and control to the entire process of writing. Prioritizing a well-developed thesis statement may be the most powerful means for promoting critical reading and thinking. We hope that, by understanding the fundamentals and mastering the techniques, students will grow to be more confident and effective writers.

Resources for Students and Instructors

Book Companion Website Visit the book companion website at www.cengage.com/english/moore to access valuable course resources. Resources for students include an extensive library of interactive exercises and animations that cover grammar, diction, mechanics, punctuation, research, and writing concepts, as well as a complete library of student papers and a section on avoiding plagiarism. The site also offers a downloadable Instructor's Manual.

Enhanced InSite™ With **Enhanced InSite for Composition™**, instructors and students gain access to the proven, class-tested capabilities of **InSite**—such as peer reviewing, electronic grading, and originality checking—*plus* resources designed to help students become more successful and confident writers, including access to the **Personal Tutor**, an interactive handbook, tutorials, and more. Other features include fully integrated discussion boards, streamlined assignment creation, and access to **InfoTrac® College Edition**. To learn more, visit www.cengage.com/insite.

Infotrac® College Edition with InfoMarks™ InfoTrac® College Edition, an online research and learning center, offers more than 20 million full-text articles from nearly 6,000 scholarly and popular periodicals. The articles cover a broad spectrum of disciplines and topics—ideal for every type of researcher.

Online Instructor's Manual Available for download on the book companion website, this Instructor's Manual provides answers to exercises in the book as well as basic classroom practices. Other features include Short Writing Prompts, Discussion Questions, Activities, Supplemental Material, Cross-References, Instruction Points, and Exercises.

About the Authors

Kathleen Muller Moore has an MA and PhD from the University of California Riverside. She has been teaching composition for more than ten years and is currently an Associate Director in the University Writing Program at the University of California, Riverside. She is also a coauthor of *Write It: A Process Approach to College Essays*, now in its second edition.

Susie Lan Cassel is Professor of Literature and Writing Studies at California State University, San Marcos. She has an MA from Harvard University and a PhD from the University of California. She is an award-winning teacher. Her first book, *The Chinese in America: A History from Gold Mountain to the New Millennium*, was nominated for the Association of Asian-American Studies Book Award in History. She has published articles in the *Journal of Asian-American Studies* (JAAS), *Frontiers: A Journal of Women's Studies*, *Reflections: On Community-Based Writing Instruction*, and the MLA's *Profession*. Her current project, "The Ah Quin Diaries," is supported by grants from the National Endowment for the Humanities, the American Philosophical Society, and the National Historical Publications and Records Commission.

Acknowledgments

In the ten years that have passed since we began writing this textbook, numerous people have offered generous support, without which this book would not have come to fruition. Our greatest thanks go to Aron Keesbury, our original Cengage editor, and Mary Beth Walden, our developmental editor. Their extraordinary vision and skill took our rough manuscript to its present coherent form. It was an honor and pleasure to work with them. Thanks also to Alexandra Kasuboske for believing in our work enough to bring it to Aron's attention. Thanks to publisher Lyn Uhl for her decision to give this book a chance; to our editor, Margaret Leslie; and to the skilled and dedicated Cengage team that guided this book through production.

We owe many students, colleagues, and friends our appreciation for their feedback on early versions of this text. Included among them are Staci Beavers, Jayne Braman, Donna Bradley Burcher, Darel Engen, Dawn Formo, Chris Johnson, Deborah MacLean Rider, Linda Strahan, Piper Ann Walsh, and Elissa Weeks. We are grateful to those whose ideas and suggestions have improved this work, including Peter Arnade, David Barsky, Stephan Cox, Thomas Dean, Denise Garcia, Sharon Hamill, Michael McDuffie, David D. Phillips, and Michael Schmidt. Kathleen's thanks go to Dorothy Delorio Muller, Susan Muller, and Bill Muller for their good suggestions and steady support. Finally, Susie would like to thank her parents, Lan Mieu Cassel and especially Russell N. Cassel, who never failed to ask about the book, no matter how long it took and how slow the progress.

We are thankful for the many insightful comments from the reviewers who have helped to shape this book. Their responses made valuable contributions to its development.

Susan B. Achziger, *Community College of Aurora*
Lisa Angius, *Long Island University*
Dean Bartow, *Laramie County Community College*
John Lansingh Bennett, *Lake Land College*
Joe Carrithers, *Fullerton College*
Anita L. Cook, *Bridgewater College*
Annamaria Deidesheimer, *SUNY Morrisville*
Magdalen Dugan Doss, *Santa Rosa Junior College*
Africa Fine, *Palm Beach Community College*
Charles Fox, *Georgia Perimeter College*
Fiona Glade, *Sacramento State University*

Katherine A. Hagopian, *North Carolina State University*
Lita Hooper-Simanga, *Georgia Perimeter College*
Sara E. Hosey, *Nassau Community College*
Mickey Kessler, *Washington State Community College*
Amy King, *Nassau Community College*
Noel Kinnamon, *Mars Hill College*
Linda L. Lawliss, *College of the Desert*
Gloria Lessmann, *Bellevue University*
Kara Lybarger-Monson, *Moorpark College*
Rachel Maverick, *Richland College*
Diana Nystedt, *Palo Alto College*
Denise Padgett, *Wallace Community College*
Roxanna Pisiak, *Morrisville State College*
Cris J. Robins, *Ranken Technical College*
John O. Rogers Jr., *Tennessee Temple University*
Richard Sabolick, *Chaffey College*
Deborah A. Scally, *Art Institute of Dallas and Richland College*
Margaret D. Smith, *Bainbridge College*
Alan Trusky, *Florence-Darlington Technical College*
Ben Varner, *University of Northern Colorado*
Carolyn K. B. Youngbauer, *Minnesota School of Business/Globe University*

Kathleen Muller Moore
Susie Lan Cassel
August 2009

Part One

THINKING THROUGH THE THESIS STATEMENT

CHAPTER 1

Defining the Thesis Statement and the Academic Essay

This textbook is designed to provide you with the tools you need to create successful academic essays and to enhance your writing in general. To become a good writer, you must develop skills in critical reading and thinking, and you must learn how to organize and present the results of that intensive study in a conventional format that communicates your ideas clearly and persuasively. To that end, this book approaches college *] college writing* writing with the understanding that the basic tool necessary to create a successful academic essay is the thesis statement. The thesis statement provides an essay with a central purpose—an organizing principle—for all of its parts. The first several chapters of this text teach you how to formulate a working thesis statement so that you can create, even at the beginning of your coursework, very effective essays. Subsequent chapters provide you with additional tools and techniques that lead you, step-by-step, toward enhancing your critical thinking and analysis skills and applying those insights to your writing. In short, in this textbook you will learn how to think through the thesis statement to write winning essays.

WHAT'S AHEAD...

► the origins of the academic essay

► overview of the academic essay

► the importance of the thesis statement

► the academic essay format

► organization and the essay's format

► the audience and effective persuasion

► an overview of the writing process

Origins of the Academic Essay

In the Western tradition, **rhetoric**, the formal study of the art of persuasive speaking and writing, began about 2,500 years ago on an island in the Mediterranean Sea now called Sicily. Two Greek scholars from that island, Corax and Teisias, initiated the systematic analysis of the elements of persuasion, and their lessons were so influential that in 427 BCE, Gorgias of Leontinoi brought this knowledge to Athens. At the time, Athens was breaking new political ground with a form of government called a democracy. Rather than be governed by a religious leader (a theocracy) or a small group of elite men (an oligarchy), Athens created an Assembly where any adult Athenian male citizen could cast a vote on matters that affected the entire city (such as laws on taxes and citizenship), as well as matters that affected individuals (such as lawsuits between neighbors). The Assembly met about forty times a year, and speakers, comparable to modern-day politicians and lawyers, took the stand to make arguments regarding whatever issue was under consideration. At least 6,000 eligible voters, the number required for a quorum, sat in the audience, and decisions were made based on a simple majority of the votes cast. The ability of a speaker to persuade an audience often made the difference between owning or losing property, establishing favorable or unfavorable laws, and even being granted life or death.

When Gorgias of Leontinoi arrived in Athens with the beginnings of rhetoric—this scholarly study of persuasive speaking and writing—it captured the interest of the leading thinkers of the day who would, in turn, further develop this important craft. Orators were eager for lessons that would help them to be more successful speakers, and scholars were excited about the systematic analysis of language, form, audience, and function. The most influential rhetoric expert during this late Classical period of Greek history was Aristotle (384–322 BCE) who synthesized and codified the beliefs of his day in his book *Rhetoric* (completed around 330 BCE).

....

DID YOU KNOW...

Aristotle was a philosopher who was born in 384 BCE at Stagira in northern Greece. At the age of eighteen, he went to Athens to study in the Academy of Plato where he learned science, mathematics, literature, and rhetoric.

....

Through his studies, Aristotle realized that all Athenian speeches relied on persuasion, so he attempted to formalize the characteristics of speeches that writers could use to persuade. He identified some twenty-eight types of logical arguments that could be used for any speech. He then prescribed a four-part format for arranging the different elements within a speech, based on the metaphor of the human body. According to Aristotle, the successful speech should begin with an *introduction* (exordium) that serves as the head of the speech. It should then *state the issue*, give the *proof* for the argument in the *body*, and end with a *conclusion* (epilogue).[1]

---

[1] See David Phillips, *Athenian Political Oratory: 16 Key Speeches* (New York: Routledge, 2004), 4.

Whether you realize it or not, you have probably used this format many times for persuasive speaking. Imagine, for example, asking your parents for extra money to meet the necessary demands of college life. You would probably frame your request with some *introduction* that softens your audience and paves the way for what follows. Once your listeners are prepared, you might *state the issue*—that you need money for unforeseen expenses. Your claim of necessity would have to be supported with evidence and explanation (*proof*). Likely, you would search for the best examples possible, ones that you think your parents would find convincing. These might include the need for additional school supplies; extra snacks for late-night studying; spending money for occasional entertainment; and unexpected transportation costs for required visits to libraries, museums, or study halls. For each of these topics, you might offer a specific example, like describing a workbook an instructor assigned, which you have not been able to afford and which you need to study for a test. Using concrete evidence like the need for a workbook shows your benefactors why extra money is warranted in more explicit terms than the general idea "school supplies." You will likely anticipate their counterargument—that they have already given you money—and you will explain carefully why you cannot afford these items on your current budget. When you have exhausted your list of examples (or your parents' time and patience), you would *conclude* by reminding them of your request and quickly summarizing your most salient points. This four-part speech format that includes (1) an introduction, (2) a statement of the issue, (3) proof for the argument, and (4) a conclusion has shown itself over thousands of years to be effective, in part because audiences have learned to expect these persuasive conventions.

While our modern cities don't hold formal assemblies to cast votes, we can see the continuing influence of Athenian democracy in terms of our reliance on persuasive communication for civic, legal, professional, and even personal matters. Our society is inundated with persuasive appeals from politicians who use it for election propaganda, lawyers who foster it for courtroom speeches, companies that perfect it for advertisement purposes, and individuals who hone it for things as various as personal ads and job interviews. In short, to have a measure of confidence—better yet, power and/or control—in a democratic society, one must be able both to create persuasive arguments and to assess arguments for their validity. These skills are often taught in college through the critical reading and writing of academic essays. As you'll soon see, democracy is not the only thing we have inherited from ancient Greece; the academic essay as we know it today is largely based on Aristotle's four-part prescription for a successful speech.

Aristotle's Four-Part Speech	Purpose	Academic Essay Part
1. Head (exordium)	thoughtful beginning	Introduction
2. State the issue	orient the audience	Thesis Statement
3. Body	give the proof for the argument	Evidence
4. End (epilogue)	thoughtful ending	Conclusion

Overview of the Academic Essay

The **academic essay** is the most commonly assigned essay format in college. Like Aristotle's four-part prescription for a speech, it provides a formal structure for presenting an argument but this time in terms of writing. It begins with an *introduction* that includes a *statement of the issue* (a thesis statement), body paragraphs that provide concrete evidence or *proof* of the argument, and a *conclusion* that purposefully and strategically closes the essay. Like speeches in Athens, the academic essay's primary goal is to *persuade*.

....

DID YOU KNOW...

Michel de Montaigne (1533–1592) was the first writer to use the French term *essai* or "attempt" to describe his short, descriptive pieces of writing in French. Several years later, Francis Bacon used the same term to describe his English-language writings. The genre of the essay, partly because of its short length, its succinct style, and its ability to contain both formal and informal arguments, was embraced by the university and eventually codified in a form that prescribes an introduction (with a thesis statement), body paragraphs, and a conclusion.

....

In college classes, instructors from across the disciplines regularly require an academic essay for the successful completion of a class. They often assign students to use it to offer an interpretation of a text, to give an evaluation of a subject or project, or to take a position on an issue. The five-paragraph essay that you may have become acquainted with in high school is a precursor to the academic essay format. However, the academic essay goes beyond the restrictiveness of the five-paragraph essay by allowing for more than just three paragraphs of support and including additional expectations for the overarching statement (the thesis statement), the level of argumentation, and the unity of the paper.

The academic essay provides an opportunity through writing to ask a critical question and develop a meaningful response, but it is important to keep in mind that literally proving something to be absolutely true is not its primary goal. When we engage in the critical thinking process with the goal of writing a persuasive essay, we hope to push the boundaries of our understanding a little further, to discover a perspective or point of view on our world or our lives that is meaningful. Therefore, the standard of proof for the academic essay is that you have made a **valid and compelling argument**, rather than an **objectively true** argument. After all, if something were "objectively true," then it would be a statement of fact and would not require an argument in the first place.

This is a difficult concept, so let's look at an example. We have said that academic essays focus on matters of interpretation rather than matters of fact, but these interpretations, to be valid, must be derived from facts. For example, several scholars may research the life of President Franklin D. Roosevelt and collect the same objectively true facts about, say, his presidency, such as the date of his inauguration, his speeches, his travels, his political platform, and his political appointees. Yet each researcher might interpret the facts of Roosevelt's presidency in a different way. Each could offer a different interpretation of what those facts add up to regarding, for example, the influence his terms as president had on the

OPINION/INTERPRETATION VS. FACTS

American Constitution, or the domestic economy, or the twentieth century. Given that these various interpretations are based on the facts of his life, they could all be equally valid and compelling. More importantly, together these various viewpoints give us a larger perspective on—and a more reliable understanding of—Roosevelt's presidency and its importance in American history.

To communicate its ideas and to present its case, the academic essay therefore relies on precise, polished language and logical, organized persuasion or argumentation. Its ultimate goal is to offer interesting ideas in a realm where there is room for multiple perspectives. Its focus on systematic reasoning and drawing sound conclusions harkens back to its ancient Greek predecessors, yet it remains a useful format for exploring a number of different topics in a variety of arenas today. This is especially true in college, as the following examples show.

English and Composition
- give an interpretation and/or analysis of a literary work (a literary criticism)
- read an essay that offers an argument (like those in the opinion or editorial pages of the newspaper) and give your own position on the subject

Social Science
- give your views on a controversial current event (that is, write your own opinion/editorial piece)
- compare the achievements of two different cultures

History
- give a viewpoint on a historical incident, person, time frame, or cultural event

Philosophy
- analyze a philosophical argument

Business
- assess the effectiveness of a program, company, strategy, or experiment

Science
- assess the value of a recent scientific or technological discovery

Art
- offer an interpretation of a work of art or cultural artifact

Any Class
- review the literature on a certain topic (a literature review)
- evaluate the contributions of a famous person
- determine the significance of a concept or special term in your field of study

It might be tempting to view the academic essay as a needlessly formal, overly prescriptive, and artificially narrow type of writing that has little to do with life outside of college. However, while learning to perfect the art of persuasive writing, you will also be learning skills applicable to the world outside of college, such as the following:

- how to communicate clearly and effectively

- how to critically analyze issues, formulate logical arguments, and persuasively express your opinions

- how to hone your own writing process by systematically considering audience, organization, style, and format

- how to evaluate the credibility of different sources of information and what you can/cannot understand at face value

- how to recognize and use a conventional format for writing

  (The professional world is filled with conventional formats for writing, including memos, proposals, year-end reports, project plans, and grants. There are even specialized writing formats associated with certain industries and local or regional offices. The academic essay format may be the most popular writing format used in college, but the sooner you learn to recognize and use writing formats, the more successful your writing will be.)

The Importance of the Thesis Statement

The thesis statement is the modern version of what Aristotle called the "statement of the issue," and it deserves special mention because it is vital to the success of persuasive appeals. In fact, *thesis* is a Greek word meaning "setting down" and, as used today, the job of the thesis statement is to focus and announce (to "set down") the argument. The thesis statement is perhaps most important for the reader because it provides an anchor early in the paper to help understand the points made throughout the essay. But the thesis statement is also important for the writer as an organizing device that helps him/her to think through the issues and decide which points are most relevant.

Said differently, the purpose of the thesis is to give order both to the reader and to the writer. It does this by clearly stating the central claim that a piece of writing will try to prove. The writer takes care in the thesis statement to articulate a paper's argument as precisely as possible, and this precision clarifies and focuses the direction of the paper. Most of the time, a writer must work with a dynamic thesis statement—one that changes and evolves during the writing process. In other words, a working thesis statement that articulates what a writer is interested in exploring will be enough to guide a writer through a draft of the essay, but the **exact words for the thesis statement are not finalized until the paper is nearly complete.**

It's easy to underestimate the importance of the thesis statement, especially if you don't realize that, when used well, it carries the burden of the entire essay. Think of it this way: The thesis statement is a *promise* from the writer to the reader. The reader expects you to make good on its claim by demonstrating with concrete details and logical reasoning how you arrived at that conclusion. Imagine your reader asking, "Why did you say that?" or "On what grounds did you make that claim?" A reader (especially one experienced with thesis-based writing) holds the thesis statement in mind while continuing to read through the rest of the paper. Judgment is delayed as the reader examines the evidence offered and the logic behind it. Once the reader comes to the end of the essay, judgment is no longer suspended. If the writer has satisfied the demands of the thesis by carefully illustrating each burden of proof with compelling evidence and sound logical explanation, then the reader will be satisfied because the expectations suggested by the claim will be met. This is the fundamental definition of a successful essay.

The Academic Essay Format

A closer look at each of the four components of the academic essay—the introduction, the thesis statement, the body paragraphs, and the conclusion—will help you better understand the unique functions that each performs in service to the essay as a whole.

The **introduction** has three primary jobs: to entice the reader to read the essay, to orient the reader to the subject of the paper, and to present the thesis statement. In this sense, the introduction sets the stage for the essay by preparing the reader for the argument that follows. The introductory paragraph (and in longer papers, there may be more than one paragraph for the introduction; see chapter 5) can be visualized as a triangle where the wide side of the triangle represents the relatively broad opening of the paper, which narrows to a point that represents the thesis statement (see figure 1.1).

The **thesis statement** is the most important component of the essay because it has the job of giving meaning and purpose to the paper. In chapter 2, we'll study the three specific parts of the thesis statement—the context, the subject, and the claim. For now, know that the thesis statement is important because it sets before the reader the paper's argument—the precise interpretation, evaluation, or position a paper will assert and develop. At its best, the thesis uses clear terms and offers an insightful assertion to draw the reader's interest. The thesis statement never states the obvious or the generally accepted viewpoint. Instead, a thesis statement is always controversial; it tries to break new ground. Although the thesis statement is generally a single sentence in the essay, it has a very large job to do in that it directs the movement of the essay and gives the paper a sense of unity.

The **body paragraphs** make up the largest part of the paper and carry the evidence and commentary that show the thesis statement to be valid. Each paragraph has two jobs: to develop one important point in support of the thesis statement and to show how that point furthers the argument of the paper. Body paragraphs open with a topic sentence and include evidence, a discussion of the evidence, and a clear link between the paragraph's subject matter and the thesis claim (paragraph development is discussed in detail in chapter 5). Perhaps each paragraph's most important duty is to explain carefully how the point developed in the paragraph helps to forge one of the logical links in the chain of the paper's argument. In the diagram of the academic essay in figure 1.1, the body paragraphs are each represented by an hourglass shape, where the topic idea, contained in the paragraph's opening and closing sentences, serves as an overarching statement for the details within each paragraph.

Finally, the **conclusion** of the paper mirrors the introduction in a way that provides closure, often bringing the discussion full circle. Here, the reader is reminded of the thesis of the paper and the context in which the paper's discussion takes place. There are many good strategies for shaping conclusions, which often include stylistic flair (see chapter 5), but one typical formula is to begin by restating the thesis statement using different words, and reviewing at a general level the evidence examined in the paper.

Fig. 1.1 Diagram of the Academic Essay

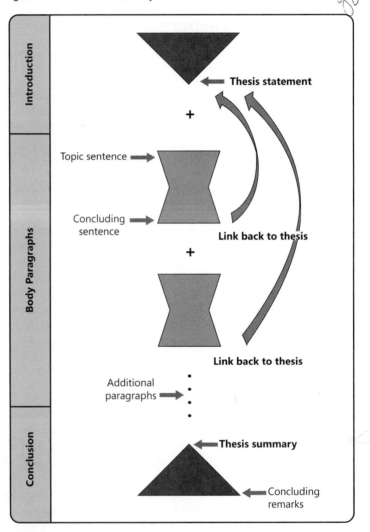

The introduction begins broadly and then narrows to a clear focus, finishing with the thesis statement. Each paragraph begins with a topic sentence that announces the idea of the paragraph and ends with a sentence that ties the paragraph back to the thesis statement. Finally, the conclusion begins by restating the thesis and summarizing the evidence and/or speculating about the greater significance of the paper's conclusions.

Practice 1.1 Recognizing the Academic Essay Format

Read the following student essay, "Homing Device for Humans." Compare the format of the essay with the diagram of the academic essay. Label the various parts of the academic essay format as you recognize them in this essay.

Homing Device for Humans

Ever imagine that you could flip a switch and know, exactly, where your child or boyfriend or best friend is located at that very minute—without them knowing that you knew? Some call it spying and criticize this new technology as invasive to personal privacy. Others see it as a profound revolution in health care, especially for keeping track of patients and loved ones who suffer from dementia and are often endangered when they wander away from home. The company calls it VeriChip, and it's a glass-encased computer chip the size of a grain of rice. It is inserted into the upper arm, where it emits low frequency radio waves associated with a personal identification number. After being read by a scanner, the number can be entered into a database that could provide personal information about medical records, government files, and physical location, just to name a few possibilities. However, the potential for the chip to serve as a personal homing device, among other juicy possibilities, is precisely why it should be available only for very restricted use and even then carefully monitored.

Thesis

Nightclubs have already used VeriChip to recognize regular customers, and police have used it to control access to a high-security office, so there are many uses for a device like this that could be linked to different databases to help improve business transactions in our modern world. But what is the cost of this improved business efficiency? It turns us all into bar-coded meat packages that are passed through scanners and given a verdict as "acceptable" or "not acceptable" based on a rice-sized chip stuck into the top of our arms. If something goes wrong, we cannot pull it out and make an adjustment. At least with hard copy identification papers, we have something to show when there is a problem. Even if the VeriChip can help to make advances in office relations, the price for those advances is too high—it turns us into packaged food with little recourse for mistakes. Therefore, allowing unrestricted development and use would be a huge mistake.

The VeriChip uses the same technology currently used to code animals for retrieval if they are lost. In San Diego, all cats and dogs in shelters are required to have the device implanted before they can be adopted. The identification number associated with the chip is linked in their database to the new owner's address and phone number. This works great until someone moves. The chip has also recently been linked to cancer in animals. Veterinarians say the likelihood of a pet getting cancer is far smaller than the likelihood of loss, so they continue to encourage people to have their pets "chipped," but is the same trade-off fair for humans? While a link to cancer in animals does not necessarily mean the chip will cause cancer in humans—under what conditions is it worth the risk? Probably only in the most extreme circumstances, when someone may be a danger to himself if he inadvertently walks out the door and doesn't know how to return. Only in the most restrictive of circumstances does the VeriChip make sense.

VeriChip provides a revolutionary way of interacting with the world around us. It can allow our bodies to speak even if our minds cannot—and that can be lifesaving for those in need—but it is invasive and risky for most others. We cannot let the excitement about these new technologies and the real improvements they can make in our lives under certain circumstances, convince us to give them free reign in all areas of our lives. The temptation is great, but the cost is even greater. We could too easily turn ourselves into bar-coded luncheon meat, waiting in the grocery line for a pass to work, travel, see a doctor, get medication, or live.

Organization and the Essay's Format

When you construct an essay, you will want to check its organization and format to ensure that your essay is as reader-friendly as possible.

essential

The Academic Essay Format Checklist

Introduction

▶ Does the introduction to the paper begin broadly and narrow to focus on the thesis statement?

▶ Does the paper draw the reader in at the beginning? Does it introduce sufficiently the subject that the paper will develop?

▶ Is the thesis statement placed at the end of the introduction to your paper? If not, consider relocating it there for optimum clarity.

Paragraphs

▶ Does every paragraph in the paper have a clear link to show the relationship between the point in the paragraph and the thesis statement?

▶ Are the paragraphs placed in an order that makes the argument easy to follow? Is the arrangement persuasive or can you imagine a better organizing scheme? Should a counterargument be included?

▶ Check to see if the order of the sentences is the best and the clearest.

▶ Check to see if every sentence sticks to the point of the paragraph.

Conclusion

▶ Are the thesis statement and major points of the essay revisited effectively in the conclusion?

▶ Are the final words of the essay convincing? Does the essay close purposefully and effectively?

▶ Is the tone of the essay appropriate, especially for the concluding remarks (i.e., not arrogant, not condescending, not doubtful)?

Because readers, especially teachers, are familiar with the academic essay format, using it to express your ideas will help your readers to grasp your insights because the information will be readily accessible in an expected and recognizable format. Spend as much time as is necessary to double-check your use of the academic essay form because this will pay dividends in terms of clarity. Clear communication is an important aspect of a successful paper.

Practice 1.2 Using the Academic Essay Checklist

Read the following essay and see if you can identify the writer's argument and supporting evidence. Run the essay through the academic essay checklist and use your results to evaluate the effectiveness of the academic essay format. To what extent does the essay follow the format? If the essay does not always fulfill the checklist criteria, do you believe the writing is still effective? Discuss your reasons with your class or with a peer.

THINKING THROUGH A READING   → Critical, active reading

1. What are the credentials of the three authors of this article and to what degree do these credentials influence you as you read this essay?

2. What evidence do the authors give to convince you that these forest fires are an important problem in Southern California?

3. Why, in their opinion, are the strategies currently being used to fight this problem inadequate?

4. What solution to this problem do they offer and how convincing is it?

Blazed and Confused[2]
C. J. Fotheringham, Jon E. Keeley, and Philip W. Rundel

In the last century, a greater proportion of Southern California has burned than that of any other part of the country. Chaparral shrublands—not forest—cover much of our landscape and account for the vast majority of what burns. The United States Forest Service, which devotes more than half of its budget to fire-related activities, spends most of that money to protect residences built in these shrublands.

Yet we have just seen, for the second time in less than a decade, wind-driven fires causing at least $1 billion in damage. The magnitude of these events makes it clear that it is time to re-evaluate the wildfire problem and how we deal with it as a matter of public policy.

There is much confusion over the causes and behavior of these fires. Some people contend that fire suppression is itself responsible for the catastrophic events, because it has allowed for an unnatural accumulation of flammable vegetation. But while it's true that fire suppression has affected fire behavior and intensity in many forests, it is not true of the chaparral that constitutes much of Southern California's undeveloped land, and more than 95 percent of what burned last week.

Fire suppression over the past century has failed to eliminate fire on these landscapes. In fact, recent estimates from the Forest Service suggest that most of the area has burned more often

---

[2]C. J. Fotheringham, Jon E. Keeley, and Philip R. Rundel, "Blazed and Confused," *New York Times* (online), November 3, 2007, http://www.nytimes.com/2007,11/03/opinion/03fotheringham .html?_r=1&pagewatnted=print

in the past hundred years than in the centuries before that. So it's not as if we have allowed more flammable vegetation to accumulate than when nature alone was in charge.

In any case, fires pushed by strong Santa Ana winds are only weakly affected by the amount of fuel in their path. This is evident from last week's fires, which consumed more than 60,000 acres of the same landscape in San Diego County that burned in the 2003 inferno.

In other words, even the extensive burning just four years ago did little to stop the recent fires. In addition to being inaccurate, the theory that fire suppression is responsible for large destructive wildfires is outright dangerous. It casts blame on firefighters and even suggests that we stop suppressing fires on these shrublands, even though they are home to a large population. And it shifts our focus away from real solutions, which are tied to local land planning and development patterns.

Large, high-intensity wildfires are a natural feature of the Southern California landscape, and we have limited ability to stop those that begin during the autumn Santa Ana winds. The best we can do is alter our behavior in ways that limit our vulnerability.

There is no one simple way to reduce fire risk, but we can learn many strategies by examining not only where houses have burned but also where they did not. It makes sense to begin by restricting the location and design of new housing developments, requiring the use of fire-resistant building materials and maintaining "defensible" space around houses. Greater use of parks and other open recreational areas on the periphery of neighborhoods that abut undeveloped lands can also contribute greatly to protecting communities from fire.

Downed power lines are responsible for igniting some of the recent large fires as well as previous catastrophic ones. Running power lines underground is expensive, but would be a worthwhile investment given the high cost of fighting fires and the billions of dollars in losses that fires cause.

Most fires in Southern California begin on roads, often when car fires ignite vegetation or when cigarettes are carelessly discarded. Low cinderblock walls built along fire-prone stretches of highways—similar to those that are used along freeways as sound barriers in cities—would greatly limit the spread of fire. And given that many fires result from sparks produced by construction equipment like welders, chain saws, mowers, and chippers, it would be useful to limit these activities during the Santa Ana winds.

Trying to eradicate all chaparral wildfires in Southern California will continue to be futile. With the population expected to double in the next 40 years, we can expect fires to only increase. We should think of them as we think of earthquakes: we can't stop them, so we must accept them as a natural hazard and figure out how to withstand them.

C. J. Fotheringham is a doctoral candidate, Jon E. Keeley is an adjunct professor, and Philip W. Rundel is a professor of ecology and evolutionary. biology at the University of California, Los Angeles.

The Audience and Effective Persuasion

In some sense, all writing is constructed to persuade an audience. After all, every time you write something, you're not only trying to communicate your ideas, but you're trying to persuade your readers that those ideas are compelling and insightful. When writing a

AUDIENCE

resume, for instance, you are hoping to convince a potential employer that you are the best person for the job. When you're writing a personal ad, your aim is to persuade a suitor to call you. When writing an e-mail message, you might be, for example, trying to persuade someone to spend an evening with you, convince a boss that you completed a task, or persuade a long-lost friend to keep in touch. Spending some time thinking about your audience will help you create an effective appeal.

Aristotle, our rhetoric expert, realized that persuasive appeals depend on the effectiveness of the speaker, the beliefs of the audience, and the quality and presentation of the evidence. Aristotle used the terms *ethos*, *pathos*, and *logos* to define different ways a speaker or writer can appeal to his audience.

Ethos refers to the ethics of the writer or the writer's credibility. How does the writer present himself/herself? Does the writer seem reasonable and knowledgeable, giving fair consideration to counterarguments? Is evidence presented in a clear and balanced way, reflecting a writer who seems well informed and clear-sighted? Is the tone respectful and thoughtful, rather than arrogant, pushy, or condescending? In considering an argument, the audience always takes into account the speaker or writer and assesses the *ethos* of the writer as well as the evidence presented.

Pathos refers to an argument's emotional appeal and can be thought of in terms of an audience's proclivities. How well will the intended audience respond to arguments about animals' rights, a company's rights, or the rights of those who are suffering and starving? Which emotions can be called on to make an issue meaningful to a particular audience? How can a writer use the information available about an intended audience to make the argument stick? How interesting would an argument be to you if it contained only facts and figures with no emotional lure?

Logos refers to the logical appeal of an argument, that is, how well a writer uses data, evidence, and step-by-step reasoning to show an audience that the facts indisputably support the position being taken. Usually, the logical appeal is the most prevalent of the three areas—it constitutes the "text" of the argument—but Aristotle made clear that it was not necessarily the most important.

To illustrate the relationship among these three areas of persuasion, scholars often represent them using a triangle and call it the *rhetorical triangle* (see figure 1.2).

Notice that the legs of the triangle are all equal, suggesting that each of the three areas of persuasion are equally important to the success of the argument. It is also true that writer-audience-text are all inextricably linked together in a web where each directly

Fig. 1.2 The Rhetorical Triangle

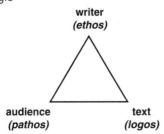

**writer
(ethos)**

*Questions
address
this*

**audience
(pathos)**   **text
(logos)**

affects the other. If an author appears to be unreasonable and untrustworthy, for example, the text put forward to support the argument may be negatively perceived. If a writer knows that an intended audience will consist of parents, he or she may be sure to include some "kid-friendly" data to help persuade this particular audience of the point.

To make best use of the *ethos*, *pathos*, and *logos* of your argument, it might help to take different points of view during the course of your writing. Taking an audience-oriented perspective as you develop and draft your argument will help you find better ways to form a bridge of communication between you and your readers. Don't worry if this seems unnatural or alien at first. During the early stages of the writing process, your focus likely will be writer oriented because that is when your ideas will be developed and shaped. During the revision process, however, your focus should become audience oriented as you make decisions about how to approach your introduction, conclusion, and evidence as effectively as possible to convince your intended readers that your argument is the most compelling. In chapter 5 we'll consider this shift more carefully and help you develop some audience-oriented revision strategies to make your writing as effective as possible.

An Overview of the Writing Process

After you've considered the format, content, and audience for your essay, just how do you begin to write it? Most people don't sit down and write a paper from beginning to end without making changes and revisions. Despite what they may say, most people don't have a complete paper "in their head" that they simply sit down and spew forth on the computer in final form. More often, writers begin with one or two vague ideas and then use the process of writing to try to uncover what, exactly, they want to say. The process of trying to write down what you think, of pinning down that sometimes-vague feeling that you are onto something interesting, takes time and hard work.

Steps of the Writing Process

▶ prewriting

▶ drafting

▶ revising

▶ editing

Experts in the field of composition studies have identified four basic stages of the writing process—**prewriting**, **drafting**, **revising**, and **editing**.

Prewriting includes clustering, freewriting, listing, and diagramming, among other semistructured writing activities. It is often—but not always—the earliest stage of the writing process where you use language to engage and attempt to draw out your ideas. The beauty of prewriting is that it can be useful at any time during the process of writing to help you think through and/or articulate your thoughts.

Drafting specifically refers to the writing of the paper, but it may also include cutting and pasting from prewriting activities. Few people will draft a paper in a linear fashion, from the beginning straight through to the end. Instead, most writers will skip sections (like the introduction) and draft easier portions of the paper first. Whatever the order used, a writer has completed this stage when a (nearly) full version of the essay has been written.

Revising refers to a global revision of the paper, not just cosmetic and grammatical changes. A good revision reconsiders the argument of the essay and examines the paper to see if the most compelling evidence has been presented in the most convincing way. It looks to the format to ensure that the essay is following an appropriate form and that exceptions to that form are made for good reasons. Before being finalized, a successful paper will often go through two or three global revisions, spaced several days apart, to allow for critical reflection.

Editing is often saved for last and refers to sentence-level changes to correct grammar and improve style. It is usually done last because so many things may change during the drafting and revision stages that it would be inefficient and therefore premature to edit except as a final step.

Researchers have taught us that writers use these four stages either explicitly or implicitly whenever they write. These stages, however, do not necessarily progress one after the other, step-by-step, from first to last in a linear fashion. Instead, they are recursive, meaning they *recur*, or show up, again and again over the course of a writing project. The recursiveness of the process is one of its strongest qualities because it keeps the door open for continual discovery and refinement. In practice, this means that you may return, for example, to prewriting even after you have already drafted and revised your paper. While revising, you may recognize an area in the essay that needs more development, so you might use freewriting or clustering to explore your ideas further. Being open to returning to prewriting at any time in the process provides the opportunity for you to develop new insights and incorporate them even after the paper has been planned and a draft written. It also gives you a system for cataloging your critical thinking process so that you can capture your good ideas and integrate them, when relevant, within your essay's draft. Finding the precise words to communicate your new ideas will further clarify them for you and may deepen and expand the insight you gain. Being aware that the different stages of the writing process are associated with specific writing goals can give you increased control over your writing as well as greater efficiency.

Our goal in this book is to combine the *form* and the *process* approach to writing so that you have the best of both worlds—a clear understanding of the conventional formats for writing joined with the best research about the writing process. To that end, we'll focus on the thesis statement as the basic building block for the essay, and we'll explore it in depth according to the steps of the writing process. Chapter 2 familiarizes you with the three parts of the thesis statement, and chapter 3 gives you some critical thinking skills to help you to develop your own thesis statements. Chapter 4 will help you to analyze your thesis statement and use it to identify critical support for the logic of its claim we call these the thesis "Burdens of Proof." Chapter 5 will help you draft the essay and provide strategies for effectively developing introductions, body paragraphs, and conclusions. Part 2 of this book gives you a closer look at how to use this thesis-centered approach to respond to writing assignments, and part 3 shows how the techniques in this book can be applied to a broader range of writing assignments. The last part, the Appendices, expands on the skills and strategies of parts 1–3. Together, the four parts of this book provide a comprehensive strategy for thinking through your thesis statement to write a successful academic essay.

Remember that the process of writing an essay isn't linear. You are therefore encouraged to use the techniques in these chapters in a fluid way, jumping back and forth between chapters as necessary. View these techniques as tools that you can draw on at any time and in any order as you develop your own essays.

APPLICATIONS AND WRITING EXERCISES

Application 1.1 Using a Writing Format

Even if you are not aware of it, you have often used conventional writing formats. When you write an e-mail to your instructor, for example, you typically begin with a salutation ("Dear Professor"), remind the instructor of your identity ("I am a student in your freshman writing class…"), tell why you are writing ("I am wondering what my overall grade is so far in the class"), give preferred ways for the instructor to reply ("You can reach me by e-mail or cell phone"), and sign the note ("Sincerely, Mary"). You might include some variations on this format—such as not reminding the instructor of your identity because you are sure the instructor knows who you are or not mentioning the best way to contact you because the instructor has contacted you before—and still be said to be using a conventional format for e-mail messages. Think of writing formats as templates to help get you started. Variation and creativity are usually anticipated—even expected—in the product.

Select one of the following personal writing formats. List as thoroughly as you can the conventions for this writing format. Depict the conventions visually, if you can (e.g., a diagram or chart). Combine your list with that of a classmate who also chose this example. On what items do you agree and disagree? Share your results with two to four additional classmates. For each format, ask the group as a whole to vote on which traits are conventional and which lie outside the convention of each writing format. How closely did your group agree? What does this tell you about the writing format selected? (Hint: Remember that *conventions* are those criteria that most people agree belong to a particular writing format.)

- a post-it note to your mother about why you are not home

- a text message sent by cell phone to your best friend

- an electronic message posted to a chat room

- a note on the top of a late paper turned in to your professor

- a blog, journal, or diary entry

- a note expressing affection to someone you are dating

- an e-mail message asking for or canceling a date

- a note asking your roommate to do something for you while you are away

- a writing format of your choice

Application 1.2 Analyzing a Student Essay

Read the following student essay, "Plagiarism: A Crime to Be Prevented." Compare the format of the essay with the diagram of the academic essay. Label (yes, write in the book) the various parts of the academic essay format as you recognize them in this essay. Does the essay have a thesis statement? If so, as a reader, did the thesis statement help you to make sense of the essay (i.e., give the essay a purpose)? Would the essay be as successful without the thesis statement? Explain. Run the essay through the academic essay checklist. Discuss your discoveries in class.

do home
★ @ home
for 1/24

THINKING THROUGH A READING

1. How does this essay define plagiarism?

2. According to this writer, who is harmed by plagiarism?

3. Who is the audience for the essay and how do you know?

4. According to this essay, what response should teachers have when confronted by plagiarism? Do you agree?

Plagiarism: A Crime to Be Prevented
Vicki Xiong

Plagiarism is an ugly word; it is an ugly act to be caught in—to have next to your name. No matter how ugly the word, students all across America continue to resort to its tempting "benefits." With the modern advent of the World Wide Web, and the accessibility of the home computer, the act of plagiarism has become an easier crime to commit. Growing up, children are taught that stealing is wrong; plagiarism is indeed just that, wrong—for it is the stealing of another's idea(s). The only way to combat the outbreak of plagiarism is through prevention. Prevention of plagiarism is our best hope in securing the honors of academia in the years to come.

Plagiarism is when someone represents someone else's creative or academic work, whether all of it or part of it, as one's own. There are several forms of plagiarism. It can be an omission, where someone fails to acknowledge or give credit to the creator of words, pictures, or ideas. Or, it can be a case where a person uses someone else's ideas and gives credit but invents the source.

Study after study has continued to show that plagiarism is a growing epidemic. Students, when surveyed anonymously, overwhelmingly admit without any reservation to having relied on plagiarism to complete their assignments. Many people have studied this growing problem, and some think that as many as 95 percent of today's students plagiarize with little hesitation.

Plagiarism is a problem because it harms all parties involved—the plagiarizer, fellow classmates, and even the entire student body. The plagiarizer, taking part in academic dishonesty, makes a conscious decision to cheat not only those involved but him/herself as well. The logic is simple. The workload (assignments, tests, quizzes, projects, etc.) of a course is designed to aid students in learning the basic fundamentals of the course. When cheating is practiced, the student robs himself/herself from the true learning experience and thus loses the chance of absorbing the knowledge that might have been drawn on for future reference.

Likewise, fellow classmates are harmed as well (especially in the college setting). When classes are graded on a curve, it is unfair to the diligent students who dedicate time and effort to do their best only to be deprived of the full benefit of the curve, as the cheaters set the curve with their added advantage. As students learn that some are plagiarizing to improve their grades, they lose faith in the integrity of the school and may decide that they have to plagiarize, too, to compete. As long as plagiarism is allowed to go on with little, if any, penalty, students will eventually lose their belief that colleges are honorable institutions and that going to one is a privilege.

On the large scale, society is harmed as well. Society is harmed when plagiarizers are not get caught. When plagiarizers are praised for their work, when they get the promotion, or when they get accepted into a professional school based on their supposed merit, they are rewarded for their dishonesty. Society is harmed when incapable, lazy people get by on their cheating ways and, when push comes to shove, are unable to perform their job to the best of their abilities because they cheated themselves from the basic training that schooling was supposed to provide. Plagiarism benefits no one. Yet it is an ever-growing problem in our constantly advancing society, where lust after the newest gadgets and tools will lead them to continue to live dishonestly to get what they want. This is not one of the lessons college graduates should be learning.

Unfortunately, academic dishonesty and plagiarism are not foreign issues in our present-day academia, but so far little has been done to stop it. On the contrary, the act of plagiarism has become a means of survival in the hostile and aggressive realities of higher education. As college admissions and professional schools admissions continue to become more and more competitive, students will be only drawn more to the temptations of cheating. Little is done by campus authority figures to combat this. They should discuss the harmful effects of plagiarism and offer alternative choices for students who are struggling and under pressure to succeed. Many times, students plagiarize because their friends all do and they just haven't thought about the seriousness of what they're doing. If this problem was discussed more openly, these students might make different choices. When students are caught plagiarizing, professors are usually lenient. They seem unwilling to confront students who cheat. As long as professors and others in authority remain unconcerned about their students relying on plagiarism to complete their assignments, it will continue to grow and eventually destroy the integrity of higher education.

Educators should make a commitment and join forces with other fellow educators across America in the fight against plagiarism. Teachers should make it a duty to teach all students what plagiarism is and to drill the ethical consequences of plagiarism into each and every student before they enter college. The conditioning should start as soon as students enter grade school. In the first grade, little lessons on cheating should be taught; as students progress from grade school, to middle school, to high school, each year, lessons in cheating, academic dishonesty, and plagiarism should be reiterated in more detail and observed under a stricter set of guidelines. The common excuse of "I was never taught that" will instantly be eliminated, as all students will be informed from an early age. The repercussions of plagiarism should be on a no-tolerance basis. If students are ensured that when caught, they will be punished to the maximum, this will undoubtedly stimulate a fear and thus draw students away from the lure of dishonesty and cheating. Teachers and professors, alike, must be firm on implementation of the consequences when occurrences do happen; they must carry out with the punishment—not just let it go with a warning. Then they will become the role models for students that they should be.

In addition to annual lessons on plagiarism, teachers at the high school level should also spend time teaching students ways to manage time. This will directly aid in the lowering of overwhelming shock students often experience when entering college and will hopefully decrease the temptation of resorting to academic dishonesty. At the same rate, teachers should teach students to think for themselves—allowing them to explore the possibilities of their imaginations. Assignments and projects should not be so strictly constrained—confined by guideline after guideline. In contrast, assignments should encourage students to think outside of the box; this will enable them to practice creative thinking and, in turn, will reduce dependency on other people's thoughts and ideas as they build confidence in their own ideas. In essence, teachers should teach students to think, not to regurgitate.

Plagiarism is a serious problem that is rapidly growing. Its appeal has drawn in students from all walks of life. The act of plagiarism is no laughing matter. It must be taken seriously. Our actions will eventually catch up with us. Excuses will eventually run out. Educators should not put off lessons in plagiarism but begin the conditioning as soon as possible—for prevention is our best bet in ending today's academic dishonesty crisis.

Application 1.3 Analyzing Your College Entrance Essay *No —*

Bring to class your college application essay (if you can't find it or didn't write one, bring to class an essay you have written recently). Examine the paper closely and try to identify the structure or writing format you used for the essay. Use the following questions to help guide your analysis:

- Does it have an introduction? What does the introduction accomplish?

- Does the essay have a thesis statement or something similar?

- Does the essay have clear support paragraphs? If not, in what format is the bulk of the information presented?

- Does the essay have a conclusion? What does the conclusion accomplish?

- Are there other sections, such as an extracurricular involvement section, a background section, an overview? Do these sections fit into the essay as a whole or do they seem to stand apart and fragment the overall effect of the essay?

If time allows, trade essays with a peer and conduct the above analysis on the essay you receive. Compare your results.

Writing Exercise 1.1 Analyzing Your College Entrance Essay (cont.) *No —*

Based on your answers to Application 1.3 on your college entrance (or other) essay, write short responses to the following questions:

1. Outline the structure used for the essay you studied.

2. How does (or doesn't) the structure of the paper suit the assignment? Discuss.

3. What modifications might you make to the structure of the paper to improve it, if you had the chance to revise this paper?

4. In what other context might you use the writing format you identified?

5. What can you conclude about the writing format you used and its effectiveness?

Writing Exercise 1.2 Responding to an Essay and Process Writing

1. Examine Kluckhohn's essay "Mirror for Man," that follows. Identify the thesis statement. Then find the supporting topic ideas and underline them. Write a brief analysis of the structure of this essay. What organizational structure does the author use? Why do you think he used this structure? How does this structure affect readers' understanding, in your opinion?

THINKING THROUGH A READING

1. How does Kluckhohn define culture?

2. What similarities does Kluckhohn find in all human groups?

3. According to Kluckhohn, how does nature restrict culture?

Mirror for Man
Clyde Kluckhohn

One of the interesting things about human beings is that they try to understand themselves and their own behavior. While this has been particularly true of Europeans in recent times, there is no group which has not developed a scheme or schemes to explain human actions. To the insistent human query "why?" the most exciting illumination anthropology has to offer is that of the concept of culture. Its explanatory importance is comparable to categories such as evolution in biology, gravity in physics, disease in medicine.

Why do so many Chinese dislike milk and milk products? Why during World War II did Japanese soldiers die willingly in a Banzai charge that seemed senseless to Americans? Why do some nations trace descent through the father, others through the mother, still others through both parents? Not because different peoples have different instincts, not because they were destined by God or Fate to different habits, not because the weather is different in China and Japan and the United States. Sometimes shrewd common sense has an answer that is close to that of the anthropologist: "because they were brought up that way." By "culture" anthropology means the total life way of a people, the social legacy individuals acquire from their group. Or culture can be regarded as that part of the environment that is the creation of human beings.

This technical term has a wider meaning than the "culture" of history and literature. A humble cooking pot is as much a cultural product as is a Beethoven sonata. In ordinary speech "people of culture" are those who can speak languages other than their own, who are familiar with history, literature, philosophy, or the fine arts. To the anthropologist, however, to be human is to be cultured. There is culture in general, and then there are the specific cultures such as Russian, American, British, Hottentot, Inca. The general abstract notion serves to remind us that we cannot explain acts solely in terms of the biological properties of the people concerned, their individual past experience, and the immediate situation. The past experience of other people in the form of culture enters into almost every event. Each specific culture constitutes a kind of blueprint of all of life's activities.

A good deal of human behavior can be understood, and indeed predicted, if we know a people's design for living. Many acts are neither accidental nor due to personal peculiarities nor caused by supernatural forces nor simply mysterious. Even we Americans who pride ourselves on our individualism follow most of the time a pattern not of our own making. We brush our teeth on arising. We put on pants—not a loincloth or a grass skirt. We eat three meals a day—not four or five or two. We sleep in a bed—not in a hammock or on a sheep pelt. I do not have to know individuals and their life histories to be able to predict these and countless other regularities, including many in the thinking process of all Americans who are not incarcerated in jails or hospitals for the insane.

To the American woman a system of plural wives seems "instinctively" abhorrent. She cannot understand how any woman can fail to be jealous and uncomfortable if she must share her husband with other women. She feels it "unnatural" to accept such a situation. On the other hand, a Koryak woman of Siberia, for example, would find it hard to understand how a woman could be so selfish and so undesirous of feminine companionship in the home as to wish to restrict her husband to one mate.

Some years ago I met in New York City a young man who did not speak a word of English and was obviously bewildered by American ways. By "blood" he was American, for his parents had gone from Indiana to China as missionaries. Orphaned in infancy, he was reared by a Chinese family in a remote village. All who met him found him more Chinese than American. The facts of his blue eyes and light hair were less impressive than a Chinese style of gait, Chinese arm and hand movements, Chinese facial expression, and Chinese modes of thought. The biological heritage was American, but the cultural training had been Chinese. He returned to China.

Another example of another kind: I once knew a trader's wife in Arizona who took a somewhat devilish interest in producing a cultural reaction. Guests who came her way were often served delicious sandwiches filled with a meat that seemed to be neither chicken nor tuna fish yet was reminiscent of both. To queries she gave no reply until each had eaten his or her fill. She then explained that what they had eaten was not chicken, not tuna fish, but the rich, white flesh of freshly killed rattlesnakes. The response was instantaneous, often violent vomiting. A biological process is caught in a cultural web.

All this does not mean that there is no such thing as raw human nature. The members of all human groups have about the same biological equipment. All people undergo the same poignant life experiences, such as birth, helplessness, illness, old age, and death. The biological potentialities of the species are the blocks with which cultures are built. Some patterns of every culture crystallize around focuses provided by biology: the difference between the sexes, the presence of persons of different ages, the varying physical strength and skill of individuals. The facts of nature also limit cultural forms. No culture provides patterns for jumping over trees or for eating iron ore. There is thus no "either-or" between nature and that special form of nurture called culture. The two factors are interdependent. Culture arises out of human nature, and its forms are restricted both by human biology and by natural laws.

Clyde Kluckhohn was born in 1905 in LeMars, Iowa. He attended Princeton and wrote two cultural works, Mirror for Man, *published in 1952, and* Culture: A Critical Review of Concepts and Definitions. *Kluckhohn felt that people think their own cultural beliefs and practices are normal and natural, and those of others are strange or even inferior.*

Based on your reading of "Mirror for Man," answer the following questions.

1. Look again at Kluckhohn's essay "Mirror for Man," above. Spend a few minutes thinking about the author's purpose for writing. Now write a two-to-three-paragraph response to the author's argument. Set your response aside.

2. It's time to reflect on the writing process you just used. Review the section in this chapter that describes the typical four-stage writing process. Think carefully about the writing process(es) *you* used in writing a response to "Mirror for Man." Did you begin at the beginning and write the entire response without ever changing a word? Did you jot down some notes, then write some ideas about the essay, then draft a response? Did you draft full sections and move things around? Refer to the steps of the writing process outlined above and describe what *your* writing process(es) were with this assignment. Did you complete (or would your response have been better if you had completed) all four stages? Was it recursive? Is this representative of the way you typically approach a writing assignment?

3. Write a paragraph about what you have learned about your own writing process and refer back to it often this term to see if it changes over the course of this writing class.

CHAPTER 2

Understanding the Thesis Statement Through Its Three Parts

An essay is not guaranteed to be successful simply because it is grammatically sound, has an introduction, a set of body paragraphs, and a conclusion. These components require a thesis statement to tie them together and give them significance. In this sense, the thesis statement is more than just a sentence—it's the central element that locks the other components of the essay together. As discussed in chapter 1, a thesis has two main purposes: (1) Most important, the thesis statement gives the reader a clear statement on the perspective or argument of the paper, and (2) the thesis statement is an organizing device to help the writer think through and present thoughts in a systematic way. To do this, *the thesis statement explicitly isolates a subject and provides a perspective on it. Implicitly, the thesis establishes the logical framework for the paper by suggesting what evidence is necessary to validate the perspective* (we'll discuss arguments in depth in chapter 4).

Thesis ★

This chapter will break the thesis statement down into its basic elements and give you examples and exercises to help you better understand how the thesis can help you in your writing process. As you will see, these examples have been drawn from a wide variety of topics and fields; we hope some will be relevant to your own work. We'll build on these lessons in the next chapter, where you will learn more strategies for developing your own thesis statements.

WHAT'S AHEAD...

► identifying the three parts of a thesis statement >main idea

► three ways to visualize your thesis statement

► the context

► the subject
  • three potential problems with the subject and how to fix them

► the claim

► three essentials for effective claims
  • four potential problems with the claim and how to fix them

write a ¶ explaining this to someone who hasn't read the book (or write a l ¶ review)

Identifying the Three Parts of a Thesis Statement

As discussed in the previous chapter, the word *thesis* comes from the Greek noun meaning "setting down" or "a placing or a position." In ancient times, this was a very popular and commonly used term for a variety of things, most of them having nothing to do with writing or the academic experience. Now we use the term *thesis* in a much more specialized way, largely owing to developments in rhetoric and essay writing. Within the framework of the academic essay discussed in chapter 1 that prescribes an introduction, body paragraphs, and a conclusion, the purpose of the thesis statement is "to set down" the argument of the paper. This can be done most clearly if you think of the thesis statement as having three parts: a **context**, a **subject**, and a **claim**, as in the following example:

In America today, the documented increase in childhood emotional disorders
    CONTEXT   SUBJECT

reflects changes in institutional practices rather than a deterioration of family values.
                                       CLAIM

Although you likely have read and written a number of thesis statements, perhaps you have never looked at a thesis statement in this way before. The *context* places the reader in the general area of discussion ("In America today"), the *subject* directs the reader's attention to the focus of the paper ("documented increase in childhood emotional disorders"), and the *claim* tells the reader what argument regarding the subject the paper will make ("reflects changes in institutional practices rather than a deterioration of family values"). After reading the thesis statement, the reader should have a clear understanding of the goals of the paper and be able to continue reading to see how compellingly the case is made.

Including context, subject, and claim—the C-S-C—in the thesis statement helps both the writer and the readers: It helps the writer to order thoughts and organize information gathered in service to the paper's goals, and it ensures that the readers clearly understand the paper's purpose at the outset. A thesis statement with these three parts will give you and your readers important signposts to aid composition and comprehension.

Three Ways to Visualize Your Thesis Statement

There are many things a writer can do to make working with a thesis statement easier. Here are three ways to work with your thesis statement:

THE SENTENCE FORMAT

Because a thesis statement is a grammatical sentence, it is most often written in sentence format. In using this type of visual representation, it may be helpful to underline and label the C-S-C in the following manner:

The most flagrant abuse of animal rights today ironically takes place in U.S. laboratories
    CLAIM   SUBJECT   CONTEXT   CLAIM   CLAIM

dedicated to the preservation of human life.

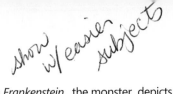

In the <u>film version of Mary Shelley's *Frankenstein*,</u> <u>the monster</u> <u>depicts the detrimental</u>
     CONTEXT   SUBJECT

<u>effects of isolation and alienation on the human subject.</u>
      CLAIM

THE GRADUATED TRIANGLE FORMAT

Imagine plotting the context, subject, and claim of the thesis statement along the base of a graduated triangle where you can more easily see how they narrow to a focus. In figure 2.1, notice that the context is the broadest aspect of the paper (represented by the far left and widest side of the triangle), the subject is centered at a level of breadth that is narrower than the context but not as specific as the claim, and the claim represents the focus of the paper—that is, its argument.

Fig. 2.1 The Graduated Triangle Format

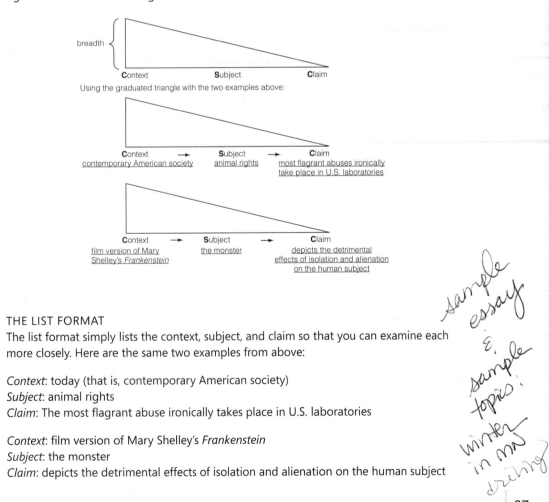

THE LIST FORMAT

The list format simply lists the context, subject, and claim so that you can examine each more closely. Here are the same two examples from above:

Context: today (that is, contemporary American society)
Subject: animal rights
Claim: The most flagrant abuse ironically takes place in U.S. laboratories

Context: film version of Mary Shelley's *Frankenstein*
Subject: the monster
Claim: depicts the detrimental effects of isolation and alienation on the human subject

Practice 2.1 Diagramming Thesis Statements

Diagram the following thesis statements using all three formats, the sentence, the graduated triangle, and the list (if you need a tip, the first one was started at the beginning of this chapter). Decide which format you prefer and explain why. It's possible that your format preference depends on your writing needs. If this is the case, try to imagine under what circumstances you would find each format most helpful.

a. In America today, the documented increase in childhood emotional disorders reflects changes in institutional practices rather than a deterioration of family values.

b. The poor food served on the campuses of most universities across the nation represents campus administrators' privileging of profit over student health.

try this together

We've shown you three ways to depict your working thesis statement, each of which offers you a slightly different perspective. Notice that the three parts may not be presented in C-S-C order in every thesis statement. It is important that all the parts are there but not that they are in a particular arrangement. Instances in which the context is implicit rather than explicit are discussed later.

Some writers may find it too prescriptive to have to think about three parts in their thesis statements, but we have noticed that the most common problem in composing them is stopping before the thesis statement is complete, usually before a claim is clearly stated. Let's examine these parts in more detail to see how you can best use C-S-C to think through your ideas and announce your argument.

The Context

The context portion of a thesis statement locates the reader in the paper's general area of discussion or frame of reference. It can be thought of as the outer limits of the paper's exploration. There is often a temptation for a writer to draw a *context* that is overly broad for a paper, such as "From the beginning of time" or "People have always desired. . . ." It is important that writers resist this temptation because it establishes a frame of reference so large that it is meaningless. How realistic is it that one essay could address any topic from the beginning of time or cover what all people have always desired?

Establishing the paper's context allows the writer to control the subject matter that might be explored within the paper and focus the essay. Again, using the graduated triangle depiction, you can imagine that the thesis statement has three levels that, when starting with the claim, are each more broad than the one before.

For instance, if you were going to write a paper about the discovery of water on Mars and how it suggests the possibility for sustaining life on the red planet, you could use the triangular image in the following way to help figure out what should be in your thesis' subject, context, and claim.

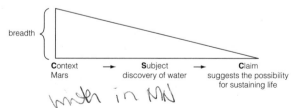

breadth {

Context	Subject	Claim
Mars	discovery of water	suggests the possibility for sustaining life

water in MN

↗ your point

Notice that the claim gives a very specific interpretation of the subject, while the context gives you a broader perspective on the subject. In other words, the claim is one step narrower than the subject, and the subject is one step narrower than the context. This configuration helps to lay the groundwork for a tightly focused thesis statement and paper.

For another example, return to the thesis statement that opens this chapter. There, "America today" gives a context for the subject's more specific concern with the documented increase in childhood emotional disorders. Orienting the reader with the phrase "America today" will give you enough space to introduce the circumstances surrounding the subject but not so much space that you lose the reader's—and possibly your own—focus.

While the subject and claim of a thesis statement are always explicitly stated, the context is sometimes implied. In other words, it may be obvious from the focus of your essay what you plan to discuss. If, for example, you are arguing that music file-sharing through the Internet should be legal, a likely context would be today's music industry. Or, if you are developing an argument that the use of steroids in college sports should be more tightly regulated, a likely context would be the wider frame of college athletics. Remember that the purpose of the context is to situate the reader and writer in the general area of the paper's discussion. Once you determine a context for your thesis statement, you will be more aware of the implications of your thesis statement for society as a whole, and this perspective will help you to focus your argument and to develop your points with a clearer awareness of the issues' ramifications. As an added practical benefit, identifying the context for your thesis statement will give you a clear place to begin your essay's introduction.

The Subject

The subject of the thesis statement is the central thing the paper is about—the topic of the paper's discussion. The subject establishes the particular focus of the paper and draws the readers' and writer's attention to the issue or matter that the paper will explore.

The subject is usually something you find particularly interesting. That is why you select it to be the topic of your writing assignment and hence the center of your thesis statement. However, beware of oversimplifying it. It is important to identify as precisely as possible the subject that you will analyze, and it is important that it be something that you can develop within the page length that you are assigned. As you will see, you will sometimes have to narrow and focus the paper's subject until it is not only clear but manageable in the amount of space and time available. In short, the scope of the subject should be appropriate; the subject should be neither too broad nor too narrow, and it should not be too vague.

Three Potential Problems with the Subject . . .

1. The subject is too broad.

2. The subject is too narrow.

3. The subject is too vague.

Three Potential Problems and How to Fix Them
Problem #1: The Subject Is Too Broad

As a student taking classes across the disciplines, you will likely find yourself writing persua-sive essays about a number of things—perhaps a novel, a social issue, a war, or a historical figure. If you are assigned a five-to-eight-page paper, a typical length for a college essay, you would have to think carefully about the appropriate scope for your subject. You should not presume that you can include everything you know or learn about a war, a novel, a social issue, or a historical figure; you must narrow the subject. For example, taking all of World War II as the subject for a thesis statement is too general and unwieldy. Instead, ask yourself what about World War II you can explore. A better paper might orient the reader to World War II in the introduction and from there direct the reader's focus to a particular battle in that war, such as the bombing of Pearl Harbor.

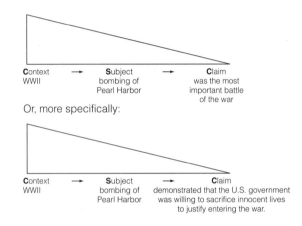

Or, more specifically:

You may decide, for example, to write about the significance of the bombing of Pearl Harbor instead of all of World War II. Because this subject is more limited, you could better focus your analysis and gain depth and insight. Narrowing the subject for a thesis statement is similar to placing a specimen under a microscope: When the focus is made more intense, the detail becomes more apparent. This results in the possibility for greater revelation, one hallmark of a successful paper.

USING THE *SHIFT LEFT* METHOD

You could choose to intensify the focus of an essay even more by narrowing the sub-ject from one battle in the war to a strategy used in a particular battle or to the role of a certain leader in a particular battle. One technique for accomplishing this is to use the *shift left* method on the graduated triangle and *shift* the subject to the *left* and into the context position of a new thesis statement. Using the example about a par-ticular battle in a war, let's begin a new thesis statement by moving the battle to the left and into the context position and then developing a new subject and claim. This time we'll focus on the battle between the ancient Greeks and Persians at the Battle of Marathon.

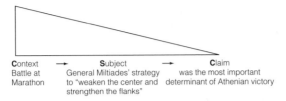

Context → **S**ubject → Claim

Battle at   General Miltiades' strategy   was the most important

Marathon   to "weaken the center and   determinant of Athenian victory

            strengthen the flanks"

This new thesis statement focuses on the successes of a particular military strategy within a specific battle of the war. It is narrower in scope than the previous examples and gives you a sense of the different levels of specificity to consider when drafting your thesis statement. In written form, the thesis might say: "The Athenian victory in the battle of Marathon can be attributed primarily to General Miltiades' strategy to 'weaken the center while strengthening the flanks' of his forces." Understanding how to narrow the subject can be an important technique because most of the time the more precise the subject, the more precise the claim, and the more compelling the paper. When a subject is too broad, the analysis will likely remain superficial.

Let's look at another example of narrowing the paper's scope. Imagine that you have been assigned to write a paper on one of the many film versions of *Frankenstein*. Taking an entire film as the subject of your five-page paper is likely too broad (although a film might be a fine subject for a longer paper). Instead, think of the *Frankenstein* film you have chosen as the context of the paper and begin narrowing the focus by selecting a more manageable subject. What about *Frankenstein* will you focus on? What specific aspect of the film will you take as the core of your essay? The subject of your paper might be Dr. Frankenstein's psychology, the role of the monster in the film, or an important difference between the film and the novel. For example, you decide to focus on the monster (as we did in an earlier example) and want to argue that the monster depicts the detrimental effects of isolation on the human subject. Your thesis might look like this:

[handwritten: focus on a particular aspect]

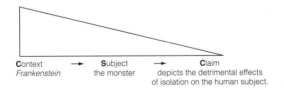

Context → **S**ubject → Claim

Frankenstein   the monster   depicts the detrimental effects

                     of isolation on the human subject.

Now, rather than trying to focus on the film as a whole—a very complex and unwieldy subject—you are able to focus on a particular aspect of the film—the monster. Again, narrowing the focus of the paper makes the essay more manageable; it identifies a particular task with very specific demands and erases some of the confusion for the writer and reader.

Practice 2.2 Narrowing the Scope   *[handwritten: —7 in class on '31]*

Try applying the *shift left* technique to each of the following prompts. Using the graduated triangle, move the subject of the prompt (underlined) to the context position and develop a new, more specific subject that will invite a level of analysis that goes beyond the surface. The first one is done for you:

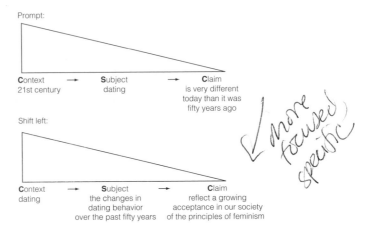

Prompt:

| **C**ontext | → | **S**ubject | → | **C**laim |
| 21st century | | dating | | is very different today than it was fifty years ago |

Shift left:

| **C**ontext | → | **S**ubject | → | **C**laim |
| dating | | the changes in dating behavior over the past fifty years | | reflect a growing acceptance in our society of the principles of feminism |

more focused / specific

1. Discuss <u>dating</u> in the twenty-first century.

2. Write an analysis of the film *Fellowship of the Ring* (or a film of your choice).

3. Write a paper that discusses the relationship between <u>clothing style</u> and identity.

4. Investigate the influence of <u>popular music</u> today.

5. Comment on the way <u>pollution</u> threatens our environment today.

Problem #2: The Subject Is Too Narrow

The subject of the thesis statement should be right for the paper. If the subject of the paper is too broad, as we saw previously, the paper may be superficial or inconclusive. If the subject is too narrow, the support for the claim may be exhausted too quickly to offer a satisfactory argument. See figure 2.2 for an example.

Fig. 2.2 Frieda Kahlo, *Self-Portrait with Thorn and Hummingbird*

....

DID YOU KNOW . . .

Frieda Kahlo (1907–1954) was a Mexican painter who is famous for her self-portraits and her marriage to Mexican muralist Diego Rivera. She painted in a style that combined Surrealism, Realism, and Symbolism. When she was about eighteen years old, she was seriously injured in a vehicle accident. Her spinal column, along with many other bones, were broken in the collision, resulting in intense, life-long pain. She depicts much of this personal suffering on her canvases.

....

[handwritten at top: Try writing about a painting > 3 small groups → 3 diff. paintings too narrow]

EXAMPLE:

> The hummingbird necklace in Frieda Kahlo's *Self-Portrait with Thorn and Humming-bird* illustrates her personal feelings of fragility.

Context: *Self-Portrait with Thorn and Hummingbird*
Subject: the necklace
Claim: illustrates the artist's personal feelings of fragility

Here is a case where the subject should be expanded. Talking only about the necklace in the portrait will limit the discussion to a small aspect of the painting and would result in a thin or misguided argument that would probably not be compelling. How can you broaden the subject so that it can include multiple aspects of the painting that can be used to support the claim that this painting "illustrates the artist's personal feelings of fragility"?

BETTER:

> The nature imagery in Frieda Kahlo's *Self-Portrait with Thorn and Hummingbird* illustrates her personal feelings of fragility.

[handwritten in right margin: takes practice?]

Notice that for this example, focusing on the nature imagery in the painting will also allow the writer to comment on the presence and arrangement of the animals, insects, and foliage in the painting. This broader thesis also invites commentary on the unexpected way that other pieces of the artist's jewelry in the painting are natural elements, such as the butterfly hairclips and the leaf hair designs, and the way in which the animals in the painting continue the theme of the association of the artist with the vulnerability of nature. Broadening the subject allows for a more in-depth and thus more compelling argument.

Problem #3: The Subject Is Too Vague

As previously noted, it is important to make sure your subject is as clear and precise as possible. You will not always have the clarity you want in a working thesis statement, so be open to troubleshooting this aspect of the thesis during the revision process. Following is a vague thesis, also based on the Frieda Kahlo painting. Try using the graduated triangle and the C-S-C technique to refine it.

EXAMPLE:

> The way Kahlo paints *Self-Portrait with Thorn and Hummingbird* illustrates a devotion to feminist principles.

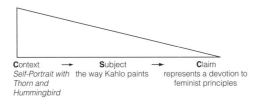

Context → Subject → Claim
Self-Portrait with the way Kahlo paints represents a devotion to
Thorn and feminist principles
Hummingbird

In this example, the context is Kahlo's painting. Does the subject of this thesis statement—the way Kahlo paints—seem clear? Do we know exactly what the author means by this phrase? Does this refer to what hours of the day Kahlo paints? Whether she uses her left hand, stands on her head, or paints in the nude? If certainty is in doubt, then it's better to be more specific; aim to clarify it. We'll assume that "the way Kahlo paints" refers to the way she depicts herself in this self-portrait, including things like her facial expression, her posture, and the background on which the figure is displayed. Can we find a more precise way to state the subject?

BETTER:

> In *Self-Portrait with Thorn and Hummingbird*, Kahlo's depiction of herself illustrates a devotion to feminist principles.

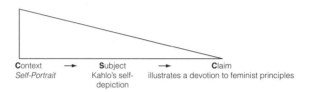

Context   →   **S**ubject   →   **C**laim
Self-Portrait   Kahlo's self-   illustrates a devotion to feminist principles
      depiction

Here, we've focused the subject in a way that is more explicit. The writer of this paper could discuss several topics in support of the claim, so it is neither too broad nor too narrow a subject.

The message in all of this is not to assume that the context and subject of a thesis statement come easily. It is usually only after careful thought and exploration, and after narrowing and systematically identifying potential topics, that you will be ready to identify a working C-S-C. Again, the challenge comes in knowing when you have found a subject that is appropriate—not too broad, not too narrow, and not too vague—for your writing assignment.

The Claim

The claim provides a point of view on or an interpretation of the subject. It is an important part of the thesis statement because it encapsulates the insights of the writer and gives relevance and coherence to the supporting paragraphs. Some instructors call this the *so what* of the thesis because it articulates the significance of the paper. Others call it the *twist* or *angle* that the thesis gives to or puts on the subject. For example, if the context is a Shakespearean play, say *King Lear*, and the subject is a character, say Lear himself, the claim is the perspective or point of view that you will give on the character. Your thesis statement might be that In Shakespeare's play *King Lear* (context), King Lear's (subject) excessive pride leads to his undoing (claim). Using a sports example, if baseball serves as your context and steroid use is your subject, then your claim might be that steroid use is appropriate for professional baseball players who are entertainers as much as athletes. The claim gives meaning to the thesis statement because it presents the paper's argument clearly and succinctly. It is the most challenging and important part of the thesis statement to develop, and it evolves from critical thinking, analysis, and prewriting.

(handwritten: read for 1/31 → journal entry)

Study the following example, paying particular attention to the subject and claim.

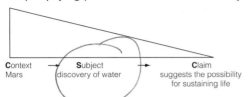

(handwritten: debatable thesis)

(handwritten: Winter in MN is cold)

Notice that the subject is not debatable—it is a topic, a fact. Although you will want to document (using credible sources) that water was, indeed, discovered on Mars, this point does not require you to develop an argument about its validity. There seems to be little dispute about this recent discovery. What is in dispute is what this discovery means, why the discovery of water on Mars may or may not be significant. Your claim—that the discovery of water on Mars suggests that life-forms could have survived on the red planet—is controversial. Some scientists agree with this idea, whereas others disagree. To support this position, you will need to review the evidence on both sides of the debate and show how the evidence best supports your view, assuming that this is what you find. If you learn otherwise, it is time to alter your working thesis statement.

Continue to focus on this difficult aspect of writing. Following are three guiding principles to help you establish effective claims.

Three Essentials for Effective Claims

For many writers, the claim is the most difficult part of the thesis statement to pinpoint. Often, writers have a sense of what they want to write about but struggle with selecting just the right words to express their thoughts. Sometimes the process of choosing words makes you realize that the idea you thought was interesting now sounds flat. Other times choosing words helps you discover an exciting path that seems well worth pursuing. Whatever your writing process, you will likely revise your claim several times before your paper is complete, so keep the following essentials in mind.

Essential #1: A claim is something that can be <u>objectively supported.</u> *(handwritten: → not too opinionated)*
A thesis claim must be based on objective evidence; it is essentially an opinion or hypothesis, but it is a type of opinion that can be supported by carefully selected and interpreted evidence from a text or other source. This is easier to explain through an illustration.

Here is a claim that cannot be objectively supported:

> The <u>architectural design</u> of the <u>new library</u> is ugly. *(handwritten: → too subjective)*
> SUBJECT   CONTEXT   CLAIM

Notice that the context and subject are clear and precise, but the claim is a distinctly personal opinion about which it will be difficult to convince readers. Your personal opinion is sometimes a good place to begin but don't stop there. Try to find out why you feel the way you do. Consider the example just stated. No matter what you say about how ugly the new library is, a person who finds it attractive will not find this claim to be persuasive. The only way to objectively demonstrate that something is "ugly" is to define criteria for what "ugly" means and then to apply them. If this is the case, then it is better to use one or more of the criteria for a more precise thesis claim. Ask yourself why you think the library is ugly. You will have to spend some time thinking about your opinion to be sure that it is based on ideas and evidence rather than an off-the-cuff response or something you heard and adopted without thought. If you think that the building is ugly because its lines are repetitive, the material used is impractical, and the space allocation is inefficient, then your thesis might look something like this:

> The architectural design of the new library is repetitive, impractical, and inefficient. The advantage of this thesis is that it sets up the essay's format and cues the reader about the major topics that will be covered.

ASKING "SO WHAT?"

There are benefits to making a thesis statement even more focused, namely that it allows you to see more clearly the significance of your claim. To illustrate, let's attempt to bring even greater focus to the revised thesis statement. We can begin by looking for an over-arching idea that encompasses the three things listed in the thesis. Ask yourself *why* it is *significant* that the library's architectural design is repetitive, impractical, and inefficient. Why would you want to draw these three issues to a reader's attention? In other words, *so what*?

Your thesis should be written so as to invite interest. When someone reads the introduction to your essay, the worst thing that can happen is that the reader shrugs and asks, *so what*? Make sure you've asked this question of yourself during the writing process. One way to respond to this question with the example at hand is to develop a point of view or recommendation based on your interrogation of the evidence. For instance:

> The architectural design of the new library is repetitive, impractical, and inefficient, so the building should not be funded.

OR

> The architectural design of the new library is seriously flawed, so the building should not be built.

Here, a reader will be asked to think beyond the criteria for a beautiful or an ugly building and think instead about the implications of those responses—that a building might not be worth erecting. This kind of writing challenges you to go beyond having an opinion—it asks you to think about the possible implications of that opinion and to draw conclusions based on careful analysis that can be reproduced in supporting your claims.

A writer can ask the *so what* question forever—part of the challenge of persuasive writing is knowing when you have reached a thesis that has fully developed the idea with which you are working. The difference between an okay thesis and a really focused thesis is often the difference between an okay paper and a really superb one. Knowing when you have found something of interest takes practice. A strong thesis is always exciting. It provokes interest and has a ring to it—a sense of resonance that invites the reader to continue reading.

You can avoid the problem of the underdeveloped thesis by becoming more familiar with the role the thesis statement plays in the paper and the three parts required for it to fulfill that job. Recognizing how your thesis statement fulfills these demands will help you to see when the thesis is fully formed.

Essential #2: A claim should be debatable; that is, valid alternative viewpoints should be possible.

A good thesis claim should elicit debate in the sense that it should suggest valid alternative viewpoints; that is, not everyone will already agree with it. Said differently, counterpositions or counterarguments should exist. A writer should anticipate the arguments that might be made by those who don't agree with the thesis claim—and, if possible, should strengthen the essay by responding to these alternative viewpoints within the paper.

Consider this thesis claim about the role of computers in our world:

> Although viewed by many as a work-saving addition to modern life, computers have, ironically, increased rather than decreased the amount of time people spend at work.

From among the possible ways to account for the impact of computers on modern society, this thesis chooses one: that computers have *increased* rather than *decreased* the amount of time we spend at work. However, there are a number of ways to counter this argument. One could argue, for instance, that computers have decreased the time required for work because people can now use e-mail as a substitute for some conferences and electronic attachments instead of delivering some documents in person. Here are some examples of alternative claims based on our computer example:

Alternative thesis #1 (positive view on computers):
Although it is widely believed that we spend more time at work than ever before, in fact, because of the wide use of computers in the workplace, the American worker today both accomplishes more and has more free time.

Alternative thesis #2 (positive view on computers):
Computers have led the way to a new sense of professionalism for the American worker.

Alternative thesis #3 (neutral view on computers):
In spite of the expectation that computers would bring greater efficiency and more free time to the American worker, computers have had very little impact on either of these.

All three of these alternative thesis statements have the same context and subject but offer different claims regarding the impact of computers on the American worker. Although we can imagine some overlap in the papers that would result from these thesis statements, these four claims would lead to significantly different papers, all of them potentially interesting and rewarding.

Essential #3: A claim should reveal a perceptive point.
In developing a claim, remember that a perceptive point is not necessarily a right point (as opposed to a wrong point) as much as it is an imaginative or provocative view on a subject. It should be interesting, have resonance, and be phrased in such a way that it

elicits interest or provokes thought on the part of the reader. It should say just enough to get the reader's interest and to make the reader want to read more.

Finding something insightful to offer is a challenge for any writer. It is important that you realize that there is no hidden "correct" answer that you are trying to uncover (and that you think the instructor may be withholding). The secret is to develop an interesting point using your own imagination and intelligence.

As discussed earlier, when a thesis statement is underdeveloped and does not yet include a perceptive point, readers will often ask writers, *so what*? In other words, the thesis statement falls flat; it may be lacking a claim, or it may have a claim that is not very perceptive. Asking, *so what*? guides the writer to focus on the claim portion of the thesis statement to push it one step further, to punch it up. Here is an example:

In *Dombey and Son*, Dickens uses the figure of the triangle in every scene.

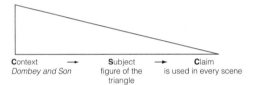

Context → Subject → Claim
Dombey and Son   figure of the   is used in every scene
                    triangle

This thesis identifies an interesting pattern in the novel, the use of the triangle in every scene. Examine this statement further using the *so what*? technique suggested above. Does the thesis tell us why the subject, the pattern of triangles, is important or significant? In this case, no. Saying that *Dombey and Son* uses the triangle in every scene doesn't answer the more interesting question of *why* the writer of the thesis thinks the presence of the triangles is important. Why should the reader care that there are triangles in each scene? What does the figure of the triangle bring to the novel, especially given its frequent appearance? In other words, *so what* that there are triangles in every scene? A claim should suggest the significance of the subject, but there is no phrase in this sentence that does this work. As a thesis, it is underdeveloped.

Now explore this thesis from the position of the reader. A reader who hasn't noticed the triangles may find this to be an insightful and imaginative observation. However, imagine the paper that would follow from this thesis. The evidence that would be used to support this claim would simply be a long list of the scenes that contain triangles. How interesting is a paper that consists of paragraph after paragraph describing the places in the novel where triangles appear? The idea of triangles in Dickens may entice a reader, yet the reader may finish the paper feeling unsatisfied because it simply exposed the triangles but did not offer an interpretation, an assertion, about why they appear so often and why they are important. A reader of this essay might be left with more questions than answers. This is a situation that can be prevented by asking the *so what* question, perhaps a few more times.

BETTER:

Throughout *Dombey and Son*, the triangle emerges as a symbol of the family, which is privileged as the ideal unit of society.

This statement is a significant improvement on the first because now there is a clear focus for the discussion about *Dombey and Son*. This paper will not only call attention to places where the triangle appears, but it will also show how the triangle contributes to the thematic aspects of the novel. According to this thesis, the reoccurring presence of the triangle symbolizes the family (mother, father, child) and suggests that this family trinity is the ideal unit in society. In imagining the paper that would result from this thesis, a writer would have to identify a number of scenes in the novel where triangles represent the family trinity and then show how this representation is privileged.

One way of determining whether you have a provocative claim is to draft the thesis statement and then step back from it for a moment. Ask yourself, does the thesis you have just written suggest a reason or interpretation for why the subject is significant? Double-check to be sure that you have an independent subject and claim (sometimes a complex subject can be mistaken for a claim, as in this example with the triangles). If you are not sure that you have both a subject and a claim, isolate the subject and then ask yourself, "What's the perceptive point I'm making about this subject? Why is this important?" If your thesis sentence contains an answer to this question, it is probably a fully developed thesis statement. If not, then it might be a *half thesis*, a thesis where the subject is clear, but the claim is undeveloped. In other words, the complicated wording of the subject fools the writer into thinking that a claim has been made.

Remember that your claim is the key to your thesis statement, and your thesis statement is the key to your essay. So, as we are directing our attention to exactly what a claim is and what it does, let us also take some time to examine what a claim is *not* and how we can fix four common problems with the claim.

Four Potential Problems and How to Fix Them

There is much overlap among the common problems with claims, especially when talking about self-evident claims, statements of fact, and statements of summary. Try not to spend too much time figuring out the nuances among these often overlapping distinctions. Instead, learn from this section how to determine the difference between a strong claim and one that still requires some work. A strong thesis statement will suggest a clear course for the paper, while a self-evident claim, a statement of fact or summary, or a statement of a plan rarely lead beyond the obvious or superficial. When used as claims, these statements lead to dead ends.

Four Potential Problems with the Claim . . .

1. The claim is self-evident.

2. The claim is a statement of fact.

3. The claim is a statement of summary.

4. The claim is a statement of a plan.

Problem #1: A claim should not be self-evident.

A claim should not be self-evident; it should be something worth writing about that is not readily apparent, something that demands thorough introspection or study, the results of which are presented in the paper. Truly interesting claims have a mark of creativity and ingenuity. They have a spark, and they invite the reader to take an interest in the paper. Admittedly, writing good claims takes practice. Most often they are the products of extensive reading, thinking, brainstorming, and prewriting—strategies that are covered in the next few chapters of this book.

EXAMPLE:

In Shakespeare's corpus of work, the play *Romeo and Juliet* is a tragic love story.

No one who has read *Romeo and Juliet* could argue with this statement; it does not generate interest or debate because it is likely that even those who have not read or seen the play would already know this statement to be true. However, with some work, it can be developed in productive ways.

Brainstorm to find a more insightful claim. Notice that "tragic love story" suggests a link between love and death. Can we think of something in the play that expands on this link between love and death? What about the last scene where the Montagues and Capulets, whose family feud has divided the city of Verona throughout the play, commiserate with one another over the double tragedy of young death?

....

DID YOU KNOW . . .

In the last lines of Shakespeare's famous play *Romeo and Juliet*, the feuding families begin to set their differences aside. Juliet's father says to Romeo's father, "O brother Montague give me thy hand" and Romeo's father replies, "But I can give thee more;/ For I will raise her statue in pure gold,/ That whiles Verona by that name is known,/ There shall no figure at such rate be set/ As that of true and faithful Juliet."

....

The final few lines suggest there will be a change in the relationship between these two powerful families, perhaps even an end to the feud. Given this, let's try to formulate a thesis statement about this new relationship and its possible effects on the city of Verona.

BETTER:

Shakespeare's *Romeo and Juliet* presents the view that love has the power to reform a community.

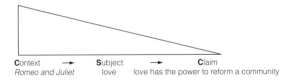

Context   →   Subject   →   Claim
Romeo and Juliet   love   love has the power to reform a community

This thesis statement entices the reader to examine the realm of human values to decide how, specifically, love might redefine the relationships within a community. Even readers who are already quite familiar with *Romeo and Juliet* may not have considered the play from this particular vantage point. A paper that develops this claim likely will reveal ideas new to the reader and, perhaps, excite a reader's interest in a way that the self-evident statement does not.

Problem #2: A claim should not be a statement of fact.

A claim should not be a statement of fact; it should be an insightful assertion that offers an opportunity for disagreement. It should not be a belief that is so widely held that it is virtually accepted as truth; you should be able to imagine at least one good counter-argument. Always test your claim to see if you can envision anyone disagreeing with it. A good claim is always more than a set of facts—it offers an interpretation based on facts.

EXAMPLE #1:
> Cell phones have changed our society.

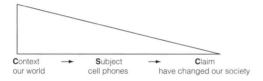

It is difficult to imagine anyone in the twenty-first century arguing with this statement. Part of the problem with this thesis claim is the overly general phrase "changed our society." Like the situation with a subject that is too broad, this thesis can be improved by using the *shift left* method to say something more specific about *how* cell phones have changed our society. This means the original claim moves to the subject position and the subject moves to the context position. Then a claim can be written about the new subject. In using this technique, be aware that a claim is typically a verb clause, whereas a subject is typically a noun clause. When you take the claim and push it left into the subject position, you will probably need to adjust it a bit by turning a verb clause into a noun clause.

BETTER:
> Although cell phones make communication easier, they in fact have brought about a society where people are increasingly isolated from one another.

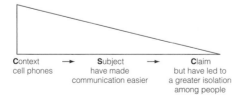

Not everyone would agree with this statement; in fact, the prevalent assumption might be the opposite, that cell phones are welcomed because they bring us closer together.

This revision of the thesis attempts to be more precise about an ironic effect that cell phones have had on our relations with one another.

EXAMPLE #2:

There is a heated debate in the United States today over whether or not to mandate greater fuel efficiency.

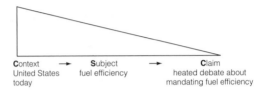

Context → Subject → Claim
United States   fuel efficiency   heated debate about
today   mandating fuel efficiency

Not only is this a statement of fact, but it is also somewhat superficial as a thesis statement—it offers no real insight about or position on the fuel efficiency controversy. Use the *shift left* method to create a space for a more appropriate claim.

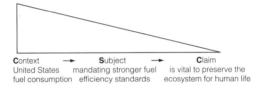

Context → Subject → Claim
United States   mandating stronger fuel   is vital to preserve the
fuel consumption   efficiency standards   ecosystem for human life

BETTER:

It is vital for the United States to mandate stronger fuel efficiency standards to preserve the ecosystem for human life.

By shifting left, this thesis statement has gone from stating a fact—that there is a continuing debate regarding fuel efficiency standards—to taking a position on the issue.

Problem #3: A claim should not be a statement of summary.

A claim should not be a statement of summary; it should be an interpretation of a subject rather than an overview of it. If the subject is a story or a novel, then the claim should articulate an opinion about it, rather than give a summary of its plot. If the subject is an event, such as a war, then the claim should offer a viewpoint about the war rather than simply present key events. If the subject pertains to a social issue, such as gun control, animal rights, or environmentalism, then the claim should offer a position or reveal some insight about the issue (or its society) rather than simply present an overview of the various arguments. In other words, a claim should not reduce the subject to a single sentence where the subject is described rather than interpreted. The claim should suggest why a subject has significance.

EXAMPLE #1:

As one of many films that depict human atrocities, Steven Spielberg's film *Saving Private Ryan* presents the horrors of war.

Context → Subject → Claim
films on _Saving Private_ presents the
human atrocities _Ryan_ horrors of war

Anyone who has seen _Saving Private Ryan_ realizes after only a few minutes that this film presents the horrors of war. Why is it significant that the horrors of war are presented in this film? What do you think the film accomplishes by showing the horrors of war? Is it attempting to show the viewer that war is horrible? Who wouldn't agree?

Let's approach this question from a slightly different angle. Rather than trying to figure out whether or not the thesis is a statement of summary (compared to a statement of fact, for instance), think for a moment about the paper that would result from this particular thesis. What would this thesis allow a writer to explore beyond the fact that horrors appear in more scenes than not in this film? In other words, supporting a thesis in which Spielberg's film serves as the subject and "presents the horrors of war" appears as the claim would lead to a list of all the scenes where war horrors are illustrated. That wouldn't result in a very interesting paper for the average reader who might find lists inconclusive. The paper would be merely a summary of scenes of the film—something that requires little analytical thought.

However, this statement of summary may be a good beginning. To help develop this thesis, use the _shift left_ method to find something insightful.

BETTER:
> Steven Spielberg's film _Saving Private Ryan_ argues that the horrors of war bring out the goodness in humans.

Context → Subject → Claim
Saving Private Ryan horrors of war bring out the goodness in humans

To support this thesis, the writer would have to examine all the ways in this film that human goodness comes through in spite of the devastation of war. Compared with the original thesis, this one promises a deeper and more satisfying treatment of this film.

Here is another example of a thesis statement that is improved by using the graduated triangle to isolate and examine the statement's C-S-C parts.

EXAMPLE #2:
> While some think a policy of open immigration is important to preserve American freedom, others see it as a dangerous assault on that freedom.

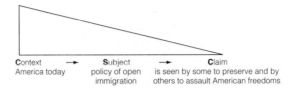

Context → Subject → Claim
America today policy of open is seen by some to preserve and by
immigration others to assault American freedoms

This thesis simply summarizes two major positions concerning immigration to the United States. While this might be appropriate for an information paper that requires you to present the major issues (see chapters 8 and 10), an argument paper should choose a position and defend it with carefully organized evidence and persuasive reasoning.

BETTER:

> While some think that a policy of open immigration will be a dangerous assault on American freedom, it is in fact necessary to preserve domestic freedom.

OR

> While some think a policy of open immigration is necessary to protect American freedom, it is in fact a threat to the very ideals protected by the Constitution.

Notice the difference between summarizing a debate and taking a position on it. For the thesis-driven paper, you would choose a position and argue persuasively that it is the best alternative given all the options.

Problem #4: A claim should not be a statement of a plan.

A claim should not be a statement of a plan where the subject of the paper is announced but its significance is not made clear. Like the statement of fact or statement of summary, the statement of a plan will not make any insightful observation or point about the issues or plan proposed.

EXAMPLE:

This paper will examine the reasons why rottweilers are chosen as pets.

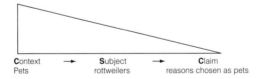

Context → Subject → Claim
Pets rottweilers reasons chosen as pets

By trying to fill in the C-S-C triangle, we can see that the claim lacks an argument, that is, an interpretation or a point of view. The writer's promise to "examine the reasons" sidesteps the need to draw some conclusions based on an examination of these reasons. This paper will likely result in a list rather than an argument. Statements of a plan can be corrected by presenting the findings rather than the plan.

BETTER:

> While insurance companies, among others, believe that rottweilers are dangerous dogs, the qualities natural to this breed make them ideal pets.

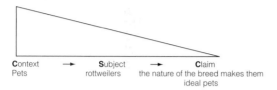

Context → Subject → Claim
Pets   rottweilers   the nature of the breed makes them
                           ideal pets

Notice that in revising this example, we have moved from examining the reasons to making a specific claim about these dogs. Rather than a listlike paper presenting why rottweilers are chosen as pets, this paper will present the unexpected—it will explain why these seemingly aggressive dogs appeal to pet owners.

THE THESIS STATEMENT CHECKLIST   *for RD 1*

▶ Isolate your thesis statement and write it down.

▶ Check your thesis statement's C-S-C to be sure it has a solid context, subject, and claim.

▶ Check to see that the insightful point that is offered pertains to the thesis statement's subject. If you can't identify both the subject and the claim, you might have a complex subject masquerading as a claim. Use the *so what?* approach to help avoid this.

▶ Check the scope of your subject to make sure it is not too narrow, too broad, or too vague.

▶ Check to make sure your claim reveals a perceptive point.

▶ Check to be sure that your claim is debatable, that it is a controversial idea rather than an obvious one. You might make a quick list of the arguments against your claim to be sure there are at least two different valid positions on the issue that you are addressing. If you can't think of any contrary evidence, you probably need to revise your claim to make it stronger.

▶ Check to be sure the argument you are making can be supported by objective criteria and that it does not simply offer your personal opinion.

▶ Check to make sure your claim is not
  • self-evident
  • a statement of fact
  • a statement of summary
  • a statement of a plan

APPLICATIONS AND WRITING EXERCISES

Application 2.1 Identifying the Context, Subject, and Claim

For each of the following thesis statements, identify the context, subject, and claim. It might help you to use one of the schematics for identifying the parts of the thesis statement: the graduated triangle, the sentence, or the list format. The first one is done for you as an example.

1. For the music industry today, copyright laws should be set aside in favor of free Internet distribution.

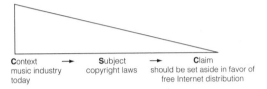

Context → Subject → Claim
music industry   copyright laws   should be set aside in favor of
today   free Internet distribution

2. Nintendo's video game *James Bond* encourages the breakdown of family values.

3. In William Faulkner's *As I Lay Dying*, the child is used as a vehicle to portray the South's arrested development.

4. Men's mental health today still depends on being the main financial provider for the family.

5. The major weakness in this department's efficiency is the lack of punctuality.

Application 2.2 Transforming Subjective Opinions into Objective Claims

For the following subjective opinions, replace each subjective term (underlined) with a term or phrase that can be objectively supported.

1. The movie that was ranked first at the box office last week is a <u>terrible</u> movie.

2. Stephen King's recent novel is his <u>best.</u>

3. Boxing is the <u>silliest</u> sport ever invented.

4. The capturing of endangered species for exotic dining is <u>reprehensible.</u>

5. My little brother is my <u>favorite</u> sibling because he is so <u>gross.</u>

Application 2.3 Considering Alternative Claims

Consider whether the following thesis statements allow for the possibility of alternative claims. What might those alternative claims be? How does the possibility for alternative claims enrich your understanding of the subject being analyzed? It might help to use the graduated triangle first to map out the context, subject, and claim of each thesis statement.

1. The television show *The Simpsons* contributes to an American cultural trend of anti-intellectualism.

2. The most important lesson of the twenty-first century is that racial equality will be the secret to world peace.

3. The Olympic ideal of the amateur athlete participating in friendly international competition has been eroded by human greed.

4. Popular performers are necessary role models for young men and women.

Application 2.4 Recognizing When a Thesis Lacks a Perceptive Point

For the following sentences, identify which are thesis statements and which statements lack a perceptive point.

1. Our local mayor, Bill Smith, is an antitax leader who confessed to using campaign money inappropriately.

2. Several new cable television programs are made to appeal to "tweens," or eight- to twelve-year-olds, a demographic group that is courted by marketers.

3. When doing home repairs, it is better to have luck than skill.

4. Children who are abducted are most often taken by someone they know.

5. The breeding of domestic cats with wild cats should be outlawed.

Application 2.5 Reviewing C-S-C

Examine the following *New York Times* online excerpts and identify the C-S-C for those that are fully developed thesis statements. For those that are not fully developed, explain why.

1. "Cutting Taxes Faster Would Help Everyone."

2. "The Bush administration strategy is to prevent criticism of what amounts to a fiscal debacle by wrapping its budget in the flag."

3. "Afghanistan will prove again that helping war-torn third-world countries is a smarter policy that running away from them."

4. "All the sound and fury about Enron . . . obscures a more basic problem that is ubiquitous in corporate life today: organizational structures that discourage honesty and suppress truth."

5. "In an era of unchecked self-expression and emotional outbursts, modesty and discretion made Sade a star."

6. "President Bush said today that a 57-year accumulation of nuclear waste from power plants and weapons should be buried in the Nevada desert at Yucca Mountain . . .."

7. "President Bush said today that a Peace Corps team would leave within three weeks for Afghanistan to assess how the program could help reconstruct the country."

8. "Lately, however, there are signs that such confidence [in clergy-penitent privilege] may increasingly be misplaced."

Do in class   *OUTLINING*

Writing Exercise 2.1 Identifying and Analyzing a Thesis Statement in an Essay

Read *The Beatles* - Rubber Soul: *The Fab Four's Transitional Near-Masterpiece*, by Spence D. Analyze the essay by answering the following questions.

THINKING THROUGH A READING

do individ. then share answers

1. What is the writer's thesis statement? Identify its context, subject, and claim. Is the thesis statement insightful? Is it debatable?

2. Identify the topics that support the claim.

3. Write an outline for this essay based on the information you found in the two previous tasks.

4. How convincing is the essay and why? *informative) knowledgeable tone*

The Beatles – Rubber Soul:[1]
The Fab Four's Transitional Near-Masterpiece
Spence D.

Thesis

One listen to *Rubber Soul* and you will immediately realize that this album marked a significant turning point in The Beatles' shifting sense of musicality. The 14 songs included here began to bridge the gap between their early blues/pop covers and subsequent short, snappy singles, but more importantly heralded the impending approach of their full-blown sonic re-discovery that would come two years later on *Sgt. Pepper's Lonely Hearts Club Band*.

Support

While an undeniable milestone in their discography, *Rubber Soul* isn't without its faults. Most noticeable is the overwhelming sense that the band was involved in a creative tug-of-war. The album is rife with subdued push-and-pull feeling: on the one hand the band seems to be pushing toward their eventual psychedelic awakening all the while being pulled back to their blues/rock roots. The result is an album that is undeniably infectious, but still only begins to hint at the brilliance the quartet would eventually unleash. Perhaps this is the true sign of the Beatles' lasting greatness, the simple fact that you can actually hear them going through their sonic education and transmogrification from album to album. Their shift was a gradual one that didn't jar the fans too much as some other outfits have been prone to do over the years. This sense of consistent growth is an all too rare occurrence in the realm of pop music.

"Drive My Car" is pretty standard Beatles fare for the time period; blues intoned piano rolling underneath twangy guitar and raspy throated vocals. It's vintage Old School Beatles. The first signs of a noticeable rift come with "Norwegian Wood," a track that not only utilizes somewhat cryptic lyrics ("I wanted a girl or should I say she wanted me/she showed me her room, isn't it good, Norwegian Wood?...") and the introduction of sitar. While the Indian instrument would come into play in a much more major way down the

[1]Spence D., review of The Beatles - Rubber Soul, http://music.ign.com/articles/681/681058p1.html

line, here it blends seamlessly with the stripped down acoustic guitars and tambourine shuffle rhythms.

By the time we reach the third track, "You Won't See Me" they've blended the two styles, adherence to the standard pop motif of verse-chorus-verse, doo-wop harmonies, and an infectious sense of what it means to make catchy, yet intelligent music. "Nowhere Man" returns them to the inklings of psychedelia, thanks to Lennon's whiny vocals which swirl over the wonderful guitar licks. It's still got the new-fangled doo-wop vocalistics working in the background and it's not quite full-tilt out of the ozone, but it's a step in the right direction.

They slip back to their roots somewhat on "Think For Yourself," although allowing some mock garage fuzz into the mix, thus morphing their standard blues based pop ditty structure into something slightly different. A wonderfully droll bop bounce energy fumigates "The Word," again another one of those tracks that struggles to break free of the band's old ways, mostly striving for the transition in the way the vocals are delivered, thin and hypnotically veiled. "Michelle," perhaps the most straightforward love song on the entire album, is a wonderfully sedate acoustic number that dips into pseudo barbershop quartet terrain thanks to the "ooh-ooh-oohs" lilting in the background.

The Fab Four then do a complete back flip and kick out a bona fide honky-tonk number in the form of "What Goes On." Having Ringo take the lead vocals certainly lends a different air to the track, but the finger picking and twang bass are what really do it. A wonderful WTF insertion that shows the boys droll sense of sonic humor was not just a fluke. "Girl" returns to the swooning yet stripped down love ballad, replete with sweet vocal harmonies. The track is given a little twist thanks to the strange sucking noises that go on in between the chorus.

"I'm Looking Through You" is a McCartney fronted number that is all acoustic shuffle and folk song sing-a-long. The lyrics are incredibly self-reflective in terms of where The Beatles were at and where they were headed: "I'm looking through you, where did you go?/I thought I knew you, what did I know?/You don't look different, but you have changed/I'm looking through you, you're not the same..." Anybody who had succumbed to Beatlemania was certainly beginning to see the writing on the wall that this album revealed.

"In My Life" follows in the vein of "Norwegian Wood," melancholic yet blissful in its simplistic construction and acoustic drift. The Mozartian piano solo in the middle again points to their sense of humor. "Wait" finds the group being pulled back to their roots and is one of the more "standard" numbers here. It's immediately backed up by the jangly "If I Needed Someone," a tune that has a distinctive pre-No Depression vibe thanks to the chime infused guitar playing. Not quite spacey, but the hints of psychedelic over-rush are beginning to shine through the widening cracks. This is one of those tunes that's a perfect bridge between the old Beatles and the new Beatles.

The final number on the album, "Run For Your Life," goes back to the band's roots, albeit substituting some of their more obvious blues and traditional rock emphasis for a decidedly more noticeable folksy extrapolation, rendered in glorious slide-styled guitar twang and a dusty boot stomping shuffle.

Rubber Soul is really the last great somewhat old-styled Beatles album, the logical stop-gap before they found "enlightenment" and began dropping Vitamin L. Anyone who first discovered the music of John, Paul, George, and Ringo via *Sgt. Pepper's* may be a bit put off at first, but chalk that up to retro shock and nothing more. In the end the sheer infectious nature of the pop song compositions is undeniable and inescapable. It may not be their greatest album, but it's still one of their best.

CHAPTER 3

Using Critical Thinking to Develop a Thesis Statement

In chapter 2 we discussed the three components of a thesis statement and the three essentials for an effective claim. Now we will build on that definition by discussing two specific critical thinking techniques—observation and abstraction—that are central to thesis statement development.

Observation is one of the most basic of techniques, but it is indispensable to analysis and critical thinking. *In this context,* observation *is a systematic and highly focused method of examining texts that requires sustained concentration, note-taking, and perception so that you can see more in what you are observing than the casual observer would see.* You can collect observations on an experiment in the lab or in the field; from research found in a library or on the Internet; from a novel, film, or television show; or from a piece of music, a concert, or a presentation. In short, observation can help you better understand almost anything. Good observation skills take practice to develop and are crucial to thesis development because your observations provide the raw materials from which your thesis statements will be derived.

Developing a thesis statement also requires a certain way of thinking called **abstraction**. Abstraction *is a type of logical deduction used to find a connection between two or more things or ideas.* Its goal is to identify something that the items share that is unexpected. At its best, abstraction relies on logic as well as creativity, and it is especially useful for finding an *insightful idea* that can serve as the backbone of your working thesis statement.

Observation and **abstraction** are *recursive processes*. This means that you will likely return to them again and again during the writing of your paper. After all, most writers begin not with a thesis statement but with an idea—even a gut instinct—about which they want to write. Observation and abstraction can help to develop that idea, that instinct, into a working thesis statement. The recursiveness of this process—the reoccurrence of critical thinking and prewriting at any stage—shows you that the proposed or working thesis statement is always open to change and refinement. Therefore, thesis statements should not be viewed in terms of being right or wrong. A more useful way to envision them is as fully developed or under developed. For now, remember that the assumption throughout this chapter (and book), is that **most writers do not have the perfect thesis statement when they begin to write a paper**. Effective theses arise, sometimes slowly, from careful and systematic thought and research—and they can sometimes transform in surprising ways as you draft and revise your paper.

A Closer Look at Observation

Often, when we observe a subject, we identify two or three details about it and then quickly categorize the subject based on this quick look and on what we already know about it. Once we have what we feel is an answer or a conclusion about what we observe, we stop examining and take our conclusion or answer to be final. Resist this urge to observe only in a superficial way. It's important to realize that the first response is likely a surface-level only, based on conventional ideas that we accept without question. Instead, we recommend that you spend time with your subject. Even after you've formed impressions and drawn conclusions based on your initial impressions, continue to look at your subject and allow your mind to see things that are not on the surface, things that are more subtle. Be patient; give yourself time to register every aspect and detail. Be creative. What is your reaction to the subject you're observing? Have you considered the subject's historical context, its foreground and/or background? Are there elements that are repeated or that form a pattern? If you give yourself time, you will notice things that you didn't immediately see and will likely identify things that casual observers would not perceive.

A useful first step toward careful observation of any subject is to write down your first impressions. List as many things as you can think of regarding the text or topic. The best lists will be unfiltered. Begin simply by describing what you see but do not stop there. Look for words or ideas that seem especially important, issues or tensions that seem pivotal or significant, or patterns that announce themselves because of their arrangement or repetition. Again, be sure to slow down and resist the urge to form general, first-response judgments. Challenge yourself to find unusual nuances and unexpected similarities or differences. The longer you observe, the more your logic and imagination will have the opportunity to work.

When using observation for critical thinking and writing, remember to use *focused attention*. Look at things carefully to avoid allowing preconceived judgments to come between you and the study of your subject. Be aware that your identity—your race, class, gender, life experience, and ideology—will unavoidably shape what you see and don't see. Therefore, different people observing the same object will likely come up with different responses. This is what makes observation such a fruitful technique. And interestingly, observing something else is sometimes the best way to learn about yourself.

Observation requires patience and the ability to suspend judgment in the interest of further exploration. To discipline yourself to be a better observer and thinker, you will have to become comfortable with confusion and indecision. It is often at the point where you think you have too many ideas and are simply confused that a pattern will emerge or an insight will come to you. Don't be afraid to wait to form a thesis statement until you have allowed your ideas time to develop. Drawing conclusions too quickly closes off the process of analysis and impedes a fuller understanding of your subject. Remember, though, that this technique requires you to plan ahead to give your ideas enough time to percolate before the paper's deadline.

Don't underestimate the power of good observation skills. In short, by becoming a better observer, you will have better ideas.

Strategies for Effective Observation

⇒ Critical Thinking

▶ Use who, what, where, when, why, and how to ask questions about your subject.

▶ Consult class notes or textbooks to see what details you can add to your list.

▶ Do library or Internet research to see what others have observed and try to add to these impressions.

▶ If you are working with a text, underline key words in a paragraph and examine them, looking for relevance to other key ideas in the text. Do any of these words play a particularly important role? Do any connections come to mind that you can list?

▶ If you are working with a cultural artifact (e.g., statue, painting, music), examine the artifact for ten minutes, listing as many traits as you can.

▶ Look for patterns. Are there repeating images, sounds, colors, themes, or shapes? Note all the similarities and differences you can find regarding the appearance of these patterns.

Practice 3.1 Practicing Observation
1. Study the image of the daffodils that follows and use the strategies just discussed to make a list of observations.

2. Review your list and search for patterns or similarities that allow you to cluster your observations into groups or sets.

3. Review the clusters and label them in terms of what you find in common.

4. Compare and contrast the clusters. Are any unexpected insights revealed?

5. Now read William Wordsworth's poem, "Daffodils." Compare and contrast your insights to his. How similar (or different) are your observations? Can you draw any conclusions or new perspectives based on this comparison?

Daffodils (1804)[1]

I wandered lonely as a cloud
That floats on high o'er vales and hills,
When all at once I saw a crowd,
A host, of golden daffodils,
Beside the lake, beneath the trees,
Fluttering and dancing in the breeze.

Continuous as the stars that shine
And twinkle on the Milky Way,
They stretch'd in never-ending line
Along the margin of a bay:
Ten thousand saw I at a glance,
Tossing their heads in sprightly dance.

The waves beside them danced; but they
Out did the sparkling waves in glee—
A poet could not but be gay,
In such a jocund company!
I gazed, and gazed, but little thought
What wealth the show to me had brought:

For oft, when on my couch I lie
In vacant or in pensive mood,
They flash upon that inward eye
Which is the bliss of solitude;
And then my heart with pleasure fills,
And dances with the daffodils.

---

[1]William Wordsworth, "Daffodils," http://www.bartleby.com/106/253.html.

A Closer Look at Abstraction

The process of abstraction begins with observation. Like observation, abstraction is something that we all engage in every day. We reason from the *particular* to the *general*—that is, we look for patterns in one particular experience and try to draw general conclusions or ideas about those experiences. When we see someone smile, for instance, we unconsciously make several observations, including what the person is wearing, carrying, or doing; what the person generally looks like; how the person is walking; and whether the person is walking with others. We then use abstraction to *interpret* or draw some conclusion(s) about the smile based on the observations we have made in an effort to decide whether the smile is meant to be a greeting, a reflection of the person's internal thoughts, or a reflection of a good mood. By finding connections among some observations, and foregrounding them over others, we come up with an interpretation of the smile and respond appropriately (e.g., smile in return, run in the opposite direction, or ignore the person). Said differently, from the variety of data we receive in any given situation, we prioritize certain details and use them to categorize and make assessments. By abstracting, or reasoning from the particular (the smile) to the general (what the smile means), we give significance and meaning to our experiences.

Abstraction also requires you to understand that every topic can be approached from one of several different levels of discussion that range from the immediacy of sense impressions to our ideas about them. Analysis operates along a continuum, beginning with direct experience, or the facts, and rising, level by level, to the increasingly complex or abstract meaning we find in that experience—the interpretations. The renowned linguist S. I. Hayakawa uses the example of a cow to show how we can classify any object or idea on different levels. This can range from the more specific level—a particular cow, Bessie—to the more general levels of livestock, asset, and wealth. He uses the image of a ladder, suggesting that we "think up" as we move from the particular to the more general. Bessie shares certain attributes with the members in each of these increasingly abstract categories, as shown in figure 3.1.

Fig. 3.1 Abstraction Ladder

At each of these levels, the cow shares certain attributes with other members of the group, and the comparison among those members brings forward certain insights and discoveries. For example, a cow, a crop of corn, and a tractor can be unified when looked at from the overarching perspective of farm assets. Looking at these items in relation to one another, as a group, and in terms of their shared quality may open new perspectives and insights on them. Notice, however, that as you move away from the specific and toward the general, more and more precise details of the cow fall away. Abstraction moves a specific thing to a level that represents it in terms of one of its integral qualities. The thesis statement functions on this relatively abstract level.

Let's turn to an example to see how abstraction can work. Think for a minute about *trees* and *shoes,* two everyday items that, on a concrete level, are distinctly unalike.

Imagine that your instructor asks you to compare shoes and trees to practice finding connections between two items that you did not at first see. In Hayakawa's terms, you are looking for levels of abstraction where both items belong. You should begin your study with *observation,* looking at each item on its own and listing the first qualities that come to mind. We have noted a few observations, but your list should be much longer.

Observation Lists for Shoes and Trees

shoes
- have shoelaces, soles, and seams

- are worn on the feet for comfort and protection

- come in different colors

- can be made of leather, cloth, or rubber

trees
- have bark, roots, and leaves

- are usually planted in the ground

- can provide shade or housing for small creatures

- provide valuable resources for humans

- have green leaves and sometimes have flowers

- require water and light

Now let's use the process of *abstraction* to compare these two items and see if we can move from the *particular* items on each of the lists to find some *general* conclusions. Abstraction will allow us to draw from the comparison a number of qualities that shoes and trees have in common. It's time to prewrite again. Examine the two observation lists and write down everything that comes to mind about what shoes and trees have in common.

Using Abstraction to Find Qualities That Shoes and Trees Share

(abstract or interpretive)
- both serve humanity
- both contribute to human survival
- both function to protect humans from the environment
- both continue to have technological developments that improve their function
- both come in brown or green
- both touch the earth
- both have texture

(specific)
- both are made of cells

Notice that we've arranged the items on this abstraction list to move from the more specific at the bottom to the more interpretive at the top. The lower levels simply *describe* what shoes and trees have in common (e.g., both come in green, both have texture and touch the earth, both are made of cells), whereas the higher levels *interpret* or draw some conclusion about both shoes and trees (e.g., both serve humanity, both contribute to human survival). The interpretive ideas are more compelling for a thesis statement because their complexity warrants further thought, but the more concrete conclusions may be necessary to get you started. After all, how would you write an argumentative paper based on the idea that both shoes and trees touch the earth or have texture? These conclusions are too factual to warrant much discovery. You could, however, develop an argument about *how* they contribute to human survival or serve humanity. Because these interpretations are intriguing and potentially insightful, they can be used to anchor your thesis statement and thus your paper. Note that some of the descriptive observations lower on the scale might be used as supporting evidence for a paper based on one of the ideas higher on the scale. Abstraction is a difficult concept to master, so study "Strategies for Using Abstraction" and then try "Practice 3.2." that follows.

Strategies for Using Abstraction

▶ Try to clarify an item by rephrasing it using different words to capture the idea even more precisely. Are there any connections you now see between this item and another on the observation list? Explore those connections.

▶ Challenge an item by asking *so what*? about a particular detail or characteristic that is there. Check to see if the significance you find relates to any of the other observations you have made about your subject. Does it put some of your observations in a new light? Develop your insights as much as possible.

▶ Question items on the observation list by asking who, what, where, when, why, and how. See if your answers to these questions illuminate something unnoticed about your subject. If so, look again at your observations to see if new connections are revealed.

▶ Do any of the observations you listed have a purpose? Try to articulate it.

▶ Who is the intended audience for your analysis? What might they be interested in seeing? Can you build on your observations in ways that your audience might find especially interesting?

Practice 3.2 Practicing Abstraction

Look closely at the following sets of items. As illustrated with the shoes and trees example, use observation and abstraction to come up with insightful conclusions for each set of items. Begin by writing down simple descriptive words (observation) and then explore your thoughts as you spend more time with each set of terms (abstract). Try to find interpretive ideas that overarch each group of terms, that is, something that all the terms in the group share.

1. prescription drugs and health insurance

2. pets and vacations

3. airports and foreign countries

4. happiness and anxiety

Thinking Critically to Develop a Thesis Statement

So what, exactly, are you trying to achieve when using observation and abstraction? Namely, you are looking for an *insightful idea* that can serve as the kernel of your thesis claim. *The insightful idea is a provocative perspective or point of view; it is something that is intriguing, that deserves further exploration. It's a particular kind of idea that lends itself to interesting—and controversial— discussion.* In short, it's the cornerstone of the claim.

For instance, in chapter 2 we examined the following thesis statement:

> The poor food served on the campuses of most universities across the nation represents campus administrators' privileging of profit over student health.

The insightful idea in this thesis is the implied promise to explain why the food on college campuses is poor and how university administrators favor profits over students' health. It will be interesting to see what evidence the writer brings forward to support this view.

In the thesis statement from chapter 2 about the discovery of water on Mars, the insightful idea put forward is also a position. This one tries to explain the significance of a finding and to overturn conventional beliefs in the process. The thesis statement declares that the discovery of water on Mars suggests that life could have existed on this planet. This thesis is insightful because it challenges the long-held belief that there is no life on Mars.

As you can see, it's not easy to come up with insightful ideas—or sometimes even to recognize them. As you familiarize yourself with observation and abstraction and their usefulness in developing an insightful idea, you may find that you customize these techniques to suit your own writing and critical thinking processes. These techniques can be relied on to help you develop a successful thesis statement, but they require persistent and focused thought—in other words, a lot of hard work. An insightful idea comes out of a lot of intensive scrutiny about a specific topic and will not likely appear early in the process. Note that the conclusions you draw from the evidence you gather are not in themselves thesis statements. You must select an idea that is both interpretive and intriguing to serve as the basis for a thesis statement and then refine the thesis to meet the requirements of your paper assignment (more on this in part 2). Abstraction, in particular, can help you to form a vision that is large enough to connect a number of seemingly unrelated details.

Considering All the Evidence

When using abstraction to come up with an insightful idea for your working thesis statement, it is important to consider all the evidence; otherwise a hasty generalization could be reached. If you consider only a select amount of evidence, then you might draw a less compelling—even invalid—conclusion. Sometimes, adding just one piece of information produces a very different conclusion.

Here's an example: Imagine that you are talking on the phone with a friend, and he is telling you about a recent camping trip he took with his mother, father, and sister. As you listen to the details he gives you, you consciously or unconsciously use abstraction to draw conclusions about the trip in general. In other words, your friend provides you with the observations about the trip. As with the earlier example of the smile, you will naturally begin to draw some conclusions as you listen to derive some meaning from the details you are given. He begins by telling you that

- the family went fishing every day

- they caught lots of fish

- they had a contest over who could catch the biggest fish

From this evidence, you abstract the overarching idea that this family likes to fish. Even though your friend might not have stated this directly, the conclusion can be validly drawn from the facts he gave you. As the conversation with your friend continues, imagine that you collect the following additional information:

- they hiked through forests

- they built campfires every night

- everyone slept until 10 each morning

From this evidence, you might formulate a number of overarching ideas, some of them descriptive and some more interpretive. For example, the trip allowed this family to get closer through shared fun, to get some healthy exercise, to experience new things, to catch up on their relaxation, or to find stress relief from the demands of their daily routines. These are all reasonable ideas that can be abstracted from this list of available facts so far. Often, as in this example, a number of equally valid claims can be formulated from the available evidence. But later in the conversation with your friend, he might, for example, reveal that he and his sister had a big fight the first day of the trip and didn't speak to one another the entire weekend.

Although only one piece of new evidence has been added, it is an important piece of the overall picture. Some of the conclusions formed before this piece of information was known must now be reconsidered. For instance, the conclusion that the trip was a chance for this whole family to get closer to one another now seems questionable. If you had continued to work with this idea of family closeness, you might have formulated a working thesis statement based on partial evidence; in other words, you might have formulated an invalid thesis statement.

As you can see, it is important to accumulate as much data as possible as you work to develop a working thesis statement. Abstracting from partial evidence can result in an invalid claim.

Putting It All Together: Using Observation and Abstraction to Draft a Thesis Statement

FIVE STEPS FOR USING OBSERVATION AND ABSTRACTION TO DRAFT A THESIS STATEMENT

1. Create an observation list.

2. Freewrite—move from observing to interpreting.

3. Use summary to identify main points.

4. Use abstraction to find an insightful idea.

5. Draft a working thesis statement using C-S-C; revise as necessary.

Here, step by step, is a student's freewriting method that relies on observation and abstraction to uncover insightful ideas about the way in which the ad in figure 3.2 uses images and text to make an argument.

Fig. 3.2 Frasier "Got Milk?" Ad

Step #1: Create an Observation List

List as many observations as you can about the ad for milk shown in Fig. 3.2. Just describe the details you see, without attempting to understand or analyze them.

Here is one list:

1. This is a picture of the main characters in the TV show *Frasier*. They look happy, comfortable, and well-groomed.

2. Frasier, Niles, Daphne, and Roz are wearing dressy, expensive-looking clothes. The two women are in dresses, Daphne has on high-heeled sandals, and Frasier and Niles are wearing shirts buttoned to the neck and seem to have on ties. All of them have milk mustaches.

3. Everyone except the father, Martin Crane, is holding a cocktail glass filled with milk. The father is holding his dog, Eddie. They are standing in front of a large window. The view in the background shows that their apartment, which looks expensive, is high over a big city.

4. Under the picture, the text reads, "The general populace isn't merely lacking culture, it's lacking calcium. In fact, 70% of men and 90% of women don't get enough. The enlightened among us, however, drink 3 glasses of milk a day. A practice that can prevent a Freudian condition known as 'calcium envy.'"

Step #2: Freewrite—Move from Observing to Interpreting

Speculate on what you have observed by exploring each detail in writing. What do the details you've listed make you think about? Let yourself respond to each detail fully. Don't filter your thoughts—just write down anything that occurs to you.

For example, each of the observations listed in Step #1 about the ad for milk can now be explored:

- *(1) This is a picture of the main characters in the TV show* Frasier *. They look happy, comfortable, and well-groomed.*
  They all look very happy to be together and they all, even Martin and Bulldog, who are wearing casual clothes, look like they have taken care with their appearance. They seem to be enjoying themselves. Anyone looking at this picture probably wouldn't mind being with them and even looking like they do. They are smiling and looking out at us, as if they are friendly.

- *(2) Frasier, Niles, Daphne, and Roz are wearing dressy, expensive-looking clothes. The two women are in dresses, Daphne has on high-heeled sandals, and Frasier and Niles are wearing shirts buttoned to the neck and seem to have on ties. All of them have milk mustaches.*
  They all look sophisticated and confident. The two women look very sexy, especially Daphne, who we can see head-to-toe. Most women probably wouldn't mind looking like the women in this picture. Frasier and Niles are also well-dressed and seem sophisticated and confident. They look a little snobbish and self-satisfied, but friendly. Knowing the TV series, I know that Martin, Roz, Daphne, and Bulldog are not smug and pretentious like Frasier and Niles, but in this picture they all seem the same. The ad associates the sophisticated and confident lifestyle of these characters with drinking milk.

- (3) *Everyone except the father, Martin Crane, is holding a cocktail glass filled with milk. The father is holding his small dog. They are standing in front of a large window. The view in the background shows that their apartment, which looks expensive, is high over a big city.*
  I think we're supposed to imagine this place to be a very modern, expensive apartment in a big city. I think it's supposed to be in Seattle, like it is in the show. The high-rise buildings that can be seen outside the window are lit, so it's nighttime, and this makes me think of night life in the city—clubs, live music, dinners—and also other people living in similar high-rise apartments. This ad wouldn't be as interesting if it showed these characters sitting at the kitchen table drinking milk out of everyday milk glasses, because it wouldn't show anything out of the ordinary. Instead, the characters are standing in a living room in front of the large picture window, holding cocktail or beer glasses. Perhaps they are getting ready to go out on the town. This setting is a place where most people would gather to have an alcoholic drink and socialize. They seem to have a fun life. Maybe we're supposed to think about sophisticated people drinking milk instead of alcohol, maybe as a part of their desirable lifestyle.
  The milk mustache makes them seem playful and not intimidating. It shows they have a common, everyday side, and this makes them easy for us to identify with, even though they are so well-dressed.

- (4) *Under the picture, the text reads, "The general populace isn't merely lacking culture, it's lacking calcium. In fact, 70% of men and 90% of women don't get enough. The enlightened among us, however, drink 3 glasses of milk a day. A practice that can prevent a Freudian condition known as 'calcium envy.'"*
  At first, I thought this was just the typical humor that *Frasier* always uses, when Frasier and Niles act snobby and conceited but in a funny, foolish way. But after thinking about it, most people probably admire the culture and sophistication of Frasier and Niles and want to be a little bit like them. If people admire them, and maybe aspire to be like them, perhaps the ad hopes that everyone will think "well, at least I can drink milk like they do." In other words, if the "general populace" is "lacking culture" and "lacking calcium," we can easily make up for lacking in calcium by drinking milk. The message that 70% of men and 90% of women don't get enough calcium is a powerful statistic inserted into this mainly humorous ad. It means that only 30% of men and 10% of women **do** get enough calcium, presumably because they drink lots of milk. I guess we're supposed to think that the "enlightened among us" will drink more milk to be a part of the elite minority who know better. Those not in this minority will want to be in it, will have "calcium envy." The text says that drinking milk is "a practice that can prevent a Freudian condition known as 'calcium envy'." This is funny because it is a play on sexy psychology terminology and reminds us that Frasier and Niles are psychologists, but it tries to give a subtle and sexy power to the importance of drinking milk.

Step #3: Use Summary to Identify the Main Point in Each Paragraph
Use abstraction to distill into one or two sentences the main or overarching idea in each freewriting paragraph. To do this, remember the abstraction scale. Move your observations away from the concrete until you find an idea or perspective that many of them share.

Here, the ideas developed in Step #2 are summarized in an overarching idea or main point:

- *(1) This is a picture of the main characters in the TV show* Frasier *. They look happy, comfortable, and well-groomed.*
  They all look very happy to be together and they all, even Martin and Bulldog, who are wearing casual clothes, look like they have taken care with their appearance. They seem to be enjoying themselves. Anyone looking at this picture probably wouldn't mind being with them and even looking like they do. They are smiling and looking out at us, as if they are friendly.

  The MAIN POINT many of these observations share: The picture of the main characters from the TV show Frasier represents many of the things that people want to identify with, that they admire and want to be like.

- *(2) Frasier, Niles, Daphne, and Roz are wearing dressy, expensive-looking clothes. The two women are in dresses, Daphne has on high-heeled sandals, and Frasier and Niles are wearing shirts buttoned to the neck and seem to have on ties. All of them have milk mustaches.*
  They all look sophisticated and confident. The two women look very sexy, especially Daphne, who we can see head-to-toe. Most women probably wouldn't mind looking like the women in this picture. Frasier and Niles are also well-dressed and seem sophisticated and confident. They look a little snobbish and self satisfied, but friendly. Knowing the TV series, I know that Martin, Roz, Daphne, and Bulldog are not smug and pretentious like Frasier and Niles, but in this picture they all seem the same. The ad associates the sophisticated and confident lifestyle of these characters with drinking milk.

  The MAIN POINT many of these observations share: This ad associates drinking milk with fun and being attractive, with sophistication and happiness.

- *(3) Everyone except the father, Martin Crane, is holding a cocktail glass filled with milk. The father is holding his small dog. They are standing in front of a large window. The view in the background shows that their apartment, which looks expensive, is high over a big city.*
  I think we're supposed to imagine this place to be a very modern, expensive apartment in a big city.
  I think it's supposed to be in Seattle, like it is in the show. The high-rise buildings that can be seen outside the window are lit, so it's nighttime, and this makes me think of night life in the city—clubs, live music, dinners—and also other people living in similar high-rise apartments. This ad wouldn't be as interesting if it showed these characters sitting at the kitchen table drinking milk out of everyday milk glasses, because it wouldn't show anything out of the ordinary. Instead, the characters are standing in a living room in front of the large picture window, holding cocktail or beer glasses. This setting is a place where most people would gather to have an alcoholic drink and socialize. Perhaps they are getting ready to go out on the town. They seem to have a fun life. Maybe we're supposed to think about sophisticated people drinking milk instead of alcohol as a part of their desirable lifestyle. Maybe milk is supposed to

be a better choice than alcohol, almost like an anti-drinking advertisement. The milk mustaches make everyone seem playful and not intimidating. They seem to have a common, everyday side, and this makes them easy for us to identify with, even though they are so well-dressed.

> **The MAIN POINT many of these observations share: Milk is shown as a better drink than alcohol; it's a sophisticated drink for successful, happy people.**

- *(4) Under the picture, the text reads, "The general populace isn't merely lacking culture, it's lacking calcium. In fact, 70% of men and 90% of women don't get enough. The enlightened among us, however, drink 3 glasses of milk a day. A practice that can prevent a Freudian condition known as 'calcium envy.'"* At first, I thought this was just the typical humor that *Frasier* always uses, when Frasier and Niles act snobby and conceited but in a funny, foolish way. But after thinking about it, most people probably admire the culture and sophistication of Frasier and Niles and want to be a little bit like them. If people admire them, and maybe aspire to be like them, perhaps the ad hopes that everyone will think "well, at least I can drink milk like they do." In other words, if the "general populace" is "lacking culture" and "lacking calcium," we can easily make up for lacking in calcium by drinking milk. The message that 70% of men and 90% of women don't get enough calcium is a powerful statistic inserted into this mainly humorous ad. It means that only 30% of men and 10% of women **do** get enough calcium, presumably because they drink lots of milk. I guess we're supposed to think that the "enlightened among us" will drink more milk to be a part of the elite minority who know better. Those not in this minority will want to be in it, will have "calcium envy." The text says that drinking milk is "a practice that can prevent a Freudian condition known as 'calcium envy'." This is funny because it is a play on sexy psychology terminology and reminds us that Frasier and Niles are psychologists, but it tries to give a subtle but sexy power to the importance of drinking milk.

> **The MAIN POINT many of these observations share: The ad is trying to suggest that drinking milk is for those smart enough to know its health benefits.**

Notice that the *main point sentences* are *abstracted* from each paragraph. They represent the ideas contained within the paragraph at a level broad enough so that everything important within the sentence fits underneath it, but not so broad that it is meaningless. Said differently, the main point sentence unifies the freewriting ideas by identifying a perspective that they all share. When locating a main point in your freewriting, remember the abstraction ladder. Try moving up a level or two to find a category that can overarch the ideas you developed in your freewriting.

Step #4: Use Abstraction to Find an Insightful Idea
Place the main point sentences next to each other for easier comparison. When you "add up" the main point sentences, or use abstraction to examine the ideas in relation to one another, are there any insights or connections that you now see? Do the main point sentences share any concepts that add up to a more general, overarching point of view or insightful idea? Remember to try out multiple perspectives and consider all the evidence.

The picture of the main characters from the TV show Frasier represents many of the things that people want to identify with, that they admire and want to be like.

+

This ad associates drinking milk with fun and being attractive, with sophistication and happiness.

+

Milk is shown as a better drink than alcohol; it's a sophisticated drink for successful, happy people.

+

The ad is trying to suggest that drinking milk is for those smart enough to know its health benefits.

= insightful idea

Several intriguing ideas are called to attention once we see the main point ideas listed together: Milk is sexy and fun; it can be associated with a sophisticated, cool lifestyle; and it is favored by people smart enough to know its health benefits. In the ad, these ideas are all linked together by the group image of the characters from *Frasier*.

Step #5: Draft a Working Thesis Statement; Revise as Necessary

To draft a working thesis, isolate one or two intriguing ideas and try to draw a connection between them. Articulate this connection in the form of a complete sentence.

WORKING THESIS STATEMENT:
The ad based on the television show *Frasier* suggests that drinking milk is an important part of the happiest and most successful lifestyles.

Of course, there are other valid and interesting interpretations of this ad for milk. The one provided here is just one possibility, discovered by systematically exploring general thoughts about the image. Although this process takes time, it yields important benefits for you when it comes time to draft the paper. In fact, some of the main point sentences can be revised to serve as topic sentences to introduce important ideas in the paper. Notice that some of the freewriting can be reformulated and included in the body of the paper as evidence in support of the thesis statement. The time spent freewriting and writing main point sentences almost never goes to waste. This technique may produce both a working thesis and a rough first draft of the paper.

Be aware that when you try this technique on your own, it may not always fall into place as nicely as it does in this example. You will likely have many notes scribbled in the margins, crossed-out sentences, underlined words, and other traces of your engagement with these ideas. Rest assured that, in its original form, this example wasn't this clean. Your observation list and freewriting will probably have ideas that aren't worth exploring or that you abandon for other reasons. Don't simply go through the process in a linear fashion, from beginning to end, and be satisfied with any conclusions you've drawn. The important thing is to keep exploring your ideas. Good thinking is always recursive; that is, it continues to explore ground already covered over and over. Keep playing with the freewriting and main point sentences to see if other connections emerge. The more you work with these exploratory strategies, the more successful you will be.

APPLICATIONS AND WRITING EXERCISES

Application 3.1 Practicing Observation

Fig. 3.3 Pablo Picasso, *Guernica*

. . . .

DID YOU KNOW . . .

Guernica is a painting by Pablo Picasso (see figure 3.3) that was inspired by the Nazi German bombing of Guernica, Spain, on April 26, 1937, during the Spanish Civil War. The air raid destroyed the city and killed an estimated 1,600 people. Many more were injured. *Guernica* is done in oil and is eleven-and-one-half-feet high and almost twenty-six feet wide.

. . . .

1. Alone or working with a group, examine Picasso's painting *Guernica*.

2. Create a list of observations. Practice suppressing judgment in the interest of creating as thorough a list as possible.

3. Select one or more ideas on the list that you think are particularly intriguing.

4. Study the ideas you have selected to see if you can see any patterns or relationships among them. Arrange the observations on your list from concrete to interpretive. Pay more attention to the general placement of your items toward one or the other side of the spectrum (concrete or interpretive) rather than trying to determine the exact location of each item relative to other items on the list. Use abstraction to try to find an insightful idea. Does one idea cause or contribute to another? You might also try making a judgment about something on your list to see if it brings any insight.

5. Do your best to write a coherent sentence using the ideas you discovered in #4. Your goal in this exercise is *not* to write a perfect thesis statement (We will explore that later) but to see if you can identify the start of one. Does your sentence contain an insightful idea? Explain why you think it does or does not.

6. Keep working with your observation list and steps 3–5 until you think you have found an insightful idea and can explain why. As needed, go back to brainstorming and adding items to your observation list if you find it inadequate. It might also be helpful to work with a peer to share ideas about whether you have found an insightful idea and how to explain why.

7. Run your working thesis statement through the thesis statement checklist at the end of chapter 2.

8. Revise, as necessary.

Application 3.2 Analyzing an Advertisement

Advertising pervades modern society and is a powerful means of persuasion. Most of us probably consider ourselves too sophisticated to be persuaded by the messages carried in ads. However, the subtler, often complex and powerful messages of advertisements influence all of us to some degree. Advertising is big business, and the money and power it commands in our marketplace testifies to its success in influencing consumers. Using the following steps, see if you can recognize some of the ways that the ad in figure 3.4 attempts to persuade viewers.

1. Examine the ad carefully. Remember that the key here is to have persistence and patience. The longer you examine the ad, the more you will notice.

Fig. 3.4 An Ad for Guinness Beer

2. Then, as a class or in a small group, build an observation list.

3. Group items from the observation list into categories and give each category a title.

4. Now look at each category label in relation to the others and see if you can abstract an overarching insight, something that several of the category labels have in common.

5. Examine your insights and see if any look promising as the basis for an insightful claim. Remember that you are looking for the argument(s) the ad is trying to persuade you to accept—the logic it is using to influence you.

6. Use C-S-C to build a working thesis statement.

7. Run your working thesis statement through the thesis statement checklist at the end of chapter 2.

8. Revise, as necessary.

9. Discuss how the categories from the observation list could be used to support the thesis statement you developed. Explain carefully the connections between observations, category labels, and an insightful claim.

Application 3.3 Practicing Abstraction and Considering All the Evidence

Films can be analyzed through a number of different traits or characteristics, including theme, graphics, characters, music, costumes, setting, and pace.

1. Examine the following sets of observations we created for three different films. As with the examples of shoes and trees, after careful observation, see what conclusions you can draw about each of these three sample films based on all the given information. Be sure to consider each item in the data set to ensure that you are drawing valid conclusions. You won't have enough information at this point to write a good thesis statement, but the conclusions you draw are an important step in the thesis-building process.

2. Compare the conclusions you abstracted with those of one or two of your peers. Look at your peers' responses to be sure each is valid; that is, each conclusion considers all the evidence and is logical based on the evidence given. How similar were your responses? Do any of the conclusions stand out as particularly interesting or insightful? Discuss.

Example Film

characters: three social outcasts and misfits

music: cacophonous music

setting: college campus

pace: neither fast nor slow

plot: moving away from home

time period: 1990s

Sample Conclusions

- This could be a film about growing up.

- This could be a film about a moment when values change.

- This could be a film about three wasted lives.

- This film could be a comedy.

Film #1

characters: wealthy, young male and female lovers

music: classical, big orchestra music

setting: outdoors, English countryside

pace: slow, meandering

plot: marriage at the end

time period: nineteenth century

    variation: female is wealthy, male is poor

    plot: lovers die at the end

Film #2

characters: various human species

music: alternating between slow and brooding and fast and dramatic

setting: new planet

pace: intense action; fight scenes

plot: exploration

time period: twenty-fifth century

Film #3

characters: nuclear family

music: low key, comic

setting: suburbs

pace: chaotic

plot: everyday life

time period: contemporary time period

    variation: The characters are a group of young women.

Writing Exercise 3.1 Reaffirming Your Thesis Statement

Read the essay "Susan Coe's *Breaking*" and then return to questions 1–5 and use them to analyze the essay.

THINKING THROUGH A READING
1. Why does this writer admire Coe's *Breaking*? Do you agree with her criteria?

2. Identify some of the reasons for seeing this essay as "writer-oriented" rather than "reader-oriented" writing. Which paragraph of the essay do you think is most clear? Why?

3. Do you think this writer finds the painting to be optimistic or pessimistic? Explain.

1. On a separate sheet of paper, describe in three or four sentences the argument you think the author of "Susan Coe's *Breaking*" is making in this paper. Describe it as though you are telling someone about the insightful point the author has discovered. If you have problems summarizing the argument, it is possible that the argument is not yet focused enough. If this is the case, try step 2, below or return to chapter 2 and use the techniques described there to develop a more focused claim.

2. From "Susan Coe's *Breaking*" copy the sentence or sentences that best summarize the argument or copy key words or phrases that you feel are important.

3. Compare the description of the argument that you wrote for step 1 with the sentences, or key words and phrases, that you believe best summarize the argument from step 2.

   a. Does one of the sentences summarize all the important aspects of the argument and invite interest? If so, that is the thesis statement.

   b. If one sentence does the best work toward summarizing the argument, but it lacks an important aspect or two of the overall argument, revise the sentence to be more inclusive. Consider incorporating some of the key words or phrases that you have identified.

   c. Remember that a thesis statement should have a context, subject, and claim, and it should avoid the weaknesses in the claim that you learned about in chapter 2. Check to make sure that the statement you identify as a thesis has a claim that is not a summary, a plan, or a set of facts. It may help to run the thesis statement through the thesis statement checklist at the end of chapter 2.

4. If you have revised the thesis statement, rewrite the introduction to include the change you made. Then read through the essay again, making sure that the body paragraphs are still in alignment with the revised thesis statement.

5. What is the impact of this new thesis statement on the essay as a whole?

Susan Coe's Breaking
Sophia Campobasso

I, myself, am not an art history major. I am also not an artist, unless we are talking about performance art. However, my opinions reflect the views of modern intelligent people, who have come into some contact with art in their lifetimes. That is where I am standing in this evaluation. Often times, when looking at modern art, I feel that there was very minimal talent required to produce the final piece, and, therefore, I write it off right away as being trash. When a painting is nothing but a black box on a piece of white paper, I think to myself, "I could do that. This piece should not be in an exclusive museum, costing more than a house mortgage." However, there are works that break the mold. I believe that a good piece of art should simply do one thing, make the viewer think. Against all of the bad pieces of modern art, I believe that Sue Coe's, *Breaking*, is an excellent piece of modern art because it makes the viewer want to take a second look and therefore draws you in and forces you to make decisions about it.

There are certain paintings and sculptures that are simply, in my mind, ridiculous. For example, *To Fix the Image in Memory* (Viga Celmins) is nothing more than a bunch of rocks laid on the floor, in what seems, to the unknowledgeable eye, no specific order. Another example would be *The Stone* (Philip Guston). This painting is merely scribbled lines of ink written on paper. There is no picture within these lines, or symbols, or even color. There are just black scribbled lines. When this is what you generally seem to find in a lot of modern art, you tend to become biased and judgmental. These paintings probably do have a meaning; however, most people will never be drawn to find this meaning simply because they are too busy complaining about how they don't see "art" when looking at this, and they ignore what was trying to be accomplished with the work. Art majors and others who specifically study this might come to a different conclusion, I understand, but this is how I feel average people respond.

That is why it is very refreshing to find a work like Coe's. This painting depicts a violent scene, where the colors are rich and bold. It seemed impossible for me to look away from this work until I at least gave some thought to what she might be saying. In the painting, there are two main people front and center, who are both upside down. One of the man's eyes is closed, and there is blood on his face. It looks as though both people have been shot because there are two yellow bolts followed by orange and then a spew of red. There is a face below them, hiding in the corner with a black cape over him, which I think could symbolize death. There is also a radio, which seems to be producing blood because of the sharp red lines coming from it. Death is near the radio, which I thought was interesting. Perhaps violence and death are coming from what-ever is on the radio. There are red lines splashing everywhere, perhaps symbolizing that violence affects everyone, not just the people involved. The setting is in some sort of subway station, which is an interesting choice because anyone can be in a subway station at one time or another and involuntarily become caught up in a violent act. The most interesting part of the painting for me, however, is located in the far left-hand corner. There is an almost ghostly woman who is holding a baby. She, too, has lines of blood strewn across her, perhaps meaning that the most innocent bystanders are affected. All of this I took in with a first glance and decided myself. This is why I found Coe's painting so intriguing. A person could spend an hour simply staring at this work, deciding on what it means.

Coe is quoted to have said, "My dream is that people don't discuss the work but discuss the content." She did not give an explanation of her work *Breaking*, so I do not know what she really wanted viewers to take from this. What I know of Susan Coe is that her paintings are politically charged, and often times she takes the victims' point of view into consideration while painting, which can be seen in the painting *Breaking*.

Coe's work is gripping and makes any audience take a second look and think. Because it does this, I would consider it a very good piece of modern art. Often times, modern art is only interesting because it is so obscure, but this does not mean that it fits the criteria for art. I was completely fascinated with Coe's work, and it alone changed my views of modern art because there are works within that category that are still masterpieces, and fit my criteria for a "good" piece. The painting forces you to think.

Writing Exercise 3.2 Practicing Abstraction

1. Examine Dana Gioia's newspaper article that follows and trace the author's use of descriptive (lower-level) and interpretive (higher-level) thinking.

2. Write a paragraph on a subject of your choice using concrete and factual think-ing only. In other words, write about your subject only at the level of sense data or description.

3. Now write a paragraph on the same subject using only interpretive thinking. Omit all description or mention of the facts about your subject; offer only insights or perspectives.

4. Write down some observations about the two paragraphs you have written. Can you draw any conclusions about the use of factual or interpretive thinking? Share these observations and insights in class discussion.

THINKING THROUGH A READING
1. Are the author's arguments based on facts or does the author allow abstractions to carry his points?

2. Why do you think the author made that choice?

3. Do you think it was the best choice for the article?

Good Books Help Make a Civil Society
NY Times April 10, 2005
Dana Gioia

In 1780 Massachusetts patriot John Adams wrote to his wife, Abigail, outlining his vision of how American culture might evolve. "I must study politics and war," he prophesied, so "that our sons may have liberty to study mathematics and philosophy." They will add to their studies geography, navigation, commerce, and agriculture, he continued, so that *their* children may enjoy the "right to study painting, poetry, music . . ." Adams's bold prophecy proved correct. By the mid 20th century, America boasted internationally preeminent traditions in literature, art, music, dance, theater, and cinema. But a strange thing has happened in the American arts during the past quarter century. While income rose to unforeseen levels, college attendance ballooned, and access to information increased enormously, the interest young Americans showed in the arts—and especially literature—actually diminished.

According to the 2002 Survey of Public Participation in the Arts, a population study designed and commissioned by the National Endowment for the Arts (and executed by the US Bureau of the Census), arts participation by Americans has declined for eight of the nine major forms that are measured. (Only jazz has shown a tiny increase—thank you, Ken Burns.) The declines have been most severe among younger adults (ages 18–24). The most worrisome finding in the 2002 study, however, is the declining percentage of Americans, especially young adults, reading literature.

That individuals at a time of crucial intellectual and emotional development bypass the joys and challenges of literature is a troubling trend. If it were true that they substituted histories, biographies, or political works for literature, one might not worry. But book reading of any kind is falling as well. That such a longstanding and fundamental cultural activity should slip so swiftly, especially among young adults, signifies deep transformations in contemporary life. To call attention to the trend, the Arts Endowment issued the reading portion of the Survey as a separate report, "Reading at Risk: A Survey of Literary Reading in America."

The decline in reading has consequences that go beyond literature. The significance of reading has become a persistent theme in the business world. The February issue of Wired magazine, for example, sketches a new set of mental skills and habits proper to the 21st century, aptitudes decidedly literary in character: not "linear, logical, analytical talents," author Daniel Pink states, but "the ability to create artistic and emotional beauty, to detect patterns and opportunities, to craft a satisfying narrative." When asked what kind of talents they like to see in management positions, business leaders consistently set imagination, creativity, and higher-order thinking at the top.

Ironically, the value of reading and the intellectual faculties that it inculcates appear most clearly as active and engaged literacy declines. There is now a growing awareness of the consequences of nonreading to the workplace. In 2001 the National Association of Manufacturers polled its members on skill deficiencies among employees. Among hourly workers, poor reading skills ranked second, and 38 percent of employers complained that local schools inadequately taught reading comprehension.

Corporate America makes similar complaints about a skill intimately related to reading— writing. Last year, the College Board reported that corporations spend some $3.1 billion a year on remedial writing instruction for employees, adding that they "express a fair degree of dissatisfaction with the writing of recent college graduates." If the 21st-century American economy requires innovation and creativity, solid reading skills and the imaginative growth fostered by literary reading are central elements in that program.

The decline of reading is also taking its toll in the civic sphere. In a 2000 survey of college seniors from the top 55 colleges, the Roper Organization found that 81 percent could not earn a grade of C on a high school-level history test. A 2003 study of 15- to 26-year-olds' civic knowledge by the National Conference of State Legislatures concluded, "Young people do not understand the ideals of citizenship . . . and their appreciation and support of American democracy is limited."

It is probably no surprise that declining rates of literary reading coincide with declining levels of historical and political awareness among young people. One of the surprising findings of "Reading at Risk" was that literary readers are markedly more civically engaged than nonreaders, scoring two to four times more likely to perform charity work, visit a museum, or attend a sporting event. One reason for their higher social and cultural interactions may lie in the kind of civic and historical knowledge that comes with literary reading.

Unlike the passive activities of watching television and DVDs or surfing the Web, reading is actually a highly active enterprise. Reading requires sustained and focused attention as well as active use of memory and imagination. Literary reading also enhances and enlarges our humility by helping us imagine and understand lives quite different from our own.

Indeed, we sometimes underestimate how large a role literature has played in the evolution of our national identity, especially in that literature often has served to introduce young people to events from the past and principles of civil society and governance. Just as more ancient Greeks learned about moral and political conduct from the epics of

Homer than from the dialogues of Plato, so the most important work in the abolitionist movement was the novel "Uncle Tom's Cabin." Likewise our notions of American populism come more from Walt Whitman's poetic vision than from any political tracts. Today when people recall the Depression, the images that most come to mind are of the travails of John Steinbeck's Joad family from "The Grapes of Wrath." Without a literary inheritance, the historical past is impoverished.

In focusing on the social advantages of a literary education, however, we should not overlook the personal impact. Every day authors receive letters from readers that say, "Your book changed my life." History reveals case after case of famous people whose lives were transformed by literature. When the great Victorian thinker John Stuart Mill suffered a crippling depression in late-adolescence, the poetry of Wordsworth restored his optimism and self-confidence—a "medicine for my state of mind," he called it. A few decades later, W.E.B. DuBois found a different tonic in literature, an escape from the indignities of Jim Crow into a world of equality. "I sit with Shakespeare and he winces not," DuBois observed. "Across the color line I move arm in arm with Balzac and Dumas, where smiling men and welcoming women glide in gilded halls." Literature is a catalyst for education and culture.

The evidence of literature's importance to civic, personal, and economic health is too strong to ignore. The decline of literary reading foreshadows serious long-term social and economic problems, and it is time to bring literature and the other arts into discussions of public policy. Libraries, schools, and public agencies do noble work, but addressing the reading issue will require the leadership of politicians and the business community as well.

Literature now competes with an enormous array of electronic media. While no single activity is responsible for the decline in reading, the cumulative presence and availability of electronic alternatives increasingly have drawn Americans away from reading.

Reading is not a timeless, universal capability. Advanced literacy is a specific intellectual skill and social habit that depends on a great many educational, cultural, and economic factors. As more Americans lose this capability, our nation becomes less informed, active, and independent-minded. These are not the qualities that a free, innovative, or productive society can afford to lose.

Dana Gioia is chairman of the National Endowment for the Arts.

CHAPTER 4

Supporting the Thesis Statement: The Burdens of Proof

In chapter 1 we defined the thesis statement as a statement of an issue that "sets down" the argument a writer will make. It may help to think of the thesis statement as the claim in the academic essay that is much like a lawyer's claim in a court of law. The writer of an effective essay, like the lawyer, presents a central argument that has certain burdens that require support. For instance, a lawyer may use several different lines of reasoning to frame or arrange evidence to show that his client is innocent. The claim of innocence is meaningful only when it is fully supported with clear evidence and logical reasoning.

Similarly, the burdens of proof in the thesis statement must be unpacked and logically fulfilled for the essay to be compelling. Because it sets down the argument of a persuasive paper, the thesis statement can be said to be the reason the paper exists. The thesis drives the paper forward because it contains the claim—the assertion that gives the paper its meaning.

However, a thesis statement does not stand alone; it is interdependent with the rest of the paper. It might help to see this interdependence in terms of an analogy. Think of the thesis statement as the engine of a car and the supporting paragraphs of the paper as the body of a car. Without an engine, a car might look like a car on the outside, but it won't go anywhere. It might look functional because it has a frame, wheels, and a transmission, but what good is it for someone who wants to travel if there is no engine to propel the body of the car into motion? Vice versa, an automobile engine without a frame, wheels, and a transmission can't take the rider anywhere. It might have the necessary power but, without the other parts, it isn't very useful. Similarly, the thesis statement alone doesn't prove much, but neither do supporting paragraphs without an overarching idea to give them significance. The thesis statement, like the engine of the car, drives the paper. And the supporting details of a paper, like the frame of a car, are necessary to carry the reader to a meaningful place. Unpacking the burdens of proof from the thesis statement will show you the direction to take your paper; it will guide your drafting.

WHAT'S AHEAD . . .

▶ the burdens of proof: what to write about

▶ four tasks to manage your burdens of proof

▶ the burden of background information

The Burdens of Proof: What to Write About

We have said that the thesis statement provides a prescription for the paper in the sense that it contains what we call the **burdens of proof**, but what, exactly, does this mean? *Burdens of proof* are the arguments or points that must be made in a paper to fully prove the thesis statement, that is, to convince a reader of a thesis statement's validity. In other words, they are the requirements that logically follow from the claim made in any thesis statement. If each burden of the thesis is not adequately discussed, the claim will be less credible, and the paper will be unsatisfying.

For instance, each of the two thesis statements below argues for one side of a controversy, so the burden of proof is to make the argument for that point of view as effectively as possible.

Example 1:
> The use of steroids in college sports should be more tightly regulated.

Burdens of Proof:
- show the reasons for, and dangers of, steroid use

- establish how steroid use is currently being monitored

- show why steroid use in college should be more tightly regulated

Example 2:
> Steroid use is acceptable for professional baseball players who are entertainers as much as athletes.

Burdens of Proof:
- show how professional baseball players are entertainers

- show how professional baseball players are entertainers as much as they are athletes

- show how steroid use is acceptable for baseball players when they are viewed as entertainers

You might think of burdens of proof as the links in the chain of logic that a writer must create to convince the reader to accept the conclusion proposed in the thesis statement. Because the burdens of proof suggest the chain of reasoning the paper must take, they also work as a structuring device for the paper— a skeleton on which the supporting paragraphs of the paper are built. In short, the burdens of proof are what you write about in the paper.

Example 3:

In the fairy tale *Cinderella*, love is a greater power than magic.

Context: fairy tale *Cinderella*
Subject: love
Claim: love is a greater power than magic

Burdens of Proof:

- show that love is a powerful force in the text

- show that magic is a powerful force in the text

- show that love overpowers magic

This chapter will provide you with tools for identifying the burdens of proof in your own thesis statements. Before we discuss these tools, however, we will further look at the burdens of proof identified above for the *Cinderella* thesis statement to see how burdens of proof (BoP) can become an organizing structure for an essay.

BOP 1: LOVE IS A POWERFUL FORCE IN THE TEXT.
Write about . . . how the story shows that love is tied to true identity rather than a magical identity.

- Discuss the fact that the magic had to end at midnight to show that the love between Cinderella and the Prince would not be founded on an identity predicated on magic—he has to love her for who she really is, not who she appears to be. **In the story, true love is not tainted by magic.**

- The fairy godmother didn't use magic to force the Prince to fall in love with Cinderella— only to get her to the ball. **True love extends beyond magic.**

- Discuss how the Prince refuses to give up on love and pursues Cinderella everywhere. Even when he finds out that she is a peasant girl, his love persists. Even though Cinderella's wealth and prestige end at midnight, the Prince's endurance demonstrates that love persists. **This shows that love is more powerful than magic.**

BOP 2: MAGIC IS A POWERFUL FORCE IN THE TEXT.
Write about . . . how magic works in the service of love; it gets Cinderella to the ball where she can meet the Prince.

- Discuss how magic serves love but only up to a certain point—magic can help to initiate love, but it cannot bring it to fruition. **Thus magic is limited in a way that love is not.**

BOP 3: LOVE OVERPOWERS MAGIC.
Write about . . . how Cinderella's goodness (loveliness) both draws the fairy godmother's help and makes her appealing to the Prince.

- The fairy godmother uses magic to help Cinderella get to the ball because she loves Cinderella. **In other words, magic works in the service of love.**

- Cinderella's enduring love wins back the Prince even after the magic is gone. **Love is more powerful than magic.**

After freewriting or outlining in this way, we can begin to see a whole essay taking shape. Identifying a thesis statement's burdens of proof—and then using them to structure your essay—are keys to creating successful essays.

You should be aware that each burden of proof will require a different amount of time to cover it. In other words, even though each burden is stated in a single line, some might take pages to explain while others may require only a paragraph. What is important to recognize is that all of the burdens of proof in a thesis statement must be discussed to prove the paper's thesis and to have a compelling and therefore successful essay.

Four Tasks to Manage Your Burdens of Proof

In the following box we outline four tasks for uncovering a thesis statement's burdens of proof and incorporating them in a paper. Not all of these steps (or techniques) will be relevant to every thesis statement. However, some of them will always be useful as strategies to help you decipher the pivotal words and phrases and the underlying logical relationships within your thesis statements. Said differently, these steps are meant to do three things: (1) They will help you to systematically analyze the demands of your thesis statement in preparation for writing a compelling essay; (2) They will help you to think through ways of logically supporting the burdens of proof you identify; and (3) They will help you to examine the thesis statement objectively to be sure that it has the focus you intend based on the evidence you have collected. Once you work through this chapter's examples, you can easily refer back to this box as a reminder of the steps of the process.

FOUR TASKS TO MANAGE YOUR BURDENS OF PROOF

1. Identify the context, subject, and claim of the thesis statement.

2. Identify key terms or phrases that help define the context, subject, or claim, such as:

- adjectives or adverbs

- superlatives (i.e., most, worst, best, always)

- specialized terms that require explanation

- terms or phrases that require background information

- introductory clauses or other key terms that limit the parameters of the argument (i.e., today, twentieth century, regarding children, in my house)

- If you are unsure whether a term is "key" or not, remove the term or phrase and see if it changes the demands of the thesis statement or the direction or the boundaries of the argument. If so, then it is a key term and probably carries a burden of proof.

3. Examine the logical relationships within the thesis statement and identify whether there are any dependent points (or arguments) that must be made in advance of other points (or arguments).

4. Decide on the most effective order for covering the burdens of proof.

Note: See appendix b for more specific examples of applying the four tasks to particular patterns of argument.

These tasks represent general techniques that, with some practice, you should be able to adopt, customize, and incorporate into your writing process. They will help you to analyze your thesis statement and identify the logical chain of reasoning necessary to offer a compelling argument.

Applying the Four Tasks

Now we will examine three examples using this four-step process.

EXAMPLE 1:

Music file sharing through the Internet should be legal.

1. Identify C-S-C.

Context: music industry's copyright laws
Subject: music file sharing through the Internet
Claim: should be legal

2. Identify key phrases. Examine C-S-C and the key phrases and articulate the burden of proof suggested by each.

Not everyone is familiar with the controversial practice of "music file sharing through the Internet" and its alleged infringement on the "music industry's copyright laws," so both the context and subject of this thesis statement will need to be discussed. The burdens of proof are as follows.

- establish what is meant by "music file sharing"

- explain the objections some have to this practice

- show why music file sharing should be legal

3. Identify whether there are any dependent points (or arguments) that must be made in advance of other points (or arguments).

To argue that file sharing should be legal, it will be important to establish what it is, so the first burden listed must precede the third. The second burden could be covered along with the first as background material, or it could be discussed after the third burden as a counterargument. These are some strategic choices a writer will have to make in responding to this prompt.

4. Decide on the most effective order for covering the burdens of proof.

Think carefully about where you would like to cover the second burden. You might have to draft the entire essay using one strategy, then just the relevant parts using the other strategy, and finally weigh the effectiveness of each.

Whatever your writing process, this step should be reexamined during the revision stage to be sure the essay is as convincing as possible.

EXAMPLE 2:
It is better to have luck rather than talent when working with computers.

1. Identify the C-S-C.

Context: usefulness of different personal skills
Subject: working with computers
Claim: better to have luck than talent

2. Identify key phrases. Examine C-S-C and the key phrases and articulate the burden of proof suggested by each.

Here is the thesis statement again but with the key terms underlined:

It is <u>better</u> to have <u>luck rather than talent</u> when working with <u>computers</u>.

Notice that there are three hurdles for this thesis statement, and all three involve telling the reader precisely what is meant by terms such as *luck, talent,* and *better.* The success of this paper hinges on the clarity of the writer's definitions—how well the writer can parcel out the distinctions between *luck* and *talent* and show how one is *better.* Here is one way to articulate these burdens of proof:

- define what is meant by *luck*

- define what is meant by *talent*

- show how it is *better* to have *luck* when working with computers

3. Identify whether there are any dependent points (or arguments) that must be made in advance of other points (or arguments).

Notice that the first and second burdens must both be fulfilled, probably in that order because that is the order in which they appear in the thesis statement, before the third burden can be discussed.

4. Decide on the most effective order for covering the burdens of proof.

It would be difficult to establish a clear chain of logic for this essay that is different from the order in which the burdens currently appear.

EXAMPLE 3:

> The most flagrant abuse of animal rights today ironically takes place in U.S. laboratories dedicated to the preservation of human life.

1. Identify the C-S-C.

Context: animal rights today
Subject: abuse of animals' rights
Claim: takes place in U.S. laboratories

2. Identify key phrases. Examine C-S-C and the key phrases and articulate the burden of proof suggested by each.

Here is the thesis statement again but with the key terms underlined:

> The <u>most flagrant abuse</u> of <u>animal rights</u> <u>today</u> <u>ironically</u> takes place in <u>U.S. laboratories</u> <u>dedicated to the preservation of human life.</u>

Notice that you will have to define what, exactly, is meant by "most flagrant" abuses of animal rights and "U.S. laboratories dedicated to the preservation of human life." One is a value judgment, and the other is vague, so it is important to explain each clearly.

- show how these animal abuses are the "most flagrant"
- show how the laboratories where these abuses are taking place are "dedicated to the preservation of human life"

There is also the word *ironically*, which qualifies the relationship between the subject and the claim. If this term was removed, the thesis statement would have less punch, so you will have to show how the abuses are *ironic*.

- explain the irony in that these "most flagrant" abuses are taking place in these particular laboratories

3. Identify whether there are any dependent points (or arguments) that must be made in advance of other points (or arguments).

To show that the animal rights abuses taking place in U.S. laboratories are the most flagrant, you will have to show, first, that abuses are taking place. You will also need to define animal abuse. It might help to add both of these to your burdens of proof.

- define what is meant by "animal abuse"
- show that animal abuse, as defined, is taking place in U.S. laboratories

4. Decide on the most effective order for covering the burdens of proof.

Given what was realized in step #3 you will probably want to discuss the last two burdens listed before the first one. Beyond that, there are a number of different ways to order the remaining burdens, so thinking about what step-by-step chain of reasoning you will use to do this might save much time in drafting. It might also help to list the burdens in the order in which you intend to cover them, so it is easier to double-check your logic.

- define "animal abuse"

- show that animal abuse, as defined, is taking place in U.S. laboratories

- show how these animal abuses are the "most flagrant"

- show how the laboratories where these abuses are taking place are "dedicated to the preservation of human life"

- explain the irony in these "most flagrant" abuses taking place in these particular laboratories

Notice that all burdens of proof are not equal in terms of the amount of time/space needed to cover them. In other words, even though each burden is stated in a single line, some might take pages to explain, while others may require only a paragraph. Remember that all of the burdens of proof in a thesis statement must be discussed to prove the paper's thesis and to have a compelling and therefore successful essay.

Again, identifying the burdens of proof in a thesis statement requires some analysis and can be challenging. Remember, however, that any thesis statement you develop comes from your own exploration and insight, and in this sense you have already gone over much of the ground needed to satisfy a thesis statement's logical demands. Because writing is a recursive process, returning to your prewriting notes often during the drafting process will help you to incorporate the relevant ideas that you have already generated.

Practice 4.1 Using the Four Tasks
Examine the following thesis statements and use the four-step process to unpack the burdens of proof.

1. Although alcohol, over the decades, has been thought to be pleasurable but unhealthy, recent research shows that the benefits of drinking red wine outweigh the risks.

2. Toothpaste, like other consumable products, has been customized for every individual need, but what appears to be scientifically improved tooth care is merely materialist exploitation.

The Burden of Background Information

When identifying the burdens of proof for your thesis statement, it would be a mistake to assume that readers will share even your most basic suppositions, so it is important to state the premises on which your claim is based. This sounds intimidating. However, you may already have done this in step 1 when you defined what you meant by "animal abuses" in example 3 and showed where they were occurring before making an argument about the "most flagrant" abuses within a particular context. Still, this is an easy point to miss and, therefore, worth a small reminder. When reviewing your thesis statement, make sure that all background information is articulated carefully so that an argument can be built from a shared platform of understanding. You should turn presumptions into burdens of proof and clearly explain them in an effort to make your argument as compelling as possible.

EXAMPLE:

> Couples who have children and want to divorce should be required by law to attend four months of couples counseling.

1. Identify the context, subject, and claim of the thesis statement.

   Context: divorce in today's society
   Subject: couples who have children and are considering divorce
   Claim: should be required by law to attend four months of counseling prior to divorce

2. Identify key terms or phrases that describe the context, subject, and claim.

   Couples <u>who have children</u> and <u>want to divorce</u> should be <u>required by law</u> to attend <u>four months</u> of <u>couples counseling.</u>

3. Examine the logical relationships within the thesis statement and identify any dependent points.

4. Decide on the most effective order for covering the burdens of proof.

When you examine the logical connection between the subject of this thesis statement, "couples who have children and are considering divorce," and the claim that they "should attend counseling for four months," you should recognize that one logical step toward proving this claim is unstated—that divorce is traumatic for children. Said differently, this thesis statement is dependent on an unstated premise—that divorce has a negative and detrimental impact on children. This supposition must be established before a convincing argument can be made. If a reader is not informed about the particular ramifications of divorce on children, there is little basis for this argument. Including this background information allows the writer to establish the urgency of this problem—that divorce is hard on children—and respond by providing a remedy. This is called a problem/solution argument (see appendix B for more details). Once the problem is brought to light (background information) and the solution is put forward in the thesis statement, the rest of the paper should show how the proposed solution is the best one. There are four burdens of proof:

- discuss how divorce is hard on children

- discuss how counseling can help families cope with divorce

- discuss why passing a law is the best way to achieve these goals

- discuss why four months of counseling is the right amount

Burdens of Proof and Logical Fallacies

Now that we have discussed strategies for using burdens of proof for constructing well-supported thesis statements, it's important to cover some common pitfalls or fallacies of logical reasoning. Logical fallacies are patterns of reasoning that lead to faulty conclusions. In other words, your argument won't make sense, and you will not be able to fulfill your burdens of proof. It is important that you learn to recognize fallacies so that you don't jeopardize or weaken your argument. Let's study some particular types of logical fallacies so that, if ever in doubt, you can double check your reasoning to be sure that it is sound.

Hasty Generalization and Overgeneralization

Avoid asserting a claim based on too little evidence. For instance, if you see two student athletes cheat on exams and then offer the claim that *all student athletes cheat on exams,* your statement would not be valid. No doubt there are many student athletes who do not cheat on exams, so in using these two incidents to generalize for the whole, you would be guilty of a **hasty generalization**. In other words, you would be judging the whole by the part. Avoid using limitless terms such as *all, every, always,* and *never* because they will often lead to overgeneralized or hasty claims; they suggest definitive results that would be difficult—if not impossible—to substantiate.

Stereotypes are a form of hasty generalization because they make assumptions about groups of people based on little or no evidence. If you argued, for instance, that *women hate math; therefore math departments at women's colleges are small,* you would be basing your argument on a stereotype. There is no compelling proof that shows that all—or even most—women hate math, so this statement cannot be supported or proven. Furthermore, the cause/effect relationship suggested in this statement—that math departments are small because women hate math—cannot be developed logically because the assumption on which it is based (that women hate math) is unfounded. If math departments at women's colleges are small, it must be attributed to causes that can be substantiated (such as budget availability or curriculum needs) rather than a stereotype about women's attitudes toward math (unless you can tie that provincial view to those in charge of funding and staffing these math departments).

False Cause

A **false cause** defines a prior event as causal when it is not (also called **post hoc,** *ergo propter hoc,* which means after this, therefore because of this). Just because one thing happens before another does not necessarily mean that it has caused it. If, for example, you broke a mirror in the morning and then failed a test later that day, false cause reasoning would be concluding that breaking the mirror caused you to fail the test. If you cannot link the cause to the effect through a valid chain of reasoning, then you may be asserting a cause when there is coincidence only. This is a very common mistake with cause/effect that you should watch for carefully. Some other examples of false cause errors include (1) arguing that because a new politician has taken office, the immediate reduction in crime or immediate increase in salaries can be directly attributable to his or her election; (2) concluding that because the United States sent a new spacecraft to Mars, the Russian economy has improved; and (3) deciding that lowering the legal blood-alcohol level for driving has increased the sale of convertible cars. In each of these three examples, the cause has little to do with the effect, even if it chronologically preceded it. Recognizing the difference between coincidence and causation is central to identifying when your cause/effect assertion is valid.

Non Sequitur

A **non sequitur** occurs when the logical connection between two or more items is not firmly established and an incorrect conclusion is drawn from the evidence. For example, you make the statement that your brother's intense athletic training this summer will make him a good father. If your paper goes into great detail about the aspects of the athletic training but fails to make clear what this has to do with sound fatherhood skills, then the paper is guilty of a non sequitur. With revision, you might be able to establish a link between athletic training and fatherhood skills and thereby erase the non sequitur, but if this link is not firmly established (or cannot be firmly established), then the paper's claim is invalid.

Slippery Slope

A **slippery slope** involves asserting that one thing will inevitably lead to a series of extreme effects. When using a slippery slope chain of logic, the causal chain is taken to such an extreme degree that the conclusions cannot be supported; in fact, the conclusions are extraordinary, even inflammatory. If you argued, for instance, that *legalizing marijuana will lead to an increase in its availability and soon the entire population will be under its influence*, you would be making a slippery slope argument. The last link in this causal chain—that legalizing marijuana will inevitably mean that the entire population will be under its influence—is so extreme that it would be impossible to prove (or even believe). Your credibility might come under attack for making such an unwarranted suggestion. Other slippery slopes include (1) arguing that stricter gun control laws mean that fewer and fewer guns will be available until the crime rate will all but disappear; (2) if we do not control our road rage, the highways will become so unsafe that no one will drive on the freeways anymore; and (3) raising the standards of the SAT test will mean that fewer students will be able to achieve a high score and eventually few people will be admitted to universities. As you can see, each of these examples posits a cause/effect relationship that might be plausible if it did not extend the effect to such an extreme. In each case, the chain of reasoning is flawed and ultimately unconvincing.

Ad hominem

An **ad hominem** argument attacks a person rather than supplying evidence to support a claim. Ad hominem arguments typically seek to discredit people to destroy their authority. It can take the form of name calling, guilt by association, or slander and is unfair because it attacks the person rather than the issue. For instance, *Martha Stewart is a felon, and therefore we can no longer trust her decorating tips*. In truth, Stewart's felony conviction has little to do with her talent for decorating. Using ad hominem attacks often reflect more negatively on the attacker than on the person assailed.

False Dichotomy

A **false dichotomy** is an either/or type of argument that offers an artificially limited number of choices, usually asserting that a thing has only two possibilities when many more options are actually available. For instance, a writer might propose that you embrace his position on global warming or else the world will immediately and irrevocably be destroyed. In the present age, there are clearly a variety of solutions being proposed to stem global warming, so no single position currently is best. Notice that this argument is unfair not only because of its reductive choices but also because it carries with it an emotional threat—a scare tactic.

Straw Man Argument

On the surface, a **straw man argument** is one that is so flimsy that it is easily knocked down. It is typically used in a self-serving context, as when you misrepresent an opponent's argument by oversimplifying or exaggerating it, or by making assumptions for an argument that make it easy to refute. The fallacy arises because, with a straw-man argument, the position you attribute to others is too reductive to be a fair representation of the argument or something that few people, in reality, believe. For instance:

Claim: Women should have the right to pursue careers outside the home.

Straw man argument: Those who advocate that women should have the right to pursue careers outside the home must believe that it is acceptable to have kids running around unsupervised.

This is a straw man argument because it misrepresents the claim. The claimant said nothing about having kids running around unsupervised nor was it a necessary consequence of that position. In fact, it is possible that while the woman pursues a career, her husband could supervise the kids at home. The straw man has attributed a position to the claimant that is easily refutable, ostensibly for the purpose of winning the argument.

Claim: Global warming is a serious issue that may irreparably alter our world and the lives of all its creatures.

Straw man argument: You know global warming is fantasy when some scientist comes on the news and says we are all going to die in five years.

This is a straw man argument because it misrepresents the claim both by exaggerating it (e.g., "we are all going to die in five years") and taking the word of "some scientist" as representative of the opinions of all scientists. Despite your feelings on an issue, be careful not to misrepresent the opposition's arguments. Give the other side a fair hearing. The purpose is to arrive at the truth, not simply to win the argument.

Burdens of Proof and the Scope of Your Thesis Statement

When you are working under time or length constraints, as almost all writers are, it is prudent to spend a moment considering the likely length of the paper you have proposed to write before you begin the drafting process. The thesis statement and its burdens of proof give you insight into the paper's length and breadth—or the **scope** of the paper. The scope of the paper concerns what will be included in the essay and what will be left out. By considering scope, you clarify the amount of evidence and discussion necessary to support the thesis statement and gain a rough idea of the likely length of the essay. As noted previously, some burdens are weightier than others, both in terms of their centrality to the argument and their complexity. Therefore, one burden of proof may require only one or two sentences, but another might require several paragraphs. It is important to understand what will be necessary to explain to the reader so that each point is supported in a logical progression in defense of the thesis statement. Once you consider scope, you may find that your working thesis statement is unmanageable given your page limitations and that it should be revised before the drafting stage begins. This realization could save you much time and frustration. If this is the case, review the techniques from chapter 2 for narrowing your scope.

Using the Burdens of Proof to Create an Outline

Using your thesis statement's burdens of proof to set up a formal or informal outline is an excellent way to begin drafting an essay. Although you may work with several different outlines before your essay is in its final version, sketching out an outline or a writing plan early in the drafting stage will enable you to order your ideas.

Outlining Guide

- Place your working thesis statement at the top of your outline and use the burdens of proof to represent the main sections of your paper.

- Study each burden of proof. Refer back to the prewriting you did while generating the thesis statement and try to imagine what you will write about to cover each burden.

- Select evidence that could be used for each burden of proof.

- Review your outline to see what might be missing, what might be irrelevant, and where best to place research and additional ideas so as to fill in the gaps and present your argument step-by-step.

You may have to adjust this outline as you draft because your ideas may continue to evolve, but it is still a good strategy to begin with a working outline, even if it is very rough. Think of it as a blueprint for the paper that you will write, a place to put your essay's building materials—your prewriting ideas—together in an order that will bring unity and clarity to the essay. You can see how this works by studying the following example.

EXAMPLE:

In spite of the excitement about genetic cloning, it should not be used right now because our limited knowledge makes it too dangerous.

Context: a society excited about genetic cloning
Subject: genetic cloning
Claim: should not be used right now because our limited knowledge makes it too dangerous

Identify the burdens of proof:

- describe what is meant by "genetic cloning"
- substantiate the general excitement about genetic cloning and show what it is based on
- describe how our knowledge about cloning is limited
- discuss why limited knowledge makes cloning too dangerous
- describe why cloning should not be used right now (but perhaps could be used at a later time)

The context can be used to set up the paper's introduction, which might begin with some remarks about the current "excitement about genetic cloning." This places readers in the vicinity of the paper's particular focus and sets the stage for the thesis statement. (See chapter 5 for how to build an introductory paragraph.) The working thesis statement's subject and claim—that cloning "should not be used right now because our limited knowledge makes it too dangerous"—establish the core of the paper's argument. The context, subject, and claim are helpful, then, in outlining the paper because they specify elements that should be included in the paper's introduction and thesis statement.

For our example about genetic cloning, the first burden of proof requires a general explanation of genetic cloning. Defining key terms is crucial, especially when the thesis statement's clarity depends on a common understanding between the writer and the reader, as it does here. You would have to decide how much information to provide about genetic cloning, taking into consideration the level of knowledge of your intended audience and the amount of information you think is required to persuade them to agree with your claim. When describing key terms, it is often necessary to do some outside research to define a term correctly and clearly.

Moving to the second burden of proof, regarding the general excitement about genetic cloning, you will see that it seems very similar to the context of the paper, which has already been addressed in the paper's introduction. But sometimes a paper's context, as in this example, may need more attention than you can provide in the introduction. Readers may not be aware of the extensive research and interest in genetic cloning. You may have to show your audience the seriousness of the issue and the significance of your argument. Therefore, you might use the next body paragraphs to offer evidence that shows readers just what has been accomplished with cloning. This section of your paper could begin with a topic sentence that reads something like this: "Genetic cloning has been successfully used in a number of animal species." Under this topic sentence, you would have to give evidence to show what species have been cloned. This would probably require a bit of research, which is usually permissible even if your instructor does not call this a research paper. Including a few well-chosen sources can only help to make your argument more credible.

Once this foundation is established, you would take up the next burden of proof, the issue of limited knowledge, and show how there is much about cloning that we still do not know. Again, outside research would likely be necessary to substantiate this part of your argument, and you would want to include sources that your readers would find reliable and legitimate (see chapter 10). This burden is very important because the paper's claim relies on the fact that our knowledge of cloning is limited. Looking again at the list of burdens of proof, you would also have to show why this limited knowledge is a danger, why the immediate use of cloning constitutes a real threat in some way. You will have to make smart choices about how many paragraphs to devote to each burden of proof.

The final burden of proof provides the focus for the last section of the paper. Here, you might offer a more positive message about the future use of cloning once more research has been done. Depending on your research, you might offer readers information about particular studies being done and/or the frontiers of genetic cloning where scientists are currently working. A full outline for this paper follows, based on this study of the C-S-C and burdens of proof.

EXAMPLE:

I. Introduction: Genetic cloning

    A. Definition of genetic cloning and its uses

    B. Example of general excitement about genetic cloning

    C. Thesis: Limited knowledge makes cloning too dangerous to use right now.

II. There is limited knowledge about genetic cloning

    A. We can clone sheep but with limited success.

    B. We can clone dogs and cats but, again, there are problems.

    C. We have not yet attempted to clone humans, although many have discussed it.

III. The risks with cloning are great, so our limited knowledge means we should not use it at all.

    A. Cloning animals is not the same as cloning humans.

    B. Cloning humans has moral and ethical issues different from those associated with cloning animals.

    C. There are different implications for cloning humans than there are for cloning animals.

        1. People could clone a human army and that could harm world peace.

        2. Children could clone their parents and "raise" them, which would confuse social and familial roles and relationships.

IV. Conclusion: The risks of cloning outweigh the benefits, so we should not use it right now because we do not have enough information. Perhaps it will be safe at a later date.

As you can see from this example, the working thesis statement with its context, subject, and claim, and its burdens of proof give you a time-saving and effective way to identify the paper's skeleton and outline a writing plan for a paper's first draft.

The Burdens of Proof Checklist

The following checklist will help ensure that you have correctly identified the burdens of proof that are embedded within your thesis statement.

- Look again at the key terms in your thesis statement. Is there a burden of proof articulated that will provide an opportunity to discuss each key term? If not, add the necessary burdens of proof.

- Look again at the argument as a whole. Are there any optional points that you would like to add, such as a counterargument? If so, add those to your burdens of proof column.

- Are there any gaps in the logic, any ideas that are required to support the argument that have not been articulated, such as background information? If so, add those to your burdens of proof column.

- Check the burdens of proof to see whether your thesis statement requires any dependent arguments. If so, is the order of the arguments made correctly in the paper?

- Are the burdens of proof placed in the best possible order that you can imagine? If not sure, you might freewrite to explore other potential arrangements.

Applications and Writing Exercises

Application 4.1 Using the Four Tasks to Unpack the Burdens of Proof

Examine the following thesis statements and use the techniques provided to identify the thesis statement's burdens of proof.

THESIS STATEMENT:
> Children should not see the Disney film *Beauty and the Beast* because it reaffirms gender stereotypes.

1. Identify the context, subject, and claim of the thesis statement.

   Context: _____

   Subject: _____

   Claim: _____

2. Identify key terms or phrases that describe the context, subject, or claim.

   _____

   _____

   Circle all key terms (adjectives/adverbs, superlatives, and specialized terms) and note whether they limit or modify the subject or the claim.

List the burdens of proof for each circled term:

_____

_____

_____

_____

_____

Discuss each burden of proof by telling what it has to show or establish and why.

3. Discuss any dependent points or arguments that must be made in advance of others.

4. What order would you use to cover these burdens of proof if you were writing this essay? If not sure, freewrite on a separate sheet of paper the chain of logic that you imagine for the current arrangement of burdens of proof. Now rearrange them in a different order that you are considering. Freewrite on the logical progression of this second order of coverage and any other arrangement that you are considering. Put the freewriting aside for a few days, or at least a few hours, and then revisit the issue. When you read the different versions of logical progression, which seems most compelling? Describe why.

THESIS STATEMENT:

The popularity of today's swing music is due to its mix of nostalgic elements with contemporary ones.

1. Identify the context, subject, and claim of the thesis statement.

Context: _____

Subject: _____

Claim: _____

2. Identify key terms or phrases that describe the context, subject, or claim.

_____

_____

Circle all key terms (adjectives/adverbs, superlatives, and specialized terms) and note whether they modify the subject or claim.

List the burdens of proof for each circled term:

_____

_____

_____

_____

_____

Discuss each burden of proof by telling what it has to show (or establish) and why.

3. Discuss any dependent points or arguments that must be made in advance of others.

4. What order would you use to cover these burdens of proof if you were writing this essay? Describe why.

Application 4.2 Recognizing When Background Information Is Required

The following thesis statement requires background information. Use the four tasks to manage your burdens of proof. Can you identify what background information is necessary?

THESIS STATEMENT:

In today's society, the U.S. government should tightly regulate the sale of firearms.

1. Identify the context, subject, and claim of the thesis statement.

Context: _____

Subject: _____

Claim: _____

2. Identify terms or phrases that define the context, subject, or claim.

_____

_____

Circle all key terms (adjectives/adverbs, superlatives, and specialized terms) and note whether they modify the subject or claim.

List the burdens of proof for each circled term:

_____

_____

_____

_____

_____

Discuss each burden of proof by telling what it has to show (or establish) and why.

3. Examine the logical relationships within the thesis statement and identify any dependent points. (Hint: when background information is required, there is some point that depends on it being established.)

- Identify the unstated assumption required. Is a particular order required for this argument?

4. Decide on the most effective order for covering the burdens of proof.

Writing Exercise 4.1 Analyzing the Burdens of Proof in Two Essays

To be a good writer, you also have to be a good reader. By focusing on the techniques that other writers use to convince readers of their positions, you can add much to your repertoire of persuasive skills. Therefore, carefully read and analyze the two essays about genetic cloning that follow. Use the "Thinking Through a Reading" questions to guide your analysis. Then answer the questions that follow the readings.

THINKING THROUGH A READING

1. What is Macklin's thesis and what are her burdens of proof ?

2. How effectively does the author address these burdens?

3. What are the ethical oppositions to cloning that Macklin addresses? How effectively does she counter those objections?

4. What is the tone of this essay?

5. How would you characterize the readers that Macklin addresses in her essay?

Human Cloning? Don't Just Say No[1]
Ruth Macklin

Last week's news that scientists had cloned a sheep sent academics and the public into a panic at the prospect that humans might be next. That's an understandable reaction. Cloning is a radical challenge to the most fundamental laws of biology, so it's not unreasonable to be concerned that it might threaten human society and dignity. Yet much of the ethical opposition seems also to grow out of an unthinking disgust—a sort of "yuk factor." And that makes it hard for even trained scientists and ethicists to see the matter clearly. While human cloning might not offer great benefits to humanity, no one has yet made a persuasive case that it would do any real harm, either.

Theologians contend that to clone a human would violate human dignity. That would surely be true if a cloned individual were treated as a lesser being, with fewer rights or lower stature. But why suppose that cloned persons wouldn't share the same rights and dignity as the rest of us? A leading lawyer-ethicist has suggested that cloning would violate the "right to genetic identity." Where did he come up with such a right? It makes perfect sense to say that adult persons have a right not to be cloned without their voluntary, informed consent. But if such consent is given, whose "right" to genetic identity would be violated?

Many of the science-fiction scenarios prompted by the prospect of human cloning turn out, upon reflection, to be absurdly improbable. There's the fear, for instance, that parents might clone a child to have "spare parts" in case the original child needs an organ transplant. But parents of identical twins don't view one child as an organ farm for the other. Why should cloned children's parents be any different?

[1] Ruth Macklin, "Human Cloning," Don't Just Say No," *U.S. News & World Report*, March 1997, http://www.usnews.com/usnews/culture/articles/970310/archive_006398.htm.

Vast difference. Another disturbing thought is that cloning will lead to efforts to breed individuals with genetic qualities perceived as exceptional (math geniuses, basketball players). Such ideas are repulsive, not only because of the "yuk factor" but also because of the horrors perpetrated by the Nazis in the name of eugenics. But there's a vast difference between "selective breeding" as practiced by totalitarian regimes (where the urge to propagate certain types of people leads to efforts to eradicate other types) and the immeasurably more benign forms already practiced in democratic societies (where, say, lawyers freely choose to marry other lawyers). Banks stocked with the frozen sperm of geniuses already exist. They haven't created a master race because only a tiny number of women have wanted to impregnate themselves this way. Why think it will be different if human cloning becomes available?

So who will likely take advantage of cloning? Perhaps a grieving couple whose child is dying. This might seem psychologically twisted. But a cloned child born to such dubious parents stands no greater or lesser chance of being loved, or rejected, or warped than a child normally conceived. Infertile couples are also likely to seek out cloning. That such couples have other options (in vitro fertilization or adoption) is not an argument for denying them the right to clone. Or consider an example raised by Judge Richard Posner: a couple in which the husband has some tragic genetic defect. Currently, if this couple wants a genetically related child, they have four not altogether pleasant options. They can reproduce naturally and risk passing on the disease to the child. They can go to a sperm bank and take a chance on unknown genes. They can try in vitro fertilization and dispose of any afflicted embryo—though that might be objectionable, too. Or they can get a male relative of the father to donate sperm, if such a relative exists. This is one case where even people unnerved by cloning might see it as not the worst option.

Even if human cloning offers no obvious benefits to humanity, why ban it? In a democratic society we don't usually pass laws outlawing something before there is actual or probable evidence of harm. A moratorium on further research into human cloning might make sense, in order to consider calmly the grave questions it raises. If the moratorium is then lifted, human cloning should remain a research activity for an extended period. And if it is ever attempted, it should—and no doubt will—take place only with careful scrutiny and layers of legal oversight. Most important, human cloning should be governed by the same laws that now protect human rights. A world not safe for cloned humans would be a world not safe for the rest of us.

Ruth Macklin has written several books on the subject of bioethics, including Mortal Choices: Bioethics in Today's World. *Professor Macklin teaches bioethics at the Albert Einstein College of Medicine in Bronx, NY.*

THINKING THROUGH A READING
1. What is Krauthammer's thesis and its burdens of proof?

2. In what situations does Krauthammer support stem cell research?

3. Where does he want to impose limits?

4. What might Krauthammer say to Ruth Macklin? What might she say to him?

Stem Cell Research Without Limits Is a Bad Idea[2]
Charles Krauthammer

It is a good idea to expand federal funding of embryonic stem cell research. It is a bad idea to do that without prohibiting research that uses embryos created specifically to be used in research and destroyed.

What is deeply troubling about the Castle-DeGette stem cell bill that passed the House and will soon roar through the Senate is that it combines the good with the bad: expansion with no limit.

The expansion—federal funding for stem cells derived from some of the thousands of discarded fertility-clinic embryos that are already slated for extinction—is good because the president's sincere and principled Aug. 9, 2001, attempt to draw a narrower line has failed. It failed politically because his restriction—funding only research on stem cells from embryos destroyed before the day of that speech—seems increasingly arbitrary as we move away from that date.

It failed practically because that cohort of embryos is a diminishing source of cells. Stem cells turn out to be a lot less immortal than we thought. The idea was that once you create a line, it could replicate indefinitely. Therefore, you would only need a few lines.

It turns out, however, that as stem cells replicate, they begin to make genetic errors and to degenerate. After several generations, some lines become unusable.

In addition, there has been a new advance since 2001. Whereas stem cells in those days had to be grown on mouse feeder cells, today we can grow stem cells on human feeder cells. That makes them far more (potentially) therapeutically usable.

For both of these reasons, the August 2001 policy is obsolete. Accordingly, Congress will soon federally fund research from embryos newly created in IVF clinics.

It simply will not do for opponents of this expanded research to say that the federal government should not force those Americans who find this research abhorrent to support it with their taxes. By that logic, we should never go to war, or impose the death penalty, except by unanimous consent of the entire population. We make many life or death decisions as a society as a whole, without being hostage to the sensibilities of a minority, however substantial and sincere.

Nonetheless, Congress' current vehicle for expanding this research, the Castle-DeGette bill, is extremely dangerous. It expands the reach for a morally problematical area of research—without drawing any serious moral lines.

The moral problem for that majority of Americans who, like me, don't believe that a zygote or blastocyst has all the attributes and therefore merits all the rights of personhood, is this: Does that mean that *everything* is permissible with a human embryo?

---

[2] Charles Krauthammer, "Stem Cell Research Is a Bad Idea, August 5, 2005, http://townhall.com/columnists/CharlesKrauthammer/2005/08/05/stem_cell_research_without_limits_is_a_bad_idea.

Don't they understand the real threat? It is not so much the destruction of existing human embryos—God knows, more than a million are already destroyed every year in abortions, thousands doomed to die in IVF clinics. A handful drawn from fertility clinics *where they will be destroyed anyway* alters no great moral balance.

The real threat to our humanity is the creation of new human life willfully for the sole purpose of making it the means to someone else's end—dissecting it for its parts the way we would dissect something with no more moral standing than a mollusk or paramecium. The real Brave New World looming before us is the rise of the industry of human manufacture, where human embryos are created not to produce children—the purpose of IVF clinics—but for spare body parts.

It is this creation-for-the-purpose-of-destruction that needs to be stopped—and it does not matter whether that creation occurs by joining sperm and egg (as the Jones Institute in Virginia has already done) or by cloning a cell from an adult, turning it into a human embryo, and then destroying it for its stem cells.

Both in my writings and as a member of the President's Council on Bioethics, I have advocated this dual policy for years: expand federal funding of stem cell research by using discarded embryos but couple that with a firm *national ban* on creating human embryos for any purpose other than the birth of a human baby. We finally have a chance to enact this grand compromise—but only if a majority of senators insist that the welcome expansion provided in the Castle-DeGette bill, which will yield a near endless supply of embryonic stem cells, cannot take place unless the door is firmly closed now, while we still have the chance, on the manufacture of human embryos for research and destruction.

Charles Krauthammer is a 1987 Pulitzer Prize winner, 1984 National Magazine Award *winner, and a columnist for* The Washington Post *since 1985. He also writes essays for* Time *and appears regularly on* Fox News's Special Report. *He earned an M.D. from Harvard University's medical school in 1975. Krauthammer was appointed by President George Bush to serve on the President's Council on Bioethics in 2002.*

Now that you have read and analyzed the two readings, write your responses to the following questions:

1. Which essay do you find most persuasive? List at least three things the author did to convince you.

2. Were any notable strategies used by the author whose essay you did not choose that made it more difficult to make your choice? Describe those techniques.

3. Describe your current position on genetic cloning as a result of reading these articles. Compare the points you list to those made in the essays. To what degree is your personal position captured in one or the other essay? What does this tell you about the way you make decisions about what you believe?

CHAPTER 5

Drafting and Revising the Essay: Supporting the Thesis Statement

When you turn to drafting your essay, you turn to matters of form. Up to this point, you've spent time working on the early stages of your paper, including writing observation lists, finding overarching ideas, and generating a working thesis statement. Now that you have an understanding of what makes a good thesis statement and the tools to help you develop one, we will look more closely at the relationship between the thesis statement and the rest of the paper. In other words, this chapter will help you bring together the lessons and ideas from chapters 1–4 into a format that your readers will recognize and understand. After all, in college (and for many professional writers), the thesis-driven essay structure is the expected format for delivering your insights and discoveries.

WHAT'S AHEAD . . .

▶ revisiting the academic essay format

▶ using an outline to draft an essay

▶ a closer look at paragraphs

- the introduction

- body paragraphs

- the conclusion

▶ putting it all together

▶ revising the essay: the basics

- moving from writer-oriented to reader-oriented writing

- time management

- peer review

Revisiting the Academic Essay Format

In chapter 1, we observed that the thesis-driven essay format includes an introduction, a thesis statement, evidence or proof, and a purposeful conclusion. It's often called the academic essay, and its primary purpose is to persuade. It might be helpful now to review the diagram of this formal essay structure, shown in figure 5.1, to refresh your memory in preparation for drafting.

Fig. 5.1 Diagram of the Thesis-Driven Essay

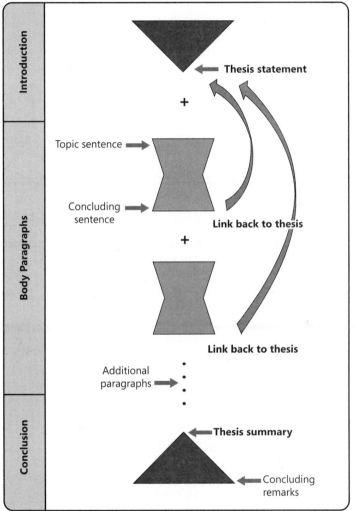

This diagram calls attention to the many elements that are included in the thesis-driven essay and how they work together to create a unified whole. As discussed in chapter 1, the job of the **introduction** is to orient the reader to the subject of the paper. It ends by presenting the **thesis statement**, which the rest of the paper will work to support. Each paragraph in the **body of the paper** focuses on one main idea that is presented using a topic sentence. Each paragraph then goes on to develop the topic idea by present- ing evidence, including a careful explanation and analysis to show how this topic helps to support or "prove" the thesis assertion. (Don't assume that this is obvious.) The essay

concludes with a quick summary of the thesis and the evidence to remind the reader of the persuasiveness of the argument and a closing comment of some sort.

Using an Outline to Draft an Essay

Drafting an essay is only part of the writing process. The first draft or initial version of your paper will likely contain rough spots and areas that need further development as well as revision. If you've built an outline before beginning to draft, you are free to draft sections or parts of the essay in any order because you can always sequence them later. Look again at the outline we created about human cloning on page 88 in the previous chapter. The outline begins to suggest how your essay might look because it creates a possible structure for the way you organize your ideas.

Don't insist on writing the draft sequentially from beginning to end. Introductions, for example, are notoriously difficult to write, so if yours is holding you up or causing consternation, skip it for now and come back to it later. Review your outline. You may want to begin with a point that you've already worked out and that you can write fairly easily. Or, you may want to go back to your observation lists and prewriting notes to find relevant sections that you can import into your draft, even if they are rough.

You may find, as you draft, that connections spring to mind that you did not anticipate in the writing plan. If so, write them out and see if they are significant to your argument. You may come to new realizations that you will want to incorporate into the paper, and those new ideas are likely to shift the working thesis statement and alter the burdens of proof. You may find yourself needing to go back and revise your thesis statement and your outline or writing plan as well. Remember that until you turn in the final version of your paper, you should think of your thesis statement as a working thesis statement and be open to modifying it as you shape your ideas and explore your subject. Writing is a recursive process, so the more time you give yourself to allow ideas to develop and be revised, the more likely you are to have a successful essay.

A Closer Look at Paragraphs: Introduction, Body Paragraphs, and Conclusion

After outlining your paper, even if it is an informal list of topics jotted down on the back of an envelope, and you have decided where to start, it's time to think about how to shape the paragraphs. Readers expect information to be broken down into bite-sized chunks to make better sense of it. Deciding how to organize a large amount of information into a unified and coherent paragraph is one of the most difficult aspects of the writing process. A paragraph usually has more than one sentence but seldom is longer than a typed page. As the building block of the essay, it is highly specialized. Each paragraph requires certain information and serves a specific purpose. The sentences within each paragraph—and the paragraphs themselves—should follow a purposeful and logical order in the essay, which is made clear to the reader through transitions and other rhetorical cues. The goals of the different kinds of paragraphs in an essay—introduction, body paragraphs, and conclusion—are important to understand.

The Introduction

Because a paper can be written about virtually anything, the introduction to a paper usually orients the reader to the general topic of discussion or its context. Think of the **introduction** as beginning the process that the thesis statement completes. It sets the stage for the paper by introducing the reader to the general subject and lays the groundwork for the claim. It does this through three discrete parts: an *opening* that "hooks" the reader and entices the audience to read the essay; a *midsection* that orients the reader to the subject of the paper; and a *focal point* that presents the thesis statement on which the rest of the essay will be built. Customarily, the last sentence of the introduction is the thesis statement.

Notice that the introduction begins broadly, setting the outer boundaries of the paper's scope, and grows more and more specific as it covers background material and creates a framework for the specific focus of the essay—its thesis. Even though the diagram in figure 5.2 is made with just one triangle, possibly suggesting that all introductions are just one paragraph in length, think of it instead as a pattern for the introductory portion of your essay. For a short essay, your introduction may be limited to a single paragraph to reserve more space for your evidence, but in a longer piece, your introduction may be several paragraphs long. Whatever its length, it should be only as long as necessary to grab the reader's attention, set the stage for your argument, and present your thesis statement.

Fig. 5.2 Diagram of an Introduction

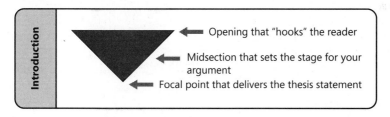

For many writers, the introduction is the most difficult part of the essay to draft. Like the conclusion, the introduction allows a writer to stray a bit into more stylistic, informal, and even personal prose as a way to accomplish the important objective of catching the reader's attention. In discussing techniques for beginning speeches, Aristotle suggested that the introduction (or exordium) should, in addition to introducing the subject, seek to remove prejudice against the forthcoming argument, clarify disputed points, and/or set up a counterattack. Aristotle allows for some pathos (emotional appeals) to be included in the introduction (and conclusion) to better appeal to audiences, but he requires strict logical reasoning within the body of the paper. If you find the introduction difficult to write, try one or more of the ten common strategies shown in the following box, but be careful to avoid the things, listed next, that can make an introduction fall flat.

Ten Ways to Begin an Introduction

▶ draft the rest of the essay and use the conclusion you drafted as your introduction; then write a new conclusion

▶ use an adage, proverb, or piece of advice in a unique way

▶ give an interesting quote

▶ narrate an anecdote

▶ state an interesting fact or unexpected detail or point

▶ use a provocative statement

▶ define an important term

▶ pose an interesting question

▶ describe an unexpected point of view

▶ show that an unforeseen problem exists

Things to Avoid in an Introduction

▶ opening with a flat explanation of what you intend to cover in the paper: "This essay is about . . ." or "I am going to inform you . . ." or "In this essay I will argue that . . ."

▶ opening with your thesis statement, unless the introduction is very brief (say, for a timed writing). When the thesis statement opens the paper, the temptation is to give more information about the thesis claim, to begin summarizing points or clarifying ideas. If the reader is shown most of the points that will be discussed in the paper in the first paragraph of the paper, what incentive is there to read the paper? It is best to place the thesis after the context of the paper is established.

▶ meaningless platitudes: "Violence is undesirable in our society. Therefore . . ." or "Man has always searched for . . ."

▶ empty statements: "Everyone knows that drinking milk is good for you."

▶ broad and sweeping statements: "Since the beginning of time . . ." or "Humans everywhere seek . . ." or "Of all studies ever done . . ."

Let's continue to build on the draft we outlined in the previous chapter on genetic cloning and try a couple of these strategies to draft an introduction.

USE A PROVOCATIVE STATEMENT
By the 1960s, scientists were speculating on the possibility that one day our society would be able to genetically engineer children so that we could "order up" the specific

gender, height, and talents we want in our offspring. Has the time come? Or do the moral and ethical issues require even more time to master than the scientific processes that would allow for this customized childbearing? Many are excited about the possibilities of genetic cloning and support its use wherever and whenever possible. However, in spite of the excitement about genetic cloning, it shouldn't be used right now because our limited knowledge makes it too dangerous.

GIVE AN INTERESTING QUOTE

At a recent biotechnology conference, one expert said, "I am convinced that human cloning is going to play a critical role in the future of our species. We cannot afford to ignore the potential benefits of this science. It may well mean the ultimate survival of our species." Many people agree with him. In fact, scientists all over the world are experimenting with animals, and even humans, to gain some of the benefits our early stages of knowledge allow. Methods of cloning are, however, still very crude, and only a mere 3% of the successfully reconstructed embryos reach the birth stage. The first attempt made to clone an animal, a sheep now named "Dolly," took 276 cloning attempts. The chances of mistakes, with such a low success rate, suggest caution is necessary. Hence, in spite of the excitement about genetic cloning, it shouldn't be used right now because our limited knowledge makes it too dangerous.

POSE AN INTERESTING QUESTION

Is it possible to have a world absolutely free of pain and suffering? Can genetic cloning, or genetic engineering, give us such a world? This is a question many are currently asking, and, although some disagree, others are excited by the possibilities genetic cloning seems to bring. Cloning techniques have been successfully used in a limited number of contexts, but cloning is still primarily a matter of trial and error, and successful attempts have been few. Although we are told that cloning will revolutionize life from medicine to agriculture, our current knowledge is in the very early stages of experimentation. The promise of cloning is still far on the horizon. Although many are excited about pushing forward, genetic cloning shouldn't be used right now because our limited knowledge makes it too dangerous.

When writing introductions, look at the suggested patterns and keep trying different ones until you find an opening that you think works well for your purposes. Your choice will depend on the information you have, your context for writing, your audience, and the tone you want to achieve. Remember to focus on providing a context for your working thesis statement and shape your opening by narrowing to this focal point.

Practice 5.1 Analyzing Introduction

1. Return to the essay in chapter 1 on "Homing Device for Humans" (page 11) and study the introduction. Does the author use a hook, a midsection, and a focal point in the introduction? Identify these components. Discuss their effectiveness.

2. Return to the essay "The Beatles-*Rubber Soul*" in chapter 2 (page 48). Does this author use a hook, a midsection, and a focal point in the introduction? Identify these components. Compare the effectiveness of the two essays' introductions.

Body Paragraphs

The **body paragraphs** make up the largest part of the paper and present the evidence and commentary that show the thesis statement to be valid. Each paragraph has two jobs—to develop one important point in support of the thesis statement and to show how that point furthers the argument of the paper. Body paragraphs open with a topic sentence and include evidence, a discussion of the evidence, and a clear link between the paragraph's subject matter and the thesis claim. Because the focus of the body paragraphs of the paper are derived from the burdens of proof inherent in the thesis statement, there is a dependent relationship established between the body paragraphs and the thesis statement. As a result, perhaps each paragraph's most important duty is to explain how the point that is developed in the paragraph forges one of the logical links in the chain of the paper's argument. In the diagram of the academic essay on page 99, body paragraphs are represented by an hourglass shape, where the evidence and its discussion are framed by the paragraph's opening and closing sentences. Figure 5.3 shows how the topic and concluding sentences serve as overarching sentences that sandwich the details in each paragraph.

Fig. 5.3 Body Paragraph Diagram: The Hourglass

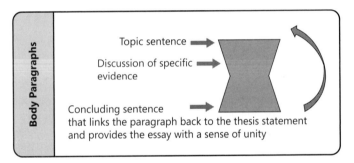

Writing a well-developed paragraph can be easy once you understand the structure that is expected. Think of each paragraph as a mini-essay: a topic sentence that functions like the paper's thesis statement followed by supporting evidence for that topic sentence. Keep in mind that the topic sentence and evidence have to support the paper's thesis statement. This is why it is best to construct an outline or writing plan from the thesis statement's burdens of proof before beginning a draft. The following acronym will help you achieve the hourglass structure of a well-developed body paragraph:

Topic sentence (a sentence that states the one point the paragraph will make)

Assertion statements (statements that present your ideas)

e**X**ample(s) (specific passages, factual material, or concrete data)

Explanation (commentary that shows how the examples support your assertions)

Significance (commentary that shows how the paragraph supports the thesis statement)[1]

---

[1] Adapted from Randy Fellows' AXES model, as described in an unpublished paper.

TAXES gives you a formula for building the supporting paragraphs in a thesis-driven essay. When beginning a paragraph, spend time writing a clear **topic sentence** that overarches the paragraph or section as a whole. It should state the one point the paragraph or section will make, a point that helps build the chain of reasoning in support of your thesis statement. Your thesis statement's burdens of proof can often be rephrased to become topic sentences.

Follow a topic sentence with strong **assertion statements** that express your ideas about the overarching topic sentence. Sometimes your topic sentence can serve double duty as an assertion sentence, especially in shorter essays where it pays to be economical. Remember, however, that just because you assert that something is so doesn't mean your readers will be convinced. Mere assertion doesn't go far enough in an argument paper to persuade readers that your thesis statement is valid and compelling.

Ground your ideas in supporting **examples**, and remember to explain carefully how the examples demonstrate the point you want to make. Examples, or evidence that backs up your assertion statements, topic ideas, and ultimately the thesis claim, can take a number of forms, depending on your writing context and purpose. For instance, you may offer a quote from the text you are interpreting, a statistic or factual detail from the research you have done, or a statement from an expert in a relevant field.

Finally, be sure to close the paragraph or cluster of paragraphs on a topic with a careful and clear explanation of its **significance** to the paper's thesis statement. This is an important, and often forgotten, part of TAXES. It can be as short as a single sentence, but without it, the paragraph hangs in limbo. Tell the reader as clearly as you can how the point you have just made furthers the argument of your paper. Often, you can restate the burden of proof that this paragraph or group of paragraphs makes.

If you weave these TAXES elements into each of your body paragraphs, they will be well developed, unified, and compelling. Following is an example from one student's essay written in response to an assignment to write an interpretation of *Devil in a Blue Dress*, a film starring Denzel Washington. Made in 1995, the film is set in the American 1940s and is the story of a black man's return from World War II and his attempt to establish himself in American society as a citizen and property owner. To do this, he is forced to abandon his job in the defense industry and learn to work as a private detective in Los Angeles, a city of crime and injustice, especially for African Americans.

The student begins the introduction with a provocative statement, leading eventually to the thesis statement:

> In Walter Mosley's film *Devil in a Blue Dress*, there is little justice for the protagonist, Easy Rawlins. The justice dispensed by the police in this film is hardly justice; it is particular, with determiners and underlying limits. A true order of justice is one that is blind to all obstacles and does not count on fame or fortune. The justice Easy sees comes through an obstructed lens, one that is trained to view life according to the white man. The form of justice he meets in his life is through crooked cops, deceiving women, and violent friends, a justice that just doesn't seem fair. The film traces his battle with injustice and his ability to prevail in spite of the forces that work

against him. *Devil in a Blue Dress* gives viewers, especially African-American viewers, a vision of pride and purpose in their struggle against social injustice.

Notice that the writer begins the introduction broadly, then narrows to a definition of true justice, which is then further narrowed to discuss the kind of justice Easy Rawlins faces. Finally, the paragraph puts forward the focus of the paper in the form of a thesis claim. In short, this introduction follows the triangular structure of the introduction discussed previously and seems to accomplish the introduction's three goals of catching the audience's attention, setting the stage for the discussion about justice, and proposing a specific argument about this film.

Now let's examine one of the supporting paragraphs from the paper to see how TAXES can be used effectively:

> **(T)** Justice in *Devil in a Blue Dress* is something that one makes for one's self. **(A)**This concept is illustrated in the film's main character, Easy Rawlins (Denzel Washington). **(X)** When Rawlins discovers that white employees are treated better on the job than black employees are, he confronts his boss, Mr. Giacome (Steven Randazzo), and makes a stand for equal rights. **(E)** He knows that this action might get him fired, as it does, but he also knows that if a person is going to receive any justice in this world, that person must be willing to fight for it. **(X)** After DeWitt Albright (Tom Sizemore) and his two goons break into Rawlins' house and threaten to cut his eyes out and kill him, Rawlins enlists the aid of his friend Mouse Alexander (Don Cheadle). **(X)** When he finds out that the police are about to frame him for the murders of Coretta James (Lisa Nicole Carson) and Richard McGee (Scott Lincoln), he takes action to find the guilty parties. He grabs Joppy (Mel Winkler) out of his bar, at gunpoint, and hunts down Albright at his cabin in Malibu. **(E)** By emphasizing Rawlins' aggressive measures to rectify the dangerous situations that he finds himself in, **(S)** director Carl Franklin illustrates an individual's responsibility to fight for justice in one's own life.

Notice the strong topic sentence that opens this paragraph, the short assertion statement that begins to develop the writer's ideas about the topic, and the use of several examples from the film to illustrate the point of the paragraph. This particular TAXES chunk is a single paragraph, yet it is well developed, and its tie to the thesis statement is clear.

Omitting one or more of the layers of TAXES often results in weak and unclear paragraphs. Try reading the preceding paragraph after eliminating one of the TAXES elements and see if you agree. Now imagine this for every support paragraph in the essay. Readers finish the essay feeling unsure and even resistant to the paper's ideas because they sense that more must be said to make the argument convincing. If your paragraphs never move beyond assertion statements, they will not persuade readers who are not already in agreement with you. Merely saying something is so won't convince anyone; you must demonstrate why it is so. This is why examples are an important element of any body paragraph.

On the other hand, paragraphs that present examples alone are equally ineffective. Never assume that your evidence, for example, a quoted passage or a piece of factual information, will be self-explanatory. You must tell your readers exactly how the quotation or fact demonstrates the point you are making in terms of your thesis statement. If you open a paragraph with a topic sentence, you get readers off to a clear start because you let them know exactly what you are going to show them in the paragraph and what the paragraph's relevance is to your overall claim. It is best not to open a paragraph with an example because readers will not understand why the example is important or what it is supposed to demonstrate. Some of the example's power will be diluted because its relevance is deferred. TAXES will help you incorporate all the steps you need to write compelling and relevant paragraphs.

Checklist for Writing Strong Body Paragraphs

Flow: Make sure each of your body paragraphs follows the TAXES format. Have you used different sentence patterns so the paragraph does not seem repetitive and bog down? Does one sentence flow to another, with appropriate transitions? Do the thoughts follow sequentially, without logical gaps, so that the point is clear to the reader?

Analysis: As you build your body paragraphs, remember that you must analyze your subject, not summarize it. If you rely on the burdens of proof for your writing plan, you will likely avoid mere summary. Using TAXES will be another safeguard against offering mere summary.

Arrangement: Think for a minute about the arrangement of your paragraphs. Is there a logical sequence or build up that will help readers follow your argument? Are there appropriate transitions between paragraphs so that one flows to the next? Have you included a counterargument? Is one necessary? There are many theories about how best to arrange the points in a paper. They include beginning with your best point, or your weakest point, or your second best point (thereby ending with the strongest point). Consider all the alternatives and make the best choices you can, given the requirements of your paper.

Research: Research can include an intense study of diverse sources, or it can be as simple as finding a pithy quote from a relevant authority on your essay topic. Your writing assignment may or may not invite or require research. Chapter 10 offers techniques for enhancing your essay with research.

Practice 5.2 Analyzing Body Paragraphs
1. Return to the essay "The Beatles-*Rubber Soul*" in chapter 2. Study one or two body paragraphs. Does this author use TAXES? Identify the components.

2. Return to the essay in chapter 4, "Human Cloning? Don't Just Say No" (page 94). Study one or two body paragraphs. Does this author use TAXES? Identify the components. Compare the effectiveness of the two essays' body paragraphs.

The Conclusion
The conclusion of an essay carries a lot of rhetorical weight because these are your last words to your reader. As illustrated in figure 5.4, conclusions typically begin by restating

the thesis statement and summarizing the evidence. However, a good conclusion should do more—it should reaffirm the validity of your thesis by reinforcing the logical reasoning you used and the conclusions you drew. Finally, the conclusion should tie up the discussion in a way that is satisfying and provides a sense of closure. Consider giving your paper a finishing touch by extending the relevance of the subject under study into contexts not covered in the paper or by considering the ramifications of the thesis now that the reader has (hopefully) been convinced of its soundness. Whatever choices you make, important to remember that the conclusion leaves the reader with a final impression of the essay and its writer. This message is also carried through the tone imparted. Style can be especially important in the conclusion. Don't try to bully your reader into agreeing with you. At the very least, you should attempt to convey an authoritative yet reasonable tone. It is best to end with grace and a balanced sense of confidence.

Fig. 5.4 Diagram of a Conclusion

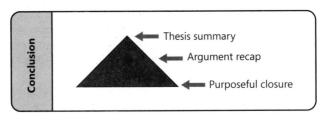

Ten Ways to Conclude an Essay

► end with an interesting quotation

► show how the argument you have made affirms an argument or issue raised by someone else

► go back to an idea or detail from the introduction and bring the essay full circle

► end by talking about the implications and/or significance of your argument

► allude to a historical idea or mythological figure to place your topic in a larger framework

► end by calling for further research

► end by urging your readers to follow your recommendation with action

► end with an anecdote or illustration

► end with an emotional statement that appeals to readers' pity, sense of justice, hopes, or fears

► end with the paper's most important point restated

Things to Avoid in a Conclusion

▶ making new points or introducing new evidence

▶ apologizing, softening, or reversing your position

▶ coming on too strong or using an unproductive tone

▶ offending the reader by making arrogant and absolute pronouncements about what you have said or proven

As with the introduction, you will have to decide on the best strategy for a conclusion, given each paper's subject, purpose, and audience. Following are two conclusions written by students. Like the introduction and body paragraphs we looked at earlier, these were written for an interpretive paper on the film *Devil in a Blue Dress*.

Notice how the first example uses the strategy of going back to an idea from the introduction and reminding readers where the argument began. With the thesis-centered essay, this means repeating the thesis statement using different words and giving a few general statements about the supporting ideas covered in the paper.

Conclusion that goes back to the introduction and brings the essay full circle:

In *Devil in a Blue Dress*, justice is served in many different ways, through many different people. Easy Rawlins must decide to take his own fate into his hands and fight for the justice that he deserves, not the mishandled justice that occurs when dealing with cops, gangsters, and even peers. Throughout the film, Easy never sees a true picture of justice. His perception of justice is gained by his involvement in solving the mystery, and he must deal with discrimination, violence, sex, and greed in the best way he can and according to his own code. He is forced to make his own justice according to his own life.

Another student chose a different concluding strategy:

Conclusion that talks about the implications of the argument:

The film *Devil in a Blue Dress* introduces a new perspective on what it was like to be a black American before the Civil Rights Movement. Using Denzel Washington, a well-known and popular star, to play the detective hero allows audiences to identify with him and to see events from his point of view. In addition to giving twenty-first century viewers historical perspective, the film shows us the struggles that the main character, Easy Rawlins, endures and overcomes, and so makes struggle and triumph more tangible for other African Americans.

In both of these examples, notice the strong tone and level of generality that help signal the end of the essay and bring readers a sense of closure. Remember, when readers reach the conclusion of your paper, they have a new perspective on your thesis statement because they have read through your ideas and learned about your subject. Consequently, you can assume a certain level of knowledge on your readers' part, and this allows you to give a perspective on the paper's subject that wouldn't be meaningful to readers in the introduction.

Remember that the conclusion is your last opportunity to persuade readers. Using clarity, grace, and balance will be most effective in compelling your readers to adopt your point of view.

Practice 5.3 Analyzing Conclusions

1. Return to the essay "The Beatles-*Rubber Soul*" in chapter 2 and study the conclusion. Identify the summary, recap, and closure. Discuss their effectiveness.

2. Return to the essay in chapter 4, "Human Cloning? Don't Just Say No." Does this author use summary, recap, and closure? Identify these components. Compare the effectiveness of both essays' conclusions.

Putting It All Together

Read the following essay, "Life in the Lap of Luxury as Ecosystems Collapse," and note how the author uses the introduction, body paragraphs, and conclusion to present and support his argument. Note the problem he identifies and the solution he proposes.

THINKING THROUGH A READING
1. What is Rees's thesis, and which sentence best presents his thesis statement?

2. What burdens of proof does this thesis entail? How effectively does the author fulfill them?

3. Consider the problem Rees puts forward in his article. How does he define the "ecological footprint" of a population?

4. What counterargument does Rees use to close his article? How effective is this conclusion? Would you recommend a different closing strategy? Explain.

Life in the Lap of Luxury as Ecosystems Collapse [2]
William E. Rees

Have you ever asked yourself how much of the earth's surface is required to support you in the style to which you are accustomed? Every free-range dairy farmer knows, within a few square meters, how much pasture of a given quality is needed to support each of his cattle, and just how many head he can safely graze on the back forty. Similar questions, however, seldom come up in relation to people.

The Cartesian dualism that underpins Western philosophy and science has been so successful in psychologically separating humans from nature that we simply don't conceive

---

[2] William E. Rees, "Life in the Lap of Luxury as Ecosystems Collapse," *Chronicle of Higher Education*, July 30, 1999, http://chronicle.com/weekly/v45/i47/47b00401.htm.

of ourselves as ecological beings, as creatures of the land. Ignoring our dependence on our environment is a serious mistake.

In recent decades, the world has experienced an event of profound significance: the massive migration of people from the countryside to the city. In 1950, New York was the only city on the planet with 10 million or more inhabitants; by 2015, as many as 27 cities—most of them in the developing world—will be that large. In the 1990s alone, the population of the world's cities will increase by 50 percent, to 3 billion people. The United Nations projects that an additional 2.1 billion people—which was roughly the population of the entire globe in the early 1930s—will be living in cities by 2025.

We usually think of urbanization mainly as a demographic or economic transition. Hardly anyone acknowledges it as a potential ecological problem. On the contrary, many observers interpret urbanization as further evidence of humanity's increasing technical prowess and independence from the land. Such technological hubris is an illusion. Separating billions of people from the land that sustains them is a giddy leap of faith with serious implications for ecological security.

For proof, let's explore the fundamental ecological question posed above. We can analyze an average person's ecological footprint to estimate how much land people actually use. The analysis involves identifying and quantifying all significant categories of materials and energy appropriated from nature to support the consumption patterns of a defined group of people. We can then calculate the area of land and water required to supply the materials and energy. For example, about 25 square meters of former tropical forest are needed just to produce the coffee beans for the average java drinker in an industrialized country. We can also estimate the ecosystem area needed to absorb certain critical wastes. Heavy users of fossil fuels need 2 to 3 hectares (4.9 to 7.4 acres) of forest somewhere on the planet to absorb their carbon-dioxide emissions alone.

In summary, the ecological footprint of a population is the total area of land and water required to produce the resources that the population consumes, and to assimilate the wastes that the population generates, wherever on earth that land is located.

As Mathis Wackernagel and I have shown in *Our Ecological Footprint* (New Society, 1995), the residents of high-income countries typically need 4 to 9 hectares (10 to 22 acres) per capita to support their consumer life styles. That area seems large. However, since our calculations assume that all the land involved is being managed sustainably (which is rarely the case), our results actually underestimate the total demand. Thus, it is easy to see that cities typically impose an ecological footprint on the earth several hundred times larger than their political or geographic areas.

Most people think of cities as centers of culture and learning, and as the productive engines of economic growth. All that is true, but they also are sites of intense consumption of material and production of waste. As the well-known ecologist Eugene P. Odum recognized in Fundamentals of Ecology, "Great cities are planned and grow without any regard for the fact that they are parasites on the countryside which must somehow supply food, water, and air, and degrade huge quantities of waste." In short, far from signaling humanity's final separation from nature, urbanization merely removes people both spatially and psychologically from the land that sustains them.

In that light, consider the following additional dimensions of urban human ecology:

- The principal material effect of technology has been to extend the spatial scale and intensity of humans' capacity to exploit nature. Contrary to conventional views, our ecological footprint is expanding, not decreasing, with increasing wealth and technological advances.

- Many croplands and forests are being used more intensively than ever to sustain the world's burgeoning urban populations. In that sense, the great plains of North America are an essential component of the urban ecosystem.

- While the citizens of urban industrial societies use up to 9 hectares of productive land and water, the earth contains only about 2 hectares of such ecosystems per capita. The consumer life styles of rich countries cannot be extended sustainably to the entire human population, using current technologies.

- In a world of rapid change, no city can be truly sustainable unless the lands in its footprint are secure from ecological change and international hostilities.

Cities have been part of the human cultural landscape for thousands of years, but only in recent decades has it become possible for the majority of people to live in cities. For better or worse, however, this phase of our development may be relatively short-lived. The recent explosive growth of the human population, our intensely material culture, and urbanization itself are all products of what the sociologist William R. Catton has called the "age of exuberance."

. . . The perspectives and skills of many disciplines are required to assess the vulnerability of urban populations in the 21st century and to determine the measures needed to enhance their security. Perhaps most important, we must develop a holistic concept of the city-as-system. Urban planning should include as much as possible of the city's ecological footprint.

. . . The time has come for us to take seriously the idea that each of us lives in a bioregion—a geographic area defined by both biophysical characteristics, including watershed boundaries, and patterns of occupancy by humans and other species—and that our urban ecological footprints should be contained as much as possible within our local bioregions. Ecologists and economists should work together to determine criteria for delineating bioregions. Geographers and urban planners might study such issues as the optimal pattern of human population distribution within various bioregions, and the appropriate size for cites. Political scientists should consider which powers federal and state or provincial governments might devolve to the local level, and which they should keep, to facilitate the planning that long-term urban sustainability will require.

In the long run, the most secure and sustainable cities may be those that succeed in reintegrating the geography of living and employment, of production and consumption, of city and hinterland. As Sim Van der Tyn and Peter Calthorpe wrote in *Sustainable Communities*, such a transformed city, "rather than being merely the site of consumption, might, through its very design, produce some of its own food and energy, as well as become the locus of work for its residents."

If we followed such ecological design principles, urban regions could gradually become not only more self-reliant, but also more socially rewarding and ecologically benign. Through greater dependence on local ecosystems, city dwellers would become more aware of their connectedness to nature. As they became more conscientious stewards of the environment, their lives would become less materialistic; in turn, that change would reduce both cities' ecological footprints and the political tensions they would otherwise foster.

To the upwardly mobile beneficiaries of the age of exuberance, all that may sound surreal, even ridiculous. We are accustomed to expecting a future of more and bigger, of freewheeling technological mastery over the natural world. But that road leads inevitably to a dead end. Accelerating global change has shown that the earth cannot keep an infinitely expanding population in the lap of luxury. Scholars should start looking for a new route now.

William Rees has a doctorate in bioecology from the University of Toronto and he is the founding member of Pollution Probe and a former president of the Canadian Society for Ecological Economics.

Revising an Essay: The Basics

Revision is arguably the most important step of the writing process. When revision is done well, you will go over an essay and make changes a half dozen or more times, each time focusing on a different attribute of the essay. This stage of the writing process is intended to be holistic—taking into account issues that are central to the essay's argument, including the **format**, **the thesis statement**, **logical development**, and **organization.** Some professional writers have been known to call revision 80 percent of the work of writing. To put this in perspective, this means that if revision is done well, 80 percent of your final essay still remains to be written even after you have a first draft of the entire essay. This is why we have included strategies for revision in each part of this book. Like everything in part 1, you may need to return often to this section as you develop your skills through the remaining sections of this book.

Revision really begins from the moment you begin prewriting, as you examine your ideas, test them against the evidence, and alter them accordingly. Throughout the writing process, whenever your current ideas are challenged by new evidence, you have to revise both your working thesis and its supporting evidence. Although the writing process is recursive rather than linear, for practical reasons, we'll talk about revision primarily as a later stage in the writing process, as the work that begins once you've written a rough draft. Revision can be hard, tedious work (a writer once called it "toiling in the muck of revision"); it can also be fun in the sense that it gives you an opportunity to experiment, take chances, and use imagination. Overall, it provides an opportunity to spend some time trying your hand at improvement to see what you are capable of making out of the rough piece of writing that you have generated. It's important to recognize that revision calls for a different point of view on your writing.

Moving from Writer-Oriented to Reader-Oriented Writing
Up until this point, you have probably been focusing on getting your ideas down as precisely as possible while trying to adhere to the academic essay format and the directions for your particular assignment. In other words, your writing has probably

been largely **writer oriented**. Revision and editing requires a change to a **reader- or audience-oriented** perspective. In chapter 1, we discussed the rhetorical triangle and the co-dependent relationship among the writer, audience, and text. We represented them with an equilateral triangle, suggesting their equal importance, as well as their intricate relationship with one another. For the text to be as persuasive as possible, then, it is important to view it from the perspectives of both the writer and the audience.

Remember to complete a draft of the essay early enough to set it aside for at least a day or two before revising. This will allow you to have a fresh perspective on your work, and you will be better able to make decisions—from a reader's point of view—about how to communicate most clearly and convincingly with your intended audience. Taking an audience-or reader-oriented perspective during revision will help give you the critical distance necessary to polish and fine-tune the good points you have already made and to see important points that you could add so that your essay is as successful as possible.

Time Management
You should try to allow enough time to do at least two complete revisions of your first draft. Each time you go over a draft, you will focus on one or two aspects, such as your use of TAXES or the way you incorporate examples. Don't try to cover everything at once. Read your draft several times, each time looking closely at one or two aspects only.

Peer Review
The goal of peer review is to have someone else read your essay while it is still a work-in-progress. You and someone else who is working on a similar project, a peer, can get together to exchange ideas about each other's writing. This can guide the process of your revision work. Your instructor may schedule a workshop in the classroom, or you may choose to set one up on your own with one or more peers.

During a peer review workshop, you exchange essay drafts with another student in your class and read one another's work for the purpose of assessing its strengths and weaknesses. We've included three revision tools at the end of this chapter. They are the Burdens of Proof Revision Checklist, the Post-Draft Outline Worksheet, and a Peer Review Workshop Worksheet, which you may use for facilitating a peer review workshop. The Burdens of Proof checklist will help you check over your own essay. To prepare for an effective peer review workshop, create a post-draft outline (template on page 126). The post-draft outline will give you an overview of your draft and allow you to fix any gaps in your paper's structure before you show it to a peer. It is always a good idea to ask for peer feedback at the stage when your draft is as good as you can make it because that is the stage when another reader can offer the most helpful advice, spotting things you are unable to see.

Be sure, before coming to the workshop, that your outline matches the draft you have so that during the workshop you can compare it to your reviewer's and see if the structure you think you have used is the one your reviewer identifies. You and your peer(s) can use the Peer Review Workshop Worksheet (on page 127) to make notes as you review each other's drafts.

PEER REVIEW WORKSHOP: THE JOB OF THE WRITER

When you are the writer, you should feel like you can speak freely in a peer review workshop, without having to filter or make excuses for your thoughts or ideas. The more you can talk about your ideas, the clearer they will become both to you and to your listener. Instead of seeing yourself in a position where you're being judged, try to picture yourself as an instructor explaining a complicated idea to your listener.

Also try not to be defensive if the listener misunderstands your ideas, doesn't give you a lot of praise, or disagrees with you about the value of a point. We learn from our critics. Although you may not agree with your listener right away, further thought about an idea may find you agreeing (and a bit embarrassed about your response) at a later date. Be as gracious and open-minded as you can during the peer review session and wait until you are actually doing the work of revision back at your computer to make final decisions about the feedback you receive. It might help to remember that this is your paper, and you are the final arbiter of what goes into it and what does not. However, if one reader is confused or misunderstands a passage or a point, chances are that other readers will feel the same way. Even if you think your essay is as convincing as possible, the fact that one or more readers miss certain points is important for you to consider, especially when your goal is to write a persuasive paper. It might also help to ask your instructor if there is time to do more than one peer review so that you can have the benefit of multiple viewpoints to consider.

It doesn't matter how well developed your ideas are when you come to a peer review session. In whatever stage you find yourself, talking about your ideas out loud and getting feedback from another can only help to improve your focus. Once you receive feedback from a peer, consider his or her responses. Did the reviewer understand your argument and find it to be relevant to your assignment? If not, what do you think went wrong? Make a list of the elements in your draft that you plan to focus on during revision. Underline those that seem most important to you and then formulate a strategy for addressing them. Determine approximately how much time you think it will take to complete the revision process.

PEER REVIEW WORKSHOP: THE JOB OF THE REVIEWER

The job of the reviewer in a peer review workshop is to ask questions, listen or read carefully, and take notes. Imagine that you are going to be tested on this material. Listen or read as fully as possible and make sure you understand completely. Ask questions regarding those things you don't understand (after all, if you were going to be tested on this material, you wouldn't have a book to study from later). Write down key terms and engage in discussion about the writer's ideas.

Imagine the kind of advice that would be useful to you in polishing your own essay as you begin to comment on your peer's essay. Find a way to speak with courtesy and honesty; don't just rubber stamp or praise everything the writer says. If you have a doubt about something you are hearing but are not sure that you are right, say it anyway. You and the writer can always explore your doubt and either dispel it or turn it into something productive for the writer. Your tenacity in gently urging the writer to think more critically and precisely can make the difference between a successful paper and a weak and underdeveloped one.

APPLICATIONS AND WRITING EXERCISES

Application 5.1 Revisiting Essay Structure

The following essay by Dana Gioia (you may recognize it from chapter 3) follows a format that is different from the academic essay format described in chapter 1. It does not state the argument at the end of the introduction in a thesis statement but instead allows the argument to unfold, paragraph by paragraph, until the thesis statement is revealed at the end.

Read the essay carefully and try to identify the structure and purpose of each paragraph. Write this in the margin. It might help to look back at the academic essay format checklist in chapter 1 for comparison. Identify the thesis statement, if you can. On a separate sheet of paper, describe in one or two paragraphs the persuasive strategy you think this author used.

Now compare this author's argumentation strategy with the format of the academic essay discussed in chapter 1. Which do you prefer as a reader? Which do you prefer as a writer? Explain your responses.

THINKING THROUGH A READING

1. Essays like this may be said to "unfold like mystery novels where the secret is revealed at the end." Do you agree? Why does/doesn't it matter that the thesis is revealed at the end?

2. How would the essay be different if the thesis statement appeared in the introduction? If this were your essay, what would you do?

Good Books Help Make a Civil Society
Dana Gioia

In 1780 Massachusetts patriot John Adams wrote to his wife, Abigail, outlining his vision of how American culture might evolve. "I must study politics and war," he prophesied, so "that our sons may have liberty to study mathematics and philosophy." They will add to their studies geography, navigation, commerce, and agriculture, he continued, so that *their* children may enjoy the "right to study painting, poetry, music…" Adams's bold prophecy proved correct. By the mid 20th century, America boasted internationally preeminent traditions in literature, art, music, dance, theater, and cinema. But a strange thing has happened in the American arts during the past quarter century. While income rose to unforeseen levels, college attendance ballooned, and access to information increased enormously, the interest young Americans showed in the arts—and especially literature—actually diminished.

According to the 2002 Survey of Public Participation in the Arts, a population study designed and commissioned by the National Endowment for the Arts (and executed by the US Bureau of the Census), arts participation by Americans has declined for eight of the nine major forms that are measured. (Only jazz has shown a tiny increase—thank you, Ken Burns.) The declines have been most severe among younger adults (ages 18–24). The most worrisome finding in the 2002 study, however, is the declining percentage of Americans, especially young adults, reading literature.

That individuals at a time of crucial intellectual and emotional development bypass the joys and challenges of literature is a troubling trend. If it were true that they substituted histories, biographies, or political works for literature, one might not worry. But book reading of any kind is falling as well. That such a longstanding and fundamental cultural activity should slip so swiftly, especially among young adults, signifies deep transformations in contemporary life. To call attention to the trend, the Arts Endowment issued the reading portion of the Survey as a separate report, "Reading at Risk: A Survey of Literary Reading in America."

The decline in reading has consequences that go beyond literature. The significance of reading has become a persistent theme in the business world. The February issue of Wired magazine, for example, sketches a new set of mental skills and habits proper to the 21st century, aptitudes decidedly literary in character: not "linear, logical, analytical talents," author Daniel Pink states, but "the ability to create artistic and emotional beauty, to detect patterns and opportunities, to craft a satisfying narrative." When asked what kind of talents they like to see in management positions, business leaders consistently set imagination, creativity, and higher-order thinking at the top.

Ironically, the value of reading and the intellectual faculties that it inculcates appear most clearly as active and engaged literacy declines. There is now a growing awareness of the consequences of nonreading to the workplace. In 2001 the National Association of Manufacturers polled its members on skill deficiencies among employees. Among hourly workers, poor reading skills ranked second, and 38 percent of employers complained that local schools inadequately taught reading comprehension.

Corporate America makes similar complaints about a skill intimately related to reading—writing. Last year, the College Board reported that corporations spend some $3.1 billion a year on remedial writing instruction for employees, adding that they "express a fair degree of dissatisfaction with the writing of recent college graduates." If the 21st-century American economy requires innovation and creativity, solid reading skills and the imaginative growth fostered by literary reading are central elements in that program.

The decline of reading is also taking its toll in the civic sphere. In a 2000 survey of college seniors from the top 55 colleges, the Roper Organization found that 81 percent could not earn a grade of C on a high school-level history test. A 2003 study of 15- to 26-year-olds' civic knowledge by the National Conference of State Legislatures concluded, "Young people do not understand the ideals of citizenship…and their appreciation and support of American democracy is limited."

It is probably no surprise that declining rates of literary reading coincide with declining levels of historical and political awareness among young people. One of the surprising findings of "Reading at Risk" was that literary readers are markedly more civically engaged than nonreaders, scoring two to four times more likely to perform charity work, visit a museum, or attend a sporting event. One reason for their higher social and cultural interactions may lie in the kind of civic and historical knowledge that comes with literary reading.

Unlike the passive activities of watching television and DVDs or surfing the Web, reading is actually a highly active enterprise. Reading requires sustained and focused attention as well as active use of memory and imagination. Literary reading also enhances and enlarges our humility by helping us imagine and understand lives quite different from our own.

Indeed, we sometimes underestimate how large a role literature has played in the evolution of our national identity, especially in that literature often has served to introduce young people to events from the past and principles of civil society and governance. Just as more ancient Greeks learned about moral and political conduct from the epics of Homer than from the dialogues of Plato, so the most important work in the abolitionist movement was the novel "Uncle Tom's Cabin." Likewise our notions of American populism come more from Walt Whitman's poetic vision than from any political tracts. Today when people recall the Depression, the images that most come to mind are of the travails of John Steinbeck's Joad family from "The Grapes of Wrath." Without a literary inheritance, the historical past is impoverished.

In focusing on the social advantages of a literary education, however, we should not overlook the personal impact. Every day authors receive letters from readers that say, "Your book changed my life." History reveals case after case of famous people whose lives were transformed by literature. When the great Victorian thinker John Stuart Mill suffered a crippling depression in late-adolescence, the poetry of Wordsworth restored his optimism and self-confidence—a "medicine for my state of mind," he called it. A few decades later, W.E.B. DuBois found a different tonic in literature, an escape from the indignities of Jim Crow into a world of equality. "I sit with Shakespeare and he winces not," DuBois observed. "Across the color line I move arm in arm with Balzac and Dumas, where smiling men and welcoming women glide in gilded halls." Literature is a catalyst for education and culture.

The evidence of literature's importance to civic, personal, and economic health is too strong to ignore. The decline of literary reading foreshadows serious long-term social and economic problems, and it is time to bring literature and the other arts into discussions of public policy. Libraries, schools, and public agencies do noble work, but addressing the reading issue will require the leadership of politicians and the business community as well.

Literature now competes with an enormous array of electronic media. While no single activity is responsible for the decline in reading, the cumulative presence and availability of electronic alternatives increasingly have drawn Americans away from reading.

Reading is not a timeless, universal capability. Advanced literacy is a specific intellectual skill and social habit that depends on a great many educational, cultural, and economic factors. As more Americans lose this capability, our nation becomes less informed, active, and independent-minded. These are not the qualities that a free, innovative, or productive society can afford to lose.

Dana Gioia is chairman of the National Endowment for the Arts.

Application 5.2 Assembling an Introduction

Examine the following sentences that come from the introductory paragraph of a student essay by Eric Strickland, "Explaining Christian Persecution during the Roman Empire" (see page 121). Revisit the techniques for writing an introductory paragraph and then place the sentences in the best order to achieve the goals for an introductory paragraph. Use the checklist on page 12 of chapter 1, if you need help.

a. However, if one considers historical evidence from other sources, it becomes clear that some responsibility for the Christians' persecution lies with the Romans, some with the Christians, and some with the cultural framework of the time.

b. For many people, however, this knowledge extends only to vague recollections of Christians being fed to lions and falls short of understanding the underlying causes and conditions that led to persecution.

c. Because Christianity is the dominant religion in the Western Hemisphere, it is not surprising that most people are aware that the early Christians were persecuted by the Romans.

d. If only Christian sources are consulted, one might conclude that this maltreatment was due exclusively to the tyranny of the Roman Empire and the treachery of Jews.

To check your answer, refer to Stickland's essay.

Application 5.3 Assembling a Body Paragraph

The following sentences are from one of the body paragraphs of the student essay, "Explaining Christian Persecution during the Roman Empire." Revisit TAXES and place the sentences in the best possible order. Use the checklist on page 12 of chapter 1, if you need help.

a. Though these remarks were ostensibly made as part of his effort to defend Christianity, they would have been highly inflammatory to many Romans.

b. For instance, of the Roman gods he writes, "I see in them merely the names of certain men long dead."[3]

c. In addition to his reasoned defense of Christian innocence, Tertullian's writing also reveals his condescension toward the Roman people and their customs.

d. Finally, Tertullian hints that the Romans are inequitable in their worship of the gods and the Emperor's genius. He writes, "You pay your obeisance to Caesar with greater

---

[3] Tertullian, *Apology* (publisher unknown), paragraph 12.

fear and craftier timidity than to Olympian Jupiter himself . . . you are lacking in religious feeling toward your gods, since you show more fear to a human lord."[4]

e. Even in the event that Tertullian was unique in his disdain for Roman religion, his position as a prominent defender of Christianity would have led many Romans to view him as representative of Christians' views toward Rome.

f. The fact that Tertullian's *Apology* has survived until now suggests that it was circulated and read by many of his contemporaries. As a result, it can be concluded that some Christians publicly declared their disdain for the Roman Imperial cult, and this was likely a contributing factor that led to their persecution by the Romans.

g. He then belittles the statues of the gods, suggesting that they are made from the same base materials used in household pots and utensils.[5]

To check your answer, refer to Stickland's essay.

Application 5.4 Assembling a Conclusion

The following sentences are from the conclusion of the student essay, "Explaining Christian Persecution during the Roman Empire." Revisit the goals for a conclusion and place the sentences in the best possible order. Use the checklist on page 12 of chapter 1, if you need help.

a. Finally, blame also lies with the Christians themselves, who not only chose to exclude themselves from many aspects of Roman society but in some cases criticized and disparaged it.

b. Certainly, Christians were wrongly blamed and overzealously punished in some instances (for instance, Nero's implication and harsh punishment of Christians as scapegoats for the fire that destroyed much of Rome), but the Romans are not exclusively responsible.

c. The persecution of Christians at the hands of the Romans cannot be attributed to any single factor, and the view that it was primarily caused by the wickedness of the Roman emperors is not accurate.

d. Another contributor was that the characteristics of Roman culture and Christian belief were incompatible, and this naturally led to conflict.

To check your answer, refer to Stickland's essay.

Writing Exercise 5.1 Writing an Introduction

Study the following outline and draft an introduction for this paper using one of the techniques described within this chapter.

Working thesis statement: Internet dating is the perfect solution for finding companionship given the harried lifestyles of twenty-first century Americans.

---

[4] Tertullian, *Apology* (publisher unknown), paragraph 28.
[5] Ibid.

1. It's efficient because it allows users to screen prospective dates for compatible character traits, education, values, and so forth.

2. It removes typical barriers to dating by leveling the playing field and making men and women equally accessible.

3. It gives people a chance to get to know one another before investing time and energy in face-to-face meetings.

Writing Exercise 5.2 Writing a Conclusion
Read again the conclusion for the essay "Plagiarism: A Crime to Be Prevented" on page 19 of chapter 1. Now write a different conclusion for that essay. Use one of the strategies from this chapter to help you.

Writing Exercise 5.3 Analyzing One Writer's Argument
1. The *Thinking Through a Reading* questions that precede William Rees's essay, "Life in the Lap of Luxury as Ecosystems Collapse," ask you to consider both the problem the author puts forward in his article and the way he defines the "ecological footprint" of a population. Explain in a paragraph or a page of your own writing how this term is central to his argument.

2. What evidence does Rees use to convince his readers that the problem is real and that it warrants our attention? Make a list of these pieces of evidence and determine which ones rely on research and which rely on his own experience and expertise.

3. Identify Rees's proposed solution. List the elements in this solution and discuss or write a summary about their overall viability.

THINKING THROUGH A READING
1. What is the thesis statement for this essay?

2. What are the burdens of proof for the thesis statement? What type of evidence is used in support of the burdens?

3. Do you find this argument convincing? What techniques does the writer use to persuade you of his position?

Explaining Christian Persecution during the Roman Empire
Eric Stickland
Because Christianity is the dominant religion in the Western Hemisphere, it is not surprising that most people are aware that the early Christians were persecuted by the Romans. For many people, however, this knowledge extends only to vague recollections of Christians being fed to lions and falls short of understanding the underlying causes and conditions that led to persecution. If only Christian sources are consulted, one might conclude that this maltreatment was due exclusively to the tyranny of the Roman Empire and the treachery of Jews. However, if one considers historical evidence from other sources,

it becomes clear that some responsibility for the Christians' persecution lies with the Romans, some with the Christians, and some with the cultural framework of the time.

One of the most revealing sources on this topic from a Christian viewpoint is Tertullian's *Apology*. His writing identifies some of the cultural motivations for Roman attitudes toward Christians. Early in the text, Tertullian indicates the major indictment of Christians, which was their "obstinate refusal to offer sacrifice"[6] to the Roman gods. Though Roman religion was not as compulsory as that seen in medieval Europe, it was customary for Romans to offer sacrifice and proclaim their loyalty to the Roman gods. In particular, it was expected that the people would revere the Roman gods, the deified past emperors, and the genius (or guiding spirit) of the current emperor. This custom was seen as a display of patriotism and loyalty to the empire and the emperor. However, the monotheistic doctrine of Christianity forbade worshipping idols and any god other than the "one true God." Though the Roman state may have been content to allow Christians to pursue their beliefs so long as they also participated in the Imperial cult, this was unacceptable to the Christians. As a result, they were perceived as unpatriotic, unsupportive of the emperor, and possibly disloyal to the empire. It is easy to understand how this perception of the Christians could lead to their maltreatment by zealous Roman magistrates.

In addition to his reasoned defense of Christian innocence, Tertullian's writing also reveals his condescension toward the Roman people and their customs. For instance, of the Roman gods he writes, "I see in them merely the names of certain men long dead."[7] He then belittles the statues of the gods, suggesting that they are made from the same base materials used in household pots and utensils.[8] Finally, Tertullian hints that the Romans are inequitable in their worship of the gods and the Emperor's *genius*. He writes, "You pay your obeisance to Caesar with greater fear and craftier timidity than to Olympian Jupiter himself . . . you are lacking in religious feeling toward your gods, since you show more fear to a human lord."[9] Though these remarks were ostensibly made as part of his effort to defend Christianity, they would have been highly inflammatory to many Romans. Even in the event that Tertullian was unique in his disdain for Roman religion, his position as a prominent defender of Christianity would have led many Romans to view him as representative of Christians' views toward Rome. The fact that Tertullian's *Apology* has survived until now suggests that it was circulated and read by many of his contemporaries. As a result, it can be concluded that some Christians publicly declared their disdain for the Roman Imperial cult, and this was likely a contributing factor that led to their persecution by the Romans.

Tertullian's less than favorable view of Roman culture was not limited to religion, as is seen when he comments on the Christians' disavowal of Roman games and events. He wrote:

> Likewise, we renounce your public shows just as we do their origins which we know were begotten of superstition, while we are completely aloof from those matters with

---

[6] Tertullian, *Apology* (publisher unknown), paragraph 2.
[7] Tertullian, *Apology* (publisher unknown), paragraph 12.
[8] Ibid.
[9] Tertullian, *Apology* (publisher unknown), paragraph 28.

which they are concerned. Our tongues, our eyes, our ears have nothing to do with the madness of the circus, the shamelessness of the theater, the brutality of the arena, the vanity of the gymnasium. How then do we offend you?[10]

After condemning Roman amusements as superstitious, mad, shameless, brutal, and vain, Tertullian's confusion as to how the Christians were offensive indicates a lack of understanding on the part of the Christians as to how they were viewed by the Romans. One historical source that reveals how the Roman magistracy viewed Christians is Pliny the Younger's request for guidance from the Emperor Trajan on how to punish those suspected of being Christians. His letter refers to people who were "virtually insane with this cult"[11] and references the "blind and over-wrought nature of their cult-superstition."[12]

The persecution of Christians at the hands of the Romans cannot be attributed to any single factor, and the view that it was primarily caused by the wickedness of the Roman emperors is not accurate. Certainly, Christians were wrongly blamed and overzealously punished in some instances (for instance, Nero's implication and harsh punishment of Christians as scapegoats for the fire that destroyed much of Rome), but the Romans are not exclusively responsible. Another contributor was that the characteristics of Roman culture and Christian belief were incompatible, and this naturally led to conflict. Finally, blame also lies with the Christians themselves, who not only chose to exclude themselves from many aspects of Roman society but in some cases criticized and disparaged it.

Part 1 Writing Assignments

1. Using "The Beatles-*Rubber Soul*: The Fab Four's Transitional Near-Masterpiece" essay in chapter 2 as a model, write an essay that presents an evaluation of a music CD with which you are familiar. Listen carefully to the CD as a whole. Try to identify several themes or motifs that unify the CD as a whole. Focus on one or two cuts that stand out and determine what sets them apart. Write an observation list. Then think about the CD overall and decide what criteria you will use as the basis of your evaluation. Draft a working thesis statement that offers an argument about the CD's success or failure. Be sure to use C-S-C to develop your thesis fully. Organize your ideas into supporting topics and then draft your paper—allowing plenty of time to revise and edit it.

2. Use "The Beatles-*Rubber Soul*: The Fab Four's Transitional Near-Masterpiece" essay in chapter 2 as a model to write an essay of your own where you offer an argument about an artist with whom you are familiar. Think about the artist's repertoire. Identify an anomaly or inconsistency in the artist's music (or film, visual art, prose, acting, etc.), something that the artist created that seems very different from the rest of his or her work. Why do you think the artist chose to do something so different? You should be

---

[10] Tertullian, *Apology* (publisher unknown), paragraph 38.

[11] Pliny, *The Historians of Ancient Rome*, ed. Ronald Mellor (New York: Routledge, 2004), 536.

[12] Ibid. 537.

able to identify at least two or three points that define the artist's general style and then two or three points to show how the thing you have isolated differs from that style. Looking at the artist's repertoire as a whole, how does this anomaly or different piece help you to make sense of the artist's achievements as a whole? Be sure to use C-S-C to develop your thesis fully.

3. Write an essay about a transitional moment. For example, you might write about a performer's music, a director's films, a model's sense of fashion, a person's character, a specific aspect of American culture, or some other topic with which you are familiar. Choose the transitional moment carefully. You should be able to make two or three points about your topic's pretransitional state and two or three about his or her post-transitional state. How does this transitional moment affect how we see the topic as a whole? Be sure to tell why this transition is important. Use C-S-C to develop your thesis statement fully.

4. Examine the advertisement in figure 5.5 or select one from a magazine, a newspaper, or the Internet that seems to warrant analysis. Use the five steps you have learned to find an insightful perspective and generate a working thesis statement (see Chapter 3, pg. 59). Write an essay with each of the following elements:

- an introduction that introduces your ad and presents your thesis statement

- body paragraphs that develop and support the thesis statement, each of which is devoted to one topic taken from your observation list

- a concluding paragraph that restates your thesis statement using different terms and that offers your readers a concluding comment or summary of your paper's argument

Fig. 5.5 Calvin Klein Advertisement

5. Use the essay "Life in the Lap of Luxury as Ecosystems Collapse" as a model of an essay that makes a proposal. Then make a proposal of your own in response to one of the following scenarios. Use the academic essay format, even if you are writing a letter. Make sure your proposal identifies the problem and argues for a particular solution. You will have to decide how much development will be required for the proposal and how much for the solution. In some cases, the identification of the problem will need extensive

discussion to convince your audience that a particular problem exists. You should also consider whether to use counterargument and offer a discussion of alternative solutions and their inadequacies. Be as clear and compelling as possible and include any additional headings or supporting documents to strengthen your presentation.

a. write a letter home proposing that a family member send you money

b. compose a letter to a friend asking for forgiveness after a fight

c. write a letter to your boss asking for a raise or for time off

d. identify a problem on campus that requires attention and write a proposal to university officials about how to address the problem

e. identify a problem in your community that requires attention and write to city officials proposing a well-founded solution

f. write a proposal for a senior project in your major field

Part 1 REVISION TOOLS

1. The Burdens of Proof Revision Checklist

2. The Post-Draft Outline Worksheet

3. Peer Review Workshop Worksheet

THE BURDENS OF PROOF REVISION CHECKLIST

When revising for burdens of proof, you should determine if your supporting ideas and your thesis statement cohere. Ultimately, you are checking to see whether your readers will be able to follow your argument step-by-step. This entails (1) double-checking to be sure you have correctly identified the burdens of proof that are embedded within your thesis statement and (2) checking the body paragraphs to be sure they address the burdens of proof persuasively and coherently.

Check the following points to see how you may be able to improve your essay by clarifying or better establishing the connection between your thesis statement and its supporting paragraphs.

✓ List your essay's thesis statement and burdens of proof. You may use the Post-Draft Outline Worksheet included in this section or some scratch paper.

✓ Revisit the burdens of proof that you wrote for your thesis statement. Trace the logical paths of each burden to be sure that you have covered every point necessary to "prove" the thesis claim. Are there any gaps in the logic—any ideas that are required to support the argument that have not been articulated—such as background information? If so, add the burden of proof that is missing.

✓ Look again at the argument as a whole. Are there any optional points that you would like to add, such as a counterargument? If so, add it to your burdens of proof column.

✓ Check the burdens of proof to see whether your thesis statement requires any dependent arguments. If so, are the arguments in the correct order in the paper?

✓ Check to be sure that you have sufficiently developed all the burdens of proof embedded within your thesis statement. Is each burden of proof addressed adequately in the paper?

✓ Are the burdens of proof addressed in the best possible order that you can imagine? If not sure, freewrite on a separate sheet of paper the chain of logic that you could use if you rearranged the burdens of proof. You might freewrite for each order that you are considering. Put the freewriting aside for a few days, or at least a few hours, and then revisit the issue. When you read the different versions of logical progression, which seems most compelling? Be sure your final paper matches the order you found most convincing in your freewriting passages.

POST-DRAFT OUTLINE WORKSHEET

Once you've drafted your essay, a post-draft outline can be invaluable for revision because it can help you to see more clearly the organization and logical progression of your argument. Complete this post-draft outline form to construct an overview of your paper's structure and identify any gaps in logic or design. This can be used individually or as part of a peer review.

Working thesis statement:

_____

_____

Context: _____

Subject: _____

Claim: _____

List the burdens of proof (that is, all points that must be addressed to prove the claim):

_____

_____

_____

_____

_____

_____

Paraphrase the working thesis statement, identifying the insightful point it makes:

_____

_____

List topics of support and evidence:

Topic: _____

Example(s): _____

Significance to the thesis: _____

_____

Topic: _____

Example(s): _____

Significance to the thesis: _____

_____

Topic: _____

Example(s): _____

Significance to the thesis: _____

_____

Topic: _____

Example(s): _____

Significance to the thesis: _____

_____

Ask yourself or a peer reviewer:

1. What are the draft's strongest elements?

2. What parts are most in need of further work?

PEER REVIEW WORKSHOP WORKSHEET

1. Introduce yourself to your peer reviewer and give your drafted essay to him or her. Depending on where you are in the writing process, you may have specific concerns about your essay that you will want to discuss with your peer before he or she reads it. It will be most helpful if you can also exchange. You may want to jot down some specific questions for your reviewer.

2. Identify the paper's thesis statement:

_____

_____

Context: _____

Subject: _____

Claim: _____

The thesis statement's burdens of proof:

_____

_____

_____

_____

3. List three things you think the essay does well.

_____

_____

_____

_____

4. What three specific things do you think are most important for the writer to work on in this revision stage?

_____

_____

_____

_____

Decide which essay you will talk about first (discuss one essay at a time) and turn to the two post-draft outlines: the one written by the author and the other written by the reviewer.

5. Did you both identify the same thesis statement? If not, which statements did you each identify and why? Look at the evidence and try to decide which thesis statement is the best one for this paper.

6. Did you each identify the same C-S-C? If not, try to reconcile your answers.

7. Did you each identify the same burdens of proof? If not, try to come to a consensus about what the burdens of proof should be for the thesis statement identified.

8. Discuss the essay's strengths and suggested areas of improvement, as articulated in steps 3 and 4. Overall, if there are things about which you do not agree, note them. If there is another peer review, the writer can compare the feedback. Otherwise, you might consult your instructor.

9. Discuss the second essay using questions 5–8.

Part Two

THINKING THROUGH YOUR WRITING ASSIGNMENT

CHAPTER 6

Developing a Thesis Statement from a Writing Assignment by Using Seven Steps

In this chapter, we will continue to work with the techniques you learned in part 1, but now we will look more carefully at the relationship between the particular demands of your writing assignment and the thesis statement you develop in response to it. A writing assignment, or a *writing prompt*, usually comes in the form of a written directive that lays out the task for the writer. Because every writing assignment has its own goals and purpose, as you go through your college classes, it will be important for you to learn to recognize each assignment's unique objectives and how to craft an effective reply. This chapter provides you with seven steps that will guide you in unpacking a writing assignment and developing an appropriate thesis statement. These seven steps build on the strategies you learned in part 1 for thesis-based writing.

As discussed in the first five chapters of this book, the most common college writing assignments require you to write an academic essay that contains a well-developed thesis statement and strong supporting topics. (For other types of writing assignments, see chapter 8 on the informative essay and the scientific essay.) So we will assume, in this chapter and the next, that the instructor is expecting a thesis-centered response (a persuasive essay). If you are unsure what is expected, ask your instructor. Understanding what type of essay you are expected to write is an important step in completing any writing assignment.

WHAT'S AHEAD . . .

► types of writing assignments

► the seven steps to develop a thesis statement from a writing assignment

► the assignment that asks you to respond to another writer's idea

► The assignment that includes a quotation

► The assignment that includes an essay

► The assignment that includes an ongoing debate

Types of Writing Assignments

A writing assignment can take a variety of forms. It can be a simple question or command; it can come as a set of step-by-step instructions, contain multiple concepts that require discussion, include a quotation that you must analyze, or have a combination of these characteristics. Whatever the case, writing assignments serve a number of different goals in the classroom, including assessing what you have learned, helping you apply that learning in situations beyond the course, and using that knowledge to improve your own critical thinking skills. You probably have already had some experience responding to writing assignments. Have you noticed that they often provide certain crucial types of information—the subject and context of the assignment, for instance—and they ask you to respond to a primary question?

Seven Steps to Develop a Thesis Statement from a Writing Assignment

It is important that you first spend some time unpacking a writing assignment to see what it is asking of you before you formulate a working thesis statement. You need to know how to use the information contained within a writing assignment to help you get started on an appropriate response. In addition to questions, the writing assignment may also offer hints that can guide you in formulating your thesis statement and supporting it.

The seven steps that follow show you strategies to identify the *subject, context,* and *primary question* contained within an assignment. This information will inform the way you develop a working thesis statement. Because a writing assignment may have many questions, the seven steps will guide you toward identifying the most important or primary question. This is the question you must answer in your essay. Notice that the first three of the seven steps are new, but the remaining four steps were introduced in chapter 3 in the Frasier example.

Seven Steps

1. Examine the assignment and underline key terms.

2. Find the context and subject of the assignment.

3. Determine the primary question, if necessary.

4. Generate an observation list.

5. Freewrite and cluster, if necessary.

6. Use abstraction to find an insightful idea.

7. Draft a working thesis statement and revise as necessary.

Step 1: Examine the Assignment and Underline Key Terms

Your goal is to understand what the assignment is asking so that you can be sure that your essay fulfills the assignment's requirements. The first step in doing this is to analyze the assignment carefully, sorting out its key terms and determining its primary task. You will likely have to read the writing prompt several times to be sure you understand what it is asking you to do. During your reading, underline terms that seem to be the focus of the assignment. Underlining these terms will help you to see the crucial elements, the important information that the assignment is asking you to consider.

EXAMPLE:

Analyze a documentary or semidocumentary film whose subject matter is central to American culture or society. Remember, this is not a review but an analysis. Identify an argument the film makes. How does the film use this argument to either affirm conventional views or challenge them? Be sure to discuss the film's formal elements and show how they are used to make this argument.

The key terms in the assignment have been underlined. Notice that the key terms in writing prompts are primarily nouns. Nouns often define the subject and context of the prompt, but you will also want to underline any direction words, that is, words that tell you what you are supposed to do with regard to the subject. Here are some possibilities:

analyze: break down into components or essential features

evaluate: make a judgment based on criteria

explain: clarify how and why; make plain and comprehensible

interpret: explain the meaning

discuss: consider or examine in writing

compare: discover similarities or differences between two or more things

describe: provide characteristics and features

These are some of the most common direction words, but remember to look for any words in a writing assignment that guide your thinking, even if they are implied. For example, look at these sample writing prompts:

Do you believe manufacturers of hard alcohol should be allowed to advertise on television?

Of the early civilizations—ancient Rome or the Han Dynasty in ancient China—which, according to a standard of measure that you choose, provided the best quality of life for the most people?

Neither of these two prompts contains direction words from the list above. You can identify the implied directions, however, by examining the prompts carefully. In the first example, you are asked to present your belief about an issue—in other words, to *analyze* the issue and *make an evaluation*. In the second, you are asked about two civilizations that you will have to *compare*. The direction words are implied rather than explicitly stated in these two examples. Remember to read writing assignments carefully to determine the action that you are expected to take.

Step 2: Find the Context and Subject of the Assignment

We defined in part 1 the terms *context* and *subject* and their place in building a thesis statement. Similarly, when you examine a writing assignment, notice the *context* of the prompt—the frame of reference within which the prompt places you. For example, you are asked to respond to the following in a sociology class:

> Discuss how one issue we studied this term impacts your neighborhood.

Once you identify the context—your neighborhood—you can focus your thinking on this specific area. You should also take note of the *subject* of the prompt because it will help to guide your attention to pertinent ideas and information. In this example, you can see that you will have to define the precise subject of your essay because the prompt calls for you to identify an issue you studied in class. You might choose something concerning gender, teenage dating, community sports, or single motherhood. As a first step, identifying the context as your neighborhood and the subject as one issue, helps you think in clear and efficient ways about how you will approach this assignment.

Step 3: Determine the Primary Question, If Necessary

Writing assignments are sometimes long and complex and can even have multiple questions. You may think you have to answer each question, one at a time, but this approach will often create an essay without unity—without a thesis statement. The best strategy to use for an assignment with multiple questions is to identify the most important question first. Sometimes it will be one of the questions in the writing assignment prompt, and sometimes you will have to derive it . You can often recognize the primary question because it will encompass all the other questions within it. After you identify the prompt's central or most important question, you should focus your response on that question. For instance, consider the following writing assignment:

> How do you feel about cheating on school assignments? How common is cheating in school? What might be the motivation of students who cheat? What strategies, if any, would you endorse to fight cheating in school? What are the ethical considerations? Who is negatively/positively affected by cheating?

Initially, you may think that your instructor wants you to answer each of these questions, one by one. But a better strategy is to recognize the primary question in the prompt— "How do you feel about cheating on school assignments?"—and develop a thesis statement that answers it. This is the one question general enough to overarch all the others, which are much more specific. All of the questions ask you to evaluate or make a judgment about cheating in school, although the secondary questions do so by giving you suggestions about different angles on the subject. Often, as in this case, the secondary questions in a writing assignment will provide potential topic ideas that you can use to support your thesis statement. This is an added bonus that should not be overlooked.

Step 4: Generate an Observation List

By the time you reach step 4, you should have a clear idea of the assignment's key terms, context and subject, and primary question. You are ready to develop your ideas in an observation list in preparation for drafting a working thesis statement. This process should be familiar to you because the next four steps were already covered in chapter 3. We'll review them here but be sure to look back at chapter 3 or look ahead to the next several prompts for more complete examples.

For the example about cheating in school, you should list any experiences you or your friends have had that involved cheating in your classes or at your school, any ideas you have about whether it is wrong and why, any motivations students might have to cheat, and anything else you can think of that is relevant to cheating in school. Creating an observation list is crucial to writing a thoughtful, well-organized essay because it gives you a forum for collecting ideas and analyzing your subject.

Step 5: Freewrite and Cluster, If Necessary

Once you have an observation list, you will want to extend its potential by freewriting and clustering. This will help you determine which of the items on the list are important and how the relevant items might be organized. Freewriting will often uncover new ideas that you will want to add to your observation list. This may lead to new perspectives on the information, new ways to cluster, and thus new insights.

Step 6: Use Abstraction to Find an Insightful Idea

Although you will have plenty of raw material after you create an observation list and cluster its items, you will not have the glue that holds these ideas together and unifies them into a coherent essay. You will have to examine the items or clusters on the list to determine what they have in common and what characteristic addresses the assignment before forming the basis for a working thesis statement. Without this unifying idea, your raw material will simply be a collection of loosely related thoughts. Use the strategy of abstraction to find an overarching idea that can hold some or all of these thoughts together.

Step 7: Draft a Working Thesis Statement and Revise as Necessary

By the time you reach step 7, you have enough material to draft a working thesis statement. It's called a *working* thesis statement because it will likely have to be revised, perhaps several times, but it will be enough to get you started drafting your response.

As you draft, you may discover holes in your logic, ideas that you haven't thought through, or parts of your claim that you cannot support. When this happens, return to your observation list, review it perhaps add to it, and see if you can develop your thoughts. Then revise your thesis statement accordingly. A working thesis should be used like a hypothesis is used in science: It should be tested and revised so that it aligns with the evidence.

Practice 6.1 Unpacking a Writing Assignment

Read the following writing assignments and underline key terms. Find the context, subject, and central question of each assignment.

Example: Discuss the role of one character in a play by Shakespeare.
Subject: role of one character
Context: play by Shakespeare
Central question: "discuss" or examine in writing

1. Evaluate the different treatments for bulimia being used today.

2. Given Franklin Delano Roosevelt's three successive presidential terms, assess his greatest contributions while in office. Begin with the years just before his election into office. Then consider his first term's agenda versus his previous political agenda. Finally, compare his last two terms in light of his first term.

3. Discuss the role of the American media in a recent international conflict.

4. It is often said that "birds of a feather flock together." How does this apply to the film *Fellowship of the Ring*?

5. According to Robert Frodensen, Alexander's claim that it is "a good idea to expand federal funding of embryonic stem cell research" is a mistake. Why does Frodensen say this? What are the implications of federal funding of stem cell research? Does Frodensen think that stem cell research will play an increasingly important role in the future of medicine? Analyze his position in this controversy.

*****

In the rest of this chapter, we will apply the seven steps to several types of writing assignments to illustrate how the same seven steps can lead you to an effective thesis statement for very different kinds of writing assignments. We have categorized assignments according to the type of information given within the prompt and therefore the type of response expected. Your writing assignments won't be titled or categorized the same way we have classified them here. We are grouping them in terms of their characteristics, but your instructors will likely title them in terms of their role in the class (i.e. short essay, midterm, research assignment). Therefore, when you are given an assignment, check to see which type of prompt it most closely resembles and use the strategies that follow to guide your thinking and writing.

The Assignment That Asks You to Respond to Another Writer's Ideas

Responding to a writing assignment that focuses on the ideas of another writer—whether those ideas are expressed in an essay, a quotation, or a position in a debate—can be a challenge because there are three distinct steps involved: (1) you must unpack the question or questions in the assignment; (2) you must make sense of the other writer's ideas; and (3) you must keep in mind the writing task in reference to the quote, essay, or debate that is being cited. The seven steps just covered will help you respond to this type of writing assignment in its various forms. The scope of relevant information differs in each of these cases, so we have customized the seven-step strategy to give you suitable guidelines for each of the possible variations for this type of assignment. As you will see, some steps take on more or less importance because prompts themselves vary in terms of how much information is given, what is being called for, and what context is provided to direct your thesis statement.

The Assignment That Includes a Quotation

Quotes are used in writing prompts in a variety of ways. Sometimes a quote is placed in a prompt as an assertion that you must support or challenge. Other times, a quote provides key terms that serve as food for thought. Quotes may focus attention on a central theme or provide a perspective for an analysis. They may even begin shaping the claim. When you are given an assignment that includes a quotation, begin by analyzing the quotation.

> Dante begins the *Divine Comedy* with the line: "Midway in our life's journey, I went astray / from the straight road and woke to find myself / alone in a dark wood. . . . But since it came to good, I will recount/ all that I found revealed there by God's grace." How is this first line representative of the *Divine Comedy* as a whole?

In this case, you can see that the prompt calls attention to one aspect of a text (here, the first sentence of the *Divine Comedy*) and suggests that the sentence is representative of the work as a whole. You must identify the importance of this quote to the text and reveal the evidence that supports your position.

Step 1: Underline Key Terms in the Prompt
Be sure to underline key terms in *both* the quotation and the assignment.

> <u>Dante</u> begins the <u>*Divine Comedy*</u> with the line: "<u>Midway</u> in our <u>life's journey</u>, I <u>went astray</u> / from the <u>straight road</u> and woke to find <u>myself /</u> <u>alone</u> in a <u>dark wood</u>. . . . But since it came to <u>good</u>, I will recount / all that I found revealed there by <u>God's grace</u>." <u>How</u> is this first line <u>representative</u> of the <u>*Divine Comedy*</u> as a <u>whole</u>?

Step 2: Find the Subject and Context of the Writing Assignment
The context is easy to identify in this case —Dante's *Divine Comedy*.

The subject is not explicitly given in this prompt, so you will have to identify a subject for your response, probably something related to one of the key terms in the quote. Keep in mind that the subject you choose should be sufficiently narrow to cover in the page length assigned. Will it be the figure of the narrator, the everyman? Will it be the journey? Will it be the vulnerability of human nature (see especially "I went astray . . . and woke to find myself *alone* in a dark wood," (emphasis added)? Will it be God's grace? When there are choices like this to make, you might list the possibilities and explore them through observation and freewriting before settling on one. Be sure that you examine each of the possibilities and choose the subject that you think is most representative of the text as a whole or that you are most comfortable writing about. For this prompt, we will work with human nature as the subject.

Step 3: Determine the Primary Question in the Writing Assignment

In this case, the primary question is very clear because only one question appears in the prompt: "How is this first line representative of the *Divine Comedy* as a whole?" You will have to show how human nature is represented in the quotation and in the *Divine Comedy* as a whole.

Steps 4–5: Generate an Observation List and Freewrite

For this kind of prompt, you may have to freewrite several times, and on different topics, before you are ready to write a working thesis statement. A good way to proceed is to list observations and freewrite first *on the quote* to find an interpretation of the quote that you think is sound. What can the common man learn from the quote? What wisdom or lesson does the quote impart? In plain language, what is the quote really saying? Try to put it into your own words.

The quote focuses on the moment at which the everyman figure realizes his own flawed human nature—the moment at which he strays from the straight road and finds himself alone in a dark wood—and sees that he comes to good only through grace.

Then examine your observations and freewriting to see if you can give the quote an interpretation; that is, *paraphrase* the quote in the form of a general lesson or a general truth. You might reword the quote so that you make an *assertion*—a plain statement that summarizes the lesson or truth the quote reveals. Be sure to use your own words without losing or changing the quote's meaning. This lesson could be paraphrased as follows: The epic shows that everyman's journey through life includes going astray and making mistakes; although humans are, by nature, flawed, they end up okay because of God's blessings. Often, quotes give insightful lessons. If you can phrase the lesson in your own words, you may be able to use it as the kernel of your thesis statement.

Step 6: Use Abstraction to Find an Insightful Idea

Look back at steps 4 and 5 where we used observation and freewriting to help us understand the quote. There, we paraphrased the quote by saying that human nature is flawed and yet comes to good. This is insightful because it offers an interpretation based on reading the *straight road* and the *dark wood* as metaphors for life. Perhaps we can take this insightful idea, combine it with the prompt's charge to show that the quote is representative of Dante's work as a whole, and draft a working thesis statement.

Using C-S-C, we have the following (so far):

Context: Dante's *Divine Comedy*
Subject: human nature
Claim: is shown to be flawed, but it comes to good through God's grace.

Thesis:

> This quote is representative of Dante's *Divine Comedy* because, like in the *Divine Comedy*, human nature is shown to be flawed but able to come to good because of grace.

This is an adequate working thesis. Remember that the prompt asks you to explain—in other words, make plain or clarify—how this quote is *representative* of the entire *Divine Comedy*. You will have to analyze the quote's depiction of human nature and then "make plain or clarify" where and how that depiction is also in the entire epic.

The thesis statement responds directly to the assignment and sets up the argument for the essay. Notice that it borrows terms such as "representative" from the prompt, which is a good strategy to use, when possible, to set up a thesis statement.

The Assignment That Includes an Essay

The difference between the writing assignment with a quotation and the writing assignment with a passage—whether the passage is a paragraph, an entire essay, or even a group of essays—is mainly one of scope. In a nutshell, you will have to put more time into analyzing the passage or essay(s) before you can respond successfully. Just as you had to first unpack the quotation in the previous example, here you need to locate the writer's controlling idea or thesis statement and understand how the evidence is used in its support. (If a writer doesn't use a thesis statement, it may be harder to identify the overall point of the essay. After you identify and understand the author's argument, you must decide whether you agree or disagree with it and then write a response that supports your view. Read the following essay and then look over the writing assignment and the seven steps for responding that follow.

THINKING THROUGH A READING
1. What does Sen mean by the term "clashing civilizations?"

2. Why does Sen think that dividing the world into discrete civilizations is both crude and absurd?

A World Not Neatly Divided
Amartya Sen

When people talk about clashing civilizations, as so many politicians and academics do now, they can sometimes miss the central issue. The inadequacy of this thesis begins well before we get to the question of whether civilizations must clash. The basic weakness of the theory lies in its program of categorizing people of the world according to a unique, allegedly commanding system of classification. This is problematic because civilizational categories are crude and inconsistent and also because there are other ways of seeing people (linked to politics, language, literature, class, occupation or other affiliations).

The befuddling influence of a singular classification also traps those who dispute the thesis of a clash: To talk about the "Islamic world" or "the Western world" is already to adopt an impoverished vision of humanity as unalterably divided. In fact, civilizations are hard to partition in this way, given the diversities within each society as well as the linkages among different countries and cultures. For example, describing India as a "Hindu civilization" misses the fact that India has more Muslims than any other country except Indonesia and possibly Pakistan. It is futile to try to understand Indian art, literature, music, food or politics without seeing the extensive interactions across barriers of religious communities. These include Hindus and Muslims, Buddhists, Jains, Sikhs, Parsees, Christians (who have been in India since at least the fourth century, well before England's conversion to Christianity), Jews (present since the fall of Jerusalem), and even atheists and agnostics. Sanskrit has a larger atheistic literature than exists in any other classical language. Speaking of India as a Hindu civilization may be comforting to the Hindu fundamentalist, but it is an odd reading of India.

A similar coarseness can be seen in the other categories invoked, like "the Islamic world." Consider Akbar and Aurangzeb, two Muslim emperors of the Mogul dynasty in India. Aurangzeb tried hard to convert Hindus into Muslims and instituted various policies in that direction, of which taxing the non-Muslims was only one example. In contrast, Akbar reveled in his multiethnic court and pluralist laws, and issued official proclamations insisting that no one "should be interfered with on account of religion" and that "anyone is to be allowed to go over to a religion that pleases him."

If a homogeneous view of Islam were to be taken, then only one of these emperors could count as a true Muslim. The Islamic fundamentalist would have no time for Akbar; Prime Minister Tony Blair, given his insistence that tolerance is a defining characteristic of Islam, would have to consider excommunicating Aurangzeb. I expect both Akbar and Aurangzeb would protest, and so would I. A similar crudity is present in the characterization of what is called "Western civilization." Tolerance and individual freedom have certainly been present in European history. But there is no dearth of diversity here, either. When Akbar was making his pronouncements on religious tolerance in Agra, in the 1590s, the Inquisitions were still going on; in 1600, Giordano Bruno was burned at the stake, for heresy, in Campo dei Fiori in Rome.

Dividing the world into discrete civilizations is not just crude. It propels us into the absurd belief that this partitioning is natural and necessary and must overwhelm all other ways of identifying people. That imperious view goes not only against the sentiment that "we human beings are all much the same," but also against the more plausible understanding that we are diversely different. For example, Bangladesh's split from Pakistan was not connected with religion, but with language and politics.

Each of us has many features in our self-conception. Our religion, important as it may be, cannot be an all-engulfing identity. Even a shared poverty can be a source of solidarity across the borders. The kind of division highlighted by, say, the so-called "antiglobalization" protesters—whose movement is, incidentally, one of the most global-ized in the world—tries to unite the underdogs of the world economy and goes firmly against religious, national or "civilizational" lines of division.

The main hope of harmony lies not in any imagined uniformity, but in the plurality of our identities, which cut across each other and work against sharp divisions into impen-etrable civilizational camps. Political leaders who think and act in terms of sectioning off humanity into various "worlds" stand to make the world more flammable—even when their intentions are very different. They also end up, in the case of civilizations defined by religion, lending authority to religious leaders seen as spokesmen for their "worlds." In the process, other voices are muffled and other concerns silenced. The robbing of our plural identities not only reduces us; it impoverishes the world.

Amartya Sen is an economist presently teaching at Harvard.

Applying the Seven Steps to a Writing Assignment on Amartya Sen's "A World Not Neatly Divided"

WRITING ASSIGNMENT:

> What is the danger of dividing the people of the world into discreet civilizations, according to Amartya Sen in "A World Not Neatly Divided?" Do you agree and why?

Following is how we might apply the seven steps toward unpacking this writing assignment.

STEPS 1–3:

The prompt's subject, context, and primary question are as follows:

Subject: dividing people by civilizations
Context: the world
Primary question: "Do you agree with Sen and why?"

Now we break down the primary question into the secondary questions contained within it:

1. Why does Sen think it is wrong to divide the people of the world into discreet civilizations?

2. Do you agree?

3. Why?

Now focus on analyzing the subject, context, and primary question in Sen's essay.

As with the Dante quotation above, read the essay carefully and underline key terms. Try to get a sense of the overall argument in the essay and the issues raised to support that argument. This will help you to identify the C-S-C of the passage. If the passage is longer than one or two paragraphs, as with the Sen example, focus most of your attention on the introduction and the conclusion when underlining key terms. It's likely that the essay's C-S-C will be most clearly stated at the beginning and end of the piece. If the thesis or argument is not stated directly, you might have to use abstraction to envision the essay's main point and then state it in your own words. After you have identified the thesis statement, locate the topics of support for the claim and construct a summary of the essay as a whole. This will help you answer the first question in the prompt, "What is the danger of dividing the people of the world into separate civilizations, according to Amartya Sen?"

STEPS 4–5:

After you have identified Sen's argument and its topics of support, create an observation list(s) about the thesis and its topics to help you decide what you think about his essay. Does he make a valid point? (This doesn't necessarily mean that you agree with his point.) Does he use the best evidence you can think of to make his argument compelling? Are there weaknesses or gaps in his evidence or his logic that you can pinpoint? Freewrite on some of these ideas if you are not sure of your thoughts and need to explore them further.

STEPS 6–7:

Examine the observation list(s) and freewriting you have done in response to Sen's essay. Decide whether, overall, you agree or disagree with his main point, or whether you agree but with some caveats or qualifications. The insight you uncover will include the reasons you give for agreeing or not agreeing with Sen's argument. Your insightful idea will serve as the basis for your thesis statement.

This sample writing assignment gives you a helpful guide for your thesis statement. It asks you to "agree or disagree with Sen's argument and to tell why." Drafting the thesis statement should be fairly straightforward. The subject of your thesis statement is Sen's essay and is the focus of your essay's discussion. The context is the subject of Sen's essay—dividing or categorizing people of the world. Anything associated with grouping people into categories, then, can be brought into your discussion, so this sets the outer parameters for your essay. Finally, your claim will present your perspective on or argument about categorizing people. You will either be in line with Sen, or you will have a different or opposing position.

If you agree with the prompt essay's argument, then your thesis can follow this simple format:

> "I agree with Sen's argument that it is impossible (dangerous?) to categorize people of the world according to a commanding system . . . and I have this insightful idea to contribute [give your insightful idea]."

If you disagree with the prompt essay's argument, then your thesis statement should go beyond simply saying that you disagree. If, for instance, you use a thesis statement that says: "I disagree with Sen because his arguments are weak and unconvincing," this will not lead to a fully developed essay because you have simply dismissed one argument without putting a more compelling argument in its place. Be sure to use C-S-C to *take a position on the issue or offer an insightful idea, not just to put forward a negative opinion about his essay.* A thesis template that may help you to take a position while disagreeing with the prompt essay's argument is the following:

"Although Sen argues that . . . I think that [and give your insight] . . . ."

This template will help you to think of an argument that will require support rather than one that simply criticizes a position another writer has taken.

There are additional conventions for responding to this type of writing prompt. Typically, you would begin with an introduction that summarizes Sen's argument and the evidence he calls forward to support it. You would then offer your own position on the subject in a thesis statement at the end of the introduction. Following this introduction, the body paragraphs of your essay would be devoted to presenting the supporting evidence for your thesis claim. By following the thesis templates and conventions for the introduction and body of this essay, you may find that your response to Sen's essay is easier for you to write and clearer for your reader.

The Assignment That Includes an Ongoing Debate

Sometimes a writing assignment will ask you to take a stand on a controversial issue about which there is much debate. This type of prompt is often assigned in a class where course materials and lectures have focused on a particular social issue about which many people disagree. Your job is to present enough information to convince your reader that your position on this issue, in contrast to the other available positions, is the most compelling one. This requires you to synthesize a large amount of information, sometimes from different kinds of sources (written articles, speeches, artwork), and to think critically about it so that you can come to some personal conclusions about it. Because both of these skills—synthesizing information and critical thinking—are central to a college education, it is likely that you will see this kind of prompt in several classes and in different disciplines. Here are some examples:

- Do you believe manufacturers of hard alcohol should be allowed to advertise on television?

- Does the Hollywood paparazzi do more harm than good?

- Should Richard Wright's *Native Son* be censured from high school classes because of its racial violence?

- Of the early civilizations—ancient Rome or the Han Dynasty in ancient China—which, according to a standard of measure you choose, provided the best quality of life for the people?

Notice that all of these prompts ask you to take a side in a controversy that already exists. Each prompt suggests that there are at least two different sides that can be argued compellingly, and you are being asked to weigh the available evidence and choose the side you have determined to be most valid. The scope of this assignment is larger than the prompt with a quotation and the prompt with an essay, but all three of these prompts require you to analyze the arguments of other writers and formulate your essay in response to their ideas. In all three cases, you must spend time studying what has been quoted or said to respond appropriately and participate effectively in the intellectual conversation.

Following is an example.

EXAMPLE PROMPT
Do you believe that Confucianism is best classified as a religion or as a philosophy?

STEP 1:
Be sure to find the key terms in the prompt *as well as* in the larger debate. The key terms in the prompt are pretty straightforward:

<u>Do you believe</u> that <u>Confucianism</u> is <u>best classified</u> as a <u>religion or</u> as a <u>philosophy</u>?

Regarding the body of work that discusses Confucianism, your job is to find the key terms in the debate, not in the sense of individual words but in the sense of key issues. This might mean that you underline the key words in the numerous articles you read and then abstract from them the larger ideas repeatedly discussed. For this example, find sources (e.g., articles, books, experts) that consider Confucianism a religion and sources that classify it as a philosophy. What reasons are given for each perspective? You will probably have to do some research and perhaps look through your textbook and class notes to identify the key terms. The information you find there will determine the depth and breadth of your essay, so it is important to spend an adequate amount of time collecting information. You will know you have enough information when the new sources you find repeat information you have already collected. When you reach a point of diminishing returns—that is, you have plenty of information for your essay and the information you are finding is largely repetitive—it is time to move to the next step.

STEPS 2–3:
Regarding the prompt, the context is Confucianism, the subject is the controversy of whether it should be classified as a religion or a philosophy, and the primary question is "With which side do you agree?" Implicitly, you should also ask yourself "so what?" because this may help to push your ideas further to find an insightful idea.

STEPS 4–5:
Because the reading and research you've done on the prompt's subject—the controversial issue you've been asked to consider—is likely extensive, you will have to consider the evidence you have found and identify the significant points. See chapter 10 for guidance on collecting, evaluating, and organizing your research.

Return to the key terms or key issues lists that you created for step 1. Now add to that list by writing observations about the key issues. Use freewriting and/or clustering if they help you decipher what you think about the information you have found. Which points seem the strongest to you? Why? Articulate your thoughts as fully as you can, even if just on scratch paper. This prewriting will come in handy when you draft your essay.

STEPS 6–7:
Look over your observation lists and decide which side of the controversy you will take. Is the evidence on one side of the controversy significantly stronger than that on the other side? You may agree with a position put forward in some of the research you have found, but be sure to use your own words to state your thesis. If you incorporate any of the research in your essay, be sure to cite it properly (see chapter 10 and appendix C for help). Your freewriting may also uncover an insightful idea that offers a new perspective on the issue, one not yet expressed in your research.

It is not enough to simply say that you agree with those who argue that Confucianism is best qualified as a religion. A more effective thesis statement will say, "I agree with those who argue . . . *because* . . ." even if not using these words. Here are some examples of possible responses:

An Affirmative Stance

Confucianism should be classified as a religion because it provides both moral and spiritual guidance.

A Example of a Negative Stance

Confucianism must be categorized as a philosophy and not as a religion because it lacks an institutionalized spiritual order.

Notice that the essays that would result from these thesis statements would take the question head on. The affirmative stance would first have to establish that moral and spiritual guidance are distinguishing factors of a "religion." It would then have to show that Confucianism is concerned with both moral and spiritual guidance and can thus be considered a "religion." For the negative stance, you would first have to argue that a religion, by definition, must have an established infrastructure with official representatives of the religion to oversee its rituals. You would then examine Confucianism and show that it does not have this kind of order; therefore, it is not a religion.

A Example of a Qualifier or a Counterargument

Another option is to suggest an answer to the prompt by proposing an alternative argument or inserting a qualifier.

Although Confucianism is often considered a religion, *it is better understood* as a philosophy.

OR

Confucianism should be seen as neither a religion nor a philosophy; it is best understood as a prescription for civic responsibility.

An Example of an Argument from "Out of the Box"

When you are sure your instructor is open to an argument that addresses the prompt but may not take a position on its primary question, consider putting forward an argument that offers an interesting and related point of view. The following example rejects the established terms of the debate as presented in the prompt and offers an unexpected perspective:

> Classifying Confucianism as either a philosophy or a religion is inconclusive, but the more important issue is that Confucianism has single-handedly shaped contemporary Chinese society.

You are probably familiar enough with the seven steps by now to see that, while it is a systematic, step-by-step approach, it also gives you a flexible strategy that can be adapted to a variety of writing assignments. As you work with these steps, you will adapt them to your own style so that they work the way they are intended—to help you understand the purpose of any writing assignment so that you can respond in a meaningful and efficient way. After you carefully examine a writing prompt and identify the key words, context and subject, and primary question, you will fully understand the assignment and will be prepared to do some critical thinking to develop a working thesis statement and offer strong supporting evidence and analysis.

APPLICATIONS AND WRITING EXERCISES

Application 6.1 Using Observation and Abstraction to Respond to Another's Ideas

For the following prompts, generate an observation list. Then use abstraction to see if you can identify any overarching ideas that might serve as the basis for a working thesis statement. Do your best to draft a working thesis statement. If possible, work in groups of two or three. Then share your group's ideas through a class discussion.

1. Bruno Bettleheim argues that fairy tales present life's problems in their most essential forms and thereby guide the development of children. Do you agree with him? Write an essay that explains your view of the role of fairy tales in childhood development.

2. According to humorist Dave Barry, we need a law that forbids brides from planning their weddings more than a week in advance. Do you think he is right in claiming that the planning and preparation for weddings have become too expensive and time-consuming and impose an unfair and even unhealthy burden on the bride, groom, and their families?

3. Steven Landsburg claims that, in all cultures, male children hold marriages together and female children break marriages apart. Is there a reason why parents who produce sons grow closer together while parents who produce girls tend to grow apart? Support your position with evidence from your own experience, including people you know or have read or heard about. You might also draw on research to support your position.

Application 6.2 Responding to the Assignment That Contains a Quotation

Briefly describe how you would use the seven steps to respond to each of the prompts below. For example, identify the key terms, as well as the subject and context. How many observation lists would you create and what would be their focus? What would you hope to find through freewriting and analysis? Compare your responses to a classmate's responses. Share what you learned with the class as part of a larger discussion.

1. It is often said that "birds of a feather flock together." How does this apply to your current set of friends or the friends of one of your roommates or family members?

2. Hollywood has convincingly argued that the Internet poses the greatest threat to the music and movie industries because of rampant and illegal file sharing. Industry officials have regularly said "all college students who copy music or movie files should be prosecuted to the fullest extent of the law" and "Universities should be held liable when students use school computers to infringe on copyright laws." How do you respond to these arguments?

3. "Although the Equal Rights Amendment was never formally ratified, the U.S. courts should make decisions as if it had become law." Do you agree with this statement? Explain.

Application 6.3 Responding to Another Writer's Ideas

1. Read the essay below by Tina Lennox (written while as a first-year business student at Santa Clara University). What is the context, subject, and primary question in Lennox's essay? What position does this essay take on the debate?

2. Write a thesis statement that expresses an alternative view on Lennox's context and subject.

3. Give three or four arguments in support of the alternative thesis statement.

4. Be as objective as you can. Which argument do you think is more compelling— Lennox's or your own? Why?

THINKING THROUGH A READING
1. Do you agree with Lennox that privacy no longer exists?

2. How much do you rely on the Internet? Do you think about the fact that your Internet usage may be monitored by various groups who have an interest in gaining access to information about you?

Privacy? What Privacy?
Tina Lennox
Many would agree that privacy is important in corporate life. According to Ferdinand Schoeman, "Privacy is important . . . for the personal or inner lives of people" (416). Schoeman believes that respecting people's privacy shows moral strength. Unfortunately, the modern world greedily seeks information about people—the more the better, and there is usually no problem getting it. Privacy no longer exists, not even in a theoretical state. From the workplace to the Internet, the invasion of personal information is at an all-time high. "A 1998 survey of 1,085 corporations conducted by the American

Management Association shows that more than 40 percent engaged in some kind of intrusive employee monitoring" (Doyle). Employers monitor actions through the "checking of e-mail, voice mail and telephone conversations; recording of computer keystrokes; and video recording of job performance" (4). The intrusion does not stop here, as random drug testing, psychological testing, and genetic testing are also practiced.

Even more pervasive and disturbing, "advances in database technology, marketing technology, and the sudden growth and capabilities of digital networks are creating new opportunities for direct marketers and raising new privacy issues" (Kirsh). The Internet is a powerful tool. Its large-scale influence has made it both a threat and a benefit. As a threat, the Internet demonstrates that privacy cannot be preserved in a high-tech age.

Simple tasks such as "surfing the net" and sending e-mails can broadcast personalized information about the sender to nosy viewers. These viewers fall into one of three categories according to Jim Aspinwall in his article, "The Complete Guide to Internet Privacy." The first is composed of "thrill-seeking kids" who merely wish "to annoy users and overwhelm networks." The second is known as the "system-crackers" or "script-kiddies." These hackers keep pushing their luck until they get caught. They find unsecured servers and take advantage of their weaknesses. Passwords are stolen, protection is disabled, systems are crashed, and network files are viewed and copied. The last group represents the serious, sophisticated cybercriminals. This group searches for vital corporate or government information. All three groups contribute to the ever-growing insecurity of Internet users.

The main targets of hackers are commercial sites. Through these sites, detailed information on an individual's credit, health, financial status, purchasing patterns, and personal preferences are made available on centralized computer databases. There are also cases of stolen identities where social security numbers and credit card numbers are used to buy goods, receive government benefits, and commit crimes. Aspinwall cites the case of BackOrifice, in which a sophisticated hacker silently recorded all activity on a personal computer and eventually took over the entire system. Often, a site uses "cookies" to retain information on individual consumers. Cookies are small text files with plain and/ or coded information on sites previously visited. They may either stay on the local hard drive for years or be stored only as temporary bits of information that disappear when the browser is closed (Aspinwall). As Steve Gibson of Gibson Research states, "when you are connected to the Internet, the Internet is also connected to you" (Aspinwall).

Through the Internet, merchants can reuse and sell personal information. Advertising companies such as DoubleClick, Inc., receive this data and use it to specialize their online billboards. DoubleClick dominates the online ad market with rapidly growing global online advertisement, spending currently up to $7.7 billion (Weston). Other companies sell customer prescription information to drug companies. HMO's, banks, and security firms have access to insurance records and, ultimately, medical records. Thought to be highly personal and confidential, medical records are one of the least protected records in America, according to Brendon Weston.

Although consumers complain about the lack of privacy on the Internet, they continue to use its resources day in and day out. A 1994 survey states that 82 percent of people polled were concerned about threats to personal privacy (Kirsh). While 51 percent were concerned about the creation of subscriber profiles on viewing and purchasing patterns online, 52 percent were interested in receiving information and advertising tailored to their particular interests (Kirsh). These two statistics contradict each other. By completing financial statements and forms through the Internet, these hypocritical consumers are dangling themselves over the open fire. Understandably, modern communities have become very dependent on the Internet for commerce and entertainment desires alike. The Internet is fast, easy, efficient, and loaded with information. The only solution now is to use this information Internet intelligently and carefully.

Federal laws now protect the rights of online users. The Electronic Privacy Commission Act (EPCA) protects consumers against the unauthorized surveillance of privileged electronic messages and the release to third parties of message content. It also restricts government access to customer records on interactive service providers. During the Clinton presidency, the national Plan for Information Systems Protection was developed. It addresses the vulnerability of systems to cyberterrorism and makes recommendations for security measures. On January 20, 2001, H.R. 237 was unveiled. Established by House of Representatives members Chris Cannon and Anna Eshoo, the Internet Privacy Enhancement Act requires commercial sites and e-businesses to disclose how they use and secure information collected. Sites must also provide ways to safeguard against inappropriate and illegal use of the information by marketers or others. The inclusion of a disclosure statement that tells customers where the information goes and gives them the right to prevent their information from going to marketing is another policy of the act. "Consumers *shouldn't have to reveal their life story every time they surf the web*. This legislation will help to assure the security that Americans expect when it comes to privacy. . . . The bill doesn't regulate the Internet; it empowers the consumer" (Eshoo). The Federal Trade Commission has increased its penalty authority in online violations, with civil penalties ranging from $22,000 to $500,000 (Eshoo). Promising future bills cover more restrictive privacy requirements, increased penalties, and greater burden on businesses through frequent reports and limits on activities.

While the government is taking small steps toward resolving consumer privacy issues, a great deal of responsibility lies on the individual, who can take steps to safeguard information from hackers and third-party onlookers. First, there are a number of Internet connection methods to choose from. With a standard modem, one anonymous dial-up customer out of millions is chosen and a random Internet protocol (IP) address is assigned to fit the computer's hardware. When logged off, the customer and address are gone completely. This type of modem is safer than a Digital Subscriber Line (DSL) or cable connection that is literally always on. DSL and cable connections use one to two permanent IP addresses and host names that work in conjunction with their specific computer. A hacker looking in on these lines of communication would find it easy to track down a user and user profile.

Second, precautionary measures can be taken by installing security patches. Practicing safe habits on computers will help guard information. With a DSL or cable connection, the modem should be disconnected from the computer when not in use. This way the hacker can get absolutely no information from the dead modem line. Programs such as

Zone-Alarm post warnings when an application tries to make a connection or external sites are trying to connect to the computer through the Internet. Virus protection programs similar to McAfee Virus Scan and Norton AntiVirus should be run weekly. Because many Internet e-mail servers are not secure, the Pretty Good Privacy (PGP) firewall Program can be used to create a private encryption key for oneself and a public key to share with others so that they can decode the mail on the other end. Clients should be wary of the file attachments sent by unknown users. Even mail from family and friends may contain viruses that a quick scan would exterminate.

The capabilities for computers and Internet servers have far surpassed consumer and producer expectations. Legislation has been passed, but to trifling ends. Ellen Alderman and Caroline Kennedy, authors of *The Right to Privacy,* make this observation:

> Perhaps the biggest problem with the statutory scheme is that there is no overall privacy policy behind it. As even a partial list of privacy laws indicates, they address a hodgepodge of individual concerns. The federal statutory scheme most resembles a jigsaw puzzle in which the pieces do not fit. That is because the scheme was put together backwards. Rather than coming up with an overall picture and then breaking it up into smaller pieces that mesh together, Congress has been sporadically creating individual pieces of legislation that not only do not mesh neatly but also leave gaping holes. (qtd. in Kirsh)

Although privacy can never again be fully preserved, one cannot give in to the pressures of the high-tech age. It is a struggle between humans and machines. Although machines have become increasingly powerful and capable, they can never compete with the abilities of the human mind. It is difficult to protect personal information in this high-tech age, but one cannot give up. It is cowardly just to lie down and let hackers and prying companies walk all over an individual's rights. Legislators need to continue passing legislation regarding Internet privacy issues, and people need to take steps to safeguard themselves and their personal information. There needs to be regularly scheduled, independent review groups to promote online privacy practices, the coalition of existing industry organizations, and privacy advocacy groups as well as individuals with support from government agencies and consumer understanding and involvement with online privacy issues. Online improvements must be demanded and new standards strictly upheld for anything to change. Although Big Brother may be watching, individual responsibility and action must still continue.

Works Cited

Aspinwall, Jim. "The Complete Guide to Internet Privacy." *Mother Earth News* Nov. 2000: 1.

Doyle, Rodger. "Privacy in the Workplace." Jan. 2001. March 2001 <http://www.sciam.com/1999/01999issue/01999numbers.html>.

Eshoo, Anna G. "Reps. Eshoo and Cannon Unveil Internet Privacy Legislation." *FDCH Press Releases* Jan. 2001.

Kirsh, Ellen. "Recommendations for the Evolution of Netland: Protecting Privacy in a Digital Age." CMC *Abstracts* 2 (1996).

Schoeman, Ferdinand David. "Privacy and Intimate Information." *Philosophical Dimensions of Privacy: An Anthology.* Ed. Ferdinand David Schoeman. Cambridge, Eng.: Cambridge UP, 1984. 402-16.

Weston, Brendan. "Cookie Recipes." *Canadian Business* Dec. 2000.

White, Fred. "The Well-Crafted Argument." Student Text, 1E. © 2002 Heinle/Arts & Sciences, a part of Cengage Learning, Inc. Reproduced by permission. www.cengage.com/permissions.

Writing Exercise 6.1 Strategies for Comprehending Another's Ideas

In preparation for responding to another writer's work, one technique that can help you to identify the key ideas in an essay is to summarize it. Summary, however, is not a simple skill to master. Try the following:

1. Write a one-paragraph summary of Amartya Sen's essay, "A World Not Neatly Divided."

2. Compare your summary paragraph to those of at least three peers. For each comparison, identify points or nuances expressed in your peers' summary paragraphs but not in yours and vice versa. For each of the points, decide whether it is or is not central to Sen's overall argument.

3. With the feedback from the three comparisons, revise your summary paragraph.

4. Now write a one-sentence statement that summarizes your new paragraph.

5. Compare both your new paragraph and your summary statement with the same three peers. How close are your results? What can you conclude about the art of summarizing?

Writing Exercise 6.2 Taking a Side in a Controversy

1. Write a definition of privacy in the context of Lennox's essay "Privacy? What Privacy?" Using that definition, discuss what importance you think it has in today's world.

2. In three or four paragraphs, discuss whether it is possible to value privacy and also use the Internet for things such as making purchases or using MySpace. How are these two things mutually exclusive? How can you reconcile the two?

CHAPTER 7

Using the Seven Steps to Develop a Thesis Statement from an Advanced Writing Assignment

In chapter 6, you began using the seven steps to develop thesis statements in response to some common types of writing assignment prompts, specifically assignments that ask you to respond to another writer's work. These assignments require you to unpack the prompt as well as the other writer's work (e.g., a quote, an essay, or a side in a debate) so you can construct an appropriate reply.

This chapter will help you identify three more types of writing assignments, which are a bit more advanced. We will look at (1) the comparison and contrast assignment that asks you to compare two or more items and to reveal something insightful gleaned from the comparison; (2) the open-ended assignment that gives you a subject but little guidance on what direction or approach to take in your writing; and (3) the assignment with multiple questions or parts, which can be confusing, so you must analyze it carefully. We will show you that, regardless of how challenging the writing assignment may be, applying the seven steps that you learned in chapter 6 will help you develop an effective thesis statement and respond successfully.

Our purpose in chapters 6 and 7 is not to be exhaustive but to give you some guidelines for responding to the most common writing assignments seen in the college classroom. You may come across assignments in your classes that do not fit clearly into one or another of these categories, or assignments that combine aspects of several of these categories, but you will see by the end of this chapter that the seven steps are flexible. With practice you will be able to rely on them to guide your response to even the most unconventional writing situation. This is especially helpful for a timed writing situation, like an exam. After all, the best antidote to writer's block or to the anxiety that often accompanies a timed essay is a clear prescription or plan for writing.

WHAT'S AHEAD . . .

▶ the comparison and contrast writing assignment

▶ the open-ended writing assignment

▶ the writing assignment with multiple questions or multiple parts

▶ the timed essay

The Comparison and Contrast Writing Assignment

A writing assignment that asks you to compare two items is difficult to handle well. The temptation is to write a thesis that promises to compare the two items' similarities and to contrast their differences, as in the following statement: "With close inspection, one can see that X and Y have interesting similarities and differences." However, this kind of thesis statement leads to an essay that often offers little more than a list of similarities and differences with minimal, if any, analysis. Using the seven steps will help you to find some meaningful insight to offer as the thesis claim. Because you are already familiar with the seven steps, we will illustrate them in abbreviated form in this chapter.

Example
Compare and contrast two American slave narratives.

STEPS 1–3:
In this sample assignment, the key terms, the subject and context, and the primary question are all fairly clear. The context is the literary and historical period that encompasses the American slave narrative, roughly the hundred-year period from 1750 to 1865. The two slave narratives are the subjects, and the primary question is what insight can be gained by comparing them with one another.

Let's say you decide to compare two of the most famous American slave narratives, Frederick Douglass's *Narrative of the Life of Frederick Douglass by Himself* (FD) and Harriett Jacobs's *Incidents in the Life of a Slave Girl* (HJ).

STEP 4:
Construct your observation list to suit the demands of this type of prompt by listing observations under two categories—the similarities and the differences between the subjects under study:

Similarities	Differences
• both are from the same time period	• the authors are of different genders
• both are first person accounts of slavery	• FD is able to hire himself for work while HJ cannot
• both are heroic stories	
• both narrators escape	• HJ escapes due to sexual exploitation while FD escapes because of labor exploitation
• both suffer under slavery	
• both learn to read and write	• HJ hides for seven years while FD's journey to freedom is fairly short
• both experience kind and cruel owners	
• both are mixed race	• FD focuses on himself while HJ focuses on the kindness of family and friends who hide her
• both work with the abolitionists	• HJ has a child but FD does not

STEPS 5–6:

After examining your observation lists, see if you can use abstraction to derive some insights. Your goal is to decide whether the similarities or the differences offer a more interesting or significant perspective. Although these two slave narratives have much in common, you have decided, for example, to focus on their unexpected differences. Looking more closely at their differences, what insightful perspectives do you observe? Using abstraction, you might realize that Douglass relies on himself, while Jacobs relies on friends and family.

STEP 7:

Taking into consideration your choice to focus on either similarities or differences, and your insightful idea to focus on the "unexpected differences in terms of Douglass's reliance on self and Jacobs's reliance on friends and family," use C-S-C to construct a working thesis statement. Because there are at least two subjects in any comparison essay, you will have to modify the C-S-C formula to accommodate both subjects. We've listed some common templates for comparing theses in the box that follows. If you choose to focus on differences, then you might try one of the first two templates; if you choose to focus on similarities, try one of the second two.

Sample Thesis Statement Templates
for a Comparison Essay

Templates That Focus on Differences:

1. Although X and Y have many similarities, their differences are more significant in terms of A.

2. Even though X and Y are similar in terms of A, B, and/or C, their differences show E, F, and/or G.

Templates That Focus on Similarities:

1. In spite of the fact that X and Y appear very different, they are similar regarding A.

2. Most people believe that X and Y are unrelated; however, a close examination reveals that they share A.

To fill in the thesis template for this step, return to the lists of similarities and differences you generated in Step 4. Because this example will focus on differences, consider choosing the most unexpected difference for which you have compelling evidence, as it will both challenge you as a writer and be rewarding for the reader.

If you use one of the first two thesis templates and insert the similarity in the first part of the template, you will draw forward an expected or commonly held assumption. This helps create a platform to dramatize the significance of the difference that will be identified in the second part of the template—the thesis statement's claim. Regardless of which template you use, you can include more than one similarity or difference. Your job in the next step will be to sculpt this information into a smooth and compelling claim. The first draft of this working thesis statement using thesis template #2 focusing on differences might look like this:

> Although Frederick Douglass's and Harriet Jacobs's slave narratives are from the same time period and present accounts of life as a slave in the United States, their differences show that Douglass's account focuses on himself and Jacobs's account focuses on family and friends.

Once the template is filled out, it is time to fine-tune it into a fully developed thesis statement. Consider the following methods:

- Look closely at the items listed as similarities and those listed as differences and find overarching ideas for each (see abstraction, chapter 3).

- Ask "so what?" to take your ideas to the next step to find a compelling claim (see chapter 2).

- Fine-tune the language and word choice (see appendix A).

Whichever technique (or combination of techniques) you choose, a comparison thesis must go beyond simply calling attention to the fact that the items being compared share certain things and not others. Saying that two things are both alike and different is a statement of fact, as this can be said about any two things. You must find something insightful to highlight, something that you have probably found using observation and abstraction.

Here's one refinement of the slave narrative example, the result of asking "so what?" and then fine-tuning the language:

> Although Frederick Douglass's and Harriet Jacobs's slave narratives present similar accounts of life as a slave in the United States, they demonstrate two equally effective and unexpected strategies for emancipation: Douglass through self-reliance and Jacobs through reliance on community.

The Open-Ended Writing Assignment

Although all prompts give directions for a writing assignment, the open-ended writing assignment gives little or no guidance on the specific aspect or angle that should be taken. It merely puts a subject before you and asks you to comment, analyze, evaluate, or interpret. You will usually have to determine the context within which you will place the subject of your thesis statement, as well as the point of view your essay will establish.

So, on one hand, the open-endedness of this type of prompt offers a chance for you to freely engage a subject in a way that appeals to you. On the other hand, the *challenge* of responding to an open-ended prompt is that you must develop a clear and defensible perspective on the subject you are exploring without much direction. The goal here is not to be intimidated by the open-ended writing assignment's lack of direction.

Sometimes you will be able to rely on course materials to guide you in responding, but other times you will be free to present the subject in whatever light you wish. Remember, though, that while you may have a wide spectrum of knowledge about the subject, you will have to use some judgment to limit what you put in the essay to those things that directly support the claim you put forward in your thesis statement. Although you may feel that your response can be taken directly from lecture notes, especially if a great deal of classroom discussion has been devoted to this subject, the success of your essay will always be greater if you can go beyond a simple regurgitation of the material to offer something new and insightful.

Example

In an essay of five pages, discuss the use of Prozac in society today.

DID YOU KNOW . . .

Prozac is a drug that increases serotonin, a chemical in the brain. A lack of serotonin is linked to depression, anxiety, and premenstrual syndrome (PMS).

STEP 1:

In an essay of five pages, <u>discuss</u> the <u>use</u> of <u>Prozac</u> in <u>society today.</u>

Notice that this prompt is asking you to discuss the *use* of Prozac, not its chemical makeup or its side effects (although these issues may come into the essay less directly). The prompt limits you to focusing on *society*—not the family or the individual—and it clarifies the time period as *today*, not Prozac's use in the past or its potential for the future. In short, the prompt has given you some clear boundaries for the essay.

STEP 2:

The subject of this prompt is the use of Prozac. As already noted, the subject of the open-ended prompt is commonly the thing you are being asked to discuss. Notice that there are no terms that give clear guidance on the direction that the claim should take. The prompt asks you to write on the *"use"* of Prozac, which could be interpreted in positive or negative ways. It does not ask you to discuss, for instance, the dangers of Prozac, which would lead to a negative interpretation. Hence, you are free to offer whatever perspective you wish. The context you are given is "society today."

STEP 3:

For this prompt, there is only one question—the primary question—so it is already quite clear. (This will not always be the case.) Notice that the direction word *discuss* can lead you astray if you do not recognize that it is calling for a discussion (or analysis) that leads to a conclusion, rather than a loosely structured discussion that might cover interesting ground but has no clear central essay.

STEP 4:

It is usually necessary to generate an observation list about the subject to help make you aware of the many characteristics that might be relevant to a essay. As discussed in the previous section, this is the first step of analysis. Bring to the surface all the information that you can think of regarding the use of Prozac. Here is a sample observation list:

- It is used by many people.
- It is effective.
- It is readily available through prescription.
- It is commonly used for depression and PMS.
- It has minimal side effects.
- Society is increasingly accepting of this and other mental health drugs.
- It can be cautiously used by children and teenagers.
- It is generally covered by insurance.
- Most people have heard of it.
- Some people are reluctant to take it.
- It was released for wide-scale use in 1987.

STEP 5:
For this example, there is only one subject term, Prozac, and brainstorming produced one list or cluster that appears fairly substantial. Try to move forward without dividing the brainstorm list into multiple clusters or freewriting to see if this list can produce fruitful overarching ideas. You can always return to this step later if you need to add ideas or explore ideas in more depth. Remember, writing is a recursive process!

STEP 6:
Look to see if there are any overarching themes suggested in the observation list. Our goal is to use abstraction to find an insightful point of view about the subject using as many of the observations as possible. In other words, the burden of this step is to articulate a relationship between the items observed and the use of Prozac in society today. What conclusion can you abstract about Prozac's use from this list?

After exploring closely the ideas in the list, you have decided, for example, to pursue two overarching ideas: (1) almost all of the items on the list suggest some benefit provided by this prescription drug, and (2) the breadth of the items suggests that this drug has revolutionized the mental health care field. If you decide to work with insight 1 and use "benefits" as the theme or insightful idea from the observation list, you can see more clearly the relationship between all the terms, that is, each demonstrates a benefit re-garding Prozac's use.

STEP 7:
Using the C-S-C approach, insert "benefits" into the claim portion of your thesis statement. If you sketch the key terms, you come up with the following:

Context: society today
Subject: use of Prozac
Claim: is beneficial

Simple Working Thesis:

> The use of Prozac in society today is beneficial.

Now imagine what this essay would look like. It would probably go through many of the items that were generated in the observation list, showing how they can be considered beneficial. Some items suggest benefits to children, some suggest benefits to those who are diagnosed as depressed, and some suggest benefits to doctors who can rely on this readily available drug. However, this thesis (and the accompanying essay) ultimately is still somewhat under-developed. This essay would take the shape of a list, discussing various groups of people who benefit from Prozac's use (e.g., children, the depressed, doctors). There is currently no final assessment or overarching evaluation of these individual examples. In other words, "so what?"

We can revise and improve upon this first draft thesis by using abstraction again to find an overarching term that can encompass all these beneficiaries of Prozac. Think about it: Prozac benefits children; it benefits individuals; and it benefits doctors . . . so what? Do these thoughts suggest that it benefits society as a whole, even those who are not involved in its use or distribution? We have inserted this more encompassing and insightful idea to see if it provides a more compelling claim.

Revised Thesis:

> The wide use of Prozac today is advantageous to society as a whole.

This thesis might be interesting to those who are resistant to wide-scale dissemination of Prozac. It takes the controversial position that such wide-scale use is advantageous, even to those who don't actually take the drug. The burden of proof for this essay is to convince resistant readers by bringing them to a better understanding of why the use of Prozac benefits the entire society (although its dangers may come up as a counter argument in the discussion). Notice that virtually all the items in the observation list can be used to develop and support this thesis. This is unusual; it may not always work out this way.

Note also that the term *wide* is a key qualification in the thesis that must be addressed specifically and must be supported in the defense of the claim. Often, a thesis will include a key term like this that qualifies the subject, and these terms should be used consciously and deliberately and with an understanding of their contribution to the claim. (See "Qualifying a Commonly Accepted Idea" in appendix B.)

This example of an open-ended writing assignment, asking us to think and write about Prozac, is a very simple one. Although open-ended, it illustrates several things: a clearly identified subject and context, no preset direction for the claim, and a case where the first or second stage of observation and abstraction reveals an insightful idea that leads to a thesis claim. As you will see next, prompts are not always this straightforward.

The Writing Assignment with Multiple Questions or Multiple Parts

In chapter 6, we examined a sample writing assignment regarding cheating in the classroom that had multiple questions in it. We said that the most common mistake made in responding to such an assignment is writing an essay that simply goes through the prompt, listing the answers to each question one by one. An essay like that would have no central point and little coherence. You would have to unpack the assignment to figure out the primary question—what is really being asked. We will use the same principle with an assignment that has multiple questions arranged in multiple parts. You will still be able to use the seven steps, but remember that these steps are tools that you are free to adjust, when necessary.

General Humanities Writing Assignment

A. Select a work of art, architecture, literature, music, theater, dance, and so forth, that serves as a good example of Modernism.

B. Think about the general definition of Modernism as a style that breaks with the past, employs experimentation, privileges subjectivity, and so forth.

C. Consult at least three sources (only one Internet source can be used) to learn more about the piece.

D. Write a detailed analysis explaining, point-by-point, how the work you have chosen represents the Modern style.

E. Include a bibliography and be sure that you cite references, when appropriate, within the body of the essay.

Study the actual assignment in the box from a freshman-level humanities class. This prompt contains a lot of information. We will use the seven steps to generate a thesis statement.

The Seven Steps

STEP 1:
A. From the field of the <u>humanities,</u> <u>select</u> a <u>work of art,</u> architecture, literature, music, theater, dance, and so forth, that serves as a good <u>example</u> of <u>Modernism.</u>

B. <u>Think about</u> the general <u>definition of Modernism</u> as a style that breaks with the past, employs experimentation, privileges subjectivity, and so forth.

C. <u>Consult</u> at least <u>three sources</u> (only one Internet source can be used) to learn more about the piece.

D. Write a detailed <u>analysis</u> explaining, point-by-point, <u>how</u> the <u>work</u> you have <u>chosen</u> <u>represents the Modern style.</u>

E. Include a <u>bibliography</u> and be sure that you cite references when appropriate within the body of the essay.

STEP 2:
Using C-S-C, part A provides the parameters for the paper. The *subject* will be the work of art you select. The *context* for this paper is the humanities, but you are being asked to

consider two specific realms of information that make up the context in which you are to view the humanities: (1) artwork and (2) theory about art (definition of Modernism). Your job will be to establish the relationship between these two realms, given the specific example of art you select as your subject.

STEP 3:

Part D contains the core of the prompt. Given the underlined terms, "how . . . work . . . chosen represents the Modern style," you could summarize all five parts of this prompt with the following sentence: How does the artwork chosen represent Modernism? This is the primary question of this prompt.

Abstracting a clear and simple sentence from this five-part prompt helps isolate the task at hand: choose a relevant piece of art and analyze its Modernist characteristics. When confused or unsure, try this technique of summarizing the whole prompt in just one sentence. You are now ready to use prewriting strategies.

STEPS 4–5:

A good way to approach this assignment is to make two observation lists. List one will be about the artwork you select. There is no need to limit your list at this stage to only those ideas you are sure represent Modernism—this may inhibit the number of observations you make. Simply list everything you observe about the piece of art you select and allow the editing of the list to happen at the next step. List two will be about the qualities associated with Modernism that you have learned from your coursework or your research. Notice that the instructor already started this list for you in part B of the prompt. Again, don't try to screen for only those qualities you also see in the artwork you selected. This will stifle potential insights. For now, simply list all Modernist attributes you can think of.

For example, you decide to use the example of Marcel Duchamp's painting *Nude Descending a Staircase* shown in figure 7.1. If you've completed the two observation lists, the one on Modernism and the other on *Nude Descending a Staircase*, try to find the overlapping ideas in the two lists. In other words, you should be able to look at list two and select qualities about Duchamp's painting that illustrate qualities of Modernism that appear in list one. Again, your lists will probably be longer than these examples. This will bring forward the characteristics of this painting that are representative of the Modernist style.

LIST ONE: MODERNISM

- style that breaks with the past

- style that employs experimentation

- style that privileges subjectivity

LIST TWO: DUCHAMP'S ***NUDE DESCENDING A STAIRCASE***

- abstract

- cubist

- uses new angles to represent the body

- represents the nude body in unconventional ways

- captures motion and time

- unique visualization of the body

Your job will be to find the issues that these clusters or realms of information share so as to support your claim that Duchamp's *Nude Descending a Staircase* represents Modernism.

Fig. 7.1 Marcel Duchamp, *Nude Descending a Staircase* (1912)

DID YOU KNOW ...

Marcel Duchamp was a French artist who became an American citizen in 1955. He is usually associated with the Dada and Surrealism movements, although much of his art is playful and shows his interest in motion. His work *Nude Descending a Staircase* was first presented in America at the 1913 Armory Show in New York City, where it generated significant controversy.

STEPS 6–7:

Note that when we restate the prompt in the form of its primary question—How does Duchamp's painting represent Modernism?—a working thesis statement is already contained within the question. By turning the question into a statement, a working thesis comes to light: Duchamp's painting *Nude Descending a Staircase* represents Modernism. Notice that this thesis would satisfy the demands for this freshman-level, general humanities assignment.

For a major's class on visual art, however, a more precise or nuanced thesis might be required. In other words, a more informed audience might find our thesis too well accepted and therefore not controversial enough for a persuasive paper. When an audience believes that a thesis is not controversial, that it states common knowledge, we call it a "soft thesis," and it requires another revision. (See appendix A for more on the soft thesis.)

To improve a soft thesis, take it one step further. In this example, you might return to your observation list and recognize that, although many of the elements of Duchamp's painting are clearly associated with Modernism, several qualities suggest ties to other styles. Noticing this, you might use the technique of qualifying a commonly held belief (see appendix B) to revise your working thesis statement into one that is broader in scope and would require the discussion of artistic periods other than Modernism. A new thesis might read, "Although Duchamp's *Nude Descending a Staircase* exhibits qualities from several artistic periods, its predominant tie is to the Modernist era." This more complex thesis would provide opportunities to exhibit a number of counterarguments while still sticking to the same primary claim—that the painting represents Modernism. This approach might be less commonly accepted and thus more appropriate for certain audiences.

Variation: Responding to an Assignment with More than One Primary Question

Sometimes a prompt may have more than one central question. When this is the case, your job is to foreground one primary question and answer it. When you foreground one question, you make it the primary purpose for your analysis and the basis for your argument, so you want to give some thought to your choice. If you are not confident about your choice, be sure to ask your instructor if she or he has a preference as to which central question you focus on in your response. It's possible that the instructor has priorities that are not well reflected in the way the prompt is written. If still unsure, use the following techniques to help you choose a primary question:

- Foreground (or make primary) the question that covers the most breadth because this may allow you to incorporate answers to the other questions as you write your response. In other words, this question is the most overarching one.

- Foreground the question that you are best prepared to answer.

- Revisit the questions in the prompt and reaffirm that your analysis is correct—that you have properly identified the question(s) that are primary and seem independent and those that are secondary and appear to be follow-ups. Choose the primary question that has the most secondary or follow-up questions associated with it because the various secondary questions may give you more hints for thesis and essay development.

- Treat the questions as a cluster and look for an overarching idea that will encompass them all. Said differently, decide which aspects the three or four questions have in common and draft a thesis that speaks to that generality.

For example:

> (1) Given its superior military might, what should be the United States' role in global affairs in the twenty-first century? (2) Should the United States begin an age of isolationism? (3) Imperialism? (4) Given the United States' moderate economic strength, should the defense budget be increased?

In this example, the first question is a primary question that is broad enough to generate an essay. The second and third questions are clearly tied to the first question and are meant to offer directions for possible responses. The fourth question seems to move the inquiry along a different path; another primary question. In this case, you should choose one of the primary questions to answer, either the first or the last question.

You might foreground the first question and use the second and third questions to give you some guidance or perspective on your topic. Then try to turn the last question into a secondary question and see if you can also respond to it in your paper, as long as you can do so in terms of your thesis claim. If not, leave it out, but double-check with your instructor to be sure that your writing plan constitutes an appropriate response. This is one strategy for composing the fullest possible answer in an essay that potentially remarks on all the questions and yet maintains a central focus and unity.

The Timed Essay

A timed essay (e.g., an in-class essay or a qualifying exam) is often a particularly stressful type of writing assignment because you may fear that you don't have the time to prewrite, plan, and revise. Although your time is limited, the trick is to parcel out the available time so you can use the seven steps and C-S-C and still leave enough time for writing. You might be surprised how little time you need for writing when the essay is well planned.

Try these strategies:

1. Decide up front how much time you will allow for each stage of the writing process.

   Be sure to give yourself enough time for prewriting/planning and writing. Decide how important it will be, given the context of the assignment and your particular strengths and weaknesses, to allow time to reread your essay to check for errors and make changes. For instance, if you have 60 minutes in which to write two essays, you might decide to devote 30 minutes to each essay. Of those 30 minutes, you might dedicate 10 minutes to planning and 20 minutes to writing. If you have a clear idea about what to write from the start, you might rethink your time allocation and allow for 5 minutes of planning, 20 minutes for writing, and 5 minutes for skimming your response to make last-minute corrections. After you make your time plan, try to stick with it as closely as you can. You might even ask your instructor to announce certain benchmarks during the writing period, such as "you have ten minutes left," in case you find yourself so engrossed in your thinking and writing that you lose track.

2. Use the seven steps quickly but effectively:

   - 1, 2, and 3: Be sure you clearly understand the assignment. If you have questions, ask your instructor or proctor for clarification so you do not lose time. Unless your instructor says otherwise, write directly on the assignment sheet so you have these notes available.

   - 4 and 5: These steps may be abbreviated, as needed, but don't skip the prewriting process simply because you are under a time constraint. The ideas you generate here will serve you well as you draft the essay. In addition, these steps give you an opportunity to review, organize, and edit your ideas before you start to write the essay. Otherwise, you may find yourself consuming even more time editing and reorganizing during the drafting process.

   - 6 and 7: Again, scribble on the assignment sheet or extra paper to draft and revise your thesis.

3. Use C-S-C to check your working thesis statement and plan your essay.

   Never begin writing without a plan, even if it is a rough outline sketched or jotted in the margin of the assignment page. Use C-S-C to begin the planning process. At minimum, you should know what you are arguing, what your major burdens of proof are, and what points you will cover first. If possible, jot down one or two less compelling points (key words are fine) so that you can quickly add or outline this evidence if you find that you have time. Without a plan, you may inadvertently find yourself wandering off point or wanting to cross off a page you have written because you find later that it is not relevant.

4. Consider beginning with your thesis statement rather than a full introduction.

Writing the introduction is often the most time-consuming part of an essay. Consider limiting the introduction to your thesis statement alone. Although this is not appropriate for a formal essay under normal conditions, for a timed essay, it is more important to spend your efforts developing the evidence rather than crafting a rhetorically interesting introduction. Ask your instructor whether this is acceptable (it might even be preferred).

5. Develop your evidence.

Presenting the evidence should be the most time-consuming part of the writing process. Be sure to allot enough time to address your burdens of proof. The success of your paper will ultimately rest on the thorough and logical presentation of your evidence and how well it supports your thesis statement. As with planning, time allocated to this step will be well spent.

6. Conclude your essay.

Write a short conclusion that restates your thesis and your evidence. This is the reader's last impression of your ideas, and it is the point in the writing process when you are probably the most familiar with those ideas and can be most succinct and/or eloquent. Never end in midstream. If you have to choose between a well-developed conclusion and completing one of your body paragraphs, give attention to the body paragraph because it is central to your argument. Then write a brief concluding sentence that simply restates your thesis and gives a sense of closure to your essay.

7. Review and revise.

Check the prompt to be sure that you have thoroughly understood the assignment and appropriately answered the question(s). Skim your essay. Clarify any words that are illegible; add or neatly strike through information you would like to alter.

....

WHAT TO DO IF YOU FIND YOURSELF RUNNING SHORT OF TIME:

DON'T	**DO**
• When two or more essays are required, don't sacrifice one whole essay to write a more complete earlier essay.	• At minimum, write an outline for the essay(s) you don't have time to complete. Give your thesis with as many briefly outlined points as possible and a one or two sentence conclusion
• Spend time developing inferior points when more important points may go unstated.	• Foreground the most important points so that you can be sure to get to them.
• End the essay in midstream.	• Outline the remaining important points and include a one or two sentence conclusion.

....

Timed essays are often very stressful because they don't allow writers the luxury of reflection and critical distance on their writing. Empower yourself by figuring out which strategies work with your natural writing process. We gave you some guidelines earlier, but you will have to experiment with them, as with all the techniques in this book, to learn how to customize them to suit your writing strengths and needs.

APPLICATIONS AND WRITING EXERCISES

Application 7.1 The Writing Assignment with Multiple Questions

For the following assignment, decide which question represents the primary question and which are supplementary questions. (Hint: the primary question is often either first or last in the series of questions.) Explain how you could tell which question is primary and which are supplementary. Once you identify the primary question, use the seven steps to generate a thesis statement. Remember that you can use the supplementary questions to help guide your brainstorming and your response.

> Should famous people (e.g., movie stars, athletes, broadcast journalists, politicians) be held to a different standard of morality than common people? Should this apply to all aspects of life equally, that is, child rearing, drugs, public and private behavior? Should their standards of morality differ depending on what kind of famous person they are? Should this standard last forever or only for the time that people recognize them in public? Should this standard apply to viewing audiences differently, according to age, for instance? What do you think?

Application 7.2 The Writing Assignment with More Than One Primary Question

Study the following prompt and cut through the wordiness to identify its context, subject, and primary question. Explain how you could use different sections or parts of the prompt to help you generate a thesis statement and essay. You may work with a peer or in a small group for this assignment. It might help to break down the prompt into its parts. Put questions, quotes, and background material together and group any other similar information so that you can better analyze the parts and the purpose they serve in the overall assignment.

Note that this prompt represents a variation of the prompt with multiple questions. However, it is distinctive for its length and wordiness, and it may even contain characteristics of several different kinds of prompts. Although this "windy prompt," as we fondly refer to it, might look intimidating, you will probably appreciate its thoroughness. Nevertheless, the essential task is to determine what question you are really supposed to answer. This prompt was actually used in a history class.

> The Gothic cathedral can be seen as the center of the late medieval world. The Gothic cathedral was at once a center of religious devotion; an achievement of civic pride; an educational institution; a tourist destination; a museum of religious history; a place for doing secular, governmental, and commercial business; and above all, a public space that expressed the whole spectrum of medieval values, beliefs,

customs, and practices. When we compare our world to the late medieval world, it's difficult to imagine any contemporary public architecture or public space that similarly captures and expresses our modern way of life, one that encompasses our various customs, practices, values, and beliefs.

Or is it? Is it possible to identify the contemporary cathedral? Is there, in the contemporary world, a public space or kind of public architecture that, like the Gothic cathedral, serves as the center of our world, capturing in one place a sense of our entire way of life? In what public space, or in what kind of public architecture, can we find an expression of our basic view of things, our overarching system of values and beliefs, our sense of who we are and where we've come from? Identify a reasonable candidate for the title of contemporary "cathedral" but go further. Offer some support for your choice. Discuss why this public space or architecture functions for us in a manner similar to the way in which the cathedral functioned for the inhabitants of medieval Europe. Why this place or building? How does it capture the basic shape of the modern world? In what ways is a given selection like or unlike the Gothic cathedral? What does it lack, compared to the earlier cathedral, or what has been gained in it? Is it complete, as a sign of modern times? What else is needed in it or around it to better express the bustle and boredom of the modern world?

Think above all about the way in which architecture can locate us—giving shape to the sense of the world, capturing the sense of our given place and time—or can dislocate us, by offering us spaces and places lacking meaning. What sort of architecture best describes our place these days? Write an essay that discusses your response.

Application 7.3 The Writing Assignment That Includes a Reading

Read Gates's essay that follows and then discuss how you might use the seven steps to plan an essay in response to the following assignment:

Why does Gates consider 2 Live Crew's music to be protected under First Amendment Rights? Do you think that all speech, no matter what form, should be protected under the rights of free speech? Support your views with examples from your own experience as well as your reading.

THINKING THROUGH A READING
1. According to Gates, the group 2 Live Crew uses "a coded way of communicating." Why does Gates believe they communicate in this way?

2. Taking Gates's points into consideration, do you think 2 Live Crew's music is obscene?

2 Live Crew, Decoded
Henry Louis Gates Jr.
The rap group 2 Live Crew and their controversial hit recording, "As Nasty as They Wanna Be," may well earn a signal place in the history of First Amendment rights. But just as important is how these lyrics will be interpreted and by whom.

For centuries, African-Americans have been forced to develop coded ways of communicating to protect them from danger. Allegories and double meanings, words redefined to mean their opposites ("bad" meaning "good," for instance), even neologisms ("bodacious") have enabled blacks to share messages only the initiated understand.

Many blacks were amused by the transcripts of Marion Barry's sting operation which reveals that he used the traditional black expression about ones "nose being opened." This referred to a love affair and not, as Mr. Barry's prosecutors have suggested, to the inhalation of drugs. Understanding this phrase could very well spell the difference (for the Mayor) between prison and freedom.

2 Live Crew is engaged in heavy-handed parody, turning the stereotypes of black and white American culture on their heads. These young artists are acting out, to lively dance music, a parodic exaggeration of the age-old stereotypes of the oversexed black female and male. Their exuberant use of hyperbole (phantasmagoric sexual organs, for example) undermines—for anyone fluent in black cultural codes—a too literal-minded hearing of the lyrics.

This is the street tradition called "signifying" or "playing the dozens," which has generally been risqué, and where the best signifier or "rapper" is the one who invents the most extravagant images, the biggest "lies," as the culture says. (H. "Rap" Brown earned his nickname in just this way.) In the face of racist stereotypes about black sexuality, you can do one of two things: you can disavow them or explode them with exaggeration.

2 Live Crew, like many "hip-hop" groups, is engaged in sexual carnivalesque. Parody reigns supreme, from a take-off of standard blues to a spoof of the black power movement, their off-color nursery rhymes are part of a venerable Western tradition. The group even satirizes the culture of commerce when it appropriates popular advertising slogans ("Tastes great!" "Less filling!") and puts them in a bawdy context.

2 Live Crew must be interpreted within the context of black culture generally and of signifying specifically. Their novelty, and that of other adventuresome rap groups, is that their defiant rejection of euphemism now voices for the mainstream what before existed largely in the "race record" market—where the records of Redd Foxx and Rudy Ray Moore once were forced to reside.

Rock songs have always been about sex but have used elaborate subterfuges to convey that fact. 2 Live Crew uses Anglo-Saxon words and is self-conscious about it: a parody of a white voice in one song refers to "private personal parts," as a coy counterpart to the group's bluntness.

Much more troubling than its so-called obscenity is the group's overt sexism. Their sexism is so flagrant, however, that it almost cancels itself out in a hyperbolic war between the sexes. In this, it recalls the inter-sexual jousting in Zora Neale Hurston's novels. Still, many of us look toward the emergence of more female rappers to redress sexual stereotypes. And we must not allow ourselves to sentimentalize street culture: the appreciation of verbal virtuosity does not lessen one's obligation to critique bigotry in all of its pernicious forms.

Is 2 Live Crew more "obscene" than, say, the comic Andrew Dice Clay? Clearly, this rap group is seen as more threatening than others that are just as sexually explicit. Can this be completely unrelated to the specter of the young black male as a figure of sexual and social disruption, the very stereotypes 2 Live Crew seem determined to undermine?

This question—and the very large question of obscenity and the First Amendment—cannot even be addressed until those who would answer them become literate in the vernacular traditions of African Americans. To do less is to censor through the equivalent of intellectual prior restraint—and censorship is to art what lynching is to justice.

Writing Exercise 7.1 A Comparison Assignment

Examine the two paintings—the first by Spanish artist Diego Rivera (figure 7.2), and the second by American artist Mary Cassatt (figure 7.3). Build an observation list where you identify first the similarities, and then the differences, between these two paintings. Imagine that you have been given an assignment to write an essay comparing the two. Examine your list and decide whether you would foreground their similarities or their differences. Write a paragraph or two explaining your choice. Then write a working thesis statement that you might use if you were to write the essay.

Fig. 7.2 Diego Rivera, *La Molendera* (1924)

Fig. 7.3 Mary Cassatt, *Five O'Clock Tea* (1880)

Part 2 WRITING ASSIGNMENTS

option 1

1. Read the following quote from the *New York Times* and write an essay that responds to its argument. Do you think enjoyment of our national parks should be broadly encouraged by relaxing bans on the use of recreational motorized vehicles such as off-road vehicles and snowmobiles, or do you think these vehicles should be banned because they constitute a threat to the preservation of the parks?

> Interior Secretary Gale Norton [in his proposed revisions for the basic management policy that guides park superintendents] is opening up the parks to off-road vehicles, including snowmobiles. The ongoing effort to revise the 2001 policy betrays a powerful sense, shared by many top interior officials, that the national parks are resources not to be protected but to be exploited. This new policy document doesn't go as far as the earlier version. But it would eliminate the requirement that only motorized equipment with the least impact should be used in national parks. It would lower air-quality standards and strip away language about preserving the parks' natural soundscape—language that currently makes it hard, for instance, to justify allowing snowmobiles into Yellowstone. It would also refer park superintendents to other management documents that have been revised to weaken fundamental standards and protections for the parks. [...] What we are witnessing, in essence, is an effort to politicize the National Park Service—to steer it away from its long-term mission of preserving much-loved national treasures.

2. Use the seven steps to write an essay in response to one of the following statements:

   A. Television advertising aimed at kids is now broadcast twenty-four hours a day.

   B. We are constantly bombarded by media images of beauty, an image that few if any of us can approximate, although most of us continue to try.

   C. The old model of living together with the contract of marriage is fading out, and many people today are choosing to cohabitate.

   D. Twenty-first century shopping malls are culture-rich centers that reflect all the diversity found in twenty-first century America.

   E. Many of the tragedies surrounding teenage drinking would disappear if we removed the age restriction regarding the consumption of alcohol so that young people could learn to drink wisely, around adults and parents, rather than on their own, where drinking becomes a form of rebellion.

3. Use the seven steps to unpack and respond to the following writing assignment on Sen's essay "A World Not Neatly Divided." (The essay can be found in chapter 6.)

   > What are the boundaries that Amartya Sen feels "separate us all into divided camps" and why does he feel they are misleading? Do you agree with his idea that these boundaries create "divided camps" and that erasing the boundaries can lead to a more peaceful world?

4. Taking into consideration Henry Louis Gates Jr. understanding of free speech in his essay "2 Live Crew, Decoded," how would you respond? Why does Gates consider

2 Live Crew's music to be protected under First Amendment Rights? Do you think that all speech, no matter what form, should be protected under the rights of free speech? Support your views with examples from your own experience as well as your reading.

5. Review or read chapter 1's essay "Plagiarism: A Crime to BE Prevented." Do you agree with the argument in this essay? Write your own essay on this subject and be sure to address the ideas in "Plagiarism: A Crime to BE Prevented" as you develop your argument.

6. Choose one of the following issues and gather information about it from the library or Internet. Then write an essay where you take a side in the debate. Be sure to support your viewpoint as well as you can. If you use research, be sure to cite your sources properly according to the MLA rules for citation (see chapter 10 and appendix C for help with doing research).

   A. Is stem-cell research an important frontier in solving human problems or is it unethical and a threat to our society's moral fiber?

   B. Is it okay for couples to live together or should they marry? Is marriage an important aspect of our society or is it okay to live together without marriage?

   C. Is capital punishment necessary in some cases or is it always an unacceptable practice no matter the situation?

   D. Are men and women treated equally in our society or are women still given the status of "second class citizens" in many ways?

   E. Should Internet file sharing be legalized or should it be considered theft and subject to criminal punishment?

Part 2 REVISION TOOLS

PEER REVIEW WORKSHOP WORKSHEET II

Find a fellow student and agree to read one another's essay to assess their strengths and weaknesses. The goal of the workshop is to give and receive feedback that can be used to guide revision.

Before exchanging drafts with a peer, complete the following:

1. Attach a copy of your assignment and underline its key terms.

2. What type of writing assignment is it? For example, does it include an ongoing debate or ask for a comparison? Is it open-ended?

3. What are its context and subject? Determine its primary question, if necessary.

4. If you have time, complete a post-draft outline (see Part 1 Revision Tools).

Exchange with a peer your responses to these items and a copy of your draft. Then complete the following:

Check the writer's understanding of the writing assignment.

1. Look over the writing assignment. Are the key terms correctly identified? If you disagree, let the writer know which terms you would identify as key.

2. Are the context, subject, and primary question (if relevant) correctly identified? Offer any suggestions you have.

Read for a first impression.

1. Read first to grasp the writer's intention. Does it respond to the writing assignment's demands? If not, give the writer some feedback.

Evaluate the thesis statement.

1. Copy the writer's thesis statement here:

_____

_____

Context: _____

Subject: _____

Claim: _____

2. Comment on the thesis statement's effectiveness.

3. Is the subject clear and does it have an appropriate scope? Does it respond to the assignment?

4. Does it make an interesting and arguable claim rather than a self-evident statement or a statement of fact?

5. Do you recommend revising any of its word choices or their order?

Evaluate the structure of the essay.

1. Identify the burdens of proof for the thesis statement.

2. Identify any special terms that will need to be explained.

3. Look closely at the essay and, for each paragraph, see if you can identify which burden of proof is being addressed. Write them in the margin. See if you can track the essay's logical progression. If a necessary step is left out of the essay or misplaced, tell the writer. If all logical steps are covered, let the writer know.

4. If you find a paragraph(s) that seems disconnected to a burden of proof, see if its presence can be justified. That is, decide if it is directly supporting the thesis statement. Explain your findings.

Look more closely at the development of individual paragraphs.

1. Mark any paragraphs that could benefit from further development, or that don't have a clear central point. Mention places where the writer might use TAXES

(topic sentence, assertion, example, explanation, significance) to fill out the discussion.

2. Point out any evidence you can think of that the writer could use to further support the essay's central argument. If you think of important contradictory evidence, mention it.

3. Are there any inappropriate sentences in the introduction? Mark any details in the intro that should be reserved for body paragraphs. Is the introduction working as an *introduction* to the essay's topic? Let the writer know your thoughts.

4. Look at the ending to see if it is too abrupt or repetitive or goes off in a new and surprising direction by positing a new claim. Make any comments you have.

Give the writer your final thoughts.

1. What is the draft's strongest element?

2. What part is most in need of further work?

Part Three

WRITING BEYOND THE COMPOSITION CLASSROOM

CHAPTER 8

Writing Across the Disciplines: Beyond Your Composition Class

Your course of study in college will include classes from across several specialized areas of academic study. These areas, called disciplines, will probably include courses in English, economics, history, biology, mathematics, and philosophy. As you are exposed to these diverse areas of study, you will learn to think about the world from different points of view. Although the disciplines themselves are diverse, and the concepts and history of each is unique, they all use conventional essay formats to communicate with those within and outside their fields. In fact, a careful survey of college writing assignments shows that, in addition to the **academic essay**, the **informative essay**, and the **scientific paper** are assigned in departments across the disciplines. In this chapter, you will study the two formats this text has not covered so far, the informative essay and the scientific essay.

In short, the informative paper is used to summarize research and convey information. You will use it when your assignment is to present, in an unbiased way, what is currently known about a subject or topic. The scientific paper is used to present and interpret the results of an experiment, study, or investigation. It can be assigned in any discipline, but it is most commonly used in the natural and social sciences and in education programs. Like the academic essay, these essay formats have established conventions that help to maximize their potential to communicate the results of systematic and sustained study.

WHAT'S AHEAD . . .

► thesis statement counterparts

► the informative essay

► using the controlling idea statement in place of the thesis statement

  • three potential problems with the CI statement and how to fix them

► distinguishing between writing assignments that require an informative essay and those that require an academic essay

---

- ▶ the scientific paper
  - using the hypothesis
  - IHMRAD: the scientific paper format
  - the scientific paper and writing assignments across the curriculum
- ▶ writing formats used for building the scientific paper
- ▶ the laboratory report
  - the format of the laboratory report
- ▶ the field notebook
  - the formats for a field notebook

Thesis Statement Counterparts

As discussed in chapter 2, the thesis statement is the central claim in the academic essay—the overarching statement that unifies all the parts of the essay. In the thesis statement, the writer clearly states the claim that the essay will develop and support. The informative essay and the scientific paper each have a unifying sentence that is similar to the thesis statement—counterparts, if you will. These counterparts function in the same overarching way. We call the overarching statement in the informative essay the *controlling idea statement*; in the scientific paper, it's called the *hypothesis*. As you learn to pursue and refine the overarching statement in these two essay types and appreciate their important differences, you will be able to write strong, coherent essays.

Essay Format		Purpose		Overarching or Unifying Statement
academic essay	⟶	to analyze evidence and persuade	⟶	thesis statement
informative essay	⟶	to summarize research and convey information	⟶	controlling idea statement
scientific paper	⟶	to present and interpret data	⟶	hypothesis

The Informative Essay

The informative essay format provides you with a systematic means of transmitting, as objectively as possible, the information currently known on a subject so as to deepen the reader's understanding. The informative essay does not take a position or put forward a controversial argument. Instead, it delivers an accessible and carefully organized view of the information that exists about a subject. Think of this essay as a means to teach or educate both your readers and yourself about something of interest or importance.

In addition to the controlling idea statement, the informative essay has two identifying characteristics. First, it should have a balanced, neutral tone that is appropriate to its purpose. Ideally, the tone of an informative essay will suggest to readers that the writer is an informed expert who writes to enlighten readers about a subject. Even when providing information on a controversial subject, the informative essay presents the various arguments fully and without bias. A second characteristic of the informative essay is its use of writing forms that help to clearly and systematically organize and present information. Organizing structures such as definition, classification, comparison, and summary are useful strategies for collecting and communicating sometimes complex information in forms that make that information more accessible to readers. Carefully **defining** special terms, sorting information into clusters or groups through a system of **classification**, **comparing** two like or unlike things to draw attention to a specific quality or aspect of one or both, and finally **summarizing** so as to give a succinct basic representation of central elements are all useful narrative devices for the informative essay.

Following are some examples of informative essay assignments that are used across the disciplines:

English and Composition
- Research a social issue currently under debate and present both sides of the argument.
- Synthesize the current scholarship on a novel, poem, short story, or play.

Social Science
- Summarize the relevant aspects of a cultural pattern or practice.
- Present the prevailing scholarship on the achievements of an ancient civilization.

History
- Give the viewpoints assessing the major achievements of an important historical figure.
- Articulate the contributing factors that led to a particular historical event.

Philosophy
- Summarize the main features of a particular philosopher's understanding of a subject or topic.
- Trace the development of a philosophical concept through a specific time period.

Business
- Present the basic features of a program, company, strategy, or experiment.
- Define the current understanding of a technical term or practice in business today.

Science
- Summarize the known results and conclusions of a recent scientific study.
- Give the prevailing belief regarding a cutting-edge development in the field.

Art

- Research the main tenets of a period in art history.
- Give the current thinking regarding the influence of an artist on a later period.

Any Class

- Research and summarize the thinking on a certain topic.
- Research a famous person and determine the significant contributions that have made him or her famous.
- Explain the basic features of a concept or practice.

The Format of the Informative Essay

The format of the informative essay is similar to the format of the academic essay, with an introduction, overarching statement,, body paragraphs, and a conclusion. The difference between them is one of purpose rather than of structure. Because the informative essay seeks to deliver information rather than to present an argument, its introduction and conclusion act as bookends that hold the essay's more detailed information between them. (For general guidelines for building introductions, paragraphs, and conclusions, see chapter 5.)

The **introduction** of the informative essay establishes a context for the subject of the essay. Thus it begins broadly, narrowing slightly to introduce the controlling idea (CI) statement, just as the academic essay's introduction puts forward the thesis statement. Its intent is to inform, which means that it will more deliberately include background information and general commentary to engage readers' interest and prepare them for the more detailed study of its subject.

The **CI statement** makes an assertion that is conclusively supported by the research; it doesn't state a claim that requires proof (as does the thesis statement). You might think of it as a summary statement or even a statement of fact concerning the topic of your essay. The CI statement unifies and gives purpose to the essay, so it must be broad enough in scope to overarch the information presented in the essay's body paragraphs.

Each paragraph in the informative essay, much like the academic essay, has an hour-glass shape. Each begins with a topic sentence and concludes with a sentence that reminds the reader how the point that was developed within the paragraph helps to explain and justify the CI statement. Each paragraph should contain concrete evidence and an explanation that shows how that evidence contributes to the topic of the paragraph.

The **conclusion** summarizes the CI statement and glosses the main points discussed in the essay.

As you may imagine, the diagram of the informative essay looks much like the diagram of the academic essay, but it is less pointed towards persuasion. Compare figure 8.1 with the diagram of the academic essay in chapter 1.

Fig. 8.1 Diagram of the Informative Essay

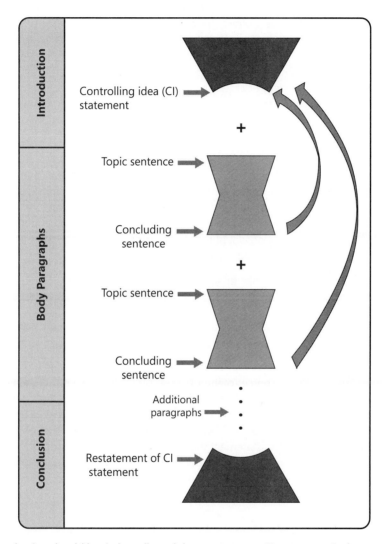

The introduction should begin broadly and then narrow to a CI statement. Each paragraph should begin with a topic sentence, narrow to develop a single point, and then use a concluding sentence to tie the paragraph back to the CI statement. The conclusion should recap the CI statement and the points made in its support and end purposefully.

Using the Controlling Idea Statement in Place of the Thesis Statement

The informative essay uses the CI statement to orient the reader to the subject of the essay and to give an overarching perspective on the essay's contents. The CI statement is a statement of fact, so it does not present an argument or make a claim, but it is just as vital to the informative essay as the thesis statement is to the academic essay. Like the thesis statement, the CI statement has a context and subject; rather than articulating a claim, however, the CI statement offers an overview or a **synthesis**. The word *synthesis* is *thesis* with the Greek prefix *syn*, which means "put together or join," so to synthesize is to join separate elements into a coherent whole. The CI statement does this by adding together the information available on a subject and offering a perspective that unifies it. The CI statement usually opens or closes the introduction; its purpose is to present the overarching idea that unifies the essay's points. In addition, the CI statement will establish the scope of the essay and thereby help you to determine what information to include, as well as what perspective to provide on that information.

The function and importance of the CI statement is easier to see in practice. If you are writing an essay on surfing, for instance, and have spent time collecting information and forming observations, your next step would be to examine the information and decide how to organize and present it. You need a frame to give your essay structure, and the CI statement will give you this frame. Without structure, without some method of organization, your information would remain scattered and listlike. Here is a list of possible CI statements for an informative essay on surfing:

> Surfing is a popular yet challenging sport.
>
> The culture of surfing includes a specialized language, dress, and etiquette.
>
> The sport of surfing draws a wide range of participants, from the casual to the professional.

You can see from these examples that each CI statement would lead to an essay that might make use of different sources of information, inform the reader about a different perspective on surfing, and have a different goal—all evident just from the CI statement. For instance, after reading that "Surfing is a popular yet challenging sport," a reader might anticipate learning more about how widespread surfing is, even though its physical demands are rigorous. A CI statement that focuses on the culture of surfing would give a reader an inside perspective of the sport itself, telling about the participants and their customs, habits, and way of life. Like the thesis statement, the CI statement gives the essay focus and direction, and it sets the boundaries for what will be included in (and excluded from) the essay.

Three Potential Problems with the CI Statement and How to Fix Them

Just as common problems arise in writing subjects and claims for thesis statements, three specific problems are common to writing CI statements. Thus, to write an effective CI statement, you should be open to revising it as you continue to explore your subject and make decisions about the information you want to include, and exclude, as you draft the essay.

PROBLEM #1: THE SCOPE ISN'T APPROPRIATE
The CI statement determines the scope of the essay—the content boundaries. In chapter 2, we discussed scope in reference to the subject portion of the thesis statement and explained techniques for recognizing when it is too narrow or too broad

for the length of the essay. You will have to think in a similar way about scope for the informative essay. The CI statement should be broad enough to encompass the prevailing points about the subject but not so broad that the reader is confused about the central perspective of the essay. On the other hand, the CI statement should not be so specific that it can be mistaken for just one of several details in the essay, leaving the essay without an overarching perspective. Consider the level of specificity of the following statement for an essay of about five pages:

> Example of a CI Statement that is too broad: *Abraham Lincoln was a famous American president.*
>
> Context: American history in the mid-nineteenth century
> Subject: Abe Lincoln
> Overarching Perspective: He was a famous president.
>
> Example of a CI Statement that is too specific: *Abraham Lincoln was the sixteenth president of the United States, and served from 1861 to 1865.*
>
> Context: American history in the mid-nineteenth century
> Subject: Abe Lincoln
> Overarching Perspective: He was president.

The first sentence is **too broad** or **too all-encompassing**. Like all sound CI statements, it is a statement of fact, but its scope is so broad that it will not serve to give the essay a clear focus. It would take you far more than five pages to discuss Lincoln's voluminous personal and political successes and failures. Where would you begin? Similarly, the terms *famous American president* will allow anything into the essay, from biographical information to his political accomplishments, his personal habits, and his religious views. To carve out one significant perspective that the essay will provide on Lincoln, the CI statement should be more selective as it sets readers up for what to expect in the essay. The second sentence, however, is **too specific** for a CI statement because it is so narrowly factual that it doesn't provide an overarching perspective for an informative essay. The most this sentence can overarch is perhaps the date of his election and his party. Any other information will go beyond the scope of this too-narrow statement. Neither of these CI statements helps you narrow and refine the very broad subject of Abraham Lincoln to select what information to include in an essay about him. Below is an improvement on the first example that focuses on one aspect of his failures:

> Abraham Lincoln persevered through many political setbacks before becoming president of the United States.

PROBLEM #2: THE UNIFYING POINT ISN'T CLEAR
Let's consider another potential problem, one having to do with word choice, when developing a CI statement for an informative essay. We discussed this strategy in chapter 2 regarding the thesis statement, and it is just as relevant to the CI statement, where clarity is always important.

Abraham Lincoln governed during a very challenging period of American history.

Context: American history
Subject: Abe Lincoln? the period of the mid-nineteenth century?
Overarching Perspective: This was when Lincoln was president? This period was
   challenging?

The sentence offers an overarching perspective, but its **unifying point is not clear**. It is hard to tell whether the essay will primarily inform the reader about Lincoln or about the tumultuous time in which he governed. Giving this statement a little more focus might help it to achieve the aims of a CI statement. Reshaping this statement so that its focus is on the subject of Lincoln will allow it to function successfully as an overarching sentence.

Abraham Lincoln governed during a very tumultuous period of American history, and he is probably best known today for the way he dealt with some of the challenges he faced.

Context: American history during the nineteenth century
Subject: Abe Lincoln
Overarching Perspective: He is best known for the way he handled this period's
   challenges

This sentence provides a subject—President Lincoln—and a perspective on his presidency. If this were your essay, you would now be able to go back to your research and decide what information would be most relevant for inclusion. You would look for information that could inform a reader about the challenges and responses that marked Lincoln's presidential term.

PROBLEM #3: THE CLAIM IS CONTROVERSIAL RATHER THAN INFORMATIVE
Let us consider another type of CI statement—one that is overarching but that makes a claim in the form of a value judgment:

Abraham Lincoln was a wonderful president.

Context: American history during the mid-nineteenth century
Subject: Lincoln
Overarching Perspective: He was a wonderful president.

This sentence suggests an overarching perspective in the sense that Lincoln is deemed a "wonderful president," but this phrase is **too subjective**; it does not summarize the research but makes an argument based on some aspects of the research. After doing some extensive research on Lincoln, you would find that there are mixed feelings about his success as a leader. Because an informative essay should summarize the research, rather than take a position or give an interpretation, the CI statement could be revised to give both sides of a controversy or identify and explain one or more particular arguments:

While some believe that Abraham Lincoln was one of America's best presidents, others judge him to have been a less than ideal leader.

Context: American history during the mid-nineteenth century
Subject: Lincoln

Overarching Perspective: Historians and scholars are divided on their assessment of his term as president.

As these examples illustrate, a CI statement should function in much the same way as the thesis statement does in the academic essay, with the exception that it informs rather than argues. Hence, the CI statement may not be fully formed until late in the writing process. Only after you have explored your subject in-depth can you make decisions about the overarching idea or perspective inherent in the information you have compiled. Therefore, you may choose to start with a working CI statement and then use an outline to draft segments of the essay before you determine the perspective you want to offer. Like the thesis statement in the academic essay, you will have to adjust your draft as your ideas evolve and as you make different choices about the perspective you want to capture in your essay.

Practice 8.1: Working with the CI Statement

Read the following informative paragraph from *The Cambridge Encyclopedia of the English Language*. Encyclopedias are by definition informative, so this is an opportunity to notice, as you read, the tone and style of this excerpt.

The Age of Dictionaries[1]

The first half of the 19th century was remarkable for the number of dictionaries that appeared on both sides of the Atlantic. Joseph Worcester provides a catalogue of English dictionaries at the beginning of his 1860 edition, and identifies 64 items published in England since Johnson's *Dictionary* (1755) and a further 30 items in America since the first Webster compilation (1806)—almost one a year. These were all general dictionaries; in addition there were over 200 specialized dictionaries and glossaries as well as over 30 encyclopedias, showing how compilers were under pressure to keep up with the increases in knowledge and terminology that stemmed from the Industrial Revolution, progress in science and medicine, and fresh philological perspectives. The world was not to see such an explosion of dictionaries and reference works again until the 1980s.

1. Identify the CI statement in this passage and tell how it organizes this short piece of informative writing.

2. Here is some information about the same subject, dictionaries. Can you determine its controlling idea? Would this information belong in "The Age of Dictionaries"?

   In the twentieth century, a debate was sparked about whether dictionaries should include forms of nonstandard speech. Dictionary writers in the eighteenth and nineteenth centuries rigidly maintained a sense of standards and correctness. Dictionary writers in the twentieth century, however, relaxed these standards, incorporating forms of nonstandard speech, such as "ain't" and "groovy," and omitting labels that identified colloquialisms. Those on one side of the debate argued that dictionary writers have a social responsibility to maintain the standards of correct speech, while those on the other side claimed that it was not the job of the dictionary writer to make judgments about what words are or are not worthy to appear in a dictionary.

[1] David Crystal, "The Age of Dictionaries," *The Cambridge Encyclopedia of the English Language.* New York: Cambridge University Press, 2003.

3. Examine Giannetti's essay, "The American Star System," that follows and see how closely its structure mirrors the diagram on page 179. Also consider how its format mirrors that of an academic essay. Pay careful attention, however, to how the CI statement differs from the thesis statement in that the CI statement doesn't present an argument, even though it functions in a similar way to unify the essay's perspective on its subject and to give the essay a distinct scope and purpose.

THINKING THROUGH A READING

1. What perspective on the Hollywood star system does Giannetti present in this essay?

2. Although much of what Giannetti says here is likely already known by his readers, what information is new to you? How does he draw you into his essay and keep your interest, even though much of this information is commonly known?

The American Star System
Louis Giannetti

The star system has been the backbone of the American film industry since the mid-1910s. Stars are the creation of the public, its reigning favorites. Their influence in the fields of fashion, values, and public behavior has been enormous. "The social history of a nation can be written in terms of its film stars," Raymond Durgnat has observed. Stars confer instant consequences to any film they appear in. Their fees have staggered the public. In the 1920s, Mary Pickford and Charles Chaplin were the two highest paid employees in the world. Contemporary stars such as Julia Roberts and Tom Cruise command salaries of many millions per film, so popular are these box-office giants. Some stars had careers that spanned five decades: Bette Davis and John Wayne, to name just two. Alexander Walker, among others, has pointed out that stars are the direct or indirect reflection of the needs, drives, and anxieties of their audience: They are the food of dreams, allowing us to live out our deepest fantasies and obsessions. Like the ancient gods and goddesses, stars have been adored, envied, and venerated as mythic icons.

Prior to 1910, actors' names were almost never included in movie credits because producers feared the players would then demand higher salaries. But the public named their favorites anyway. Mary Pickford, for example, was first known by her character's name, "Little Mary." From the beginning, the public often fused a star's artistic persona with his or her private personality, sometimes disastrously. For example, Ingrid Bergman's much-publicized love affair with Italian director Roberto Rossellini created a scandalous uproar in the United States in the late 1940s. It nearly wrecked her career, not to speak of her psyche. She was a victim of her own public image, which had been carefully nurtured by her boss, producer David O. Selznick. In the public mind, Bergman was a wholesome, almost sainted woman—modest and simple, a happy wife and mother. This image was buttressed by her most popular roles: the radiantly ethereal Ilsa in *Casablanca*, the fervent political idealist in *For Whom the Bell Tolls*, the warm indomitable mother superior in *The Bells of St. Mary's*, and the notable warrior-saint of *Joan of Arc*. In reality, Bergman was an ambitious artist, anxious to play a variety of roles, including villainess parts. When she and Rossellini met, they soon fell in love, and though still married to her first husband, Bergman became pregnant with Rossellini's child. When her condition became public, the press had a field day, indulging in an orgy of lurid speculations and attacking her for "betraying" her public. She was reviled by religious groups and even denounced from the floor of the U.S. Senate, where she was described as "Hollywood's apostle of degradation" and "a free-love cultist." Bergman and Rossellini married in 1950, but their joint movies were boycotted in the United States, and she remained out of the country for several years. She was apparently "forgiven" in 1956, when she won her second Academy Award (best actress) for her performance in *Anastasia*, a big box-office success.

Unless the public is receptive to a given screen personality, audiences can be remarkably resistant to someone else's notion of a star. For example, producer Samuel Goldwyn ballyhooed his Russian import, Anna Sten, without stinting on costs. But audiences stayed away from her movies in droves. "God makes stars," the chastened Goldwyn finally concluded. "It's up to the producers to find them."

Sophisticated filmmakers exploit the public's affection for its stars by creating ambiguous tensions between a role as written, as acted, and as directed. "Whenever the hero isn't portrayed by a star the whole picture suffers," Hitchcock observed. "Audiences are far less concerned about the predicament of a character who's played by someone they don't know." When a star rather than a conventional actor plays a role, much of the characterization is automatically fixed by the casting; but what the director and star then choose to add to the written role is what constitutes its *full* dramatic meaning. Some directors have capitalized on the star system with great artistic effectiveness, especially studio-era filmmakers.

Distinguishing Between Writing Assignments That Require an Informative Essay and Those That Require an Academic Essay

At first, it may be difficult to distinguish between an informative essay and an essay that requires an argument; in fact, we have found this to be one of the major stumbling blocks for students in successfully completing their writing assignments. Recognizing this distinction will keep you from offering a summary when you have been asked to give an analysis, or vice versa. Again, with an informative essay, your purpose is to *inform* your readers; with an academic essay, your purpose is to evaluate, interpret, or state a position in a way that *persuades* your readers. To help you to better differentiate between the two, look at these examples of overarching statements for each type.

EXAMPLE:
Discuss the economic policies of the current president.

CI statement (found in an informative essay):

Like other presidents, the current president believes that one important way to improve the American economy is to reduce taxes on small businesses.

Thesis statement (found in an academic essay):

> Like other presidents, the current president believes that the best way to improve the American economy is to reduce taxes on small businesses, and he is right.

OR

> As the economy recovers from this unprecedented recession, the best way to foster economic growth is to reduce taxes on small businesses, as the current president has done.

Notice that the assignment asks you to "discuss" the economic policies of the president and doesn't clarify whether an informative essay or a persuasive essay is required. Also, it is impossible to tell if you are required to write a full essay or something shorter, such as a response essay or a short answer. Before moving forward, ask your instructor to say more about the goals of the assignment so that you can (1) determine the proper format for fulfilling the assignment; and (2) if an essay is required, determine whether to use the informative essay or the academic essay format.

If you are doing an *informative essay* in response to this assignment, your job will be to present the ideas of the current president regarding tax reduction. Whether you agree with him or not is irrelevant. The essay's purpose is to inform the reader as objectively as possible about the president's views on tax cuts.

However, if you're writing a *persuasive essay* about the relationship between tax cuts and the American economy, you would use a thesis statement and the academic essay format. This would require you to go beyond merely summarizing and synthesizing the information for your reader; you would also need to show, as the thesis says, that "he is right," that the president's policy on tax cuts is the best policy for the economy. This adds an additional layer or burden of proof to the essay. Now your explanation of the ideas will include an argument about what makes these policies sound.

....

DID YOU KNOW . . .

When your assignment is not clear about whether you should write an informative essay or an academic essay, you can examine the assignment's word choices for clues. Some terms suggest an informative essay that requires a synthesis of information. Other terms invite interpretation and analysis that call for an academic essay. The following gives examples of both types. Be sure to check with your instructor if you are not clear about your assignment.

Informative Essay	Academic Essay
illustrate	evaluate
describe	analyze
explain	interpret
summarize	determine significance of
synthesize	argue
collect	assess
present	respond to

....

The Scientific Paper

The scientific essay format gives a writer a structure for presenting the **results and significance of primary research**. Like the academic essay, the goal of the scientific paper is to present a compelling argument. In the scientific paper, however, the argument is presented in a format that accommodates the step-by-step investigation of the particular problem or gap in knowledge that the experiment seeks to resolve. In fact, the rigors of the scientific method, with its focus on the objective testing of a hypothesis using a systematic and rigorous experimental approach, are well accommodated by the scientific paper's format, which demands a clear context, a focused question for the experiment, the systematic recording of results, and an analytical discussion.

The conventional subheadings of the scientific paper format are especially well suited for reporting information clearly and efficiently; yet the scientific paper's format is flexible enough to adapt to a variety of studies or experiments. Typically, an *introduction* sets the stage for the study, followed by a description of the *methods* used to attain the data. Then the *results* and a *discussion* of their significance are given. In short, this format requires a level of care and accuracy that helps to ensure the integrity of the research.

A misconception you may have about the scientific paper is that it is used only in the natural sciences, when a scientific experiment has been completed and the results merit reporting. In fact, the scientific paper format is regularly required in courses across the curriculum when an assignment involves primary research in the lab or in the field. Here are some across-the-discipline examples of when the scientific essay format may be used:

Sociology class
- to report the results of a field study about the behavior patterns among adolescent youths in a computer gaming arcade

English class
- to report the results of your study of the effectiveness of the campus Online Writing Lab (OWL)

Business class
- to report the findings of a study about where it would be best to build the next fast food franchise in your neighborhood

Teacher education class
- to report the results of a study on the reading patterns of accelerated learners

Those of you who are studying natural science, business, social studies, or teaching will frequently use this format beyond your college years, such as when you perform research and present your findings in a public forum. The scientific essay format is assigned because it allows you to systematically present the purpose and context of your study, the methods/materials you used, and the results that you discovered and their significance. It even accommodates the use of charts, graphs, and diagrams. Although the academic essay format could be used to investigate the above assignments, it doesn't accommodate as well the types of information associated with a study involving primary research.

Using the Hypothesis

The scientific paper is much like the academic essay in the sense that both writing formats have the goal of presenting a clear and compelling interpretation of evidence. Therefore, both essay structures rely on a precisely articulated overarching statement to unify the essay and give it significance. The overarching statement for the scientific paper is called the *hypothesis*. The hypothesis establishes a framework for the study, overarches all parts of the paper, and gives the paper purpose.

In Greek, the word *hypo* means "under," so a *hypo*thesis is a type of thesis that lays the groundwork or foundation for the paper by putting forward a claim that serves as a basis for further investigation. A good hypothesis offers a testable theory about the physical world; it proposes an explanation that requires proof concerning how one aspect of the world operates. Like the thesis statement in the academic essay, the hypothesis represents an interpretation of facts made after long and careful study, and the hypothesis has the responsibility of organizing and unifying the scientific paper's information. In other words, it gives the paper a clear purpose.

....

DID YOU KNOW . . .

The scientific essay began about 300 years ago and was modified by Louis Pasteur in the nineteenth century. In attempting to defend his findings, Pasteur added a detailed "methods" section in his reports that allowed his doubters to replicate his experiments and corroborate his results. In doing so, he helped to pave the way for the scientific paper whose form is codified today and known widely by the acronym IMRAD.

....

IHMRAD: The Scientific Paper Format

There are five basic building blocks in the scientific paper: the **I**ntroduction, the **H**ypothesis, the **M**ethods and Materials used in the study, the **R**esults achieved, **A**nd a **D**iscussion of the significance of those results (**IHMRAD**).[2] Each of these basic sections carries the responsibility of responding to one of the central questions required to complete a study involving primary research. Here are the questions that shape each of the basic parts of the scientific essay.

---

[2] We have found Robert A. Day's use of the acronym IMRAD effective (see *How to Write and Publish a Scientific Paper*, Oryx Press, 1998). According to Day, the IMRAD acronym was codified in 1972 and again in 1979 by the American National Standards Institute. To call attention to the hypothesis' important role in the paper, we have modified the acronym by adding an "H" to allow for the isolation and discussion of the important role of the hypothesis in the scientific paper.

The Five Basic Questions for the Scientific Paper	Where to Put the Answers
1. What concept, question, or procedure was studied?	Introduction
2. What answer did you expect to find?	Hypothesis
3. How was the question, concept, or procedure studied?	Methods & Materials
4. What were the findings?	Results
5. Were these findings expected? What do the findings mean?	Discussion

Although the IHMRAD sections represent the conventional building blocks for the scientific paper format, in practice the writer has some freedom to modify this form. For example, you may decide that an abstract or bibliography must be added to best display the significance of your project, so your paper may be A-IHMRAD (abstract added) or IHMRAD-B (bibliography added). Occasionally, your instructor may ask you to present the details of your experiment using added subheadings—for instance, a background section may be included in the introduction. Or you may be asked to organize your paper using headings such as data rather than results and significance rather than discussion. The flexibility of these section titles testifies to the flexibility of this essay format. IHMRAD's five basic building blocks represent the material that is critical to fulfilling the expectations of readers by contextualizing the hypothesis and supplying the information necessary to test its validity and identify its significance.

The purpose of the *introduction* in the scientific paper is the same as that of the introduction in academic and informative essays. That is, it sets the context for the essay by providing enough background information so that readers can understand the significance of the study, and it presents the paper's argument, often in the form of a prediction, called the hypothesis. The introduction bridges whatever information gap may exist between the reader and the paper's subject matter; it prepares the reader to fully understand the importance of the study and the significance of its results.

The *methods and materials* section recounts in as clear and objective a manner as possible the design of the study undertaken and materials used. The narrative should generally be chronological, giving the reader the step-by-step procedures used in the study. The focus here is on a systematic recounting of the step-by-step methods used to gather the data. Save the presentation of the data for the results section and the analysis of the data for the discussion section. If done well, the reader will be able to duplicate the study exactly and corroborate its findings, which itself can be an important contribution.

Describing the steps of a study is not always as easy as it sounds. Narrative strategies such as summarizing and describing will help you communicate this information clearly and systematically. You may want to include subheadings, numbering, and visual depictions as well. For instance, if your study involves a variety of materials, you may want to create a subheading for materials that is separate from methods.

Again, this type of adaptation is common to IHMRAD and, when well chosen, works in the interest of both reader and writer. Of course, it will improve the accuracy of your methods and materials section if you are neat, meticulous, and systematic when you are conducting the study.

The *results* section is where the data are presented to the reader. This section may open with a brief summary (usually a sentence or two) of the overall results. The data should be displayed in as accessible a form as possible. Sometimes the best choice of display is a narrative form; other times, the data may be arranged through the use of charts, graphs, tables, or other means of illustration to give the reader a clear, condensed overview of the results of the study. Rely on writing strategies such as clear description, summary, classification, and comparison to help you to negotiate this important section of the paper. Creative illustrations can be used if they can better help you to organize complex or confusing sets of information. Be careful, however, to remain as objective as possible—no opinions or analysis should appear in the results section, only objective data.

In the *discussion* section, the data are analyzed, and conclusions are drawn. Here, the writer should return to the hypothesis and discuss its validity (or its lack of validity) by revisiting the background material and comparing the results of this particular study to previous studies. In giving your analysis, be sure to include enough detail from the results to make your interpretation of the evidence compelling. Your reader wants to know why and how you came to the conclusion that you did. The burden is on you to describe, step-by-step, the chain of logical reasoning that led you to your interpretation. Again, this final section should present a discussion of the results, not a summary of them. It should explore the significance of the results in relation to the hypothesis, not reiterate what data were discovered in the experiment. Explore any new questions or problems that your study has provoked. When appropriate, suggest the direction future research might take to build on the knowledge gained by your study. See figure 8.2 for a diagram of a scientific paper.

The Scientific Paper and Writing Assignments Across the Curriculum

Here we illustrate the versatility of the scientific paper writing format by giving examples of assignments from across the curriculum where the instructor may expect the scientific paper format or a customized version of it. We hope that the following illustrations will give you a better overview of when you might be asked to use this paper structure and affirm the usefulness of this writing format for presenting empirical research. These examples are based on actual assignments.

Example 1: A Class on Business Statistics
This assignment follows the IHMRAD structure exactly, but it doesn't use the conventional IHMRAD subheadings. If you look closely, you will see that each of the five basic parts of the scientific paper is required in this assignment, as well as two add-on parts.

Fig. 8.2 Diagram of a Scientific Paper

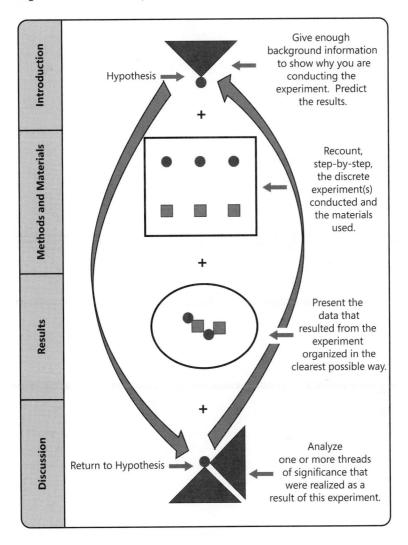

ASSIGNMENT:

The final project for this class requires you to apply one or more of the statistical tools you learned in class to a real-world problem. You can work in groups and choose any real-world business problem you want. The final report should take the following format:

1. *Executive Summary* (include the real-world business problem identified, research questions proposed, and quick summary of findings).

   This section is added onto the six basic parts of the IHMRAD structure. It Summary is basically a discipline-specific abstract that, in the field of business, is used to give an overview of a research study.

2. *Purpose and Focus of Study* (business problem, motivation for problem, research question)

> *This is a standard introduction, including the background, context, and a hypothesis for the study. It asks for the "problem," "motivation for problem," and "research question," but on closer inspection you should see that these requirements are the basics of IHMRAD's introduction.*

3. *How the Study Was Conducted* (choices of design, how the questionnaire was developed, how the data were collected, how respondents were sampled, how the data were analyzed, possible limitations)

4. *Findings* (answer to research question)

5. Conclusion

6. *Appendix* (survey, computation of sample size, pretest results)

> *This is another add-on section that gives the reader additional materials and data that the instructor considers to be somewhat peripheral to the basic design of the study, but important for the larger project.*

You can see from this assignment for a business class that this project represents a typical use of the scientific paper format—it calls for the application of course concepts to the real world—even if using subheadings different from IHMRAD.

Example 2: A Sociology Class on Social Norms

This assignment asks you to conduct interviews in the field to determine the most common criteria for choosing a mate in the United States. None of the typical IHMRAD subheadings are mentioned in this assignment sheet. However, the design of the assignment—which requires a primary research study and a writing format that can accommodate the information generated—lends itself to using the scientific paper format. Note the way your awareness of the IHMRAD structure helps you understand some of the more obscure aspects of the assignment and gives you a clear and compelling format for responding to this assignment.

ASSIGNMENT: WHO WILL BE YOUR MATE?
1. Reread the section in your textbook that discusses the issue of choosing a marriage partner or mate. In your paper, discuss the norms for choosing a marriage partner or mate that exist within U.S. culture. Specifically, design a field study that will answer the following question: In the United States, what characteristics are most important when choosing a marriage partner or mate?

> *Instead of subheadings, this instructor gives numbered sections. Because you are familiar with IHMRAD, you would know that the expectation is for you to propose a response to this question in the form of a hypothesis. Notice that the instructor expects much of the background information to come from the course text and discussions. It might be a good idea to do some background research in addition to the textbook to strengthen your introduction and discussion sections.*

2. Consider the following list of social characteristics:

age	athletics	social class
education	race	ethnicity
chemistry	beliefs	physical appearance
gender	hygiene	
political views	religion	

3. Design a study to determine which five characteristics are most important for marriage/mate selection. Consider interviewing those who are single and those who are married, collecting information from dating services, conducting a survey or experiment, and so forth.

> It will be helpful if you recognize that steps 2 and 3 are actually the basis for IHM-RAD's methods and materials section. It will be important here to identify what methods you will use to collect the desired information. What materials will you require (e.g., a survey instrument, a tape recorder, a chart, interviewers)? How you design your experiment is the core of the study. Although the assignment doesn't explicitly ask you to recount in your paper the design and implementation of your study, it is assumed that you will describe the study undertaken in enough detail to shed light on the reliability of the data gathered as well as allow another researcher to replicate the experiment and confirm your results. Because the quality of the results will be directly linked to the quality of the study you conduct, be sure to keep careful records regarding the experiment (say, in a field notebook) since they will be invaluable when it comes time to write this section of your paper.

4. Select the five characteristics your study reveals to be the most important in marriage/mate selection. For example, will similarity of age be an important factor in your study? Why? Do your data suggest that it is important that potential mates be from the same religious background? Why? From your research, does someone's physical appearance make the top 5 list? Discuss.

> Notice that this section calls for both the results of your study as well as some analysis of those results. Typically, these two types of information are separated in the scientific paper format. However, this instructor seems to prefer that the analysis of each characteristic follow its listing. We have already mentioned that this format is often customized to suit the goals of the assignment, so you might ask your instructor if she or he wants the results and the analysis within the same section. If your instructor has little preference, then we recommend that you present the results and analysis separately since this will give you a very clear structure for presenting what is likely to be complex information. When writing your analysis, don't forget to discuss your results with reference to your hypothesis. How did your study prove or disprove your hypothesis?

5. Based on the findings of your study, discuss the ways in which social norms influence the choice of a marriage partner or mate, if at all. Can you conclude that marriage or mate selection is an act of free will or is it dictated by social norming?

These questions call for an add-on section, a conclusion, where you use the results of your study to speculate further about the possible implications of what you have found. You are not given a lot of direction for answering this complex question. Consider going back to the course textbook and class notes to find ways to build on your analysis to speculate about the implications for your study's results. Often, this section will suggest new directions for future research.

Notice that even though this instructor never mentions the conventional subheadings for the scientific paper, these basic parts are suggested by the requirements of the assignment. This is a good example of an assignment that requires a student to "read between the lines" to determine what, exactly, are the general goals of the assignment, what should be discussed in the final paper, and what format should be used for the paper's presentation. Many writing assignment prompts are thin, but an instructor will usually provide further details in class to clarify the expectations and goals. It's very important that you fully understand these expectations and goals before attempting an assignment. You can help yourself by asking questions about an assignment when it's unclear and then aligning an assignment's goals with the conventions of the appropriate writing format discussed in this chapter.

Example 3: A Course in Developmental Psychology

The goal of this paper is to assess the appropriateness of a toy for a particular developmental stage of a child. The assignment requires you to make a toy and test its viability for its target age group and document the results.

ASSIGNMENT: MAKE AN AGE-APPROPRIATE TOY

1. Select an age group between one and six, review the developmental qualities associated with this age group, and make a toy appropriate for a child in this age group. Be sure to consider safety first in selecting the materials you will use.

2. Provide an overview of the developmental stages for a child in your age group.

3. Identify the age group for which your toy is appropriate and briefly give your rationale.

   You can see that both steps 2 and 3 require the basic content of the introduction portion of IHMRAD. Your understanding of IHMRAD's structure and the purpose of the assignment should give you enough information to confidently complete this portion of the paper. You should recognize, for instance, that step 3 is asking for a hypothesis, even if that word is never used.

4. Test the effectiveness of your toy. Explain the methods you used to test the toy. You might use techniques such as field observation (e.g., length of play, how toy is used, success of the toy to amuse), interviews, interaction, and so forth. Be sure to include a description of your toy and be careful to organize your data so that it is clear.

This is the methods and materials section of this paper. It must describe the materials used to create the toy (a reader might even expect an illustration of it) and includes a full discussion of the methods used to test its age-appropriateness.

5. Present your conclusions. Based on your findings, discuss whether the toy is age appropriate. Were there any negative aspects of the toy that deserve consideration? Are there any modifications to the toy that you would recommend?

Here you will have to first present your results and then discuss of those results. As you know, we recommend two separate sections for this. Consider presenting your data using pictures, graphs, charts, and other visual mediums for clarity and efficiency. In the discussion, be sure to return to your hypothesis to discuss its viability and speculate, as the prompt urges, about whether there are modifications that might improve the toy.

Again, although this study didn't mention IHMRAD explicitly, using it will help you successfully complete this assignment.

We hope that this focus has shown you the ways that IHMRAD is used across the curriculum and that you are now better prepared to recognize when it might help you complete college writing assignments. Knowing the fundamental purpose of each section of IHMRAD will help you unpack a writing assignment, complete a study using the scientific method, and document a study and its significance.

A Note on Purpose and Audience

With the scientific paper, it may be particularly easy to assume that good writing isn't as important as the ability to do careful research—that the research data will speak for itself. Yet, even the best research may go unrecognized or be misunderstood if the researcher cannot show the value of a study through clear and persuasive writing. Unlike the academic essay that often uses rhetorical devices to persuade, the scientific paper does not make use of rhetorical flourishes, such as metaphor, figures of speech, colorful openings, quotes, or colloquial language. Instead, it should be as direct and objective as possible. Generally speaking, when writing the scientific paper, you should use language that is clear, simple, and precise. However, sometimes anecdotes or creative analogies might be effective in drawing the reader's interest. After all, some of the best ideas may be lost because they are not effectively conveyed. The best advice is to consider using rhetorical devices in the scientific paper only when you are sure they will further the readers' understanding of the purpose, design, and significance of your experiment.

Writing Formats for Building the Scientific Paper

We have discussed the importance of careful record keeping concerning the methods and materials used for empirical research. There are two standard formats—one geared toward laboratory experiments and the other for work in the field—used for collecting evidence and recording reflections about that evidence. These two standard formats—the laboratory report and the field notebook—are used in college classes across the disciplines. They can be assigned as independent assignments or as building-block assignments for a formal scientific paper or an academic essay Each has its own particular conventions, but they are flexible and may be modified to suit particular writing contexts and objectives.

The Laboratory Report

The **lab report** is a detailed record of a scientific experiment that generally follows the scientific paper format and represents an experiment from its inception to its conclusion. Lab reports should be detailed, accurate, and thorough, as they provide the basis for the conclusions that you will draw from experiments. Lab reports do the following:

- Help you practice the scientific method through precise, meticulous, and thorough data recording/

- Give you a means for systematically keeping track of data, observations, results, and other details of an experiment or laboratory assignment/

- Give you a systematic format through which to test ideas and informally speculate and comment on the results of an experiment/

- Help you master the conventional format for recording a scientific experiment by using the IHMRAD structure/

Laboratory reports can be used by instructors as stand-alone assignments, but they are often used as a means of collecting evidence for the formal scientific paper assignment that will follow. A series of lab experiments, captured in lab reports, often become the means of arriving at an informed hypothesis and a formal paper. The lab report is usually assigned in courses in the natural or social sciences where students are required to do first-hand, empirical research. As a record of empirical research, it serves as the bedrock of the scientific process, which requires you to be objective, precise, and thorough regarding both the experiment and the recording of it.

Although the lab report mirrors the format of the scientific paper, there is an important difference between the two. The lab report uses what we call a *naïve hypothesis* as opposed to the *informed hypothesis* used in the formal paper. In other words, the hypothesis in the lab report presents your best prediction of the results based on the background material you have read. In the lab report, you test your best guess with an experiment. In the end, the experiment may not support your hypothesis, and further study will be required. Your job in the discussion section is to decide how well the actual results of your experiment aligned with the results you predicted in your hypothesis. You will comment meaningfully on the insights you've gained. In the scientific paper, however, the experiment or experiments have already been completed and the hypothesis you present will be based on the supporting data collected from all these experiments.

The Format of a Laboratory Report

The lab report is a less formal version of the scientific paper, but it retains the scientific paper's five-part structure. The lab report typically begins with an *Introduction* that provides background on the experiment. Every lab experiment seeks to answer a question, and the introduction to the lab report puts forward a context for the question being tested. In short, it summarizes the information we already have and speculates about why further investigation is necessary. The *Hypothesis* is stated at the end of the introduction. It tells the reader what you, the experimenter, expect the answer to be to the question that you are investigating. A section on *Methods* and *materials* then details the design of your experiment, exactly what steps you followed, and what materials you used to perform your study. The *Results* section records your findings. *And* finally, you discuss your experiment as a whole in a *Discussion* section, including a review of the validity of your hypothesis given the results of the experiment. These five standard parts combine to form the conventional format both for the scientific paper and for its less formal version, the lab report.

Characteristics of a Successful Lab Report

▶ The level of detail reflects systematic, meticulous research.

▶ The aim of the research is clearly stated, as are the methods used to test them.

▶ The data collected are precisely and clearly recorded.

▶ The observations about the experiment are detailed and consistently recorded throughout the experiment.

▶ The IHMRAD format or an alternative format is followed, as per the instructor's directions.

Characteristics of a Weak Lab Report

▶ The level of detail in the notebook is unreliable because it is too general to see what procedures were followed in the experiment.

▶ The aim of research is unclear, as are methods used to test them.

▶ Important data from the experiment are missing.

▶ Observations about the experiment are too vague, subjective, or inconsistent to be meaningful.

▶ The format prescribed by the instructor is not followed.

Because the lab report is generally less formal than the scientific paper, data may be recorded using lists, random notes, marginalia, graphs, diagrams, rough charts, sketches, or other visual depictions. Instructors may also choose to vary the IHMRAD structure based on the objectives for a particular experiment. At minimum, though, the lab report will include an experiment's methods, data, and observations.

In your lab classes, you will often be asked to do some preliminary work before coming to the lab. This work will likely be divided up according to the IHMRAD structure. For example, you might be asked to read the background material and instructions for the lab and draft the IHM (introduction, hypothesis, methods and materials) sections in the lab notebook. Mastery of the lab report is essential for the scientist because it provides a systematic format, through its five-part IHMRAD structure, that ensures a thorough accounting of the experiment performed. You will have to be meticulous in completing the report. As much as possible during the experiment, record the results as you go. This is one way to maximize accuracy. Waiting until the end of the experiment to record all the methods you used or results you found risks missing important details or making errors. Also, keep in mind that the results section is meant to record—as objectively as possible—the outcomes of your experiment. This is not the place for your opinions or interpretations—save those for the discussion section.

Example of a Student Lab Report

Ashley Gungle

Lab #1 Drosophila Cross

PURPOSE STATEMENT [HYPOTHESIS]:
The purpose of this lab is to cross a wild type *Drosophila* parent with a recessive parent to produce an F1 generation. The F1 generation will then be self-crossed to produce an F2 generation to study Mendelian patterns of inheritance.

INTRODUCTION:
Like the pea plants used by Mendel, the *Drosophila melanogaster* or fruit fly is important for understanding and investigating genetic principles. *Drosophila* are a good model organism because they are easy to rear in the lab, have short life cycles, and reproduce prolifically. As well as being a good model organism, *Drosophila* are relatively easy to sex because males and females differ in several ways. Females have an elongated abdomen, seven abdominal segments, and no sex comb. Males have a rounded abdomen, five abdominal segments, and a sex comb made up of ten black bristles on the front pair of legs. The entire *Drosophila* genome has been sequenced. *Drosophila* contain 170×10^6 nucleotide pairs and 13,792 genes.

In this lab, I will be performing a dihybrid cross to produce an F1 and F2 generation. A dihybrid is an individual that is heterozygous for two pairs of alleles. The progeny of a cross between homozygous parents differing in two respects are also called dihybrids.

METHODS:

This lab was performed over several weeks to allow for the growth of each generation of flies. During the first week of this experiment, the flies were first examined to compare any differences between the wild type flies (+) and the apterous, sepia flies. During this examination, the flies were examined for phenotype to be used in the first test cross. In the first test cross, one or two apterous, sepia males were crossed with five to eight wild type virgin females. This vial was labeled F1 and left to reproduce and grow. The following week, week 2, the parental flies were removed from the F1 vial. The F1 flies were then allowed to hatch and grow. The next week, week 3, the F1 phenotypes were observed and recorded. The F1 flies were then sexed, and F1 males were crossed with F1 females. During week 4, the parental (F1) flies were removed. The F2 larvas were then left to hatch and grow. During the final week, week 5, the F2 offspring were observed, and it was determined which gene(s) are recessive.

RESULTS:

P: ♀ +/+, +/+ (x) ♂ ap/ap, se/se

possible gametes +/+, +/+ and ap/se, ap/se

+/+, +/+ ap/se, ap/se

F1*:

	+/+	+/+	+/+	+/+
ap/se	+/ap, +/se	+/ap, +/se	+/ap, +/se	+/ap, +/se
ap/se	+/ap, +/se	+/ap, +/se	+/ap, +/se	+/ap, +/se
ap/se	+/ap, +/se	+/ap, +/se	+/ap, +/se	+/ap, +/se
ap/se	+/ap, +/se	+/ap, +/se	+/ap, +/se	+/ap, +/se

*All F1 progeny are +/ap, +/se.
*All F1 progeny show the wild type phenotype.
*All red eyes and normal wings.

Chi squared test

obs	Exp
14	9
2	3
0	3
0	1
16	16

$$\frac{(14-9)^2}{9} + \frac{(2-3)^2}{9} + \frac{(0-3)^2}{3} + \frac{(0-1)^2}{1}$$

2.78 + .11 + 3.00 + 1.00

$$x^2 = 6.89$$

$$cv = 3.84/df = 1$$

F2:

	+/+	+/se	ap/+	ap/se
+/+	+/+, +/+	+/+, +/se	+/ap, +/+	+/ap, +/se
+/se	+/+, +/se	+/+, se/se	+/ap, +/se	+/ap, se/se
ap/+	+/ap, +/+	+/ap, +/se	ap/ap, +/+	ap/ap, +/se
ap/se	+/ap, +/se	+/ap, se/se	ap/ap, +/se	ap/ap, se/se

* 9:3:3:1 ratio

actual*

14	9	+/_, +/_
2	3	+/_, se/se
0	3	ap/ap, +/_
0	1	ap/ap, se/se

*ap and se are recessive.

DISCUSSION:

From our knowledge of *Drosophila* and their modes of sexual inheritance, we expected that the progeny of the F2 generation would show Mendelian inheritance with a 9:3:3:1 ratio of +/_, +/_ : +/_, se/se : ap/ap, +/_ : ap/ap, se/se. We counted a total of 16 flies in our F2 progeny. Of these flies, the ratio was 14:2:0:0 instead of 9:3:3:1. With such a small sample size, this is understandable. With a larger sample size, possibly hundreds or thousands of flies, we would expect to get closer to the 9:3:3:1 ratio. Even compiling our class data may have improved the validity of our ratio. Because our chi squared value was 6.89, we can conclude that our data did not fit the 9:3:3:1 Mendelian ratio.

The Field Notebook

The **field notebook** is typically less structured than the laboratory notebook, and it is used to record evidence gathered in the field rather than in the laboratory. A student researcher might sit on a bench in a shopping mall, for instance, and record observed behaviors between mothers and their children for a sociology project concerning parent/child interaction. A professional archaeologist studying the culture of an ancient village might use a field notebook to draw a diagram of a dig site, including a description of artifacts discovered and the locations where they were found. A behavioral psychologist may use it to record chimpanzee behavior in response to a stuffed teddy bear. The use of the field notebook can vary widely from course to course and among different academic disciplines and professions. In developing a field notebook, you will do the following:

- Systematically gather and precisely record data and evidence.

- Develop the art of objective observation.

- Connect observations about an environment outside the classroom to lessons within the classroom (e.g., lectures, course readings, scholarly research).

However the field notebook is used in your course, the most important thing to remember is that careful, objective, detailed observation is a skill that requires practice. The challenge is to train yourself to set aside your personal biases to examine the world from as neutral a position as possible. Only in this way will you collect reliable data that can be corroborated by other researchers.

The Formats for a Field Notebook

Because the field notebook must accommodate different academic research situations, its format can vary widely. Instructors assign the field notebook with different goals in mind, so its scope and structure can vary. Instructors may ask you to turn in sections of your notebook as a way to check your progress on an assignment; they may want it turned in at the end of the project to corroborate the formal write-up of the results of your study; or they may not require you to turn it in at all because they are more interested in seeing the final results of your research than your rough record of data collection. Make sure you are clear about your instructor's requirements when you are assigned a field notebook because this format is especially adaptable.

When beginning an assignment that requires research in the field, begin with a controlling idea—some question or problem that shapes your fieldwork—and, if possible, a *tentative hypothesis* that your fieldwork is meant to verify. The field notebook, then, serves as a repository for systematic record keeping. It will likely give some remarks about the context and design of your study—the *introduction* and *methods/materials*— and offer a thoughtful *discussion* based on the *results*—the data collected.

Collecting data in the field can present unique challenges. Whenever working in the field means making detailed notes quickly to isolate specific events within a complex environment, the format of the field notebook may be open-ended and draftlike. (In other words, you may be frantically making notes.) The field notebook can be written in paragraph form, especially those sections devoted to reflecting on the data, but it may also include lists, random notes, marginalia, graphs, diagrams, rough charts, or interview questions. In some cases, instructors will require you to use the IHMRAD format.

The written record in your field notebook may serve as the first steps toward refining your understanding of the problem you set out to solve. You can use the recorded experiments in your field notebook to refine your tentative thesis and establish its validity using the data and insights you explored in your field research. Hence, the field notebook, like the laboratory notebook, contains the basic building blocks for a formal academic essay or scientific paper.

If no set format has been assigned to your field notebook, it is a good idea to establish one for yourself before beginning your project. You may want to consider working with three components: (1) the purpose of the study; (2) the methods you will use to conduct the study; and (3) after considering the type of data you expect to collect, the format you will use to record the data. Simply writing down observations with no plan may leave you with more questions than answers when you are through. Write as you go, if at all possible—don't wait until you return home and then try to capture your observations through memory. In addition to taking notes, use recording devices, if appropriate. Review the recording and document important information not captured in your original notes. When your evidence is numerical, consider using charts, graphs, pie charts, or other visual depictions. Give some thought to the kinds of information you are trying to record and choose a format that helps you make the most sense of this data later. Are you observing a mother/child interact? Are you digging up an artifact? The real point here is to think beforehand about how you might organize and systematize the types of evidence you are likely to be collecting.

Characteristics of a Successful Field Notebook

▶ The level of detail reflects systematic, objective research.

▶ The aim of research is clear, as are the methods used.

▶ The data collected are precisely and clearly recorded.

▶ The observations are detailed and consistent.

▶ An IHMRAD format or alternative format is followed, when required.

Characteristics of a Weak Field Notebook

▶ The level of detail in the notebook is unreliable because it is too general to see what procedures were followed in the experiment.

▶ The aim of research is unclear, as are the methods used.

▶ Important data from the experiment are missing.

▶ Observations about the experiment are too vague, subjective, or inconsistent to be meaningful.

▶ The format prescribed by the instructor is not followed.

Summary

In conclusion, there are three primary essay forms used for college writing. While the informative essay, the academic essay, and the scientific paper draw on somewhat different organizational structures, they all depend on the same skills of clarity, logic, purpose, and unity to put forward an author's discoveries. Because an essay's agenda is so critical to clear communication, each of these essays requires an overarching statement. In the informative essay, the *CI statement* is used to convey information rather than overtly interpret that information in the form of an argument. In the academic essay, the thesis statement is used to interpret evidence to persuade the reader of a particular position. In the scientific paper, the hypothesis is used to predict the results of a primary research study. Because the informative essay, the academic essay, and the scientific paper represent long-established conventions for writing, using these forms to share the conclusions drawn from extended critical thinking will predispose your readers to better comprehend and accept your ideas.

APPLICATIONS AND WRITING EXERCISES

Application 8.1

Study the following sentences and then discuss what makes them likely candidates for a successful CI statement. What kinds of information would you expect to find in each essay?

1. Artist George Segal's works of the mid-twentieth century are often noted for the way they capture the period's mood of alienation and anxiety.

2. By the middle of the twentieth century, American architecture often reflected an international quality.

3. The various processes that a utility company must be involved with to collect and deliver natural gas to its customers make up the company's main source of income.

4. Today, Igor Stravinsky is known as one of the most influential figures in the history of twentieth-century music.

5. Eighteenth-century scientists made notable advances in the field of biology.

Application 8.2

Study these sentence pairs. Determine which of each pair is a CI statement and which is a thesis statement. Explain your choices.

1. (a) The eighteenth century is generally thought to be history's greatest age of satire.

   (b) The eighteenth century is history's greatest age of satire.

2. (a) Although scholars agree that Freud has significantly influenced the way we understand ourselves and the working of the human psyche, many now believe that he made some questionable judgments and was wrong in some of his formulations.

   (b) Freud has significantly influenced the way we understand ourselves and the working of the human psyche, but he made some questionable judgments and was wrong in some of his formulations.

Application 8.3

For the following sample essay assignment, decide which essay format—the academic essay, the informative essay, or the scientific paper—should be used and why.

> In heterogeneous groups of three to four students, you will develop as a group a multicultural research paper. Your research should include at least three sources from the Eric database, at least three sources from the Internet, at least three print media sources, and at least one of the texts used in class. The paper will include the following:
>
> 1. A cover page listing the title and a 200-word abstract consisting of two or three paragraphs
>
> 2. A narrative that describes the issue, including its historical context

3. A description of why the issue is significant in the field of education

4. Your position on the issue and why you have taken that position

5. A defense or rationale for taking the position, with appropriate references

6. A conclusion regarding the issue with recommendations for action

7. An annotated bibliography of all references consulted and attachments such as your visual aids, graphic organizers, or any supplementary material developed to enhance student learning

The length of this essay is determined by the degree to which you articulate the requirements outlined above. Depth of analysis is more important than providing in-depth description. In other words, your essay should tell why and how more fully than it tells who, what, when, or where. Put your effort into articulating the issue, rather than into developing a fancy cover for your essay.

Writing Exercise 8.1

Look again at the essay that appears on page 184, "The American Star System" What is the essay's CI statement? Does it overarch the information contained in the essay? In one or two paragraphs, describe how each paragraph fits within the scope of the CI statement.

Writing Exercise 8.2

1. Design a field notebook for the following assignment. What section headings would you use? What would you expect to record in each section?

Problem: How important is a nickel? A dime? A quarter?

In class, discuss the attitudes toward loose change in your community. How much effort do you think people are generally willing to expend for free money? Would it be worth their effort to pick up a penny? A nickel? A dime? Remember, do not impose your own ideas regarding the value of a coin. Will the responses differ based on gender, age, social class, place, time of day? Make a prediction (i.e., offer a hypothesis). Now design a small experiment to test your hypothesis. You might find a spot in a public place where you can sit comfortably and overlook people's reactions to coins on the ground. Will they notice them with interest? Will they bother to pick them up and keep them? You might vary the place, the time of day, and the coin to see if you observe any consistent responses to coins on the ground.

2. Design and carry out an experiment in response to this prompt.

In a few paragraphs, discuss your results and what was useful regarding your field notebook format. Compare your responses with your peers.

CHAPTER 9
Writing about Literature

You do not have to be an English major to write a successful essay about literature. In this section, we'll show you how the basic principles we have explored in previous chapters, including C-S-C, the seven steps, and managing burdens of proof, can guide you in writing an interpretive essay about a short story, a novel, a poem, a film, or a play. This is most often done by exploring a work's metaphors and analyzing its literary techniques—such as plot, setting, character, and theme. The goal of this kind of essay is to reveal insights that enhance a reader's enjoyment and appreciation of the work.

When we read literature, we respond to it personally. We like or dislike its characters, we are touched by its passion and joy, we appreciate its humor, and we understand its sorrow. When you are asked to write an essay about literature, however, your job is to say **how** and **why** the work had these effects on you. This requires you to think critically about the work to discover the means by which an author, a director, or a playwright achieved these effects. When you begin to look closely at a work, to read critically and observe in a detailed way how and why it achieves its effects, you begin asking what the work **means**.

yes

A literary work is always open to new interpretations, and good literature is rich enough to evoke a variety of insightful and valid claims that are equally interesting. Your goal is to offer a perspective that your readers will learn from—an interpretation not easily recognizable on a first reading of the work. The seven steps can guide you to systematically think through the ideas you have about a text but don't be alarmed if your essay doesn't develop along a straight and narrow path from conception to final product. Unexpected and insightful interpretations often require you to take a circuitous route of discovery and often the less-traveled paths. When you are armed with both reason and imagination, these paths are the most productive.

WHAT'S AHEAD . . .

▶ thesis statements about literature

▶ developing a thesis statement about plot

▶ developing a thesis statement about a character

▶ developing a thesis statement about a theme

▶ developing a thesis statement from a personal opinion

Thesis Statements about Literature

As with any academic essay, when you write an essay that offers an interpretation of literature, you use a thesis statement to present your point of view—your claim about what you think the story or some part of the story is illustrating. The thesis statement, like any thesis statement, carries burdens of proof that the supporting paragraphs in the body of the essay must fulfill. As you have learned, interesting thesis statements can develop in any number of directions. However, your specific goal with an interpretive claim isn't so much to offer the *best* interpretation as it is to offer a *provocative* perspective—one that is insightful, well supported, and unique in the sense that it's presented from your individual point of view.

To show you how to generate, develop, and support a thesis statement about literature, we'll turn again to the seven steps discussed in chapter 6, this time pausing on steps 4 and 5 to introduce another strategy for exploring thesis statement development by asking questions. Our intention is to illustrate the patterns of questioning in hopes that you will begin to develop questions of your own and use them to generate insightful essays.

Developing a Thesis Statement about Plot

Often, interesting thesis claims come from a close examination of the plot development of a novel or a story. One way to do this systematically is to think about the three, four, or five events that propel the story forward, the significant events that must be included if you are telling the story to a friend who hasn't read it. These are called the **plot points**. You can develop a thesis statement by asking a question about a plot point and then exploring it.

We illustrate the application of the seven steps to a writing assignment about one of the most popular novels of the twentieth century: *The Great Gatsby.*

> Write an analytical essay giving an interpretation of Fitzgerald's novel The Great Gatsby. The essay should open with a clearly stated thesis statement that makes a claim of interpretation about the novel. The thesis should be supported in the essay with explanation and examples from the text.

Steps 1, 2, and 3

For this assignment, the key terms are analytical essay—interpretation, and *The Great Gatsby.* The context is Fitzgerald's novel *The Great Gatsby,* and the insightful idea you find in steps 4–6 will become the subject of your thesis statement. The primary question is clear: You must write an analytical essay that gives an interpretation of this important work. Notice that this is essentially an open-ended prompt where you are free to choose your own focus for the essay.

Step 4

Your observation list should consist of any important plot events. These might be events that help shape the action of the story, or they may be details about the story that seem strange or unexpected, for instance:

- Gatsby's first meeting with Daisy after a long separation

- Nick's move to West Egg

- Tom's affair with Myrtle

- Myrtle's death

- Jay Gatsby's death

Step 5

In this step, you select a plot point from your observation list and freewrite about the following questions in an effort to move from observing to interpreting.

a. *How would the story be different if this event were not present?*

b. *What are the plot details that surround this event?*

c. *What are the effects of this event on the rest of the novel?*

For this example, we are exploring the issue of Gatsby's death at the end of the novel.

a. *How would the story be different if Gatsby did not die?*

> If Gatsby did not die, then we would not see how truly empty and pitiful his life is-that those who cling to his wealth in life desert him in death.

b. *What are the details that surround Gatsby's death?*

> He is murdered, killed in a moment of misplaced vengeance. He is shot in the swimming pool by a man nearly deranged, in a moment when Gatsby is completely vulnerable.

c. *What are the effects of that death on the rest of the novel?*

> The effects include seeing that he has no real friends in the world—even Daisy, the woman for whom he does everything, lets him take the blame. Gatsby's death brings his father into the novel, and his father shows the reader the book that Gatsby inscribed when he was young. The inscription shows how conscientiously Gatsby fashioned himself after the American dream. His death reveals, ironically, that everything that Gatsby has lived for has been meaningless. His American dream is shown to be bankrupt of people who care.

Step 6

Examine your freewriting to see if there is an insightful idea that can be abstracted.

In examining the answers to the previous questions, one of the promising observations has to do with the author's use of Gatsby to represent and critique the American dream—the myth of rags-to-riches. If we summarize the most promising points, they might look like this:

> Gatsby's murder shows that the American dream is dark, empty, and meaningless. It ultimately sheds light on Gatsby's society and shows that he/they live for money instead of good human relationships.

Step 7

Using C-S-C, if we place Gatsby in the subject position of the thesis and condense the stated conclusion into a precise claim, we come up with the following:

Context: *The Great Gatsby*
Subject: Gatsby or Gatsby's death
Claim: Gatsby's death at the end of the novel reveals a critique of the American dream of rags to riches

Working Thesis:
> The character of Gatsby in Fitzgerald's *The Great Gatsby* acts ultimately as the vehicle to critique the American dream.

It is interesting to note that this example began by asking questions about a plot point but ultimately led to a thesis that offers an interpretation of a character. As with all complex literature, there are many other directions this example could have taken to formulate a thesis statement. Rather than focusing on the American dream, for instance, it could have isolated the theme of violence from the plot points we wrote. This might have led to a thesis that explored the numerous examples of violence in the novel, including Tom punching Myrtle, two car accidents, and Gatsby's murder. Such a thesis claim might call attention to the irony of so much bloody violence in a society that appears on the outside to be so refined and its members so fulfilled. This thesis was developed by asking questions about a plot point in a novel, but this method of questioning can be applied in other ways, as well.

Developing a Thesis Statement about a Character

The thesis claim may also come from a character analysis, in which you select one persona in the book for careful study. A character analysis can represent an ethical, psychological, moral, sociological, or cultural position or argument. Or, a character can be used as an allegory, a metaphor, or an archetype to further a theme or message. There are many things characters can bring to a text. Asking questions about what a character represents in a literary text is another way of working toward a thesis statement.

Following is a writing assignment about *Lord of the Flies*, by William Golding, that demonstrates one way to use the seven steps to build a character analysis.

> Choose a character from Golding's *Lord of the Flies* and write a five-page essay that interprets his role in the novel.

Steps 1–3

The key terms in this prompt are choose a character—interpret his role and *Lord of the Flies*. Although the context and primary question can be spotted easily, the subject is not stipulated, except that it must be one of the characters from the novel. Again, think of this as an open-ended prompt where your job, in part, is to determine the subject you will write about.

Step 4

Your observation list should include all the characters you might have an interest in exploring. These may be characters who are important for the moral of the story, ones that help to shape the action of the story, and/or characters who seem unusual or unexpected, for instance:

Ralph	Roger
Jack	Sam
Piggy	Eric
Simon	

Step 5

To help select one character, freewrite about several of the characters. You might try to answer the following questions:

a. *What are the character's dominant traits or characteristics?*

What associations does this trait have in society (e.g., positive or negative aspects or any connotations this trait has)? Determine which of the associations apply to the character you have chosen. Can you conclude or abstract anything about the character based on this comparison?

b. *Why is this character in the text? How does the character add to the story's message?*

c. *How would the story be different if this character were omitted?*

This is one way you might begin the freewriting for the *Lord of the Flies* writing assignment:

Ralph: He is twelve years old with blond hair and is the most popular of the group. He is described as strong, and he is chosen as the leader because he has many positive qualities. He and Jack are always in conflict because Ralph wants order but Jack doesn't.

Jack: He is skinny with red hair and freckles and is not very attractive physically. He seems angry and savage. When he becomes the leader of some of the boys, they turn to hunting. Jack doesn't care about having a peaceful society and seems to want the strong to dominate using aggression and brutality.

Piggy: He is short, overweight, and wears glasses. He has asthma and can't do hard work. He tries to keep peace among the boys, but he isn't popular and no one listens. He is smart and tries to have a system of fairness and order.

Continue with the rest of the characters listed in step 4.

Let's imagine that you choose Jack to explore further because you think that there are some interesting tensions in his character that might be fruitful to investigate.

a. List the character's dominant traits or characteristics.

skinny

red hair and freckles

wants power

likes hunting

Write an observation list about the trait itself (that is, think of it apart from the text). Below we use *likes hunting* to exhibit the process:

- Hunting is associated with violence because it involves deadly weapons and the destruction of animals.

- Hunting requires aggression and determination.

- People who hunt are thought to leave behind most of the conveniences and conduct of civilized life and enter the world of nature and the animals.

- Hunters rely on their physical qualities—strength, endurance, agility and skill with weapons.

- Hunting has been associated with social importance because hunters historically provided food for their societies, and this gave the hunter authority and great stature.

- Hunters were also revered for character traits such as courage, determination, and instinct, traits that were associated with a hunter's success.

Determine which of the associations that you listed apply to the character you have chosen.

- Hunting is associated with violence because it involves deadly weapons and the destruction of animals.

  This is true of Jack; He's a good hunter who revels in the blood and gore of the chase and kill. He destroys not only animals—but goes after a human.

- Hunting requires aggression and determination.

  Jack is the leader of the hunters, and he is fearless when it comes to getting his prey. He's the epitome of aggression and determination in the novel.

- People who hunt are thought to leave behind most of the conveniences and con-duct of civilized life, and enter the world of nature and the animals.

  The island is a nature preserve away from civilization, and this is where Jack is able to cast off the civilized life with a sense of relief rather than retaining feelings of loss or nos-talgia. When in nature, like an animal, he operates by primitive instinct and seems to be in tune with—rather than alien to—the forces around him. He even casts off his clothing, wearing only paint, and dresses like a savage to experience the "fun" of the hunt.

- Hunters rely on their physical qualities—strength, endurance, agility, and skill with weapons.

  Jack has all of these—strength, endurance, agility, and skill with weapons—he's the leader of the hunters, an exemplar of physicality.

- Hunting has been associated with social importance because hunters historically provided food for their societies, and this gave the hunter authority and great stature.

  Jack's skill at hunting and his physical agility convince the other boys that he can protect them. Eventually he gets so much mastery over the group that they start addressing him as "chief" and following his orders. Jack's stature and authority are so admired that he slowly but surely entices Ralph's followers to his side.

- Hunters are also revered for character traits such as courage, determination, and instinct—traits that are associated with a hunter's success.

  All of these traits are all also true of Jack.

b. Why is this character in the text? How does the character add to the story's message?

Jack serves as a foil for Ralph and Piggy because his ideas and qualities are seen as extreme when compared with the choices of other characters in the story. He represents one among a range of options, and seeing him in relation to the others brings out the strengths and weaknesses, as well as the problems, of all of their ideas.

c. How would the book be different if this character weren't present?

If not for Jack, Ralph and Piggy would be able to lead the group and probably form a society that is much less violent and more democratic. Perhaps without Jack, Ralph might even find the skill to hunt for food and be able to balance the violence necessary for hunting with the reason and compassion that make for a good society. Ralph's leadership would be much more civilized; and because he is more moderate, he might not be challenged. In short, without Jack, the book would have a completely different plot and ending.

Step 6

We isolate, for more focused study, some interesting ideas developed in steps 4 and 5.

1. Jack is a good hunter who revels in the blood and gore of the chase and kill. He destroys animals—and he even goes after a human.

2. Jack is the leader of the hunters, and he is fearless when it comes to getting his prey. He's the epitome of aggression and determination in the novel.

3. The island is a nature preserve away from civilization. This is where Jack is able to cast off the civilized life with a sense of relief. He seems to have no feelings of loss or nostalgia for the society he left behind. When in nature, like an animal, he operates by primitive instinct and seems to become in tune with—rather than alien to—the forces

around him. He even casts off his clothing, wears only paint, and dresses like a savage to experience the "fun" of the hunt.

4. Jack has all of these—strength, endurance, agility, and skill with weapons—he's the leader of the hunters, a model of physical strength.

5. Jack's skill at hunting and his physical agility convince the other boys that Jack can protect them. Eventually he gets so much mastery over the group that they start addressing him as "chief" and following his orders. Jack's stature and authority are so admired that he slowly but surely entices Ralph's followers to his side.

We can use abstraction to find some connections among the items on the list. We can identify at least three overarching topic ideas:

1, 2, and 4. Jack is by nature a skilled and dedicated hunter.

3. Because of his nature, he is more at home when away from civilization, where he can freely use his hunting instincts and skills.

5. In the wild, Jack's skills allow him to have influence over the group and become their leader.

One conclusion that can be drawn from these ideas is that hunting makes Jack more and more uncivilized. The more he calls on violence and aggression for hunting, the less able he is to restrain himself when dealing with others. His obsession with hunting causes his aggressive and violent side to take over, and this consumes him and those around him. This preoccupation reduces existence to a life of savagery. Once he takes up the role of leader for the group, he establishes a society based on the aggressive and violent qualities that are Jack's priority as a hunter. This society is self-destructive because it is outside the controls of a lawful civilization.

If life itself is reduced to an aggressive impulse, then Jack represents only one part of human nature—a part, however, that takes over the rest. He gives in to the part of us that is animal-like or savage. Ultimately, he shows that if we allow one side of our nature to dominate us (unlike a character like Ralph who shows more balance), destruction cannot be far behind. This last idea seems very insightful. Notice how this example used freewriting and an observation list in a recursive way, moving back and forth between them until an insightful idea developed.

Step 7

Let's use C-S-C to shape our insightful idea into a working thesis statement:

Context: Golding's *Lord of the Flies*
Subject: Jack
Claim: allowing violence and aggression to take over ultimately leads to destruction

Working Thesis:
> In William Golding's *Lord of the Flies*, Jack shows that allowing violence and aggression to take over the self ultimately leads to the destruction of society.

If an in-depth exploration of one character trait for one character doesn't produce useful results, you can ask yourself any number of questions to help unpack that trait or the character more fully. For instance, you can examine other characters in terms of the same trait or delve into their own dominant traits (e.g., How does this character's dominant trait compare with the virtues and vices of other characters? What message is revealed as a result of this comparison?).

Or, you might use the observations you've made about one character as a foil for the other characters in the text. Here, Jack's affinity for hunting makes him appear even more violent, aggressive, and dangerous when compared to Piggy. On the other hand, Piggy's dominant traits—his physical weakness and intellectualism—are more pronounced when compared with Jack. We see the extent of Jack's cruelty in his treatment of Piggy. The comparison shows how extreme Jack is, especially when compared with a more balanced character, like Ralph. You can see how, by asking questions about the observations you make, new and interesting ideas will come to light, any of which might lead you to an insightful perspective and a working thesis statement.

When using these questions to help generate a thesis statement, remember that they are meant to be adapted to your writing needs. Depending on your task, you may need to revise some of the questions, create new ones, skip some, or tackle them in a different order. Whatever the case, they are simply tools that can help you work through the process of analyzing a character in a systematic and productive way.

Developing a Thesis Statement about a Theme

A theme is an idea that is given significant attention in an artistic work. Sometimes when working with literature, it is relatively easy to recognize a theme, such as jealousy, love, race relations, family unity, or identity struggle. Most works have more than one theme, but usually one or two are dominant. Because dominant themes are often easy to spot, they may be a natural place to begin when generating a thesis statement.

Notice that we pause at steps 5 and 6 to show you how to use questioning to come up with an insightful idea. For this focus on a theme, questions a, b, and c will get you started with your analysis. Questions d and e may be appropriate only for certain situations, and you may have to develop additional questions on your own. As you work through this examples, the real goal is to become skilled at asking and answering questions that will lead you to develop a working thesis statement.

We use a popular fairy tale to illustrate how asking questions about a theme can lead you to generate a thesis statement.

> Write a five-page essay on a theme from the fairy tale *Snow White*.

Steps 1–3
Although steps 1–3 may seem unimportant because they are obvious in this sample writing prompt, the prompt will often be more complicated, and you will need to unpack it carefully before beginning the assignment. Prompts frequently contain helpful hints as

well as precise requirements that your instructor will expect you to take into account (see Chapters 6 and 7 for more on prompts).

Step 4

List themes, or if themes are a challenge to identify, begin by listing all the major events and plot points in the story. This may look like a summary of the story, but it will be a useful start if you are having trouble thinking of themes. Here is a list of the major events in *Snow White*.

- Snow White lives with her father and stepmother.
- She is beautiful, and her stepmother is vain and jealous.
- Her stepmother sends Snow White away to be killed so she won't compete with her beauty.
- The huntsman doesn't kill Snow White.
- Later, using the Magic Mirror, the stepmother learns that Snow White is alive and has grown up to be beautiful.
- Her stepmother learns where Snow White lives, poisons an apple, and, disguised as a peddler, gives the apple to Snow White.
- Snow White is put to sleep for a long time.
- Snow White is ultimately awakened by a kiss from a prince; she marries him and lives happily ever after.

Step 5

If your observation list is full of events and plot points rather than themes, begin the freewriting step by trying to identify any themes connected to the events listed in your observation list. For instance:

> The story may be about leaving home for the first time, following one's own conscience, or facing one's fears. Looking at the observation list created for *Snow White*, I can identify the theme of kindness when the huntsman preserves Snow White's life, the theme of true love when the prince kisses Snow White and awakens her, the theme of innocence in Snow White herself and her ability to avoid the tragic fate her stepmother desires for her, and the theme of vanity in the stepmother's self-absorption and love of herself beyond all others.

After you begin to focus upon one particular theme, try asking some of the following questions:

a. *Which characters seem most closely associated with this theme?*

b. *In which scenes does the theme appear important?*

c. *Does the presentation of the theme emphasize a particular message or point of view? Does the dialogue, plot, or tone, for example, give you a certain impression or insight about the theme?*

d. (optional) *How do descriptions of the setting add to or reinforce your impression of the theme?*

e. (optional) *Are there any recurring symbols that represent the theme? Why do you think these symbols, in particular, are effective?*

For this example, we will explore the theme of vanity and work through some freewriting questions, to find an insightful thesis statement.

a. *Which characters seem most closely associated with this theme?*

Vanity is most closely associated with the stepmother, and it is associated with everything that she does—arrogance is apparent in all of her conversations with her magic mirror, the huntsman, and Snow White.

b. *In which scenes does the theme appear important?*

There are three scenes where the theme of vanity is foregrounded. First, when the stepmother sees that Snow White is growing up to be beautiful, she becomes jealous and sends the huntsman to kill Snow White; second, when the stepmother looks into her magic mirror and is told that Snow White is still alive and is the "fairest of them all"; and third, when the stepmother tries to kill Snow White with the poisoned apple to succeed her as the most beautiful in the land.

c. *Does the presentation of the theme emphasize anything in particular about it? Does the dialogue, plot, or tone, for example, give you a certain impression or insight about the theme?*

In all three scenes, the traits of the stepmother associated with vanity include intolerance, arrogance, violence, selfishness, and competitiveness. She is driven by her vanity—her need to be the most beautiful—and this compels her to violence and hatred. She is consumed with unhappiness over her need to kill Snow White rather than be bested. The scenes seem to be saying that vanity is destructive; it destroys everyone's happiness, including the person consumed by it.

d. *How do descriptions of the setting add to or reinforce your impression of the theme?*

Vanity is tied much more directly to character and plot in this fairy tale than it is to setting. In an essay of, say, ten to fifteen pages, this could be a productive area to explore.

e. *Are there any reoccurring symbols that represent the theme? Why do you think these symbols, in particular, are effective?*

The symbol of the magic mirror comes up repeatedly in the story, highlighting the stepmother's vanity. Hypothetically, the stepmother could have asked her pet dog or her tarot cards or her crystal ball "who is the fairest of them all," but the story always returns to the symbol of the mirror. Like Narcissus in the ancient Greek myth, the stepmother's fixation with seeing herself in the mirror is an act of excessive (and destructive) self-absorption. Ironically, it reflects her moral ugliness time and time again.

Step 6

After answering these questions, notice that responses c and e hint at a claim: "The scenes show that vanity is destructive; it destroys everyone's happiness, including the person consumed by self-love." We have put vanity in the subject position of a thesis to see if we can arrive at a claim based on our responses to the questions, especially to question c, which appears most promising.

Step 7

Context: the fairy tale *Snow White*
Subject: vanity
Claim: destroys everyone's happiness, including the person consumed by self-absorption

Working Thesis:
> In the fairy tale *Snow White,* vanity destroys everyone's happiness, including that of the person consumed by self-love.

Note that you could refine this thesis statement by substituting *stepmother* for *person* because in this thesis they are one and the same. However, the purpose of an analytical essay is to shed light on an idea. If the term *stepmother* is used in this thesis statement, then the scope of the essay would be limited just to this stepmother rather than to the larger issue she represents—human vanity. In this case, and this is a minor point, we think it better not to mention the stepmother by name (other characters are not mentioned by name, either) to give the thesis wider application.

Developing a Thesis Statement from a Personal Opinion

good for Blue book

This method will work best when you find yourself reacting strongly to a work—either pro or con—and you need help channeling those strong feelings into an objective claim.

Many instructors begin a discussion about a text by asking students whether or not they liked the reading. Although personal opinions do not make for good thesis statements, they are often an effective strategy for finding a more objective claim. Your personal response to a film probably does not come from out of the blue. Although it is possible that your response will change as you analyze your personal impressions, it is more likely that asking questions about how you feel about a reading or a film will help you articulate ideas that are more objective. After you identify the objective reasons behind your personal response, you are much closer to a defensible thesis claim.

The Seven Steps

STEPS 1–3:
Steps 1–3 help you unpack the prompt.

try this together

STEP 4:

Your observation list should include any personal opinions about the text and your reasons for listing them. Don't hold back; list contradictory opinions, too. Include as many adjectives as possible that accurately describe the text. Use the following questions if they are helpful:

- How did you feel about the text? At minimum, did you like it?

- What about the text, specifically, caused you to feel this way? Try to go below the surface and get to the origin or root cause of your like or dislike.

goo apr. ?s to your topic

STEP 5:

In this step, select an opinion from your observation list and freewrite about why you liked or disliked that particular aspect of the text. This should help you move from observation to interpretation.

STEP 6:

Examine your freewriting to see if there is an overarching or insightful idea that can be abstracted. If so, move to step 7. If not, return to step 5 and choose a different opinion to explore.

STEP 7:

We have worked through just a few of the myriad working thesis statements that could have been developed from these examples through the technique of asking and then answering questions. The important thing to notice is that this technique is not a formula but rather a process that uses questioning as a productive tool. The more you practice, the better you will become at customizing the questions you ask. You might be as surprised by the moment of insight as your reader is.

When you begin to write an essay about literature, do not put pressure on yourself to write a perfect thesis statement on your first attempt. The only thing that kind of pressure readily creates is writer's block. Instead, use the seven steps to draft a working thesis. Expect to fine-tune the thesis (and the essay that develops) several times. As you go through this process, you will deepen your analysis and clarify your ideas. In other words, your essay will get better and better.

Checklist for Writing about Literature

▶ **Take the time necessary to familiarize yourself with the work you are interpreting.** Never try to put forward an interpretation without first carefully reading and studying—and rereading, several times if necessary—the poem, play, story, or novel you are writing about. The more time you spend with the text, the more insightful your interpretation will be.

▶ **Be an active reader.** Read with a pen in your hand and make notes in the text's margins about any ideas or responses you have. Note your observations, even if they are scattered across a page and seemingly disorganized. These will be useful later as you begin to ask questions about the text and try to generate a thesis statement.

▶ **Assume readers have read, or at least are generally familiar with, the work you are interpreting.** There is no need to provide a summary of the story or parts of the story except when you want to help your reader recall a point in the literature from which you are providing an example or quotation.

▶ **Limit your use of quotations.** Use only what directly demonstrates your point. Avoid lengthy quotations because often the point you want to make will be lost in the lengthy quote. (See appendix C for help with how to quote and cite using MLA and APA guidelines.)

DID YOU KNOW . . .

There are specific academic guidelines on how to quote material from literature in your essay. The guidelines for poetry are different from the guidelines for other forms of literature. See appendix C for complete details.

APPLICATIONS AND WRITING EXERCISES

Application 9.1 Freewriting about Plot
Choose a novel or short story you have read recently and do some freewriting in which you explore a question about a plot point. Develop your ideas as far as you can.

Application 9.2 Developing a Thesis Statement about Plot
When you are finished freewriting, use step 6 to examine what you have written and to see if any patterns emerge. Use abstraction to find an insightful idea. Then use C-S-C to build a working thesis statement and list its burdens of proof.

Writing Exercise 9.1 Observing, Abstracting, and Freewriting about a Character
Read William Faulkner's short story, *A Rose for Emily.* Answer the Thinking Through the Reading questions with a paragraph or less of writing for each question and then discuss your answers with others in the class.

THINKING THROUGH THE READING
1. What would be on your observation list of Miss Emily's qualities, including her physical characteristics?

2. How would you describe the townspeople's view of Miss Emily?

---

3. Describe the relationship Miss Emily had with her father. With Homer.

4. How is the South portrayed in this short story?

5. Who is narrating this story? Whose perspective does he represent?

6. We never hear Miss Emily's thoughts. If you had to speculate, what might some of these thoughts be? How might the story be different if Emily were its narrator?

7. What is meaningful about the strand of "iron-gray" hair on the pillow at the story's end?

8. Is this story completely depressing?

A Rose for Emily (1931)[1]
William Faulkner

When Miss Emily Grierson died, our whole town went to her funeral: the men through a sort of respectful affection for a fallen monument, the women mostly out of curiosity to see the inside of her house, which no one save an old manservant—a combined gardener and cook—had seen in at least ten years.

It was a big, squarish frame house that had once been white, decorated with cupolas and spires and scrolled balconies in the heavily lightsome style of the seventies, set on what had once been our most select street. But garages and cotton gins had encroached and obliterated even the august names of that neighborhood; only Miss Emily's house was left, lifting its stubborn and coquettish decay above the cotton wagons and the gasoline pumps—an eyesore among eyesores. And now Miss Emily had gone to join the representatives of those august names where they lay in the cedar-bemused cemetery among the ranked and anonymous graves of Union and Confederate soldiers who fell at the battle of Jefferson.

Alive, Miss Emily had been a tradition, a duty, and a care; a sort of hereditary obligation upon the town, dating from that day in 1894 when Colonel Sartoris, the mayor—he who fathered the edict that no Negro woman should appear on the streets without an apron—remitted her taxes, the dispensation dating from the death of her father on into perpetuity. Not that Miss Emily would have accepted charity. Colonel Sartoris invented an involved tale to the effect that Miss Emily's father had loaned money to the town, which the town, as a matter of business, preferred this way of repaying. Only a man of Colonel Sartoris' generation and thought could have invented it, and only a woman could have believed it.

When the next generation, with its more modem ideas, became mayors and aldermen, this arrangement created some little dissatisfaction. On the first of the year they mailed her a tax notice. February came, and there was no reply. They wrote her a formal letter, asking her to call at the sheriff s office at her convenience. A week later the mayor wrote her himself, offering to call or to send his car for her, and received in reply a note on paper of an archaic shape, in a thin, flowing calligraphy in faded

[1] William Faulkner, "A Rose for Emily" In *Collected Stories of William Faulkner*. New York: Vintage, 1995.

ink, to the effect that she no longer went out at all. The tax notice was also enclosed, without comment.

They called a special meeting of the Board of Aldermen. A deputation waited upon her, knocked at the door through which no visitor had passed since she ceased giving china-painting lessons eight or ten years earlier. They were admitted by the old Negro into a dim hall from which a staircase mounted into still more shadow. It smelled of dust and disuse—a close, dank smell. The Negro led them into the parlor. It was furnished in heavy, leather-covered furniture. When the Negro opened the blinds of one window, they could see that the leather was cracked; and when they sat down, a faint dust rose sluggishly about their thighs, spinning with slow motes in the single sunray. On a tarnished gilt easel before the fireplace stood a crayon portrait of Miss Emily's father.

They rose when she entered—a small, fat woman in black, with a thin gold chain descending to her waist and vanishing into her belt, leaning on an ebony cane with a tarnished gold head. Her skeleton was small and spare; perhaps that was why what would have been merely plumpness in another was obesity in her. She looked bloated, like a body long submerged in motionless water, and of that pallid hue. Her eyes, lost in the fatty ridges of her face, looked like two small pieces of coal pressed into a lump of dough as they moved from one face to another while the visitors stated their errand.

She did not ask them to sit. She just stood in the door and listened quietly until the spokesman came to a stumbling halt. Then they could hear the invisible watch ticking at the end of the gold chain.

Her voice was dry and cold. "I have no taxes in Jefferson. Colonel Sartoris explained it to me. Perhaps one of you can gain access to the city records and satisfy yourselves."

"But we have. We are the city authorities. Miss Emily. Didn't you get notice from the sheriff, signed by him?"

"I received a paper, yes," Miss Emily said. "Perhaps he considers himself the sheriff . . . I have no taxes in Jefferson."

"But there is nothing on the books to show that, you see. We must go, by the—"

"See Colonel Sartoris. I have no taxes in Jefferson."

"But, Miss Emily—"

"See Colonel Sartoris." (Colonel Sartoris had been dead almost ten years.) "I have no taxes in Jefferson. Tobe!" The Negro appeared. "Show these gentlemen out."

II

So she vanquished them, horse and foot, just as she had vanquished their fathers thirty years before about the smell. That was two years after her father's death and a short time after her sweetheart—the one we believed would marry her—had deserted her. After her father's death she went out very little; after her sweetheart went away, people hardly saw her at all. A few of the ladies had the temerity to call, but were not received, and the only sign of life about the place was the Negro man—a young man then—going in and out with a market basket. "Just as if a man—any man—could keep a kitchen properly," the ladies said; so they were not surprised when the smell developed. It was another link between the gross, teeming world and the high and mighty Griersons. A neighbor, a woman complained to the mayor, judge Stevens, eighty years old.

"But what will you have me do about it, madam?" he said.

"Why, send her word to stop it," the woman said. "Isn't there a law?"

"I'm sure that won't be necessary," judge Stevens said. It's probably just a snake or a rat that nigger of hers killed in the yard. I'll speak to him about it."

The next day he received two more complaints, one from a man who came in diffident deprecation.

"We really must do something about it judge. I'd be the last one in the world to bother Miss Emily, but we've got to do something." That night the Board of Aldermen met—three gray-beard and one younger man, a member of the rising generation.

"It's simple enough," he said. "Send her word to have her place cleaned up. Give her a certain time to do it in, and if she don't. . ."

"Dammit, sir," judge Stevens said, "will you accuse a lady to her face of smelling bad?"

So the next night, after midnight, four men crossed Miss Emily's lawn and slunk about the house like burglars, sniffing along the base of the brickwork and at the cellar openings while one of them performed a regular sowing motion with his hand out of a sack stung from his shoulder. They broke open the cellar door and sprinkled lime there, and in all the outbuildings. As they recrossed the lawn, a window that had been dark was lighted and Miss Emily sat in it, the light behind her, and her upright torso motionless as that of an idol. They crept quietly across the lawn and into the shadow of the locusts that lined the street. After a week or two the smell went away.

That was when people had begun to feel really sorry for her. People in our town, remembering how old lady Wyatt, her great-aunt, had gone completely crazy at last, believed that the Griersons held themselves a little too high for what they really were. None of the young men were quite good enough for Miss Emily and such. We had long thought of them as a tableau; Miss Emily a slender figure in white in the back-ground, her father a spraddled silhouette in the foreground, his back to her and clutch-ing a horsewhip, the two of them framed by the back-flung front door. So when she got to be thirty and was still single, we were not pleased exactly, but vindicated; even with insanity in the family she wouldn't have turned down all of her chances if they had really materialized.

When her father died, it got about that the house was all that was left to her; and in a way, people were glad. At last they could pity Miss Emily. Being left alone, and a pauper, she had become humanized. Now she too would know the old thrill and the old despair of a penny more or less.

The day after his death all the ladies prepared to call at the house and offer condolence and aid, as is our custom. Miss Emily met them at the door, dressed as usual and with no trace of grief on her face. She told them that her father was not dead. She did that for three days, with the ministers calling on her, and the doctors, trying to persuade her to let them dispose of the body. Just as they were about to resort to law and force, she broke down, and they buried her father quickly.

We did not say she was crazy then. We believed she had to do that. We remembered all the young men her father had driven away, and we knew that with nothing left, she would have to cling to that which had robbed her, as people will.

III

She was sick for a long time. When we saw her again, her hair was cut short, making her look like a girl, with a vague resemblance to those angels in colored church windows-sort of tragic and serene.

The town had just let the contracts for paving the sidewalks, and in the summer after her father's death they began the work. The construction company came with niggers and mules and machinery, and a foreman named Homer Barron, a Yankee—a big, dark, ready man, with a big voice and eyes lighter than his face. The little boys would follow in groups to hear him cuss the niggers, and the niggers singing in time to the rise and fall of picks. Pretty soon he knew everybody in town. Whenever you heard a lot of laughing anywhere about the square, Homer Barron would be in the center of the group. Presently we began to see him and Miss Emily on Sunday afternoons driving in the yellow-wheeled buggy and the matched team of bays from the livery stable.

At first we were glad that Miss Emily would have an interest, because the ladies all said, "Of course a Grierson would not think seriously of a Northerner, a day laborer." But there were still others, older people, who said that even grief could not cause a real lady to forget *noblesse oblige*—without calling it *noblesse oblige*. They just said, "Poor Emily. Her kinsfolk should come to her." She had some kin in Alabama; but years ago her father had fallen out with them over the estate of old lady Wyatt, the crazy woman, and there was no communication between the two families. They had not even been represented at the funeral.

And as soon as the old people said, "Poor Emily," the whispering began. "'Do you suppose it's really so?" they said to one another. "Of course it is. What else could. . ." This behind their hands; rustling of craned silk and satin behind jalousies closed upon the sun of Sunday afternoon as the thin, swift clop-clop-clop of the matched team passed: "Poor Emily."

She carried her head high enough—even when we believed that she was fallen. It was as if she demanded more than ever the recognition of her dignity as the last Grierson; as if it had wanted that touch of earthiness to reaffirm her imperviousness. Like when she bought the rat poison, the arsenic. That was over a year after they had begun to say "Poor Emily," and while the two female cousins were visiting her.

"I want some poison," she said to the druggist. She was over thirty then, still a slight woman, though thinner than usual, with cold, haughty black eyes in a face the flesh of which was strained across the temples and about the eye-sockets as you imagine a lighthouse-keeper's face ought to look. "I want some poison," she said.

"Yes, Miss Emily. What kind? For rats and such? I'd recom—"

"I want the best you have. I don't care what kind."

The druggist named several. "They'll kill anything up to an elephant. But what you want is—"

"Arsenic," Miss Emily said. "Is that a good one?"

"Is . . . arsenic? Yes. ma'am. But what you want—"

"I want arsenic."

The druggist looked down at her. She looked back at him, erect, her face like a strained flag. "Why, of course," the druggist said. "If that's what you want. But the law requires you to tell what you are going to use it for."

Miss Emily just stared at him, her head tilted back in order to look him eye for eye, until he looked away and went and got the arsenic and wrapped it up. The Negro delivery boy brought her the package; the druggist didn't come back. When she opened the package at home there was written on the box, under the skull and bones: "For rats."

IV

So the next day we all said, "She will kill herself"; and we said it would be the best thing. When she had first begun to be seen with Homer Barron, we had said, "She will marry him." Then we said, "She will persuade him yet," because Homer himself had remarked—he liked men, and it was known that he drank with the younger men in the Elks' Club—that he was not a marrying man. Later we said, "Poor Emily" behind the jalousies as they passed on Sunday afternoon in the glittering buggy, Miss Emily with her head high and Homer Barron with his hat cocked and a cigar in his teeth, reins and whip in a yellow glove.

Then some of the ladies began to say that it was a disgrace to the town and a bad example to the young people. The men did not want to interfere, but at last the ladies forced the Baptist minister—Miss Emily's people were Episcopal—to call upon her. He would never divulge what happened during that interview, but he refused to go back again. The next Sunday they again drove about the streets, and the following day the minister's wife wrote to Miss Emily's relations in Alabama.

So she had blood-kin under her roof again and we sat back to watch developments. At first nothing happened. Then we were sure that they were to be married. We learned that Miss Emily had been to the jeweler's and ordered a man's toilet set in silver, with the letters H. B. on each piece. Two days later we learned that she had bought a complete outfit of men's clothing, including a nightshirt, and we said, "They are married." We were really glad. We were glad because the two female cousins were even more Grierson than Miss Emily had ever been.

So we were surprised when Homer Barron—the streets had been finished some time since—was gone. We were a little disappointed that there was not a public blowing-off, but we believed that he had gone on to prepare for Miss Emily's coming, or to give her a chance to get rid of the cousins. (By that time it was a cabal, and we were all Miss Emily's allies to help circumvent the cousins.) Sure enough, after another week they departed.

And, as we had expected all along, within three days Homer Barron was back in town. A neighbor saw the Negro man admit him at the kitchen door at dusk one evening.

And that was the last we saw of Homer Barron. And of Miss Emily for some time. The Negro man went in and out with the market basket, but the front door remained closed. Now and then we would see her at a window for a moment, as the men did that night when they sprinkled the lime, but for almost six months she did not appear on the streets. Then we knew that this was to be expected too; as if that quality of her father which had thwarted her woman's life so many times had been too virulent and too furious to die.

When we next saw Miss Emily, she had grown fat and her hair was turning gray. During the next few years it grew grayer and grayer until it attained an even pepper-and-salt iron-gray. when it ceased turning. Up to the day of her death at seventy-four it was still that vigorous iron-gray, like the hair of an active man.

From that time on her front door remained closed, save for a period of six or seven years, when she was about forty, during which she gave lessons in china-painting. She fitted up a studio in one of the downstairs rooms, where the daughters and grand-daughters of Colonel Sartoris' contemporaries were sent to her with the same regularity and in the same spirit that they were sent to church on Sundays with a twenty-five-cent piece for the collection plate. Meanwhile her taxes had been remitted.

Then the newer generation became the backbone and the spirit of the town, and the painting pupils grew up and fell away and did not send their children to her with boxes of color and tedious brushes and pictures cut from the ladies' magazines. The front door closed upon the last one and remained closed for good. When the town got free postal delivery, Miss Emily alone refused to let them fasten the metal numbers above her door and attach a mailbox to it. She would not listen to them.

Daily, monthly, yearly we watched the Negro grow grayer and more stooped, going in and out with the market basket. Each December we sent her a tax notice, which would be returned by the post office a week later, unclaimed. Now and then we would see her in one of the downstairs windows—she had evidently shut up the top floor of the house— like the carven torso of an idol in a niche, looking or not looking at us, we could never tell which. Thus she passed from generation to generation—dear, inescapable, impervious, tranquil, and perverse.

And so she died. Fell in the house filled with dust and shadows, with only a doddering Negro man to wait on her. We did not even know she was sick; we had long since given up trying to get any information from the Negro. He talked to no one, probably not even to her, for his voice had grown harsh and rusty, as if from disuse.

She died in one of the downstairs rooms, in a heavy walnut bed with a curtain, her gray head propped on a pillow yellow and moldy with age and lack of sunlight.

V

The Negro met the first of the ladies at the front door and let them in, with their hushed, sibilant voices and their quick, curious glances, and then disappeared. He walked right through the house and out the back and was not seen again.

The two female cousins came at once. They held the funeral on the second day, with the town coming to look at Miss Emily beneath a mass of bought flowers, with the crayon face of her father musing profoundly above the bier and the ladies sibilant and macabre; and the very old men—some in their brushed Confederate uniforms—on the porch and the lawn, talking of Miss Emily as if she had been a contemporary of theirs, believing that they had danced with her and courted her perhaps, confusing time with its mathematical progression, as the old do, to whom all the past is not a diminishing road but, instead, a huge meadow which no winter ever quite touches. Divided from them now by the narrow bottleneck of the most recent decade of years.

Already, we knew that there was one room in that region above stairs which no one had seen in forty years, and which would have to be forced. They waited until Miss Emily was decently in the ground before they opened it.

The violence of breaking down the door seemed to fill this room with pervading dust. A thin, acrid pall as of the tomb seemed to lie everywhere upon this room decked and furnished as for a bridal: upon the valance curtains of faded rose color, upon the rose-shaded lights, upon the dressing table, upon the delicate array of crystal and the man's toilet things backed with tarnished silver, silver so tarnished that the monogram was obscured. Among them lay collar and tie, as if they had just been removed, which, lifted, left upon the surface a pale crescent in the dust. Upon a chair hung the suit, carefully folded; beneath it the two mute shoes and the discarded socks.

The man himself lay in the bed.

For a long while we just stood there, looking down at the profound and fleshless grin. The body had apparently once lain in the attitude of an embrace, but now the long sleep that outlasts love, that conquers even the grimace of love, had cuckolded him. What was left of him, rotted beneath what was left of the nightshirt, had become inextricable from the bed in which he lay; and upon him and upon the pillow beside him lay that even coating of the patient and biding dust.

Then we noticed that in the second pillow was the indentation of a head. One of us lifted something from it, and leaning forward, that faint and invisible dust dry and acrid in the nostrils, we saw a long strand of iron-gray hair.

Writing Exercise 9.2

1. Look over the story "A Rose for Miss Emily" again and list Miss Emily's dominant traits or characteristics. You might also want to consult the answers you gave to the questions in Exercise 9.1 that refer to the character Miss Emily.

2. Now choose a character trait that seems dominant in "A Rose for Miss Emily" and write an observation list about the trait itself; that is, think of it as a quality or character trait on its own, apart from the text.

3. List all the associations this trait has in society (e.g., positive or negative aspects, any connotations this trait has). Determine which of the associations apply especially to Miss Emily. Can you conclude or abstract anything about her character based on this

comparison? Do some freewriting to develop your ideas. If you reach a dead end, go back to the list of traits and explore another. Write answers to the following:

- Why is this character in the text? How does the character add to the story's message?

- How would the story be different if this character were omitted?

4. Examine your list and freewriting and use abstraction to formulate a working thesis statement using C-S-C. List the burdens of proof.

Writing Exercise 9.3 Writing about a Theme

Read the beginning of Stephen Crane's "The Open Boat" that appears below and then read the in-class student essay about a theme of the story. Use the peer review form in chapter 5 to evaluate the student essay for insight, clarity, development, and structure. We have started the review for you with a few comments in brackets. When you have completed the peer review, revise this essay based on your own recommendations. As a part of the revision, extend it to five double-spaced pages. Compare some of the resulting essays (a Web-based application such as Blackboard or an overhead projector might be useful). How similar were the revised essays in your group or class? If you were to revise the essay again based on the discussion, what would you change and why?

do this part if there is time

THINKING THROUGH THE READING

1. The preface of "The Open Boat" is often referred to as being written in "journalistic style" (or sometimes "mock journalistic style"). Why do you think Crane included these words before his short story? What do you think is being mocked, if anything?

2. Why do you think the oiler is the only man in the boat who is given a name? Is it significant that his name is "Billie"?

3. Characterize each of the men in the boat. Does each get his due in terms of poetic justice?

4. Why does Crane repeat this phrase in the text: "If I am going to be drowned . . . why in the name of the seven mad gods, who rule the sea, was I allowed to come so far and contemplate sand and trees?"

p. 127

The Open Boat (1897)
Stephen Crane

A Tale Intended to be after the Fact:
Being the Experience of Four Men
From the Sunk Steamer Commodore

None of them knew the color of the sky. Their eyes glanced level, and were fastened upon the waves that swept toward them. These waves were of the hue of slate, save for the tops, which were of foaming white, and all of the men knew the colors of the sea. The horizon narrowed and widened, and dipped and rose, and at all times its edge was jagged with waves that seemed thrust up in points like rocks.

Many a man ought to have a bath-tub larger than the boat which here rode upon the sea. These waves were most wrongfully and barbarously abrupt and tall, and each froth-top was a problem in small-boat navigation.

The cook squatted in the bottom, and looked with both eyes at the six inches of gunwale which separated him from the ocean. His sleeves were rolled over his fat forearms, and the two flaps of his unbuttoned vest dangled as he bent to bail out the boat. Often he said, "Gawd! That was a narrow clip." As he remarked it he invariably gazed eastward over the broken sea.

The oiler, steering with one of the two oars in the boat, sometimes raised himself suddenly to keep clear of water that swirled in over the stern. It was a thin little oar, and it seemed often ready to snap.

The correspondent, pulling at the other oar, watched the waves and wondered why he was there.

The injured captain, lying in the bow, was at this time buried in that profound dejection and indifference which comes, temporarily at least, to even the bravest and most enduring when, willy-nilly, the firm fails, the army loses, the ship goes down. The mind of the master of a vessel is rooted deep in the timbers of her, though he command for a day or a decade; and this captain had on him the stern impression of a scene in the grays of dawn of seven turned faces, and later a stump of a topmast with a white ball on it, that slashed to and fro at the waves, went low and lower, and down. Thereafter there was something strange in his voice. Although steady, it was deep with mourning, and of a quality beyond oration or tears.

"Keep 'er a little more south, Billie," said he.

"A little more south, sir," said the oiler in the stern.

A seat in this boat was not unlike a seat upon a bucking broncho, and, by the same token, a broncho is not much smaller. The craft pranced and reared and plunged like an animal. As each wave came, and she rose for it, she seemed like a horse making at a fence outrageously high. The manner of her scramble over these walls of water is a mystic thing, and, moreover, at the top of them were ordinarily these problems in white water, the foam racing down from the summit of each wave, requiring a new leap, and a leap from the air. Then, after scornfully bumping a crest, she would slide and race and splash down a long incline, and arrive bobbing and nodding in front of the next menace.

A singular disadvantage of the sea lies in the fact that, after successfully surmounting one wave, you discover that there is another behind it, just as important and just as nervously anxious to do something effective in the way of swamping boats. In a ten-foot dinghy one can get an idea of the resources of the sea in the line of waves that is not probable to the average experience, which is never at sea in a dinghy. As each slaty wall of water approached, it shut all else from the view of the men in the boat, and it was not difficult to imagine that this particular wave was the final outburst of the ocean, the last effort of the grim water. There was a terrible grace in the move of the waves, and they came in silence, save for the snarling of the crests.

In the wan light the faces of the men must have been gray. Their eyes must have glinted in strange ways as they gazed steadily astern. Viewed from a balcony, the whole thing would, doubtless, have been weirdly picturesque. But the men in the boat had no time to see it, and if they had had leisure, there were other things to occupy their minds. The sun swung steadily up the sky, and they knew it was broad day because the color of the sea changed from slate to emerald-green streaked with ember lights, and the foam was like tumbling snow. The process of the breaking day was unknown to them. They were aware only of this effect upon the color of the waves that rolled toward them.

In disjointed sentences the cook and the correspondent argued as to the difference between a life-saving station and a house of refuge. The cook had said: "There's a house of refuge just north of the Mosquito Inlet Light, and as soon as they see us they'll come off in their boat and pick us up."

"As soon as who sees us?" said the correspondent.

"The crew," said the cook.

"Houses of refuge don't have crews," said the correspondent. "As I understand them, they are only places where clothes and grub are stored for the benefit of shipwrecked people. They don't carry crews."

"Oh, yes, they do," said the cook.

"No, they don't," said the correspondent.

"Well, we're not there yet, anyhow," said the oiler in the stern.

"Well," said the cook, "perhaps it's not a house of refuge that I'm thinking of as being near Mosquito Inlet Light; perhaps it's a life-saving station."

"We're not there yet," said the oiler in the stern.

II

As the boat bounced from the top of each wave the wind tore through the hair of the hatless men, and as the craft plopped her stern down again the spray slashed past them. The crest of each of these waves was a hill, from the top of which the men surveyed for a moment a broad, tumultuous expanse, shining and wind-riven. It was probably splendid, it was probably glorious, this play of the free sea, wild with lights of emerald and white and amber.

"Bully good thing it's an on-shore wind," said the cook. "If not, where would we be? Wouldn't have a show."

"That's right," said the correspondent.

The busy oiler nodded his assent.

Then the captain, in the bow, chuckled in a way that expressed humor, contempt, tragedy, all in one. "Do you think we've got much of a show now, boys?" said he.

Whereupon the three were silent, save for a trifle of hemming and hawing. To express any particular optimism at this time they felt to be childish and stupid, but they all doubtless possessed this sense of the situation in their minds. A young man thinks doggedly at such times. On the other hand, the ethics of their condition was decidedly against any open suggestion of hopelessness. So they were silent.

"Oh, well," said the captain, soothing his children, "we'll get ashore all right."

But there was that in his tone which made them think; so the oiler quoth, "Yes! If this wind holds."

The cook was bailing. "Yes! If we don't catch hell in the surf."

Canton-flannel gulls flew near and far. Sometimes they sat down on the sea, near patches of brown seaweed that rolled over the waves with a movement like carpets on a line in a gale. The birds sat comfortably in groups, and they were envied by some in the dinghy, for the wrath of the sea was no more to them than it was to a covey of prairie-chickens a thousand miles inland. Often they came very close and stared at the men with black, bead-like eyes. At these times they were uncanny and sinister in their unblinking scrutiny, and the men hooted angrily at them, telling them to be gone. One came, and evidently decided to alight on the top of the captain's head. The bird flew parallel to the boat, and did not circle, but made short sidelong jumps in the air in chicken fashion.

Naturalism and "The Open Boat"
Jason Nichols

The naturalist agenda was to demonstrate that free will did not exist in a world that was determined by the environment and heredity. *[good, short introduction that stipulates the definition of naturalism being used]* "The Open Boat" by Stephen Crane clearly demonstrates the naturalist's philosophy concerning nature versus free will by its fatalistic conclusion. *[good thesis]*

In the story, we are shown a scenario of four characters stranded in the sea. All characters are described via their professions: the cook, the captain, the correspondent, the oiler. By placing these characters in this environment, the reader is immediately given the naturalists' streamlined hypothetical. Nature versus willpower is the obvious antagonistic relationship in this dichotomy.

The use of professions to describe and distinguish the characters is in keeping with the naturalist belief that there are no real choices, hence names denoting individuality are not used by Crane to distinguish this character from that one. *[So this is really the end of the first point (despite the paragraph markings) and it sets a broad stage for more specific points that will follow.]*

Nature is personified, and the "oiler" is immediately portrayed by Crane as having an antagonistic view of nature when he says to the gull on page 506, "Ugly brute, you look as if you were made with a jackknife."

Later, on page 513, the "oiler" is distinguished with the name "Billie." The name itself can be seen as particularly important. "Billy" or "Billie" is also the name of Freddie's alter-ego in London's "South of the Slot." Both naturalists, the coincidence of the choice of name is given meaning when we observe that Billy/ie is a variant of William. Just as Shakespeare's sonnets played on the name William (or Will) with the notion of a person's will, so too do Crane and London.

The death of "Billie" then, a representation of free will, at the conclusion of Crane's "Open Boat," demonstrates the naturalists' resolve that there is no free will or that free will is inconsequential compared to nature. *[The three previous paragraphs are wrapped up here with this very significant and insightful point about free will.]*

Nature, personified as an antagonist, is the destroyer of Billie. For Billie, the oiler, Crane offers a revelation that best communicates the naturalists' philosophy on page 515, "When it occurs to a man that nature does not regard him as important . . . ."

This passage explains the death of Billie to serve the Naturalists' agenda. No matter how much Billie rowed, no matter how important he was to the other character's survival, nature disposed of him with callous ambivalence. *[And here the point is brought full circle back to the thesis statement; the essay has been unified.]*

[As a side note, in timed writings paragraph structure is often imperfect. More often writers err on the side of no paragraphs—which is as unbeneficial as too many paragraphs.]

CHAPTER 10
Writing a Research Paper

A **research paper** is not a discreet essay form. It is simply another name for one of the three essay types—the academic essay, the informative essay, or the scientific paper—where it includes a research component. Any of the three essay formats can accommodate research; more importantly, each may be enhanced by using outside sources. For example, the purpose of the informative paper is to present the available information on a subject. To feel confident in writing this essay, you will often have to do some research to ensure that you can write about the subject with accuracy. The scientific paper, whose purpose is to presen t and interpret the results of an experiment, study, or investigation, will sometimes require a research component to provide enough background information to establish the importance of the project and the significance of its results. The academic essay's primary goal, to persuade, will sometimes benefit from the corroboration and insights of others to accomplish that goal most effectively.

Writing a research paper can be challenging, given the amount of information available to you in the library, online, and from experts both on and off campus. Therefore, you should begin with a clear plan for finding and organizing potentially large amounts of information. Having a good system for organizing your research will be important later, too, when it comes time to document and credit your sources according to the rules of a style manual.

WHAT'S AHEAD...

▶ including research in the three essay formats
  • the academic essay that includes research
  • the informative essay that includes research
  • the scientific paper that includes research
▶ methods for doing and using research
  • developing an overarching idea using research
  • selecting a topic and developing a research plan
  • how to include research in your paper: quoting
  • evaluating sources
  • using a style manual to appropriately document research

Including Research in the Three Essay Formats

The Academic Essay That Includes Research

When including research in an academic essay, you must include information only that supports your thesis statement and fulfills its burdens of proof, as direct evidence, as necessary background information, or as the basis for a counterargument. Think of it this way: Once the thesis statement puts forward a claim that requires proof, readers expect you to make good on that claim by demonstrating with concrete details and logical reasoning how you arrived at that position. Imagine your reader asking, "Why did you say that?" or "On what grounds did you make that claim?" Sometimes, research can help you answer those questions by giving you solid evidence for your argument. Look, for example, at the following thesis statement and its C-S-C:

> With regard to current debates about deforestation, it is clear that the redwoods should be left untouched because the benefits of allowing the redwood forests to grow far outweigh the benefits of harvesting them.
>
> *Context*: current debates about deforestation
> *Subject*: the redwood forests
> *Claim*: they should not be cut down because the benefits of leaving them
>   untouched outweigh the benefits of harvesting them.

Here is one way to think about the burdens of proof for this thesis statement:

- Give some general information about the redwood forests.

- Give some background information about the debate over whether these trees should be cut down.

- Show the benefits to the individual, society, and/or the earth if the redwoods are saved.

- Show the benefits to the individual, society, and/or the earth if the redwoods are harvested.

- Point out how the benefits of allowing the redwoods to grow outweigh the benefits of harvesting them.

It is easy to see from these burdens of proof how research might play an important part in fulfilling them. This sample thesis statement takes a clear position on this controversy—that it is more beneficial to allow the trees to grow than it is to cut them down—so the paper will have to consider the positive effects of both leaving the trees alone and cutting them down. Then it will have to show how the information about leaving the trees alone is more compelling than the information concerning the benefits of harvesting them. The writer of this essay will want to be fully informed so as to show that the evidence adds up to the conclusion drawn in the thesis statement.

It is likely, with a subject such as the redwood forests, that your prewriting process will be linked to the research you do because at least some of your ideas will take shape from the research you consult. Only after collecting information in an observation list, freewriting to develop your ideas, and using abstraction to find overarching ideas will you be ready to formulate your working thesis statement and have the necessary information to develop and support its claim.

Thoroughly researching your subject might also allow you to use a counterargument in your paper, which will significantly strengthen your argument. Researching a counterargument is an especially good strategy when you know that many of your readers will, in fact, favor a position contrary to the one you take in your paper. For the redwood forest example, research will increase your understanding of the issue. It might also allow you to challenge some of the benefits many people associate with cutting down the trees and show, instead, that these benefits are actually detriments.

Fig. 10.1 Diagram of the Academic Essay That Includes Research

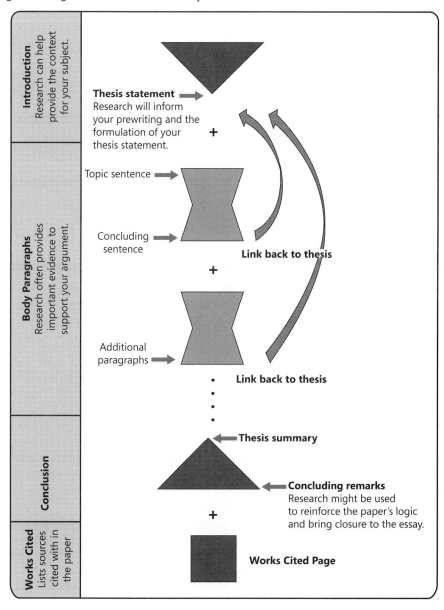

Practice 10.1 Analyzing Research and the Burdens of Proof

1. Read the following student essay and run it through the academic essay checklist in chapter 1. To what degree does it follow the academic essay format?

2. Now isolate the places where research has been included. In the margin of the page or on a separate sheet of paper, note whether the research strengthens the argument, is neutral, or distracts from the argument.

3. Review each instance where you think the research strengthens the argument and describe why/how it helps to make the overall point.

4. Revisit each instance where you thought the research was neutral or distracting and tell whether you think the paper would be improved by revising the presentation of the research or by deleting it entirely. Explain your responses.

> THINKING THROUGH A READING
>
> 1. What problem does this essay identify? What solutions does it propose?
>
> 2. Although readers are already aware of the problem of traffic congestion, what are some of the issues surrounding traffic congestion that you didn't know or hadn't thought about before reading this paper?
>
> 3. Of the solutions discussed, which do you think is most compelling and why?

Alleviating Traffic Congestion
Patrick Sweeney

Almost every person in Southern California has his or her life affected by traffic each time he or she ventures outside the house. We all loathe traffic and how it makes us late, wastes our time, and just generally frustrates us. What many people do not realize are the society-wide implications of excessive traffic congestion. Traffic is a monumental problem in our region, and it will take a wide range of solutions coupled with coopera- tion from all sectors of society to eradicate this affliction.

Redesigning the motorways of Southern California will be expensive but not redesigning them will cost us even more money. In "Traffic Congestion," Charles S. Clark declares that "The time people spend twiddling their thumbs in gridlock amounts to 510,000 hours per day, which costs the state an estimated $4.8 million daily in lost productivity." Every day, commuters are late to work because of traffic, and once they arrive, have lowered productivity due to the stress and frustration from sitting in traffic all morning. In addi- tion, companies in the shipping business lose money every time their trucks are sitting on the freeway not moving and have to raise prices because of the time lost and gas used while stuck in traffic. This puts a strain on all other businesses because they have to wait longer for shipments and pay more for them. Rearranging our roads and redesigning traffic flow will alleviate those problems and will create jobs that will stimulate the local economy. Rebuilding will require more spending by local and state government but will have the added benefit of increased tax revenue from the purchase of materials used in the construction of roads and employment of engineers, planners, and workers.

Curbing traffic congestion will help the environment as well. Marcia Clemmit states in "Climate Change" that global warming is "mostly due to increased atmospheric concentration of so-called greenhouse gases . . . like carbon dioxide, which is emitted during the burning of fossil fuels." The less time cars spend on the road, the less harmful pollutants are emitted. We can start to limit the damage to our atmosphere by limiting the time vehicles spend idling on the freeways, a major contributor to the emission of carbon dioxide. Carbon dioxide is the primary greenhouse gas that can affect global temperature and lead to disastrous consequences for our planet. Furthermore, other air pollutants, like carbon monoxide, volatile organic compounds, oxides of nitrogen, sulfur dioxide, and particulate matter, are released in the burning of gasoline. The Environmental Protection Agency asserts that 43% of air pollutants are released by mobile sources like cars (14). Decreasing the time spent in traffic would be a major step in the fight against global warming.

Along with the environmental effects of air pollution are those that encroach on human health. Not surprisingly, Carol Potera explains in "The Freeway Running through the Yard" that "the Children's Health Study has indicated that air pollution in Southern California communities reduces lung growth and development, raises the risk of developing asthma, and increases school absences due to respiratory illnesses" (A305). No one wants to breathe exhaust fumes, and those that live or work near busy roads are hit the hardest. If fewer vehicles are out driving, fewer pollutants will be released into the nearby air, contributing to the overall health of our area. Reducing the time we spend in traffic will help to greatly diminish air pollution near roadways and therefore help lessen the incidence of respiratory illness in children and adults.

Traffic congestion is a leading cause in the rise of incidences of road rage and contributes to stress. When motorways are clear and empty, much less road rage is found. This is not necessarily because there are fewer people around to get mad at; more likely it is because traffic flows easily and quickly, and motorists are able to reach their destinations in a timely fashion. Furthermore, traffic congestion is a major cause of stress for Americans today. Multitudes of workers are frustrated and tired of the traffic they're stuck in every morning and every night, and this harms business, as mentioned earlier. Stress can accumulate from many sources and lead to major mental health issues. Emotional breakdowns and even physical manifestations such as high blood pressure, heart attacks, and substance abuse can all be caused by stress. Improving traffic flow could greatly improve the health of our region and nation.

Attacking the problem of traffic congestion requires private citizens and businesses to work as a team in addition to the efforts of the government. The government should build more roads and more public transportation; businesses should allow for more employees to work at home and encourage carpooling and citizens should try to decrease their vehicle usage by using public transportation, walking, riding a bicycle, or carpooling. Also, communities need to be redesigned to allow for less use of cars for transportation and provide more opportunities for public transportation and pedestrian traffic. Altogether, these solutions can dramatically reduce the amount of traffic we encounter.

Simply building roads has been tried before as a solution to traffic congestion, and it has failed. This technique has been shown to merely spread out traffic over a larger area instead of alleviating it. For traffic congestion to be truly lessened, new roads need to be combined with other efforts to actually decrease the number of cars using the road. We need to put into effect public education programs that show the benefits of driving less. These campaigns could focus on saving money, helping the environment, and improving our health. Employers need to encourage carpooling, stagger their start times so employees don't arrive all at once, and allow more workers to telecommute and work from home. Together, these solutions can make a dent in traffic congestion.

Along with the expansion and urban sprawl that has occurred in city planning, car use has exploded. No longer do cities have central downtowns where residents can buy all they need from local producers. Instead, mega stores are spread out over the urban landscape and have products trucked in from all over the world. The layout of towns today forces people to use their cars more than was ever intended. Cities are spread far apart and people have to drive across town to get their basic needs met. In addition, American society values motor vehicles as a status symbol. Americans are fixated on car ownership, car use, and the sense of freedom or independence owning one gives us. If we are to lessen traffic congestion, we have to change the way Americans view their vehicles, and show them that public transportation is not just for the poor. A smart traffic elimination program will implement programs to encourage carpooling, bicycle use, and walking. Americans need to realize that, although their motor vehicles are useful and helpful, they aren't for everyone and every situation. Using them less will help the environment and help with traffic congestion.

A large amount of money would have to be spent to build roads and educate the public. This could be paid for by raising taxes, especially on vehicles and gas. This would encourage people to drive less or discontinue driving altogether. The government should also have tax breaks for people who rely solely on public transportation and go without cars. Some of the roads built should be toll roads to help ease the cost of construction. The public will most likely be supportive of small tax increases to help alleviate traffic congestion, and the majority already want to change the way traffic affects their lives.

Some of the solutions suggested may take years to implement. However, many of them, including carpooling, telecommuting, staggered work schedules, toll lanes, and tax incentives, could be put into place tomorrow. More than anything, Americans have to want to plan for the future, and make changes now to create less traffic congestion later.

Works Cited

Clark, Charles S. "Traffic Congestion." *CQ Researcher* 4.17 (1994): 385–408. 15 Feb. 2007 <http://library.cpress.com/cqresearcher/cqresrre1994050600>.

Clemmitt, Marcia. "Climate Change." *CQ Researcher* 16.4 (2006): 73–96. 15 Feb. 2007 <http//library.cpress.com/cqresearcher/cqresrre2006012700>.

Environmental Protection Agency. "The Fundamentals of Air Pollution and Motor Vehicle Emissions." 1997. 15 Feb. 2007 <http://www.epa.gov/otaq/consumer/fapmve2.pdf>.

Potera, Carol. "The Freeway Running Through the Yard." *Environmental Health Perspectives* 114.5 May 2006 <http://links.jstor.org/sici?sici=0091-6765%28200605%29114%3A5%3CA305%4ATFRTTY%3E2.0.CO%3B2-N>.

The Informative Essay That Includes Research

When including research in an informative essay, you will have to consider the CI statement so that the research stays within the essay's scope. Begin by collecting information on your topic and then categorize that information to create a focus and scope for your essay. Often, you will not use all of the information you have collected in your final essay—but resist the urge to include it simply to get credit for finding so much good material. Instead, use discretion. Excess or irrelevant information detracts from an essay's overall effect, weakening rather than strengthening it. Incorporate only those ideas that work within the scope of your essay to keep it focused and unified. For example, look at the following CI statement:

> The prevailing view today is that one of the distinguishing characteristics of American folk music that was popular during the 1940s and 1950s is its social-political content.
>
> *Context*: folk music tradition
> *Subject*: prevailing view of folk music of the 1940s and 1950s
> *Controlling idea*: one of the distinguishing characteristics is its social-political content

This is a CI statement because it overarches and unifies the information in the paper, rather than a thesis statement that puts forward an argument. However, it still contains certain burdens that must be fulfilled for the essay to be satisfying. We can make some predictions about the kind of information you would include, and your readers would expect to find, in this essay, given this CI statement. For instance, you would have to define the term *folk music* especially folk music of the 1940s and 1950s and perhaps give a general overview of its history and typical characteristics. You would need to inform readers about some of the major songs and performers of the 1940s and 1950s and discuss the social-political messages in their lyrics. And you would have to present scholars' analyses of the music's political content. The more your essay meets the readers' expectations, given your CI statement, the more successful your essay will be.

A controlling idea like this one will require some research on your part before you can provide enough factual support to verify that this is the prevailing opinion, rather than simply one you think is correct. Even if you are a bit of a folk music buff, you will want to be sure that the research agrees with your assessment. Otherwise, your overarching idea may be a thesis statement—something not everyone will agree with— rather than a CI statement. In that case, rather than writing an informative essay, you would be writing an academic essay. Again, it is always important that you understand the expectations of your instructor when you are given a writing assignment. If the instructor expects an informative essay, be sure that your essay synthesizes the information that is available.

Because the CI statement is a statement of fact—one with a large enough scope to overarch the essay's content—the informative essay format lends itself most readily to a research component. It is almost an integral requirement of the informative essay; however, there are exceptions. Say you are a habitual player of computer games, and you are writing an essay on the specific design of a game that you often play. Your intimate familiarity with the game, and with computer games in general, may make you enough of an expert to write the essay without incorporating outside research. But even in this case, think about how much more complete your essay will seem if you bring in outside sources, even if those sources are the statements of a couple of your friends who are also expert players. When writing an informative essay, it is important to remember that you are simply transmitting the information and ideas of others. Unless you are confident that you are an authority on your subject, you should turn to research to develop your CI statement and fully inform your readers.

Fig. 10.2 Diagram of the Informative Essay That Includes Research

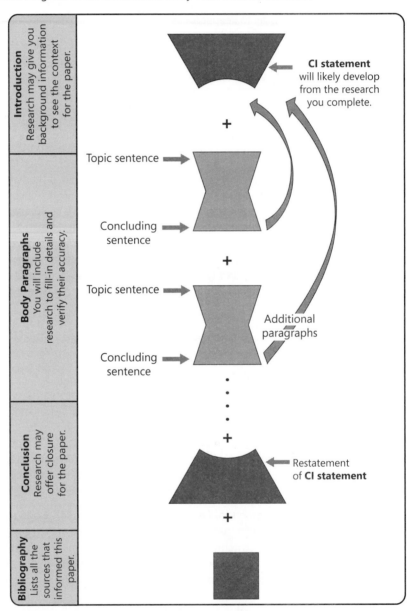

The Scientific Paper That Includes Research

When writing a scientific paper, research may be useful, or even necessary, when you provide readers with the necessary background information to justify your study or experiment and give a perspective on the significance of its results. The introduction is the primary place to offer research relevant to the focus of your project, although the discussion section may provide additional information that opens your study to future research. You might recall from chapter 8 that the introduction answers two questions: (1) What concept, question, or procedure was studied? and (2) What answer do you expect to find? You may have to do some research to provide full and clear answers to these questions.

Just as with the academic and informative essay formats, you will have to consider the scope of your scientific paper's overarching idea—its hypothesis—to determine what outside research is appropriate. Any research you include should directly bear on your hypothesis, both justifying the importance of your study and showing why you make the prediction you do. For example, examine this hypothesis:

> Children ages 3–5 will like this newly designed toy because it has many of the qualities that appeal to this age group's stage of cognitive development.
>
> *Context*: stages of childhood cognitive development
> *Subject*: a newly designed toy
> *Claim*: children 3–5 should like it because its qualities are suitable for the level of cognitive development of children ages 3–5
> *Purpose of the study*: to test the viability of the toy for children in the target age group

There are certain burdens of proof that are embedded within this claim. First, some background information is required. To prepare readers for your study and its results, they will need a brief discussion of childhood cognitive development, as well as the information that is currently known about the cognitive development of children between the ages of 3 and 5. To do this well, you might research the studies that have been done in this area and quote what they have established regarding the cognitive abilities of this age group.

Using the scientific paper format, you will probably present this information in the paper's introduction, making sure that you site all outside sources appropriately. Research may be useful in any section of the scientific paper, especially the introduction and the paper's discussion, where you explore the viability of your hypothesis and speculate on what further studies might be done to help answer the question or problem that your study addresses.

Fig. 10.3 Diagram of a Scientific Paper That Includes Research

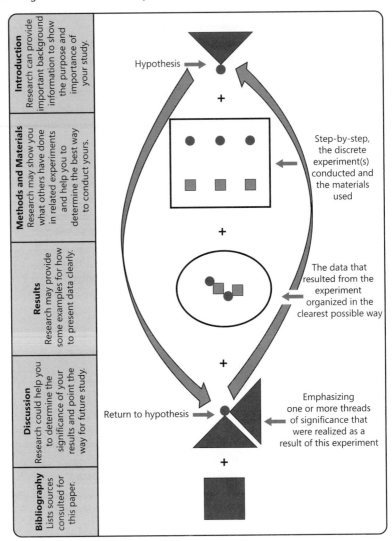

Introduction	Research can provide important background information to show the purpose and importance of your study.
Methods and Materials	Research may show you what others have done in related experiments and help you to determine the best way to conduct yours.
Results	Research may provide some examples for how to present data clearly.
Discussion	Research could help you to determine the significance of your results and point the way for future study.
Bibliography	Lists sources consulted for this paper.

Hypothesis

Step-by-step, the discrete experiment(s) conducted and the materials used

The data that resulted from the experiment organized in the clearest possible way

Return to hypothesis

Emphasizing one or more threads of significance that were realized as a result of this experiment

Methods for Doing and Using Research

Selecting a Topic and Developing a Research Plan

If an essay that includes research seems intimidating to you, try to break the task up into smaller, more manageable steps. The first step is to examine the assignment and make sure that you understand its purpose and goals. Before you begin, you should know the type of essay format to use, how long the paper should be, and any limitations or requirements concerning the research you are to do. As you select the topic for your paper, check the assignment to make sure you respond directly to its questions or demands. We recommend turning back to chapters 6 and 7 to review strategies for unpacking a writing assignment.

Whether you are writing an academic essay, an informative essay, or a scientific paper, it is likely that you will have to spend some time choosing a topic. This can be intimidating when the assignment has left the choice wide open, but think of it as an opportunity to investigate something that is of particular interest to you, even if you are limited by a specific area of study.

Magazines, newspapers, the Internet, material from your course, conversations with family and friends, television, and reference books in the library are all places where you might find a topic that interests you. Start with a couple of topics that seem intriguing and then explore them a little to see if one stands out as more promising than the others. For each tentative topic, freewrite to explore the questions it raises, the ideas you have about it, and the interest it might hold for the reader. Then pause and do some exploratory research on the Internet or in the library databases to see if there is plenty of information available about the topic.

Your choice of a topic is important; it should be something that you want to know more about. If you are writing an academic essay or a scientific paper, you will have to work carefully with your topic in steps 4–6 of the seven steps to narrow the focus and identify a specific subject for the argument you will express in the paper's thesis statement or hypothesis. If you are writing an informative paper, scope will also be a concern. You will have to find a subject that you can present fully within the prescribed length of your assignment. In other words, choosing a topic gives you a general focus. From there, you will narrow your focus to identify a more specific subject, something that suits the scope of your paper. We've done this many times in earlier examples, such as when we began with the topic "World War II" and narrowed the scope to a battle within that war, or when we began with "surfing" and narrowed it to "the culture of surfing." The challenge here is that you will likely begin with a topic and a large scope, so you will be working with a large amount of research material in the early stages of your research. After you narrow your scope and identify your subject, you will be able to identify the research you will need for your paper and eliminate all the information that is outside this scope.

If you are working on an academic essay, after you have your tentative topic, you can use the seven steps in chapter 6—with some modifications that include research—to develop your ideas and formulate a thesis statement that can be supported with solid evidence. It might go something like the following.

Using the Seven Steps with Research

STEPS 1–3:
After you have identified the subject of the assignment and the central question, you can begin thinking about how to develop your ideas about the subject and start to shape an answer to the primary question.

Think about how research will help you accomplish your task. What do you want to know more about before you write on this subject? What sources might you consult to find this information? Write out a research plan before you go to the library or consult the Internet.

Remember that research is not limited to the library or the Internet. You might consult an expert in the field, your textbook or instructor, your own knowledge, or any number of information venues. Take a few minutes to think deliberately about the information sources you will consult because some of the best sources for your subject might be nontraditional ones.

When you go to the library, consult a librarian for research advice and for the location of reference materials.

STEP 4:
Check out or get an electronic copy of all promising research material.

Compile a list of the resources you find, even if you're not sure you will use them. Check your handbook to be sure that you write down all the information about author, title, publisher, and so forth that you will need for a citation. Do this for all of your sources, because you may end up using material that you don't initially anticipate using. Create your own system, such as index cards containing bibliographic information and a few comments about what seems interesting or important in the research material (see figure 10.4).

Fig. 10.4 Using Index Cards to Capture Your Research

www.eharmony.com Sept. 09	www.match.com Sept. 09
potential dates are pre-screened	Site has dating articles and advice,
have to register and fill out questionnaire,	including safety tips.
which is extensive and, they claim,	They pioneered on-line dating in 1995.
the cornerstone of their success	a member's profile can include up
scientific matching based on 35 years	to 26 photos and a variety of free
of clinical research	writing forms
they offer a Guided Communication	every profile and photo is screened
option to take the stress from the first date	communication between members takes
they claim chemistry is not enough;	place via an anonymous email system
compatability is also important	seems most intent on protecting privacy
must be at least 18 to register	of members
	must be at least 18 and single or
	separated to become a member

STEP 5:
Organize the items on your observation list by clustering like items together. Use abstraction to title the clusters so they have an organizing or overarching principle that unifies them.

If necessary, freewrite with several of the items or clusters from your list.
If new questions arise, consult the research again.

Organize research notes into the categories or clusters you have developed. You may have to add some categories once you look back at your research notes.

STEP 6:
Here is where you will identify the subject you'll focus on, which will allow you to narrow your essay's scope. As your scope takes shape, you will be able to cull the research that you will use from among all that you found.

STEP 7:
Use C-S-C and the insightful idea you found in step 6 to put your thesis statement together.

Write a rough outline or plan for your paper using the overarching idea and the clusters or categories you developed in steps 4 and 5.

Developing an Overarching Idea Using Research

For example, you have been asked to write a research paper on Internet dating. You have completed steps 1–3 and have determined that the assignment is asking for an academic essay. You are ready to jot down some ideas and create a research plan. Your topic is Internet dating, but you will have to look for a way to narrow this broad scope. As you research a topic and develop your own ideas, you will often discover several ways that a topic can be narrowed to a sharper focus. You will have to freewrite and work closely with your observation list, adding to it as your ideas develop and working with it in different ways to creatively cluster the items. Your work at this stage will help you find a subject with an appropriate scope for your writing assignment.

Begin building an observation list with ideas/questions drawn from what you already know, just as we used questions to fill-out these steps when writing about literature (see chapter 9).

How many people use Internet dating sites as a way to meet people?

> I know a couple of people who have used these sites, and they like them. But I'm not sure that that many people use them. Are statistics available?

Is there a particular type of person who likes to meet people through the Internet or do many different types of people do this?

> This seems important to find out because it suggests how widespread and lasting this will be as a means for getting people together.

How dangerous is Internet dating?

> This might have something to do with the way each site operates. Personal information should not be given out, and people using a dating site should use caution when meeting. Investigate crime-related statistics associated with Internet dating.

What do you have to do to register for these Internet dating sites? Is it difficult? Is there security? How do you actually get together with someone for the first time?

> Better explore a couple of these to see what I can find out. Perhaps I can ask a friend who has used one of these and get his/her experiences.

How successful are these sites for getting people together?

> What statistics are available about the number of lasting relationships begun on any particular dating site?

What do psychologists say about Internet dating? Do they think it is healthy? Do people who have antisocial tendencies use these sites?

> Perhaps people who are very outgoing use them. Investigate the profile of the average user.

Now you are ready to go to the library and begin researching your questions.

Looking through the library's databases, imagine that you find fifteen sources about Internet dating. It's a good idea to summarize each one on an index card or a spreadsheet, being sure to include the title, author, and bibliographic information you will need if you use the source in your paper. It's important to go through the sources carefully, using the information they contain, as well as your own ideas, to build an observation list. When you finish, your observation list might be very long and contain a variety of information and ideas about Internet dating. Now you are ready to organize the information and ideas into categories. Look for ways to group items on your observation list into clusters. For the subject of Internet dating, you discover that many of the items fall into two clusters:

Attitudes of Experts toward Internet Dating

1. In favor of Internet dating

2. Mixed/undecided attitude toward Internet dating

3. Against Internet dating

Types of Internet Dating Sites That Are Available

1. Internet dating sites that have photos and profiles only

2. Internet dating sites that also include real-time chat rooms

3. Internet dating sites with photos, profiles, real-time chat rooms, and streaming video/voice mail

4. Internet dating sites with built-in privacy protection so that photos (and other more personal information) are not immediately released to viewers

You can see that the cluster and/or category titles you use to organize the ideas and information you have collected will significantly shape your project's scope and point of view. If you are writing an informative essay, for example, you can turn one of the cluster titles into a CI statement and then use the items under it as the structuring topics for the essay. For this assignment, your CI statement might be: "There are many types of Internet dating sites available and those interested in using them can choose the one they are most comfortable using." This summary-like statement narrows the scope of the essay and focuses the information on a particular aspect of Internet dating. Now you can sort the original research sources you found according to which ones contain information about the types of Internet dating available and put the rest of the research material aside.

If your assignment is to write an academic essay, you will have to offer an argument or interpretation of Internet dating, so the way you work with the observation list and clusters will be somewhat different from that used for the informative essay. For this essay, you will have to look over the clusters and think about which of them (one or more) can narrow the scope of your topic "Internet dating" and form the basis for an argument. You might find "Attitudes Toward Internet Dating" a provocative cluster, and you decide to explore it more to see if you can develop an argument. Here's what you have found so far:

Context: modern American society
Subject: Internet dating
Claim: ?

Now you will have to look over the sources you found and select those that are relevant to the narrowed scope of "attitudes toward Internet dating." You can then consult the sources you selected to see what arguments others are making about whether or not Internet dating is a good idea. You will have to decide what assessment of Internet dating you want to offer in your essay. By developing overarching titles for each of your clusters, you can classify your data in a meaningful way. Here is an example:

Attitudes toward Internet Dating Sites

1. In Favor of Internet Dating (ID)

   - articles on ID as a good investment opportunity for those interested in investing in a Web-based company

   - articles on ID as *the* twenty-first century dating tool

2. Mixed/Undecided Attitude toward Internet Dating

   - articles on ID marriage successes and failures

   - articles that praise ID for access but fault it for its potential for misrepresentation

3. Against Internet Dating

   - articles on dangers of ID

   - articles on ID as social taboo/unnatural way to meet people

Now, you will have to decide which position is more compelling. Imagine that you decide to argue in favor of Internet dating. For your thesis statement, it would not be enough to state: "Based on the research I have found, I am in favor of Internet dating." Being clear about your overall position is a good strategy, but this statement doesn't go far enough; it's undeveloped. Use C-S-C to sharpen your claim:

Context: today's American society
Subject: Internet dating sites
Claim: perfect solution for companionship

Possible working thesis statements:

Internet dating sites offer the perfect solution for finding companionship given the harried lifestyles of twenty-first-century Americans.

or, by qualifying a commonly held belief:

Although many will argue that Internet dating is a fad, Internet dating sites are the best way to meet a marriage partner.

or:

The opportunity to meet people through an Internet dating site is the best means of empowering women in their search for a life partner.

Notice that these thesis statements give a clear sense of what position will be argued—in favor of Internet dating—but they also go one step further to give a particular angle on Internet dating that shows why Internet dating sites are favored within a particular context. Your job as the writer is to isolate the evidence in the research you found that supports your thesis and incorporate it as evidence for your own supporting paragraphs.

Practice 10.2 Developing a Research Plan

For each of the following research paper topics, develop a research plan by beginning an observation list with what you already know and what questions you will need to research:

1. steroid use in athletics

2. antismoking campaigns

3. prescription drugs versus over-the-counter drugs

Evaluating Sources

An outside source is anything a writer consults when doing research for an assignment. *Where* you look for sources depends on the subject of your paper. If you are writing a paper on competitive surfing, for instance, some of your best sources may come from the Internet or personal interviews. On the other hand, for a paper on Babylonian history, your best sources will likely be found in the library. You can gather information about your subject from a number of places, including your own experience, the experience of others, your professors, class notes, your textbook, field research (observation), the Internet, or the library. Be creative when seeking information on a subject.

The number of sources you use for a paper will depend on the paper's subject and scope, as well as on the assignment. Often, your instructor will tell you exactly how many sources are required. A good rule of thumb is to examine enough sources to get an overview of the subject of your paper. You will know you have a solid overview when the new sources you consult largely repeat the information you have already found. When you are finding little new information, and the new information you do find seems peripheral rather than central, you can feel confident that you have consulted enough sources.

A source's quality or "goodness" can be determined by its *credibility* and *relevance*.

Credibility

Anytime you ask a reader to accept as reliable the information you are offering, be sure to evaluate the integrity of the source. This will help ensure the authenticity of the information that you offer. Ask the following questions of all sources, even those from the library:

- Who is the publisher of this information? Is it a scholarly or otherwise reliable source? Books published by university presses (e.g., University of California University Press, Temple University Press) are among the most authoritative because university presses are not special interest groups. They call for expert review of manuscripts, so these books are generally accepted as credible. Journals that are associated with academic organizations (e.g., *PMLA* is the *Publication Manual of the Modern Language Association*) also require articles to be peer reviewed and are considered scholarly.

  However, some publications, as well as most Internet sites, are paid for by groups or individuals who are interested in promoting a particular agenda, but their bias may not be obvious in the information they put forward. A Web site paid for by a religious group or a powerful industry, such as the oil or tobacco industry, may have special interests they are promoting through publication. Hence, they cannot be relied on to present all the available information, so you will have to do some additional research to assess the credibility of the material.

- Who is giving me this information? What is his/her level of expertise? What are the writer's credentials? Is the writer a PhD or otherwise known as an expert in the field?

- If you are using this information as a widely accepted standard, have you found other sources that agree? That is, can you corroborate the information? This will help illustrate that it is valid or that there is a consensus.

- If you are quoting information that has not been corroborated widely, you may be quoting something that is controversial (or misguided). Just because it is published does not mean that it is accurate. If you find a dissenting view, your original assertion may not be as widely accepted as you think. Take extra care to evaluate its legitimacy and consider either dismissing the dissenting view or incorporating it as an informed but controversial opinion.

- Check the publication date. Be sure that the information is not too old to be considered accurate. For instance, a paper about the Internet or about technology probably requires sources that are no more than a year or two old, because these fields change so quickly. However, information about ancient Greece may still be current even if it is one or two decades old. Be sure to consider your subject when assessing the currency of your sources.

- You should also look carefully at the references or data that the information source has used as the basis for the information it provides. If you are using the results of a study, for example, you might assess the credibility of the results based on who paid for the study, how many participants were included, whether the test group was representative, the reputation of the study administrators, and so forth. If the source cites references, you might ask these same questions of those references to further ensure reliable information.

Relevance
You probably won't be able to determine how relevant the source will be to your project when you first start your research. When you are closer to formulating your thesis statement, hypothesis, or CI statement, you'll have a better sense of the scope and focus of your paper, so you can better determine which sources will be directly useful. Some sources may not be quoted directly in your paper but might still be considered valuable. A source is valuable if it helps you shape and refine the ideas that do make it into your final paper. In short, you aren't wasting your time when you look at a large number of sources—in fact, it is necessary to shape your focus.

Practice 10.3 Evaluating Internet Sites
Find and evaluate five Internet sites for a college research paper on the use of steroids in athletics. Use the criteria listed previously to make your assessment. Which sites provided the most and least useful information? Who owned these sites? What lessons can you extrapolate based on this limited research?

How to Include Research in Your Paper: Quoting

When using the words or ideas of others in your paper, you must be careful to do so in an appropriate way. In short, you can either use direct quotations from a source or paraphrase the information. Quote directly from research material when you want to

- Affirm your statements.

- Capture the precise language of an expert who made the point particularly well.

- Put a dissenting view in the voice of the dissenter so that you can maintain a narrative distance that allows you to discuss all sides of the debate in a way that will be perceived as more objective.

- Discuss the source's exact choice of words to better understand complex subjects or specialized language.

- Draw attention to an important point.

A quotation needs some introductory commentary to give it context and should always be followed by an explanation of the idea the quotation is meant to demonstrate. Never let a quotation "speak for itself" because it likely won't. Be sure to use your own voice to make the point. And, be careful not to read more into the quotation than is there. Study the quotation carefully to make sure it clearly substantiates the point you are trying to make. Quotations shouldn't just float into and out of your paper. They require context, but they have a lot of flexibility; they can appear at the beginning of a sentence, at the end of a sentence, or in the middle of a sentence, or they can be set off by themselves. Here are some examples:

- *A quotation at the beginning of a sentence*:

  "You must not tell anyone . . . what I am about to tell you," writes Maxine Hong Kingston in the first line of her famous book, *The Woman Warrior* (3).

- *A quotation at the end of a sentence*:

  Robert Tellman writes that the river in Mark Twain's *Old Times on the Mississippi* becomes a "metaphor for the fluid, unbounded possibilities thought to be available in the American west" (195).

- *A quotation in the middle of a sentence*:

  Maxine Hong Kingston complains that a traditional Chinese saying, "Girls are maggots in the rice. It is more profitable to raise geese than daughters," (43) denigrates women by devaluing them.

- *A quotation longer than four typed lines*:

  Thomas Paine in "Rights of Men" writes about one difference between natural law and social law:

  > Whatever each man can separately do, without trespassing upon others, he has a right to do for himself; and he has a right to a fair portion of all which society, with all its combinations of skill and force, can do in his favour. In this partnership all men have equal rights; but not to equal things. He that has but five shillings

in the partnership, has as good a right to it, as he that has five hundred pound has to his larger proportion. But he has not a right to an equal dividend in the product of the joint stock; and as to the share of power, authority, and direction which each individual ought to have in the management of the state, that I must deny to be amongst the direct original rights of man in civil society; for I have in my contemplation the civil social man, and no other. (235)

As is clear from this quotation, Paine believed that people have different rights within a society, even as they all have certain common rights....

Blending Quotations Smoothly into Your Own Text

Quotations shouldn't be dropped into a text without warning or commentary. When using direct quotations, be sure to make their purpose clear by providing surrounding discussion and explanation for readers. Here are some strategies you can use to incorporate them smoothly into your essay.

- *Use that*

  Gloria Fiero writes that "the tragedy of Antigone springs from the irreconcilability of Antigone's personal idealism and Creon's hardheaded political realism" (79).

- *Use a comma*

  According to Edward Hallowell, instructor of psychiatry at Harvard Medical School, "e-mail and voice mail are efficient, but face-to-face contact is still essential to true human communication" (1).

- Use a colon

  Hallowell defines the "human moment" as having two prerequisites: "people's physical presence and their emotional and intellectual attention" (2).

How to Use Brackets or Ellipses to Alter a Quotation

Sometimes, a text from which you would like to quote has awkward changes in tense and person that make the passage confusing. Following is an example:

In Jack Kerouac's novel *On the Road*, he describes how he and his friends "bounced the car up on the Algiers ferry and found ourselves crossing the Mississippi River by boat" (239).

Use brackets to change the quoted material so that your sentence flows smoothly.

In Jack Kerouac's novel *On the Road*, he describes how he and his friends "[bounced] the car up on the Algiers ferry and [find themselves] crossing the Mississippi River by boat" (239).

When you want to omit parts of a passage because of relevance or length, use ellipsis marks—three periods preceded and followed by a space—to indicate where a word or words have been omitted. Some instructors will expect you to use brackets to enclose the ellipsis marks if they are yours, that is, if they are not part of the original quotation.

In his "Autobiographical Notes," James Baldwin writes: "I began plotting novels at about the time I learned to read . . . and my first professional triumph, in any case, the first effort of mine to be seen in print, occurred at the age of twelve or thereabouts, when a short story I had written about the Spanish revolution won some sort of prize in an extremely short-lived church newspaper" (26).

Paraphrasing and Summarizing

Quoting isn't always the best way to incorporate research into your paper. Quoting extensively will leave your paper choppy, so use quotations to supplement or affirm your points but don't allow them to take control of your essay. Because the success of an essay is, in part, contingent on the presence of an effective and consistent authorial voice, sometimes it is better to incorporate research material by paraphrasing summarizing it. However, you will still have to give credit to the source.

Paraphrasing and summarizing are not the same. When you paraphrase a passage rather than quote it, you use your own voice to restate another's ideas. You bring in all the ideas of the passage without breaking up your voice as the paper's author. When you summarize a passage, you give a condensed version that contains the main ideas only. Sometimes, a summary is all that is necessary to support your argument or explain your point.

Here is an original quotation, followed by a paraphrased version, and then a summary. Notice the difference in tone between the quotation and the paraphrased version and the way the paraphrased version captures all the ideas of the original but in different language. Also notice what is left out of the summary and think about situations when this might be more desirable.

- *A quotation*:

    "Color tends to be a subconscious element in film. It's strongly emotional in its appeal, expressive and atmospheric rather than intellectual. Psychologists have discovered that most people actively attempt to interpret the lines of a composition, but they tend to accept color passively, permitting it to suggest moods rather than objects. Lines are associated with nouns; color with adjectives. Line is sometimes thought to be masculine; color feminine. Both lines and colors suggest meanings, then, but in somewhat different ways" (Giannetti 24).

- *The quotation paraphrased*:

    According to Louis Giannetti, color in film influences viewers in a way they may not be consciously aware of. Color affects viewers' emotions and creates a mood more than it affects their intellects. Psychologists believe that, when looking at a painting, people automatically have an emotional response to color, while they respond intellectually to objects or things. Giannetti ties color to adjectives and femininity, and lines to nouns and masculinity (Giannetti 24).

- *The quotation summarized*:

    Louis Giannetti writes about the unconscious, emotional responses viewers have to color in films, and he associates color with what are for him "feminine," rather than "masculine," qualities (Giannetti 24).

Using and citing the ideas of others in your own writing is not a sign of weakness in your scholarship; it is a sign of your commitment to learning more about the subject and doing so through systematic research. Using the ideas of others is a weakness only if there are too few ideas of your own in the paper or if the ideas of others so far outweigh your own ideas that the paper shows signs that you have given the subject little thought.

Using a Style Manual to Appropriately Document Research

A style manual is a publication that contains the rules for documenting research used in a paper. There are several style manuals, so it's always best to ask your instructor which one to use for a writing assignment that includes research. Generally, academic disciplines tend to use certain style manuals; for example, the MLA manual is used in English and the general humanities, the APA manual is used for psychology, and the Chicago Manual of Style is often used for social sciences. Handbooks will give you abbreviated versions of the MLA and APA style rules, but when that isn't sufficient for your needs, consult the full text or online publications for any of the three major style manuals. You can also examine the sources relevant to your research and see what style manual those sources are following.

Properly citing the ideas of others within your paper will help you avoid the dangers of plagiarism. Plagiarism, defined as representing the ideas or words of another as your own, is against the law, and all colleges have established procedures for disciplining offenders. Typical penalties include failing the assignment, failing the class, and/or being expelled from the institution. In other words, plagiarism—whether deliberate or inadvertent—is a very serious ethical offense, and few instructors have patience for writers who attempt to take credit for ideas not their own. Beyond the academic environment of a college or university, plagiarism can have even more dire consequences. It is against the law and can bring stiff penalties.

In addition to citing quotations or paraphrased ideas within your paper, you will also have to include a Works Cited list and/or bibliography at the end of your paper. This is where you give credit to any outside sources that you relied on for the paper. If you are not sure whether something requires a bibliographic citation, it is better to be safe than sorry—cite it within the paper and in the bibliography. Appendix C contains more information on how to cite your research properly.

APPLICATIONS AND WRITING EXERCISES

Application 10.1
Use the library's search databases and select one of each of the following types of works. Create a Works Cited page using the appropriate format for each type of source. See appendix C if you need further help.

- a book by a single author

- the introduction in an edited volume

- a professional journal article

- a newspaper article

- a Web site

- a personal interview

- a film

- a poem

Writing Exercise 10.1

Look back at the essay "Alleviating Traffic" (see page 234).

1. For each paragraph that contains research, identify the type of source used (book, Internet, expert, etc.).

2. Paraphrase the third paragraph. Does this writer use paraphrasing or summarizing in the essay? Where? Is it effective?

3. What contributions does research make to this paper? Would it be significantly less compelling without the use of research? Explain.

4. Create an informal outline of the essay (you may want to use the post-draft outline form at the end of chapter 5), noting topic ideas and research contributions. Then try to identify the clusters this writer used to organize the essay's information and ideas.

Writing Exercise 10.2

Read the following essay and write a one-page summary of it as if you needed to support an essay you are writing. Summarize without quoting or paraphrasing any particular part of the piece. In writing your summary, keep in mind the IHMRAD structure so that you include all, and only, the pertinent information appropriate for a summary.

THINKING THROUGH A READING

1. This essay won the Eppendorf and *Science* Prize for Neurobiology in 2006, an international prize established to encourage the work of promising young neurobiologists by providing support in the early stages of their careers. Contestants submit a 1,000 word essay based on the research they have performed during the past three years. The winner is awarded $25,000 and publication of his or her essay in *Science*. Why do you think this essay was the 2006 Eppendorf winner?

2. What is the essay's hypothesis? Where is it located? Locate and label the other IHMRAD subheadings.

3. What are some of the questions this research project opens up for our understanding of human adaptation and survival?

A Dedicated System for Processing Faces
*Doris Tsao**

If you're planning to rob a bank, there's one thing you must not forget: to cover your face. Otherwise, just a brief glance will allow all the other social animals around you to identify you. What is the neural basis of the extraordinary ability of humans to recognize faces? Localized strokes can selectively destroy face recognition abilities while preserving the ability to recognize other objects ("prosopagnosia") (1). Furthermore, functional magnetic resonance imaging (fMRI), a technique that measures blood flow changes induced by brain activation, consistently reveals several discrete brain regions that respond more to faces than to other objects (2). One of these regions, the fusiform face area, shows increased blood flow even when subjects merely imagine faces (3). These findings suggest that face processing is mediated by specialized modules inside the human brain. Such specialization is surprising since, from introspection, it seems that our recognition of faces flows seamlessly into that of all the other objects in the world.

Are face-selective regions unique to humans? Charles Gross and co-workers studied a large region in the macaque brain known as the temporal lobe and reported in 1981 that this region contains some cells that respond exclusively to faces and not to other visual forms (4). This was a remarkable finding: How can a single cell be wired to detect something so complex as a face? The discovery immediately turned fuzzy questions about holistic integration and gnostic units into a concrete research goal: What are face cells detecting, and how are they wired?

One problem, however, stood in the way of understanding these cells: It was difficult to find them. In single-unit recording experiments, one can see only as far as the tip of one's electrode (≤ 100 μm wide). Several groups that studied face cells reported that they were scattered throughout the temporal lobe, with at most 10 to 20% of the cells in any one region being face-selective (5-7). Meanwhile, the discovery by fMRI of face-selective regions in humans generated great interest in understanding what is being coded by these regions. One might guess that the fMRI-identified face-selective regions contain lots of face cells. Alternatively, they could contain cells activated by any animate object, or by symmetrical objects, or by the behavioral process of fine scrutiny. Indeed, fMRI evidence was marshaled for several competing theories about face-selective activation.

In order to clarify the link between face cells and fMRI face areas, I performed fMRI experiments in alert monkeys to look for face-selective regions (8). Comparing activation to faces versus five other object categories (fruits, bodies, gadgets, hands, and scrambled patterns) across the entire macaque brain, I identified face-selective activation in three discrete regions of the temporal lobe (see the figure, left, panel A). These regions showed a blood oxygen level-dependent (BOLD) response to faces that was stronger than the response to any of the nonface categories by a factor of 7 (see figure, panel B). This suggests that face processing in monkeys is performed by specialized regions, possibly homologous to those found in humans. Furthermore, the arrangement of the face regions along an anterior-posterior axis suggests a hierarchy, given that we know from other studies that complexity in shape selectivity increases from the back to the front of the visual system.

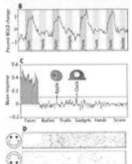

Recognizing faces: (**A**) Three patches of face-selective fMRI activation (yellow regions) in the macaque temporal lobe. (**B**) Time course from the face patches. Blood flows to these regions only when the monkey views faces. (**C**) Average response across 182 cells from the middle face patch of one monkey to 96 different images. The first 16 images are faces. (**D**) Responses of a face cell to repeated presentations of an upright and an inverted cartoon face. Each dot represents an action potential.

Having found these fMRI face regions in monkeys, I then asked: What is the selectivity of single neurons within an fMRI-identified face patch? I started by recording from single neurons—almost 500 of them—in the middle face patch of two monkeys, and found 97% of the visually responsive neurons to be face-selective (9) (see figure, panel C). These cells responded almost 20 times as strongly to faces as to other objects, and many were even suppressed by nonface objects. Up to now, one major difficulty with understanding object recognition has been the problem of determining which object, among an infinite number of possible objects, a single cell in the temporal lobe might be coding. The existence of a region in which all the cells are coding faces goes a long way toward overcoming this difficulty.

What is it about a face that these cells like? Surprisingly, most cells responded to human, monkey, and even highly simplified cartoon faces (see figure, panel D). In fact, many of the cells showed a weak but significant response to a few particular nonface objects; all of these objects turned out to be round (see figure, panel C). The weak but significant responses to round clocks and fruits in this area, as well as its relatively posterior position within the temporal lobe, indicate that it constitutes an early stage in the form-processing hierarchy. Recording from this area is a bit like peeking into a carpenter's shop and seeing the rough frame before fine chiseling—exactly what one wants for piecing together the basic mechanisms underlying face selectivity.

How do face cells encode specific faces? Early recordings in the middle face patch suggested that face cells distinguish faces on the basis of visual shape (e.g., the cells responded weakly to the round outline in a clock and an apple). To explore shape tuning of these cells quantitatively, I took advantage of their robust response to cartoon faces, which can be easily parameterized. I probed face cells with a cartoon face space consisting of 19 different feature dimensions, each sampled at 11 values; the space thus contained 11^{19} possible different faces. The cartoon dimensions included ones describing the overall facial shape, the shape of individual features (e.g., iris size), and the relationship between features (e.g., intereye distance). Across the population, a vast majority of cells showed strong tuning to at least one cartoon dimension, and no cell was tuned to more than eight dimensions. The two most popular dimensions were face aspect ratio (i.e., Bert versus Ernie) and iris size. Most cells responded best to extreme features such as large irises, Ernie's or Bert's face, etc. These results show that we can understand face cells: Each cell acts as a set of face-specific rulers, measuring faces along multiple distinct dimensions. By combining the measurements of all these little rulers, it should be possible to reconstruct any face (including a bandit's, if not covered well).

My experiments show that the neural machinery for face processing in macaque monkeys consists of a set of discrete brain regions packed with highly dedicated components. This system offers a unique opportunity for exploring high-level form perception. By recording from several large, homogeneous populations of face cells identified through monkey fMRI, we can now understand the process by which the brain synthesizes the percept of a face in terms of underlying single-cell components.

References and Notes

1. J. Bodamer, *Arch. Psychiatr. Nervenkrankh.* 179, 6 (1947).

2. N. Kanwisher, J. McDermott, M. M. Chun, *J. Neurosci.* 17, 4302 (1997).

3. K. O'Craven, N. Kanwisher, *J. Cogn. Neurosci.* 12, 1013 (2000).

4. C. Bruce, R. Desimone, C. G. Gross, *J. Neurophysiol.* 46, 369 (1981).

5. D. I. Perrett *et al.*, *Hum. Neurobiol.* 3, 197 (1984).

6. R. Desimone, T. D. Albright, C. G. Gross, C. Bruce, *J. Neurosci.* 4, 2051 (1984).

7. G. Baylis, E. Rolls, C. Leonard, *J. Neurosci.* 7, 330 (1987).

8. D. Y. Tsao, W. A. Freiwald, T. A. Knutsen, J. B. Mandeville, R. B. Tootell, *Nat. Neurosci.* 6, 989 (2003).

9. D. Y. Tsao, W. A. Freiwald, R. B. H. Tootell, M. S. Livingstone, *Science* 311, 670 (2006).

10. All the experiments here were performed together with Winrich Freiwald. I owe deepest thanks to my adviser Margaret Livingstone and to my father Thomas Tsao.

The author is at the Institute for Brain Research and Center for Advanced Imaging, University of Bremen, D28359 Bremen, Germany. E-mail: doris@nmr.mgh.harvard.edu

Writing Exercise 10.3 Analyzing Internet Sources

Evaluate the home page for one of the following organizations by answering the following questions. When finished, choose a second Web site and run the same analysis. Compare the results.

MTV   CNN   NASCAR   The NFL

1. *What is the purpose of the Web site?* The quality of the information on a Web site is often influenced by its purpose. The purpose of most Web sites is *not simply "to inform,"* so try to find out *why the Web site wants to inform* the public about something. Is its purpose to promote a product for sale; a religious belief; or a personal, social, or political agenda? If so, the information on the Web site will most likely (though not necessarily) be presented in such a way as to further the purpose of the Web site, rather than simply to offer the most accurate, objective, and useful information possible.

2. *What kind of organization is responsible for the Web site?* By identifying the kind of organization that is responsible for a Web site, one can often get a better idea of the Web site's purpose and point of view. A good clue to identifying the kind of organization is the URL. Is it a .org, .com, .edu, or .gov address? An .edu address, for example, indicates an educational institution, which is less likely to be selling something and, therefore, more likely to provide objective information than, say, an institution with a .com address.

3. *Who is the intended audience for the Web site?* Is the Web site aimed at children, students (high school, college), scholars, or the general public? The intended audience will often determine the level or sophistication of the information on a Web site.

4. *Does the Web site have a date?* Without a date (copyright, last update, etc.) there is no telling how old, or obsolete, the information is.

5. *Is the author of the information identified on the Web site?* If the author is identified, does he or she have any credentials (a Ph.D. in history, for example) that indicate expertise on the subject or a reputation for credibility?

6. *Is the information supported by rational analysis and clearly cited evidence (particularly from primary sources)?* Information on the Internet should be subject to the same standards of reason and evidence as information in print.

7. *Are differing opinions or interpretations respectfully presented?* Rarely do all historians agree on one interpretation of historical evidence. If the Web site does not present alternative interpretations (even of so-called "facts") or presents them in a disrespectful way, then it is likely that the information presented is not very objective or has not been thoroughly researched.

8. *Are there any obviously outlandish, false, or biased statements on the Web site?* One does not need to be an expert to detect the ridiculous (e.g., space aliens built the Egyptian pyramids).

9. *Is the information professionally presented and clearly written with proper spelling, grammar, and punctuation?* Chances are that the quality of the information is as good or bad as the presentation and writing.

10. *Does the Web site use garish graphics?* If something other than well-substantiated information catches your eye on a Web site, you might be suspicious of why the graphics are being used.

Writing Exercise 10.4

Using the library or Internet, locate twelve credible sources that contain relevant information for the working hypothesis that follows. Because this will use the scientific paper format, how might this research help you present important background information in the paper's introduction?

> Children ages 3–5 will like this newly designed toy because it has many of the qualities that appeal to this age group's stage of cognitive development.

Part 3 Writing Assignments

1. Look at the scientific paper sample writing assignments in Chapter 8 titled "Who Will Be Your Mate?" (p. 192) and "Make an Age-Appropriate Toy" (p. 194). Choose one of the assignments and complete it using the scientific paper format. Use the research strategies in chapter 10 to obtain background information in the appropriate subject area and include at least three credible outside sources to help you develop the introductory paragraph (you will not have the benefit of course material). Use chapter 8 for help with the IHMRAD format and be sure to follow the guidelines in this chapter for finding and using research materials in your paper.

2. Find a topic that you want to know more about. This is an open-ended assignment, so you are free to choose your own research topic. Once you have chosen a topic, narrow it by adjusting the scope to suit the essay's length and then decide on a purpose for your essay. Determine which essay format—the academic, informative, or scientific—will best serve this purpose. Your essay should incorporate a minimum of seven credible outside sources. They may be from the library, the Internet, an expert on your topic, or field research. Formulate a research plan and consult the guidelines in this book for developing your ideas and generating an outline. Here are some topic ideas:

- Yoga

- Bulimia

- Wii

- MySpace

- Discrimination

- Environmentalism

- Pressure on high school graduates to go to college

- Courses taught online

- Bilingual education

- Affirmative action

- Stereotyping

- College admissions requirements

- Female athletics

- Standards-based education

3. Write an essay that offers an interpretation of "A Rose fir Emily" (page 219) or "The Open Boat" (page 226). Be sure to use the strategies in chapter 9 for developing a thesis statement about literature using a theme, a character, a plot point, or a personal opinion. Use the seven steps to take you through the writing process. Before submitting your essay, participate in a peer review workshop (see Revision Tools in chapter 5, 7, and the end of this chapter) to get some suggestions for revising your draft.

4. Write a comparative evaluation of no more than five pages on the information contained on two different Internet Web sites that are devoted to the same historical subject. You may want to use the questions in writing exercise 10.3 on page 255 to guide your evaluation. Your comparative evaluation must be written as a scientific paper with the following organization:

- Begin with a brief introduction to the topic and state the hypothesis of your essay (e.g., Web site x is likely to be better than Web site y because . . . .)

- Provide a brief summary of the information on each Web site

- Evaluate the information on each Web site on the basis of the questions listed in Writing Exercise 10.3.

- Compare the two Web sites in the light of your evaluations.

- Determine which Web site is likely to contain the better information and discuss this conclusion in relation to the hypothesis you offered in the introduction.

Part 3 Revision Tools

Anytime you bring outside information into your paper, you should think carefully about the best way to use it. Following is a checklist you can use during the revision process to help you determine how effectively you have incorporated research into your paper:

RESEARCH PAPER CHECKLIST

✓ Review the sentences, phrases, and passages you incorporated into your paper. Is a context provided for each quotation and commentary given afterward?

✓ Decide, based on length and type of information, whether you have made good decisions about when to quote and when to paraphrase the information you have used from outside sources.

✓ Examine quotations and paraphrased information to be sure you have represented the relevant information only and in a way that does justice to the outside source's intent. Make sure that you haven't quoted more of the research material than is necessary because this will distract your readers from the point you are making.

✓ Decide if the placement of your quotations is correct. Have you used correct strategies to include quoted material within your own sentences by putting it at the beginning, middle, or end of your sentence? If the quotation is longer than four typed lines, have you set it off from the main text as a block quote? (Remember that the MLA guidelines for quotations of over four typed lines must be indented ten spaces and set off in a block. No quotation marks are used unless dialog is involved. This form signals to readers that you are quoting extensively.)

✓ Check sentences that include research material to be sure that they are grammatically correct. Make sure that you've opened and closed the quotation with quotation marks and used commas and periods correctly. Be sure that the quotation is cited correctly. (If you are not sure how to do this, see appendix C. For more help, consult a handbook.)

✓ Read aloud the section that includes the quotation, listening to see if you have provided graceful transitions into and out of the material. Does the quotation serve its purpose in the paper as a whole?

✓ Review your Works Cited pages for accuracy and prescribed style manual concerning formatting.

PEER REVIEW WORKSHEET

For the research paper writer:

1. What essay format did you use and why?

2. What do you hope to achieve with your readers?

3. Identify a problem you see in your draft that you'd like your reviewer to help you with. Describe it briefly.

For the research paper reviewer:

1. Read the essay through once and describe the overall dominant impression you receive.

2. Assess the essay's format and unity.

   a. Write what you understand the overarching statement to be. Indicate any confusion you have about the idea. Is it fully developed? Does the writer use the appropriate form, that is, C-S-C for an academic essay, CI for the informative essay, or the hypothesis for the scientific paper?

   b. Mention any revision of the overarching statement that you think is needed.

   c. If this is an academic essay, list the burdens of proof, as you see them. Then comment on how well the writer addressed these burdens. Are any missing? Are any underdeveloped?

3. Comment on the essay's content. Do you find it interesting? Does the writer need to develop ideas more fully to offer something less commonplace, less predictable? Offer any suggestions you have.

4. Evaluate the organization of the essay. Look at the way the essay is organized by making a scratch outline. Does the information seem to be logically ordered? If not, suggest a better way to organize it.

5. Comment on the strategies the writer uses in the introduction and conclusion. Make any suggestions you have for revision.

6. Look at each paragraph and see if the writer made effective use of TAXES. Mark any paragraphs that are underdeveloped and offer suggestions for revision.

7. Evaluate the use of research.

   a. Has the writer used research effectively to add to the essay's purpose?

   b. Has the writer incorporated quotations clearly? Are there places where a paraphrase or a summary would be preferable?

   c. Did the writer give proper citations for all quoted sources?

   d. Look over the list of research sources the writer used. Does the list seem balanced and are the selections appropriate, in your opinion? Be as specific as possible.

8. What parts of this essay are strong?

9. What parts are most in need of further revision?

Troubleshooting the Thesis Statement: Common Pitfalls

This appendix gives you some additional strategies for fine-tuning your thesis statement by putting the focus directly on the wording of the statement to identify rhetorical, syntactical, or grammatical weaknesses. The list that follows of ten thesis statement pitfalls might appear to contain simple stylistic considerations. However, if you consider that the alteration of a single word or phrase in your thesis statement can significantly alter its burdens of proof, you will recognize the potential importance of this fine-tuning process for your argument and for your essay as a whole.

We recommend that you revisit this section as you move through the revision process for any essay. As you become familiar with the strategies listed here, you will see that there is flexibility in how you use and apply them. These pitfalls are meant to call attention to *potential* problems. They are not meant to be used as fixed rules but as a way to make knowledgeable choices. For instance, you may decide after careful study of "the problem of because" that using the word *because* in your thesis statement is effective and appropriate for the particular essay you are writing, which is okay. Like all the techniques in this book, these are meant as guidelines to be adapted by the writer to each writing circumstance.

THE TEN THESIS STATEMENT PITFALLS

1. The problem of "these three things"

2. The problem of "because"

3. The problem of stating something in the negative

4. The problem of "no need to read"

5. The problem of "I will. . . ."

6. The problem of relative or abstract terms

7. The problem of passive voice

8. The problem of "to be" verbs

9. The problem of "did you know. . . ."

10. The problem of the soft thesis

The Problem of "These Three Things"

Example

> Controlling violence in the media will require a three-stage effort: increasing community awareness, raising enough money to spearhead a media campaign, and enlisting the support of powerful political allies.

You'll recognize this thesis statement by its characteristic promise to prove "x, y, and z." Because it is easy to formulate, it is often one of the first kinds of thesis statements we are taught to write and therefore one of the most familiar. When you are writing about a very complex issue, a "these three things" thesis statement may be perfectly fine, but in most cases it falls short in two ways. It makes a paper too predictable because it announces the topics up front. Readers, therefore, may be less inclined to read the essay. More importantly, it often lists three topics without tying them together with a strong "so what?" or statement of significance.

Of course, this thesis format might be varied to propose more or fewer than three topics. Whatever its manifestation, the "these three things" thesis can be improved by using abstraction to find a more interesting overarching claim that encompasses all three ideas.

The thesis statement above can be improved as follows:

> Controlling violence in the media requires the intervention of unlikely allies, including politicians and community members.

The Problem of "Because"

Example 1

> Drugs are bad because they kill you.

Using the word *because* in a thesis statement often leads to a thesis that summarizes the argument or makes a statement of fact and leaves you with little to prove. What you are trying to produce instead is a thesis that, like a drum roll, announces itself as a provocative claim. Often, for a more compelling thesis statement, you will have to revise to eliminate the word *because*. If you do use *because* in a thesis statement, be sure that it is followed by an interesting claim.

> Drugs are so overprescribed today that physicians and drug companies are increasingly seen as enablers instead of healers.

Example 2

Original:

> Although pornography is a controversial social issue, it is hard to resolve because of the ambiguity that surrounds it.

Revision:
  Pornography's associations with individual rights as opposed to community values makes it an irresolvable controversy.

Example 3
Original:
  A Women should never take her husband's name when she marries because then she loses her own identity.

Even in thesis statements where the "because" phrase does not summarize the argument, some rewriting can improve the strength of the statement:

Revision:
  A Women who takes her husband's name when she marries loses her own identity.

The Problem of Stating Something in the Negative

  Despite Smith's analysis, Kate Chopin's *The Awakening* is not a Realist novel.

Although there are exceptions (like the thesis that disproves a widely held notion), thesis statements should be phrased positively. A claim that says "This is not an apple," doesn't get us very far. If it is not an apple, what is it? Try to say what something *is* rather than what it is not. Use the technique of asking "so what?" to see what you discover.

For this thesis statement, the key burden of proof is to show that *The Awakening* is not a Realist novel, which is difficult, if not impossible, to prove. For a writer to convincingly argue this thesis, she would have to describe *all* the elements of a Realist novel and show how Chopin's work *cannot* fit into this category. This is a slippery slope that can be avoided easily by rephrasing the thesis in positive terms, as follows.

  Despite Smith's analysis, Kate Chopin's *The Awakening* is better categorized as a Modernist rather than a Realist work.

With this thesis, a writer could argue that Chopin's work does not fit traditional criteria for Realist works. The burdens of proof entail illustrating that there are significant elements associated with Modernism that better define *The Awakening*.

The Problem of "No Need to Read"

Example 1
Original:
  In the *Autobiography of Benjamin Franklin,* the narrator portrays a false sense of modesty by using the following rhetorical devices: his proclamation of himself as the ideal role model for young American men, his practice of name dropping for the purpose of creating a heightened level of importance, and his use of epistles as a method of self-praise easily masked by the voice of others.

Similar to the "these three things" thesis, this type of thesis statement summarizes the argument rather than asserting or posing an argument. Often long and windy, the "no need to read" thesis statement reveals all the main ideas encapsulated in the essay. This thesis does not entice readers into the essay and many readers will not read beyond it. To improve this thesis, look for a statement that overarches its points. First isolate the key terms and ideas, and then use abstraction to formulate a more succinct and provocative thesis statement. A revision follows:

Revision:
> Franklin portrays a false sense of modesty as a way to engage the good will of readers so that they accept Franklin as a role model.

Example 2
Original:
> Although Jade Snow Wong insists that her book was written in an attempt to create a "better understanding of the Chinese culture on the part of Americans," it is clear by the various references to her family's adoption of Christianity, her interest in American activities, her unfailing support of America, and her entrepreneurial spirit, that Wong is attempting to prove herself to her mainstream audience with hopes of convincing them that she is loyal to America.

Revision:
> While Jade Snow Wong insists that her book was written in an attempt to create a "better understanding of the Chinese culture on the part of Americans," it is clear that Wong has a personal—and problematic—agenda to be accepted by a mainstream audience.

The Problem of "I Will . . ." (Analyze, Discuss, Explain, Examine . . .)

Example 1
> In this essay I will explore the similarities and differences between a documentary film and a Hollywood film.

At best, "I will . . ." is gratuitous when included in a thesis statement. By definition, the paper promises to present and explain your thoughts, so there is no need to remind readers whose thoughts these are. At worst, the phrase "I will . . ." may lead you into a statement of intention rather than a claim, a plan rather than a provocative argument. The revision explains a particular comparison point:

Revision:
Although the genre of documentary film purports to capture an honest, untouched picture of life, it is actually as much a re-creation of life as many genre Hollywood films.

Example 2

Original:

> I will discuss how the themes of the film *Titanic* relate to the culture we are living in today and why the movie appealed to an array of audiences.

Revision:

> The film *Titanic* appeals to an array of audiences because its theme of a strong female protagonist relates directly to present-day culture.

Example 3

Original:

I will analyze the film *Casino Royale* to show that it is not well made.

Revision:

> The pedestrian qualities of the film *Casino Royale* make it a disappointment.

The Problem of Relative or Abstract Terms

Example 1

> Hawthorne's tale "Young Goodman Brown" portrays the presence of evil in all humans.

Subjective terms such as wonderful, good, justice, evil, beauty, and love mean different things to different people; they may also mean different things in different situations. Generally speaking, a thesis will improve with the writer's use of concrete terms that can be objectively proven, as follows:

Revision:

> In "Young Goodman Brown," Hawthorne presents a disturbing allegory about the desire in all of us to violate moral codes.

Example 2

Original:

> In the marathon race between Al Burns and Anna Johnson, the referee committee made a terrific decision.

Revision:

> The controversial finish in yesterday's marathon race was resolved fairly by the referee committee.

In some cases, abstract terms may be included in the thesis statement for provocative effect or when an abstract term best represents the scope of the subject under scrutiny. In these cases, writers must be aware that the crux of their proof will rely on how well they define the abstract term. If you use abstract terms without discussing them thoroughly in the essay, then have not not fulfilled an important burden of proof.

The Problem of Passive Voice

Example 1
Original:
> In Kate Chopin's *The Awakening*, physical love is allowed outside of marriage.

Passive voice disguises agency and often leaves writing flat (see appendix C), but it can also interfere with the clarity of your thesis statement. Passive construction, like that used in the current example, places the emphasis of the argument on the receiver of the action rather than on the agent of that action. This may cloud your argument and rob it of its punch, or worse, preclude you from making a clear claim. The following revision solves this problem:

> Kate Chopin's *The Awakening* embraces physical love outside of marriage as a legitimate bond between men and women.

Example 2
> Gun control has been thwarted by the lobbying of a powerful minority. Media violence has been supported by advertising dollars.

There is another aspect to consider regarding passive construction in your thesis statement. As you know from studying thesis statements' burdens of proof and their role in shaping your essay, the term in the subject position of the thesis statement plays an important role in establishing the focus and shape of the essay. If you use passive construction in your thesis statement, see if revising to active voice will foreground the subject that is the focus of your essay and make it a more precise statement of your argument.

> The lobbying of a powerful minority has rightly thwarted gun control. Advertising dollars support media violence.

The Problem of "to Be" Verbs

Example 1
Original:
> Primetime television is filled with violence.

Verb forms of "to be" (am, is, are, was, etc.) in your thesis statement sometimes allow you to make a declarative statement of fact without including an interpretive claim. This is especially true with the verb form "is," which, in addition to promoting passive tense within a sentence, can also serve as a reflexive verb that replicates that which is on one side of the sentence with its equal on the other side of the sentence. In other words, using "is" often leads to a claim that is a statement of fact rather than a statement that warrants debate. The following revision gives credence to a particular issue:

Revision:
The significant amount of violence in primetime television makes the V-chip blocking device an important requirement in homes with young children.

Example 2
Original:
Gun control is a concern of the American public.

Revision:
The issues surrounding gun control well illustrate the American concept of democracy.

Example 3
Original:
Shrek is a film that combines computer animation with computer-enhanced reality.

Revision:
The use of computer-enhanced reality in the film *Shrek* signals the film's message to escape our social problems rather than to commit to social reforms.

Example 4
Original:
Homeless shelters are in every city and offer meals and a place to sleep to the poor.

Revision:
Many of the homeless shelters in our major cities offer the economic, physical, and psychological support that the poor need to escape the cycle of poverty.

The Problem of "Did You Know . . ."

Example 1
The Japanese bombed Pearl Harbor to cripple the U.S. fleet and therefore gain naval supremacy in the Pacific.

This thesis often highlights an interesting point or fact but gives little or no interpretive viewpoint. No knowledgeable person could argue against it. It is ultimately a good CI statement or statement of fact but a poor thesis statement. The following is a clear thesis statement:

Believing that overseas expansion was the only solution to its domestic problems, the Japanese attacked Pearl Harbor to remove the greatest obstacle to its imperial ambitions, the Pacific Fleet of the equally imperialistic United States.

Example 2

Original:

The ancient Greeks were the first people who instituted a democratic government.

Revision:

The ancient Greek invention of democracy was not the result of a popular uprising but arose from infighting for political supremacy among aristocratic families.

The Problem of the Soft Thesis

Example 1

Cigarette smoking can lead to serious health problems.

The soft thesis presents an argument that is so close to a statement of fact, summary, or a plan that some audiences would not consider it controversial; they would receive it as common knowledge. To avoid this pitfall, think more carefully about your audience and the level of knowledge they are likely to have about your subject. If it is a general audience, then a soft thesis might be acceptable. If the audience is more specialized, then a soft thesis probably needs to be revised or stepped up to a more debatable claim. Although it is possible to imagine a general audience for whom this thesis statement about cigarette smoking could be interesting—an audience of young adult smokers, for instance—for most audiences this statement is not controversial enough to generate interest as an argument.

A thesis needs to have a reason for existence, as exemplified below:

The social stigma attached to cigarette smoking today will eventually lead to its eradication.

The claim in this thesis statement is controversial. That is, many people will likely question the idea that social pressure will be powerful enough to make cigarette smoking disappear. A claim such as this one will draw readers' interest in a way that the soft thesis will not.

Example 2

Original:

Martin Luther King Jr.'s commitment to nonviolent forms of protest led to history's assessment of him as a great man.

Revision:

Martin Luther King Jr.'s commitment to nonviolent forms of protest was paradoxically both his greatest strength and his greatest weakness.

Example 3

Original:

The abuse of prescription drugs can cause serious health problems for the user.

Revision:

Because of the serious health risks that come with the long-term use of prescription drugs, it is time to fund research to find herbal and homeopathic replacements.

Patterns of Argument in Your Thesis Statement: More on Burdens of Proof

As you learned in chapter 4, identifying the burdens of proof in a thesis statement requires some analysis, but using strategies such as the Four Tasks to Manage Your Burdens of Proof can help make the process easier. Here we will help you identify six logical patterns that are inherent in thesis statements. Each of these six patterns lends itself to specific writing techniques and, once you are familiar with them, you will see that writers use them all the time to accomplish their goals. They will probably all be familiar to you, even if you do not call them by these names or think of them as conventional patterns of reasoning. Use them in conjunction with the four tasks in chapter 4 to identify what type of logical relationship is at the core of your thesis statement. Then decide how best to organize and cover your burdens of proof to make your argument compelling for your readers.

Occasionally, a thesis statement may require two or more of these argument patterns working in conjunction. Thesis statements always carry inherent burdens of proof, and taking the time to identify them will help you draft a well-developed and compelling paper.

SIX PATTERNS OF ARGUMENT

1. An argument that establishes a cause-and-effect relationship

2. An argument that takes a position or proposes a solution

3. An argument that gives an interpretation

4. An argument that qualifies a commonly held belief (the Contrarian's Argument)

5. An argument that makes a claim of relative value (the best, the worst, the most)

6. An argument that proposes a definition

Establishing a Cause-and-Effect Relationship

The burden of proof for a cause-and-effect thesis statement entails explaining how, exactly, a particular cause is connected to a specific effect. To make the case, it is necessary to explain—through logical, step-by-step links between the cause and the effect—that these two things are not simply related by correlation or coincidence; one directly and unavoidably *leads to* the other.

These arguments seek to uncover why something happened and are well supported by factual evidence, such as examples and statistics. Notice in the following examples that the words *cause* and *effect* are rarely used, but the expectation is that the writer will establish a direct correlation between the cause and the effect to prove each thesis statement. If you are unsure whether you have this type of claim, check the examples and the box below for common synonyms for cause and effect.

An example will help here:

The <u>alarm clock's ring</u> <u>woke me</u> up.

    cause   effect

In this sentence, you can imagine how the alarm clock's ring (the cause) produced the effect of waking up. If you were to explain the step-by-step logic involved in this cause-and-effect relationship, you might say that (1) at a preset time, the mechanism in the alarm produced a noise, (2) the noise was received by your ears, (3) the sound traveled

---

SOME SYNONYMS FOR CAUSE AND EFFECT

Cause:

(nouns)	(verbs)
issue, idea	generates institutes
source	brings about
origin	gives rise to
agent	raises
mover	induces
producer	produces
creator	creates
contributor	contributes

Effect:

achievement	conclusion	aftereffect
accomplishment	end	fall out
result	sequel	wake of
consequence	aftermath	by-product, side effect
production	outgrowth	offshoot
outcome	turnout	repercussion
reaction	impact	implication

to your brain, (4) your brain registered the sound, and (5) you woke up. According to this rationale, the alarm clock's ring—and nothing else—caused you to wake up.

Most writing projects will entail more complicated cause-and-effect explanations than this one, such as the following:

> Nintendo's *James Bond* video game encourages (causes) the breakdown of family values (effect).

> Computers have led the way (caused) to a new sense of professionalism for the American worker (effect).

Cause-and-effect reasoning is important because being able to establish a causal link between two things allows you to demonstrate how change is effected. In other words, if we can understand how a cause has led to an effect, then we may be better able to produce desired results in the future. You've heard the saying that "a chain is only as strong as its weakest link." So it is with cause-and-effect relationships—it's essential that each step (link) in your chain of reasoning is solidly forged.

Cause versus Coincidence

Don't confuse coincidence with cause and effect. Correlation is not causation. When illustrating the chain of logic that ties cause to effect in your essay, be sure each link on the chain is clear. If links in your chain have a relationship of coincidence rather than cause and effect, your argument will collapse. For example,

> My favorite basketball team is playing in the national championship tonight; therefore I better not eat sauerkraut. Every time I eat sauerkraut and they play, they lose.

Just because you observe what you think is a correlation between the team's results and your eating habits doesn't mean that a cause-and-effect relationship exists. You need more evidence to establish such a relationship. You would have to show by careful step-by-step reasoning how your eating habits directly impacted the players and the outcome of the game. It's more likely that the outcome of the game was a result of factors other than what you had for dinner, such as the performance of the star players, the leadership of the coaches, and so forth. This assertion is an example of coincidence, superstition, and "false cause." For more on the "false cause" pitfall, review the logical fallacies section in chapter 4.

Applying the Four Tasks

> Men still find today that their mental health depends on their being the main financial provider for their families.

STEP 1:

Context: American society today

Subject: men's mental health

Claim: still depends on being the main financial provider for the family

STEP 2:

"Men's mental health" is an example of a specialized term (or phrase) that requires explanation. Because the thesis claim is dependent on the reader's understanding of this concept, it is important that you provide a definition of what you mean by men's mental health early in the essay. Hence, defining men's mental health is a burden of proof for this thesis statement.

Notice that the word *today* establishes the context for this argument in contemporary society (rather than a past or future society), and the prepositional phrase *for the family* limits the subject to men who *provide for a family*. These terms inform all the burdens of proof because the argument must take place within these parameters. (It is also likely that these terms will be addressed in the introduction of the essay because part of the function of an essay's opening paragraph is to describe the circumstances in which the argument takes place.)

According to this thesis, men's mental health is dependent on continuing—today—to inhabit the traditional role of financial provider—presumably, despite the large numbers of women today who work full-time. Therefore, the burden of proof connected to this adverb must establish a link between past and present showing that even though men and women are increasingly equal in our workplaces, men in our culture still see their value in terms of being the family provider.

Notice, too, the superlative *main* provider. This key term acknowledges that there may be multiple financial providers in a family, but men's mental health is dependent on being the *primary* one.

Thus, the burdens of proof (so far) are as follows:

- define what is meant by men's mental health in the context of today's society

- show that even though women are increasingly considered equal to men in our society, men's psychological health is still dependent on an older model of gender roles

- show that, according to this thesis statement, a partner can contribute to the household income, but when she becomes the main financial provider instead of the man, his mental health suffers

STEP 3:

As discussed in step 2, the terms that require definition, such as men's mental health, must precede the discussion of the claim.

Notice, too, when examining the relationship between the subject and claim, that the underlying argument is one of dependence. The paper must prove that men's mental health *depends* on being their families' main financial provider.

STEP 4:

- define what is meant by men's mental health in the context of today's society

- show that even though women are increasingly considered equal to men in our society, men's psychological health is still dependent on an older model of gender roles (dependent argument)

- show that, according to this thesis statement, a partner can contribute to the household income, but when she becomes the main financial provider, his mental health suffers (dependent argument)
- Show that men psychologically depend on their role as main financial provider for their families

Notice that this thesis statement is predicated on two qualifiers—a specialized term (men's mental health) and a superlative (main)—each of which suggests important burdens of proof that must be fulfilled to address a reader's expectations and make a compelling argument. Specifically, you must give clear criteria for how the superlative is being defined. If a pie is judged to be the best, then you must explain the criteria you are using to evaluate pies. After defining the subject, it is most important to include a thorough discussion of the various qualifiers involved in the thesis statement. The order in which the qualifiers are discussed is less important.

Taking a Position or Proposing a Solution

When proposing a solution or taking a position, you will have to identify both the problem and the solution. The crux of the argument, your key burden of proof, will be to show how the solution or position you propose, from among the realm of possible proposals, is the best one according to criteria you establish. Many potential solutions may be valid, but your job is to tell, as precisely as possible, on what terms your proposition is the most compelling.

This type of argument usually applies to something in the real world (rather than the world of a novel, a film, or a painting) and uses evidence such as statistical data, surveys, studies, government documents, and authoritative opinions. Most often, the essay will describe the problem first and the proposed policy or solution second. To be convincing, this type of argument often requires the writer to describe other possible solutions (that is, potential counterarguments) and show how the proposed solution or alternative is the best.

STRATEGIES FOR SUPPORTING CAUSE-AND-EFFECT THESIS STATEMENTS

- Use the cause-and-effect synonyms on page 271 to help decipher your writing assignments.
- Don't confuse coincidence with cause and effect (correlation is not causation).
- Be sure to establish cause-and-effect relationships without missing any important links in the chain of logic.
- Be open to seeing more than one cause or more than one effect.
- Recognize the difference between multiple causes or effects and subordinate or secondary links within the causal relationship.

Look at the following thesis statements that propose a solution or take a position and notice how they highlight both the implied problem and the solution or position proposed.

> For the music industry today, copyright laws should be set aside in favor of free Internet distribution.

- *Problem*: Internet file sharing has led to an increase in copyright violations and a decrease in profit in the music industry.

- *Solution*: set aside copyright laws just for Internet distribution because mass marketing can increase rather than decrease profits (presumably copyright laws would remain intact for retail sales and other forms of distribution).

> It is vital for the United States to mandate stronger fuel efficiency standards to preserve the ecosystem for human life.

- *Problem*: Wide-scale fuel usage is threatening the ecosystem and human survival, and the United States is one of the biggest consumers.

- *Solution*: the United States should mandate stronger fuel-use standards to promote global health.

Thesis statements or arguments that take a position often presume that a reader has enough knowledge about the controversy or issue under discussion that the claim will make sense—but this is not always the case. For these arguments, it is important to spend some extra time assessing the audience and deciding how much context is required for your writing circumstance. Regarding the thesis statement about file sharing, for instance, you will likely have some readers who think there is nothing wrong with sharing files on the Internet. You will have to spend some time convincing them that file sharing is a problem that affects a significant portion of our society before they will be ready to consider a solution.

Applying the Four Tasks—Example 1

> The Electoral College that determines U.S. presidential elections is obsolete and should be disbanded.

STEP 1:

Context: U.S. presidential elections

Subject: the electoral college system

Claim: is obsolete and should be disbanded

STEP 2:

In examining this thesis sentence, note that the general reader may not know much—or anything—about the Electoral College that currently determines U.S. presidential elections. For this reason, "Electoral College" functions as a specialized term that requires some definition and thus generates a burden of proof.

STEP 3:

Note that the writer must first explain how the Electoral College is obsolete and then, based on its obsolete status, argue that it should be disbanded. The word *obsolete* implies that there was once a time when the Electoral College served an important purpose. The essay must therefore discuss the original purpose of the Electoral College and then show that this purpose is no longer necessary or that it is potentially fulfilled by other means, making the Electoral College antiquated. In other words, the writer must give some background information. He or she might even go on to conclude that there are other more democratic ways to determine a president (e.g., the popular vote) or that the inefficiency of the system renders the Electoral College cumbersome and needlessly expensive. Now we can articulate the burdens of proof we have identified.

- explain the concept of the Electoral College

- describe why the Electoral College was necessary when it was established

- show that this necessity no longer exists (dependent argument)

- show that it should be disbanded because its necessity no longer exists (and we are better off without it) (dependent argument)

STEP 4:

As discovered in step 3, the first three burdens of proof should be covered first and then the last one should be covered.

Applying the Four Tasks—Example 2

In spite of the excitement about genetic cloning, it shouldn't be used right now because our limited knowledge makes it too dangerous.

STEP 1:

Context: a society excited about genetic cloning

Subject: genetic cloning

Claim: shouldn't be used right now because our limited knowledge makes it too dangerous.

STEP 2:

In spite of the excitement about genetic cloning, it shouldn't be used right now because our limited knowledge makes it too dangerous.

The first phrase of this thesis statement—"in spite of the excitement about"—is an introductory phrase that helps to set the context for the thesis statement by calling attention to the widely held enthusiasm about genetic cloning in which this claim—that cloning should not be used—is situated. This introductory phrase focuses on the fact that the claim is going against a current trend. This essay will not simply discuss the current trend of excitement and the reasons for its existence, but it will go on to argue that in spite of this excitement, our limited knowledge about genetic cloning makes it too dangerous to use. According to this thesis, the dangers outweigh the potential benefits. The introductory phrase adds a burden of proof to the essay—it must substantiate this general excitement for cloning and show why it exists. Imagine the thesis statement without this introductory phrase, and you can better see what it adds to this argument. Whenever there is an introductory phrase, it is important to examine it closely because there may be key terms that add a burden of proof.

Note that the subject of this thesis statement, genetic cloning, refers to a specialized subject that, unless the audience is highly knowledgeable, requires definition. Although many people will undoubtedly have heard about this concept, few will know exactly what the writer means by it, so it is important to give readers a basic understanding of what is meant by genetic cloning. This specialized term therefore imposes another burden of proof on the essay.

In examining the claim, notice that it contains three key phrases that help to define its limits. The thesis statement puts forward an argument that genetic cloning shouldn't be used, and it stipulates the temporal terms of the claim—that it shouldn't be used *right now*—suggesting that this writer might advocate for its use at a future time. There is also a rationale given for the claim that cloning should not be used right now—because there is *limited knowledge* and therefore cloning is *too dangerous*. These three phrases help to establish the line of reasoning this argument must take, and therefore they each constitute burdens of proof for this essay. Imagine if the thesis claim said something different—that cloning shouldn't be used because it is morally wrong or because the potential for abuse is too large. These ideas would set forth very different burdens of proof and generate very different essays. Thus, the burdens of proof are as follows:

- describe what is meant by genetic cloning
- substantiate the general excitement about genetic cloning and show what it is based on
- describe how our knowledge about cloning is limited
- discuss why the limited knowledge makes cloning too dangerous
- describe why cloning should not be used right now (but perhaps should be used at a later time)

STEP 3:
As discussed earlier with problem and solution arguments, you must first state the problem before making an argument for your solution. Therefore, to support the argument that a lack of information makes cloning so dangerous that it should be curtailed, the writer must first show that we have only a limited understanding of cloning. The writer can't assume that readers know about these limits, and this knowledge is one of the

steps on which this thesis is based. Once this foundation is laid, it is easy to move to the next burden of proof, which is the central one—that, given these dangers, cloning is best curtailed.

STEP 4:
The writer must decide how to organize these burdens and how much of the essay is devoted to each one. These decisions are a matter of evidence, style, and approach. For instance, one writer might combine the first two burdens of proof for this thesis statement and cover them both in an introductory paragraph. Another writer might leave the issue of widespread excitement until the end and spend the bulk of the introduction giving background on the nature of genetic cloning. These choices are made based on the subject matter, the evidence, the audience, and the writer's interests and experience. What is important is that all the burdens of proof are meaningfully covered and that independent arguments are addressed before dependent arguments.

Giving an Interpretation

Certain subjects, such as works of literature, film, or music, require students to write essays supporting thesis statements that offer an interpretation. Here are some examples:

• In director Kenneth Branagh's film version of Mary Shelley's *Frankenstein*, the monster depicts the detrimental effects of isolation and alienation on human beings.

- In William Faulkner's *As I Lay Dying*, the child is used as a vehicle to portray the South's arrested development.

- The television show *The Simpsons* contributes to a dangerous trend of anti-intellectualism in American society today.

- The music and lyrics of the newly released CD by Eric Clapton and J. J. Cale send a clear message that the simple life offers the most rewards.

- Edward Hopper's painting *Nighthawks* captures post–World War II American life as entrapped in isolation and sterility.

For any one such subject, there may be a number of valid, well-supported, and persuasive interpretations. When you develop an argument in this context, your goal is not so much to offer the *best* interpretation, as it is to offer a *provocative* interpretation, one that adds to readers' appreciation of the subject. In short, if you are writing an interpretive essay, your burdens of proof should show how and why your interpretation is supportable and therefore valid; but you do not have to show that your interpretation is better than other possible interpretations. The evidence used for arguments of interpretation is often from primary texts (such as a novel or a film, philosophy or theory) or secondary sources (such as literary critical articles and historical analysis). For more on interpretive writing, see chapter 9.

For interpretive claims, the crux of the argument is to be sure that you have an insightful kernel—a "so what?" in your thesis claim. It is particularly easy to mistake a statement of fact or a statement of summary for an interpretive claim. For instance, if you argue that the television show *The Simpsons* illustrates an American theme of anti-intellectualism, you would simply be offering a summary of the show rather than an interpretation of it. Any regular viewer of *The Simpsons* will recognize this as a statement of fact. To develop a full thesis statement, you will have to include a claim about your subject: What does *The Simpsons* say about anti-intellectualism? If you modified your statement to say that "*The Simpsons* contributes to a dangerous trend of anti-intellectualism found in prime-time television shows that are popular today," then this unexpected argument would constitute an intriguing claim because it would bring a new viewpoint to bear. What is dangerous about anti-intellectualism? Few people who watch this show may have thought of it in this way, so this might be an interesting perspective for readers to consider.

Applying the Four Tasks

We will use Mary Shelley's Frankenstein thesis as an example of the steps to take.

> In director Kenneth Branagh's film version of Mary Shelley's *Frankenstein,* the monster depicts the detrimental effects of isolation and alienation on human beings.

STEP 1:

Context: film version of *Frankenstein*

Subject: the monster

Claim: depicts the detrimental effects of isolation and alienation on human beings

STEP 2:

This analysis should focus only on Branagh's film version of *Frankenstein* (not the book version or a different film version, although these may be mentioned briefly for a purposeful comparison on a specific point).

The essay will have to define exactly what is meant by detrimental effects, rather than, for example, catastrophic or tragic effects. It will have to make clear why this particular adjective was chosen to represent this insight.

Also, the essay will have to make clear what is meant by "isolation and alienation on human beings." Remember that the burden of an interpretative claim is to reveal a compelling and insightful perspective, not to prove that your interpretation is the best or the only one that is compelling. Therefore, in addition to providing clear criteria for complex terms, such as *isolation* and *alienation*, there is a burden to show—not merely assert—through a careful explication of textual evidence how these ideas can be seen in the text, as denoted by the burdens of proof below:

- make clear in the context of the film what is meant by detrimental effects

- make clear in the context of the film what is meant by isolation and alienation

- make clear in the context of the film how these effects apply to human beings

STEP 3:

One way to approach this claim is to cover these burdens of proof vertically, instead of horizontally, by sculpting paragraphs in such a way that they support each of the three burdens of proof. To do this, you would decide which examples of isolation and alienation you will discuss in the essay. Then give one example in each paragraph. In the discussion part of the paragraph for each example, show how the example represents isolation and alienation and, furthermore, the detrimental effects on the human subject that result. The strength of this essay will be found in how well you make the connections among these three burdens of proof for each example and the number of compelling examples you bring forward.

STEP 4:

If you decide to cover the burdens of proof vertically—that is, in each paragraph—then the order of the essay will be determined by the order in which you introduce your examples. Some writers advocate starting with your second best example so that you end with your strongest example. Other writers believe in leading with your strongest example. Also consider issues such as the storyline, the chronology of the text, and the accessibility to the reader of the example/argument in choosing how you organize the evidence in your paper.

Qualifying a Commonly Held Belief (The Contrarian's Argument)

Many excellent thesis statements begin with a commonly held belief that the writer seeks to overturn. The thing that makes this thesis interesting is precisely the fact that it

STRATEGIES FOR SUPPORTING A THESIS STATEMENT THAT GIVES AN INTERPRETATION

- Have a C-S-C in your thesis statement.

  It is particularly easy to mistake a complex pattern or subject for an argument with significance. Take extra care to check that your thesis statement has a clear C-S-C so that your argument will be satisfying.

- Know your subject area.

  Sometimes you discover after doing some research that an idea that sounded like a compelling claim is actually a statement of something so commonly accepted that it is considered to be truth. In these cases, you can attempt to qualify the statement by adding one or more carefully selected adjectives or by overturning the belief entirely.

- See chapter 9 on writing about literature for more tips on interpretive writing.

flies in the face of conventional wisdom. Because a commonly accepted idea is not, by definition, debatable, the key burden of proof for this kind of thesis statement is to show that what has often been accepted as truth should, instead, be questioned and possibly displaced by a different point of view. Because this argument is *contrary* to the general thought about an issue, we also call this the Contrarian's Argument. This type of thesis may take any of the following forms:

Although X . . ., Y . . .

Even though X . . ., Y . . .

Despite the fact that X . . ., Y . . .

In spite of X . . ., Y . . .

X . . .; however, . . . Y

This is not to say that simply beginning with the word *although* or placing a *however* in the middle of the thesis statement will result in a compelling claim. Templates give you a format for writing; they don't help you to analyze the content of your work. These templates should signal you to look for an argument against a commonly held belief, but they don't guarantee that one is present.

Following are some examples of commonly held beliefs paired with examples of thesis statements that qualify that belief.

History

Commonly-Accepted Idea: The Japanese attacked Pearl Harbor out of naked aggression.

Thesis Statement: A common assumption is that the Japanese attacked Pearl Harbor out of naked aggression; however, because of a U.S. embargo, they had little choice.

Social Science

Commonly Accepted Idea: Charles Darwin developed a theory based on the "survival of the fittest."

Thesis Statement: The widely used phrase *survival of the fittest* misrepresents Darwin's theory, which is actually better represented by the phrase *reproduction of the fittest*.

Science

Commonly Accepted Idea: Red meat is thought to be the key to good health due to its high protein and iron content.

Thesis Statement: Although red meat has been considered one of the keys to good health because of its high protein and iron content, recent studies have shown that it is, in fact, one of the most harmful things you can eat.

Literature

Commonly Accepted idea: Oedipus's murder of his father and marriage to his mother suggest that he is crazy, immoral, or both.

Thesis Statement: Despite the fact that Oedipus murders his father and marries his mother, he is the noble hero in Shakespeare's *Hamlet*.

Architecture

Commonly Held belief: The Cathedral of Notre Dame is considered a Gothic cathedral.

Thesis Statement: The Cathedral of Notre Dame, characterized by most art historians as Gothic, exhibits enough anomalies to the Gothic style of architecture to render this characterization misleading.

Politics

Commonly Held Belief: Thomas Jefferson was democratically minded.

Thesis Statement: History has identified Thomas Jefferson as a democratically minded U.S. president; however, a number of his political views were more autocratic than democratic.

Sports

Commonly Held Belief: The athletes in the Olympic games manifested good sportsmanship.

Thesis Statement: Although many of the athletes in the Olympic games manifested good sportsmanship, skater Michelle Kwan could easily be cast as this year's ideal role model.

Generally speaking, you can refute a commonly held assumption, challenge it, or qualify it. Adding strong qualifying adjectives to the commonly held idea can open up a space for argument, if those adjectives qualify the issue at the heart of the claim and are chosen with a thorough understanding of the assumptions underlying the belief. The best adjectives to choose are ones that are extreme, exciting, controversial, or dramatic because these single words or short phrases will clearly define your burdens of proof and make your argument interesting. One danger of this technique is that it may lead to a thesis that flirts with personal opinion. Another is that extreme terms such as *ideal* or *quintessential* may be very difficult to prove. Be sure to consider the limits of your support before you use an extreme term to qualify your thesis claim.

Applying the Four Tasks—Example 1

We will use an example from science to illustrate the key steps.

> Although red meat has been considered one of the keys to good health because of its high protein and iron content, recent studies have shown that it is, in fact, one of the most harmful things we can eat.

STEP 1:

Context: good health

Subject: red meat

Claim: red meat is one of the most harmful things we can eat

STEP 2:

The phrase *Although red meat has been considered one of the keys to good health because of its high protein and iron content*, sets the context for this claim because this is the commonly held belief against which this claim argues. It will be important to stipulate this argument carefully and objectively, probably in the essay's introduction, to establish a context as well as credibility with your readers—some of whom subscribe to this position and whose minds you hope to change. (Review the Straw Man Argument, in particular, in the logical fallacies section of chapter 4.) Note that your job in setting forth this commonly held belief is explaining how red meat's protein and iron content have convinced many of its key role for good health.

Your burdens of proof include showing that red meat is not only harmful to consume but also among the *most* harmful things a person can eat. You must do this by calling the reader's attention to recent studies. This then produces the following burdens of proof:

- establish the commonly held belief that red meat is considered to be one of the keys to good health because of its high protein and iron content

- use recent studies to show that consuming red meat is harmful

- use recent studies to show that red meat is among the most harmful things we can eat

STEP 3:

As with the problem/solution argument, the commonly held belief must be clear before the claim can be meaningful. You should gauge your audience to decide how much context to give but, at a minimum, articulate what you think is the generally held belief to orient your reader.

STEP 4:

As always, you will need to take into account the weight and strength of your evidence to best organize your paper.

STRATEGIES FOR A THESIS STATEMENT THAT CHALLENGES A COMMONLY HELD BELIEF

- Begin with a belief that is, indeed, commonly held.
- Place the commonly held belief or assumption in the subject position of the C-S-C and the a qualification of that subject in the claim.

STEP 5:

To be compelling, a thesis statement that makes a claim of relative value relies on carefully drawn definitions and comparisons. These arguments claim that something has a certain degree of value, so the key burden of proof involves a comparison to other possible values. Terms such as *good, bad,* and *best* are relative terms on their own because they are applied very differently by each of us. These arguments' burdens of proof require that you first establish clear terminology and criteria for assessing the value of your subject. Then you must systematically apply those criteria to your subject to prove your overall point.

For instance, if you describe a CD as the best of the year, someone else might consider it the year's worst. If you both can first agree on the criteria that define best and worst, your reasoning and meaning would become clearer to one another. You could then have a more meaningful conversation about the different ways to appreciate and evaluate musical CDs. Research may be required because this kind of thesis statement assumes a particularly wide breadth of knowledge about the subject under study.

In the following examples, the value-laden term or phrase is in **bold**.

- In *Guernica*, Picasso's style **effectively** protests war.
- The Bombing of Pearl Harbor was **the most important** battle of World War II.
- The **most important** lesson of the twentieth century teaches that racial equality will be the secret to world peace.
- Eating constitutes the **best** pleasure in life.
- The **ideal** mate surprisingly exhibits one's opposite qualities.
- The **best** education focuses on the humanities.
- She gave the **most valuable** statement of the campaign in the opening speech.
- The **kindest** act we can do sometimes seems to be the **cruelest**.
- Joseph Campbell's work comprises the **most compelling** study of the hero figure in mythology.

If you are to support the burdens of proof for a claim of this kind, you will have to rely on logic and the careful articulation of your definition of the value-laden term. For instance, if your roommate, acting as a peer editor to help you revise a rough draft, wrote on your paper that you did not use evidence effectively, but you believe you did, it will be important for each of you to define exactly what you mean by effective evidence usage so that you can reconcile the disagreement. You might argue that effective usage means integrating appropriate quotations, explaining their significance, and tying them back to the argument at hand. Your roommate may believe that effective usage entails finding relevant sources, selecting inspiring quotations, and integrating the selections in a way that aids the flow of your essay. You both have valid viewpoints. Even if you do not see eye to eye, the logic and criteria used to arrive at your claim of value should be clear and reasonable. This is the crux of a value-based claim.

Applying the Four Tasks—Example 2
We use the statement about the bombing of Pearl Harbor to illustrate the steps.

> The Japanese attack on Pearl Harbor started **the most important** battle of World War II.

STEP 1:
Context: World War II

Subject: Japanese attack on Pearl Harbor

Claim: The attack started the most important battle of the war.

STEP 2:
This thesis statement hinges on the idea that of all the battles of World War II, the battle at Pearl Harbor was the most important. Ostensibly, this essay will have to answer why this is so. It will do that by giving clear criteria for what makes a battle important. Is a battle important because of the implications for the rest of the war? Is it important because it caused the entrance of American involvement in this war? Is it important because of the use of particular artillery or ammunition?

In addition, this essay will have to consider likely counterarguments both in terms of its definition of *important* and its isolation of Pearl Harbor as *the most* important, according to those criteria. Critics may argue that there are alternative, better ways to define a battle as important, and that other battles in WWII were more significant—so this essay should anticipate those arguments with well thought-out counterarguments. This leads to two burdens of proof.

- define what constitutes an important battle
- show how, of all the battles in World War II, the battle at Pearl Harbor was the most important (dependent argument)

STEP 3:
The criteria for "most important" must be defined before they can be applied to the battle at Pearl Harbor, so there is a dependent argument.

STEP 4:

Just as there are many ideas about the placement of evidence, there are many theories about the best place to introduce counterarguments. Often counterarguments are given at the end of the essay, just before the conclusion, but there is no golden rule. For this essay, you might integrate counterarguments into the discussion regarding how you decided to define "most important battle" according to certain criteria and not other criteria. You could also discuss Pearl Harbor's impact on World War II by comparing it with other significant battles. Like the order of evidence, the way you acknowledge and deflect counterarguments is an important strategic choice that can be made only holistically—that is, by looking at the paper as a whole.

Proposing a Definition

Often, thesis statements hinge on specialized terms that require clear definition for the argument to be compelling. The definition of a term or concept is the central burden of proof. Even in cases where the claims are not considered to be claims of definition, there may be terms that must be defined before the central argument of the thesis can proceed. In these cases, you must be careful to identify the terms that require definition, and position the definition correctly—namely, before the argument that depends on it (the dependent argument). Here are two examples:

Mark Twain's *Huckleberry Finn* is a racist text and should not be read in schools.

The prevailing standards for college admission are unjust and should be redefined.

Applying the Four Tasks

In *Hamlet*, Shakespeare's famous play, Hamlet is mad and should not be held accountable for his actions.

STEP 1:
Context: Shakespeare's *Hamlet*

Subject: Hamlet

Claim: is mad and should not be held accountable for his actions.

STEP 2:
In the claim portion of the thesis statement, the specialized term—*mad*—requires discussion. Therefore, one of the burdens of proof of this thesis claim is to define the meaning of madness in terms of the play.

STEP 3:
You must first define madness in terms of Hamlet's characterization in the play and then show that this madness means he should not be held accountable for his actions. As you identify a dependent logical relationship, at least two burdens of proof are already apparent: the background information required to make the argument (defining what you mean by "Hamlet is mad") and the dependent argument (that because of his madness, Hamlet should not be held accountable for his actions). The burdens of proof can be broken down as follows:

- define madness in the context of *Hamlet*

- prove that Hamlet exhibits this type of madness in the play

- given that Hamlet is mad, show why he should not be held accountable for his actions (dependent argument)

If you had trouble unpacking the thesis statement's burdens of proof, you can also arrive at them by asking questions about pivotal terms or phrases in the thesis statement. Following is an example of the questioning method:

What's the definition of madness?

What scenes show madness?

In *Hamlet*, Shakespeare's famous play, Hamlet is mad and should not be held accountable for his actions.

Why not?

- your definition of madness in the context of *Hamlet*

- in what scenes Hamlet exhibits these traits

- given that Hamlet is mad, why he should not be held accountable for his actions

STEP 4:
The definition of madness must precede its application to Hamlet's actions in the text. But how do you handle the burden of proof that requires you to identify scenes in the text where this kind of madness is displayed (burden 2)? Looking at the burdens of proof

listed in step 3, you could follow the order of the burdens as they are listed, or you could reverse or intertwine the discussion of the first two burdens. It is important, though, that the third burden is discussed last because this is a dependent argument in which you must establish that Hamlet is mad before you can discuss why he should or should not be held accountable for his madness.

One final point: laying out the burdens of proof in this way helps determine the outline of the essay—and it may also serve as an excellent prewriting strategy. Often the burdens of proof can be used as the basis for topic sentences and help to organize the essay from a bird's-eye view. They may also tell you that the thesis statement you have just unpacked does not match the evidence you have collected, and so revision might be necessary.

STRATEGIES FOR SUPPORTING THESIS STATEMENTS THAT PROPOSE DEFINITIONS

- Clearly define your central term.

  Be sure that your readers understand what you mean when you use a term on which your argument hinges.

- Think carefully about your readers.

  Do not take for granted that your readers share your understanding of the central term you are using. Get rid of all assumptions and build a careful definition from the ground up, so that your argument has a firm foundation.

Grammar, Style, and Rules for Citation

Editing Your Paper

If you think you are done with your paper after you have drafted and revised it a few times, you're missing an opportunity to fine-tune it at its most basic and perhaps obvious level—the level of grammar and style. Review these ten grammar points and the eight style points and then reread your essay with an eye toward improving your paper at the sentence level.

TEN GRAMMAR POINTS

1. usage errors:

   - it's and its

   - their, there, they're

   - your and you're

   - then and than

   - between and among

2. apostrophe placement

3. pronouns and antecedents must agree in number

4. subject/verb agreement

5. mixed construction

6. sentence fragments

7. run-on sentences

8. comma rules

9. faulty parallelism

10. dangling participle or dangling preposition

Grammar Points

1. USAGE ERRORS

it's and its

- The word is always a contraction for **it is**. For example, "**It's** cold today."

- The word is a possessive pronoun. For example, "The play is bad; **its** plot makes no sense."

When in doubt, replace the words **it is** for **it's** or **its** and see if it makes sense. If it makes sense, use **it's**.

their, there, they're

These words all sound alike—they are homophones—but they mean very different things.

- **Their** is a possessive pronoun, as in "**Their** tickets were no good at the show."

- **There** is usually used as an adverb, as in "Put the desk over **there**."

- **They're** is always a contraction for the words **they are,** as in "**They're** going to throw a party next week."

Here's an example that uses their, there, and they're all in one sentence:

> If a couple put a picture of themselves kissing on **their** MySpace page, **their** friends may say **they're** hamming it up too much, and **there** would be no end to the teasing for the rest of the year.

your and you're

These words also sound alike but have different meanings.

- **Your** is a possessive pronoun, as in "**Your** textbooks were all resold by **your** girlfriend."

- **You're** is a contraction for "you are," as in "**You're** not to blame for the car fire."

Both your and you're can appear in the same sentence:

> **Your** video game is played best when **you're** in the mood to aim and shoot.

then and than

- Use **then** to signal that something comes later or after: "Turn left at the corner, **then** go around the block and park."

- Use **than** for comparisons: "X is better **than** Y."

Signal words and comparison words can be used in the same sentence. For example,

> I believe butter is healthier **than** margarine, but when I eat too much of it, **then** I have to take a nap.

between and among

- Use **between** when comparing two items and **among** when comparing more than two items.

A sentence may have two different kinds of comparison. For example,

> If I have to choose **between** Coke and Pepsi, I will always take Coke; however, if I have the chance to choose from **among** all the drinks in the vending machine, I will pick water.

2. APOSTROPHE PLACEMENT

Be especially careful in your use and placement of apostrophes. Apostrophes are used to indicate either **possession** or a **contraction**.

For example, apostrophes are used in the following: "**Fred's** bicycle" for "the bicycle of Fred" or "she **can't**" for "she cannot." Possessive plural nouns also take apostrophes, such as "the **women's** center" (not "womens' center") or the "**geese's** nest" (not "geeses' nest"). When the last letter is an "s," the apostrophe goes after it: "**Robert Jones'** car" or the "**skiers'** hotel room." (However, some instructors accept either formation: "**Robert Jones's** or "**Robert Jones'**.")

Apostrophes are **not** used to indicate plurals: for example, the plural of "bicycle" is "bicycles," **not** "bicycle's."

3. PRONOUNS AND ANTECEDENTS MUST AGREE IN NUMBER

Make sure that **pronouns** and their **antecedents**, the nouns to which they refer, **agree** in number. Here are some examples that will clarify the usage.

> **Rome** was important because **they** produced many influential cultural achievements.

This sentence is grammatically flawed because the pronoun, "they," is plural in number, whereas its antecedent, "Rome," is singular in number. The sentence should be either: "**Rome** was important because **it** produced many influential cultural achievements" or "The **Romans** were important because **they** produced many influential cultural achievements."

> One often only sees the good a person has accomplished after they are dead.

Here, the antecedent, "a person," is singular in number whereas the pronoun, "they," is plural. The sentence should say, "One often only sees the good **a person** has accomplished after **he or she** is dead."

> Each character in the movie actually has their **[correction: his/her]** own designated type of makeup.

> When a writer writes an autobiography they are **[correction: he/she is]** not trying to give the reader just facts.

> Did everyone bring their **[correction: his or her]** books to class?

4. SUBJECT/VERB AGREEMENT

Subject/verb agreement is sometimes a challenge, especially when a prepositional phrase or another long phrase obscures the subject or places great distance between the subject and the verb. Double-check to be sure you are conjugating the verb to agree with the subject of the sentence. Remember that subjects separated by "or" usually take singular verbs, whereas subjects connected by "and" take plural verbs. For example,

> The sound of the narrator's voice and what it is saying is important to the film.

This sentence has a double subject—the "sound of the narrator's voice" and "what it is saying"—so it should use a plural verb. A correct version of the sentence is "The sound of the narrator's voice and what it is saying **are** both important to the film."

> Jake Gittes's pride and need for a good reputation outweighs the higher, less egotistical qualities within his character.

This sentence uses the singular conjugation of the verb "to outweigh" instead of the plural, even though there is a double subject ("pride **and** need for a good reputation"). A correct version is "Jake Gittes's pride and need for a good reputation **outweigh** the higher, less egotistical qualities within his character."

> The debates concerning the young people's riots in France was difficult to resolve.

The subject, the "debates" (plural), should agree in number with the verb, "was" (singular). The distance between the subject **and** verb can sometimes make it more difficult to recognize that the verb is not conjugated correctly. A correct version of this sentence is "The debates concerning the young people's riots in France **were** difficult to resolve."

5. MIXED CONSTRUCTION

A mixed construction occurs when a sentence's parts don't fit together logically or grammatically. In other words, a mixed construction sentence starts one way and then, part way through, it shifts direction so that it ultimately doesn't make sense. For example, the sentence may begin in one verb tense and switch to another for no clear reason, or there may be an unnecessary preposition or a dependent clause trying to stand alone as a sentence. The following sentence pairs show a mixed construction followed by their respective revisions.

> In "Privacy? What Privacy?" by Tina Lennox claims that privacy no longer exists in today's society.

In "Privacy? What Privacy?" Tina Lennox claims that privacy no longer exists in today's society.

All of Buddy Holly's immediate and extended family (with the exception of his father) had the ability to sing or play a musical instrument and did so at every family event and was a favorite past time.

All of Buddy Holly's immediate and extended family (with the exception of his father) had the ability to sing or play a musical instrument, and they often played and sang together at family gatherings.

6. SENTENCE FRAGMENTS

A complete sentence includes a subject and a predicate. A sentence fragment is missing one or both of these parts, or it might include both but contain a word that signals dependency. In this case, it is a subordinate clause rather than an independent clause and it cannot stand alone as a sentence. To fix sentence fragments, add the missing subject or predicate to turn them into independent clauses. When they are subordinate clauses, attach them to a full sentence. For example, three sentence fragments are followed by possible revisions.

- All of which are key factors in the category of health care reform.

- Which leads to my conclusion that we are all wrong.

- It also requires knowledge. Knowledge of the various strategies to utilize. [the second sentence is the fragment]

- **Prescription drug controls, physician referrals, and tax write-offs for medical necessities are** all key factors in the category of health care reform. [correction: added a subject and predicate]

- **My computer search comes up with different answers**, which leads to my conclusion that we are all wrong. [correction: attached the fragment to an independent clause]

- It also requires **knowledge of the various strategies to utilize**. [correction: removed the repeated term and omitted the period to attach the fragment to the preceding independent clause.

7. RUN-ON SENTENCES

Run-on sentences are the opposite of fragments in the sense that they combine two or more independent clauses without proper punctuation or conjunctions. To fix them, either formally combine them using **conjunctions** such as *and* or *because* or split them using a semicolon or period. Run-on sentences can occur easily, as these examples attest. Possible revisions are given after the run-ons.

- The film ends showing the viewer one of the most influential waves ever surfed in Loftus's review it is described as "perfect."

- It was dark, you could not see the tropical, mountainous lush lands of the island but you could feel the energy of the island and the people around you.

- I had no idea what I was in for I knew that I was going to be a grown-up and living on my own.

- The film ends showing the viewer one of the most influential waves ever surfed in Loftus's review; it is described as "perfect." [added semicolon]

- It was dark. You could not see the tropical and mountainous lands of the island, but you could feel the energy of the island and the people around you. [substituted a period for the comma, thus eliminating the comma splice; added comma]

- I had no idea what I was in for, **but** I knew that I was going to be a grown-up and living on my own. [added a comma and the conjunction "but"]

8. COMMA RULES

Many commas are optional, but many are also required. Review the following most common comma rules for times when a comma is necessary.

- Use a comma before a coordinating conjunction that joins two independent clauses. Coordinating conjunctions are sometimes referred to as FANBOYS, an acronym that stands for "for," "and," "nor," "but," "or," "yet," and "so."

  I always drive carefully, **but** it is harder to do when I am in a hurry.

- Use a comma after introductory phrases.

  Once I am home, I can relax with my cat.

- Use a comma between items in a series.

  The fruit bowl was filled with **apples, oranges, pears, peaches, and grapefruit**.

- Use a comma to set off a nonrestrictive clause—a clause that gives additional information that is unnecessary for the sentence to be clear. If you can remove a phrase in the sentence without changing the meaning of the sentence, you have likely identified a nonrestrictive clause. Commas should also be used to set off parenthetical phrases, which are similar.

The novel *The Bluest Eye*, **by Toni Morrison,** is an elaboration of a scene from Ralph Ellison's *Invisible Man*.

My Uncle Jimmie, **who loved sweets,** was always happy to see me.

- Use a comma to set off a direct address, the words yes, and *no* interjections, and questions embedded within the sentence.

Billie, will you please come here.

Yes, I will help with the meeting.

Well, well, it's sometimes so hard to make a decision.

I wish it wasn't so cold, **don't you**?

- Commas should not be used to separate two independent clauses (two full sentences). This is a misuse of the comma and is called a comma splice. Either a period or semicolon should be used instead.

We couldn't wait to get to the club, almost everyone was already there and dressed to kill.

We couldn't wait to get to the club; almost everyone was already there and dressed to kill.

9. FAULTY PARALLELISM
When multiple words, phrases, or clauses are used within a sentence, they should be balanced or expressed in parallel form. For example,

Becausee I was still underage, I had to coerce my stepmother into allowing me to get my tongue pierced but also having a tattoo around my belly button.

I had to coerce my stepmother to allow me to get **my tongue pierced** and **my belly-button tattooed** because I was still underage. [each of these phrases is made parallel with a pronoun, noun, and verb, e.g., "my tongue pierced"]

By documentary form, I mean a director will storyboard the scenes chronologically or in any way that presents the materials accurately and comprehensible to the viewers.

By documentary form, I mean a director will storyboard the scenes chronologically or in any way that presents the materials **accurately** and **comprehensibly** to the viewers. [the noun *comprehensible* was turned into an adverb to parallel *accurately*]

10. DANGLING PARTICIPLE OR DANGLING PREPOSITION

A dangling participle is when the conjugated verb "to be" is left hanging at the end of the sentence. In such cases, the reader is likely to ask, "is what?" or "be what?" A dangling preposition is when a preposition is left hanging at the end of the sentence, and the reader is likely to ask, "for what?" or "into what?"

- She was selfish, and this is the way she always was. [**correction**: She was always selfish.]

- I do not know what his favorite cake flavor is. [**correction**: I do not know his favorite cake flavor.]

- The search for the house is what we went for. [**correction**: We went to search for the house.]

- Who is the gift from? [**correction**: From whom is this gift?]

EIGHT STYLE POINTS

1. introduce and give context for quotations

2. use past tense for historical events and present tense

3. avoid excessively informal language, slang, and abbreviations

4. avoid long summaries of information that the reader is likely to know already

5. avoid wordiness, redundancy, and repetition

6. avoid passive construction

7. don't overuse "to be" verbs

8. use varied sentences

Style Points

1. INTRODUCE AND GIVE CONTEXT FOR QUOTATIONS.

Try to **incorporate quotations** into your text **naturally**. One way to do this is to state who said the quotation. The first quotation is poorly incorporated; the revision incorporates the quotation within a more natural feel:

> Livy was one of Rome's most important historians. "There is this exceptionally beneficial and fruitful advantage to be derived from the study of the past, that you see, set in the clear light of historical truth, examples of every possible type" (Livy, Mellor p. 171). He believed that the study of history was beneficial.

Livy was one of Rome's most important historians. He believed that the study of history was beneficial, **going so far as to say that** "there is this exceptionally beneficial and fruitful advantage to be derived from the study of the past, that you see, set in the clear light of historical truth, examples of every possible type" (Livy, Mellor p. 171).

2. USE PAST TENSE FOR HISTORICAL EVENTS AND PRESENT TENSE WHEN TALKING ABOUT TEXTS.

Generally speaking, use the past tense to describe events that actually took place in the past, as when you are writing about history.

During the Puritan Era of American History, women were expected to play the traditional roles of housewives and mothers. They awoke early, they worked hard, and they slept well at night with the sense that they had well cared for their families.

Use the present tense when you are explicating texts.

When John Bogan writes about the Puritan tradition in colonial America, he describes the place of women as a lonely one. He argues that women's location in the home separates them from the community and leaves women to depend on the companionship of children. His view of Puritan motherhood is pessimistic, making you glad that you did not have to live then.

If you have a paper that mixes historical events with textual explication, you will have to make conscious choices about what tense(s) to use. If large sections of your paper are historical or text based you may decide to use the past tense in a large section of your paper, and then the present tense in a large section of your paper. In any case, avoid switching verb tenses within paragraphs. Do your best to make sure that the tenses of your verbs are logical and as **consistent** as possible.

3. AVOID EXCESSIVELY INFORMAL LANGUAGE, SLANG, AND ABBREVIATIONS.

Abbreviations might appear too informal or unprofessional to some readers. In addition, avoid the use of slang. Some readers might appreciate the use of slang, while others might not. Formal language is not likely to offend anyone, so it is the preferred choice. Here are two examples of slang that have been revised:

Jim Smith is, hands down, the most powerful person in the room. He can't leave or the meeting would abruptly end. [**correction**: Everyone recognized that Jim Smith was the most powerful person in the room. He cannot leave or the meeting would abruptly end.]

Bob Brown is not that kind of guy; he wants to know everything and hates being caught off guard and out of it. [**correction**: Bob Brown especially dislikes being uniformed and put at a disadvantage.]

4. AVOID LONG SUMMARIES OF INFORMATION THAT THE READER IS LIKELY TO KNOW ALREADY.

Assume that the reader is familiar with the issue at hand and provide summaries of information only when it is likely that the reader is not familiar with that information or when it is absolutely necessary for you to make your arguments. **Summarized information cannot by itself prove your thesis. You must provide analysis** that relates such information back to your thesis and explains how or why it supports your thesis.

5. AVOID WORDINESS, REDUNDANCY, AND REPETITION.

A reader will likely stop reading a paper that goes on too long and/or repeats itself. This can take place at the sentence or paragraph level of a paper. Here are two examples:

> This morning the lesson will begin at 10:00 a.m. [better to delete "a.m."; it's redundant because the sentence already states that it is a morning lesson]

> List the items carefully, one-by-one. [better to delete "one-by-one" as this is implied by "carefully"]

When a sentence seems to have excessive detail, readers will be turned off. The revisions that follow the next three examples present the text succinctly.

> The director of the documentary will usually always create a film that he or she is interested in or has a different point of view that they feel they need to show.

> When one decides to watch a movie, deciding which movie to watch is the obstacle in whether the movie will be a good movie or something one wouldn't pay for again.

> Because reality can be manipulated and biased in accordance to the way the director of the documentary desires and still preserve the feeling of truth, that is the biggest advantage of documentary films.

- A director of a documentary film usually creates films that he/she feels have a new point of view, a view he/she believes needs to be shown.

- When planning to watch a movie, the process of deciding which movie to watch can influence whether you think it is a good movie or one not worth the price.

- The biggest advantage of documentary films is that a director can manipulate reality and still preserve the feeling of truth.

6. AVOID PASSIVE CONSTRUCTION.

Use the active voice whenever possible because it keeps your writing lively and clear. A verb is in the active voice when the subject of the sentence does the acting. A verb in the passive voice leaves the subject in the position of being acted on by an agent that either is not expressed or is identified in a prepositional phrase. Use the passive construction when you want your sentence to emphasize the receiver, rather than the doer, of the action. In the following example, the first sentence uses a passive format, while the second sentence uses an active format. Notice how the second sentence seems more lively than the first sentence.

> The DNA double helix was discovered by James Watson and Francis Crick.

> James Watson and Francis Crick discovered the DNA double helix.

7. DON'T OVERUSE "TO BE" VERBS.

Sentences that use "to be" verbs, such as "is," "are," and "was," tend to be lifeless, and the overuse of this verb will make your writing seem dull and primary. Whenever possible, replace "to be" verb forms with an active verb.

> Sylvia Plath **is** a poet who often wrote about death.

> Sylvia Plath frequently **explores** death in her poems.

8. USE VARIED SENTENCES.

A reader can easily get bored reading a paragraph that employs the same sentence structure over and over again. To keep the prose lively—and your reader interested—try to vary your sentence structure.

> I think regular exercise is the best thing in the world. I used to think doing exercise was too much trouble, but now I know differently. I once had a roommate who seemed like an exercise fanatic to me, but now that I have formed the habit of regular exercise, I can see how different my life is now that I exercise compared to when I did not exercise. I wish everyone knew how much better life is with regular exercise, but I know some people will never try it.

This example repeats a simple sentence structure that begins with a noun/verb phrase, "I know" or "I think" or "I have," too often. It also relies on a sentence pattern that includes coordinating conjunctions and repeating word choices. This repetitive style makes the paragraph seem overly simplistic. Vary the sentence style to improve it.

> I used to think that doing exercise was too much trouble. My roommate, who jogged regularly, seemed like an exercise fanatic to me. Now that I have formed the habit of working out regularly, I can see how it improves my life. Everyone should do something physically challenging every day.

Using a Style Manual

Whenever you write a paper that includes outside sources, you will be expected to follow the rules of a style manual regarding elements such as the physical format of the paper, the proper use of quotations, the meticulous documentation of print and electronic sources, and the standards for avoiding plagiarism. Style manuals, in other words, show you how to prepare a piece of writing. Although there are several accepted systems for using and acknowledging sources, this section will focus on two: the **Modern Language Association (MLA)**, used primarily in the humanities, and the **American Psychological Association (APA)**, used primarily in the social sciences. For most of your essay assignments, you will follow one of these. If you are required to use another, do not worry. Once you are familiar with how a style manual works, you can use alternative manuals with confidence. If you follow the rules of an accepted system for using and acknowledging sources, your research papers will reflect responsible and reliable scholarship and will win serious consideration from your readers.

If you have formatting questions that go beyond the scope of this appendix, the reference section in your campus library will have the *MLA Handbook for Writers of Research Papers* and *The Publication Manual of the American Psychological Association*. These publications contain the complete rules for writers. Both of these guides are also available online.

Basic Guidelines for Formatting a Paper

- Use a computer to type your paper and print it out on standard 8.5 × 11-inch white paper.

- Double-space the entire paper. Use a standard font such as 12-point. Times New Roman or Courier and set the margins on all sides to 1 inch. Indent the first line of each paragraph five spaces. When using the APA style, single-spacing can be used when it will improve readability, such as for table titles and headings or for long quotations.

- Number all pages in the upper right-hand corner, one-half inch from the top and flush with the right margin (use the header feature in your word processing program). When using MLA style, include your last name with the page number. When using APA style, include a shortened version of your paper's title.

- Italicize the titles of books, plays, periodicals, Web sites, films/television shows, and works of visual art included in your paper. Use quotation marks around titles of essays, articles, chapters of books, pages on Web sites, television episodes, and unpublished works (lectures/speeches).

Formatting the First Page of Your Paper in MLA Style (Figure C.1)

- Do not make a cover page for your paper unless your instructor requires one. Instead, type your name, your instructor's name, the course, and the date in the upper left-hand corner of the first page. Don't forget to double-space this information.

- Create a header in the upper right-hand corner, one-half inch from the top of the page, that includes only your last name and a page number. This header should appear on every page of your paper (even the first page), with each page numbered consecutively.

- Under your name, the course information, and the date, center the title of your paper. Do not underline or italicize it. Do not put it in quotation marks. Capitalize the first letter of all major words. Do not capitalize articles (a, the, an), short prepositions, or conjunctions unless it is the first word in a title.

- If your title contains a title, italicize the included title. The titles of short works, such as a poem or a short article, get quotation marks.

Formatting the First Pages of Your Paper in APA Style

- The APA format requires a title page. The paper's title should be centered horizontally and vertically on the page, followed on the next line by your name (also centered horizontally), and on a third line by your course and section number. You may also be asked to include your instructor's name and the date. The title page should be double spaced.

- Create a header in the upper right-hand corner, one-half inch from the top of the page and flush with the right margin, that includes a shortened version of your paper's title followed by five spaces and then the page number.

- Page two typically gives an abstract—a brief (100–150 words) comprehensive summary—of the research paper. The word *Abstract* is centered as the first line of type on this page. Type the abstract as a single paragraph in block format.

- Page three is the beginning of the body of the paper. The title of the paper should be centered at the top, and the first line of the body of the paper should be double-spaced below the title.

Acknowledging Sources

Plagiarism and How to Avoid It

In general, plagiarism is using someone else's words or ideas—whether done deliberately or accidentally—as if they are your own. Your responsibility to give appropriate credit for someone else's words or ideas covers anything from entire papers to paragraphs and even sentences or special terms. It also covers spoken or written material in any

Fig C.1 Sample of a First Page in MLA Style

Patrick Sweeney

Professor _____

English 1B

February 18, 2009

Alleviating Traffic Congestion

Almost every person in Southern California has his or her life affected by traffic each time he or she ventures outside the house. We all loathe traffic and how it makes us late, wastes our time, and just generally frustrates us. What many people don't realize are the society-wide implications of excessive traffic congestion. Traffic is a monumental problem in our region, and it will take a wide range of solutions coupled with cooperation from all sectors of society to eradicate this affliction.

Redesigning the motorways of Southern California will be expensive, but not redesigning them will cost us even more money. In "Traffic Congestion," Charles S. Clark declares that

"The time people spend twiddling their thumbs in gridlock amounts to 510,000 hours per day, which costs the state an estimated $4.8 million daily in lost productivity." Every day, commuters are late to work because of traffic, and once they arrive, have lowered productivity due to the stress and frustration from sitting in traffic all morning. In addition, companies in the shipping business lose money every time their trucks are sitting on the freeway not moving and have to raise prices because of the time lost and gas used while stuck in traffic. This puts a strain on all other businesses because they have to wait longer for shipments and pay more for them. Rearranging our roads and redesigning traffic flow will alleviate those problems and will create jobs that will stimulate the local economy. Rebuilding will require more spending by local and state

form, from statistics and spreadsheets to artwork, interviews, lectures, and electronic material. You must not only give appropriate credit to words and ideas from professional and nonprofessional writers and publications, but you must also credit a friend or classmate, or even a paper-writing service you may have found online if you use their words or ideas.

You do not have to credit information considered to be *common knowledge*. If you are writing a paper on Ernest Hemingway, for example, and you read in three or more sources that he was a cat lover, you do not have to credit the sources of this information because it is widely known and accepted. Generally speaking, information that you find in more than three sources can be considered common knowledge and does not require a citation. In addition, familiar sayings, well-known quotations, and common proverbs or tales generally do not require a citation.

Use common sense and your own ethics when deciding whether documentation of information is necessary. Keep in mind that it must always be clear to your readers which ideas are your own and which ideas are those of others. Even if you change the wording and omit some of the details, you must let your reader know by clearly and carefully citing the ideas of others that you incorporate into your paper. It isn't enough to list your sources at the end of your paper or to tack a citation at the end of a section of your paper, leaving it unclear as to which ideas are another's and which are yours. Your college or university puts the burden of responsibility on you, so claiming that you "didn't plagiarize deliberately" or "didn't realize that you weren't supposed to do that" will not be a reasonable justification. Always ask your instructor if you are unsure about the rules of citation.

How to Include Others' Ideas in Your Paper

BASIC IN-TEXT CITATION RULES USING MLA
When following style rules, you must use what is known as *parenthetical citation* when referring to the works of others in your text. Immediately following quoted or paraphrased material from a source, use parentheses to give the author's name followed by a space and the relevant page number(s).

> One writer claims that, for the artist, "the things that hurt him and the things that helped him cannot be divorced from each other" (Baldwin 9).

If you identify the author in your text, give only the page number in the parenthetical citation.

> According to writer James Baldwin, for the artist, "the things that hurt him and the things that helped him cannot be divorced from each other" (9).

Or, when using paraphrase,

> According to James Baldwin, life's challenges as well as life's blessings make the artist what he is (9).

When the author is unknown, give a shortened title of the work instead of an author's name. Put the title in quotation marks if it's a short work; italicize it if it is a longer work.

> Our country's park system is being eroded by a lack of funding on the national level ("National Parks").

When you are using sources by two authors with the same last name, include a first initial in all citations.

> Ancient kings were commonly called priests; this was "no empty form of speech but the expression of a sober belief" (Frazier, J. 8).

When you are using two or more works by the same author, put a comma after the author's last name and give a shortened version of the title.

> In many mythological stories, "the hero becomes, by virtue of the ceremonial, more than man" (Campbell, *Hero* 22).

When you are using an indirect source, that is, a source cited in another source, use "qtd. in" (which is short for "quoted in") to indicate that you did not consult the original source. Because you are responsible for your research, you should always try to locate and verify the original source.

> Robert Barnam writes that myths are "human stories created to help us understand ourselves and our place in the universe" (qtd. in Summers 87).

When you cite lines of poetry, mark the ends of lines using a slash.

> Sylvia Plath, creating poetry from her experience as a woman, wife, and mother, wrote that "A certain minor light may still / Lean incandescent / Out of kitchen table or chair" (56).

All parenthetical citations (all sources you referred to and cited within the text of your paper) must be included in the Works Cited page(s) at the end of your paper so that readers can find enough information about any of your sources to verify your understanding or use them in their own scholarly work. There will be more on this later.

BASIC IN-TEXT CITATION RULES USING APA
Using the APA system, the citation contains the last name of the author and the year of publication of the original work. If the cited material is a quotation, you should include the page numbers, too. Use commas to separate the author, year, and page and precede the page number with a *p.* for a single page or *pp.* for a range. Join the names of multiple authors with an ampersand (&).

> One historian claims that Samuel Johnson was considered by his peers to be the "reigning arbiter of all things of the mind, and no easy judge of men" (McCullough, 2005, p. 5).

If you identify the author in your text, cite the year in parentheses directly following the author's name and give the page reference in parentheses before the sentence period.

> According to Briggs (2005), "Lincoln achieved an oratorical distinction in the prepresidential years that may yet be underestimated" (p. 1).

Citations with unknown authors and works with two or more authors follow the MLA guidelines except that you must include year of publication and page numbers to conform to APA guidelines.

HOW TO INCLUDE LONG QUOTATIONS IN YOUR PAPER
For quotations *longer than four typed lines,* use the *block form* if you are using the MLA style rules. Indent the long quotation 1 inch from the left margin and double-space as shown in figure C.2.

Fig. C.2 Using a Block Quotation in MLA Style

It seems that 1892 to 1896 were years of great struggle for James. He was forced to abandon his ambition to become a successful dramatist. He had to come to terms with the suicide in 1894 of his good friend Constance Fenimore Woolson and the death of his sister just two years earlier. He wrote in his notebook, on 9 January 1894, from Venice:

> Last night, as I worried through some wakeful hours . . . I was turning over the drama, the tragedy, the general situation of disappointed ambition—and more particularly that of the artist, the man of letters: I mean of the ambition, the pride, the passion, the idea of greatness that has been smothered and defeated by circumstances, by the opposition of life, of fate, of character, of weakness, of folly, of misfortune . . . Then I thought of the forces, the reverses, the active agents to which such an ambition, such pride and passion, may succumb—before which it may have to lay down its arms: intrinsic weakness, accumulations of misfortune, failure, marriage, women, politics, death. (416)

> James seems to have his own experiences in his mind as
>
> he begins to sketch an idea for this story. His own life as an
>
> actor clearly led to some difficult decisions on his part and

When using APA style rules, block quotations include those that are *more than 40 words in length*. The entire block should be indented five spaces and single-spaced (double-spaced in papers for publication); see figure C.3.

If an indented quotation comes from two or more paragraphs, indent the first line of each paragraph an additional one-quarter inch using MLA, or half-inch using APA.

PUNCTUATION CONSIDERATIONS
Always italicize the titles of long works. Put the titles of short works, or titles within titles, in quotation marks.

Time Magazine

The Complete Works of Edgar Allan Poe

"The Raven"

"An Analysis of Time" in Charles Dickens' *A Tale of Two Cities*

Use double quotation marks for quotes; single quotation marks are only used for quotations within a quotation.

According to Deborah Mix, Zimmerman "holds up *Zami* as a model of the 'more complex search for the source and meaning of identity' lesbian writers of color must undertake" (223).

Periods and commas always fall inside quotation marks, but colons, semicolons, exclamation points, and question marks fall outside of them, unless they are part of the quote. (You might remember this rule by saying, "if it's short, it's inside; if it's tall, it is outside.")

Fig C.3 Using a Block Quotation in APA Style

It seems that 1892 to 1896 were years of great struggle for

James. He was forced to abandon his ambition to become a

successful dramatist. He had to come to terms with the sui-

cide in 1894 of his good friend Constance Fenimore Woolson

and the death of his sister just two years earlier. He wrote in

his notebook, on 9 January 1894, from Venice:

> Last night, as I worried through some wakeful hours . . .
> I was turning over the drama, the tragedy, the general
> situation of disappointed ambition—and more particu-
> larly that of the artist, the man of letters: I mean of the
> ambition, the pride, the passion, the idea of greatness
> that has been smothered and defeated by circum-
> stances, by the opposition of life, of fate, of character, of
> weakness, of folly, of misfortune. . . . Then I thought of
> the forces, the reverses, the active agents to which such
> an ambition, such pride and passion, may succumb—
> before which it may have to lay down its arms: intrinsic
> weakness, accumulations of misfortune, failure, mar-
> riage, women, politics, death. (Edel, 1986, p. 416)

In James Frazier's book on the roots of religion and folklore, he claims that ancient folk customs show a tendency, with the growth of civilization, to shrink from "solemn ritual" into "mere pageantry."

Can we agree with Freud's statement that human actions are not simple "thanks to the discrepancies between people's thoughts and their actions and to the diversity of their wishful impulses"?

Freud's intriguing question for scholars is "What do women want?"

Formatting the Works Cited Page(s) of Your Paper Using MLA

The last section of a paper using the MLA style guide should be titled Works Cited. This is where you give a list of the reference sources you used in writing your paper. The words *Works Cited* should be centered at the top of the page. Note that this page has the same one-inch margins and header requirement a the rest of the paper. All lines in this section should be double-spaced, including the lines between entries. See figure C.4.

- Capitalize each word in the titles of articles, books, and so forth, except for prepositions, conjunctions, and articles (unless it is the first word of a title):

The Portrait of a Lady

The Fundamentals of a Working Society in the Twenty-first Century

- Entries are listed in alphabetical order by authors' last names (or editors' names):

Horner, James T.

Muller, Susan Marie, ed.

- Do not list authors' titles or degrees but do include Jr. or Sr. when given.

- For each entry, indent all lines after the first by one-half inch.

Fig C.4 An MLA Works Cited Example

Cantor, Norman. *Imagining the Law: Common Law and the Foundations of the American Legal System*. New York: Harper Collins Publisher, 1997.

Dimock, Wai Chee. *Residues of Justice: Literature, Law, and Philosophy*. Berkeley: UC Press, 1996.

Scholes, Robert. "Toward a Semiotics of Literature." *Critical Inquiry* 4.1 (1977): 105-20. 2 Feb. 2009 http://www.journals.uchicago.edu/action/jstor?doi=10.1086%2F447926

Generally speaking, always provide enough information so that readers can locate cited articles—whether in print or electronic form. Remember that a work should not appear on the Works Cited page(s) unless it is cited in your paper, and vice versa.

SOME TYPICAL ENTRIES USING MLA STYLE

For a **single-author book,** the name is written with last name first followed by a comma and the first name. Then comes the book's title followed by a period, the city of publication followed by a colon, the name of the publisher followed by a comma, the date of publication followed by a period.

> Dove, George. *The Reader and the Detective Story*. Bowling Green: Bowling Green State UP, 1997.

For an **edited volume**, cite the book as you normally would, but add "ed." next to the editor's name.

> Cucinella, Catherine, ed. *Contemporary American Women Poets*. Westport: Greenwood Press, 2002.

OR

> Bishop, Elizabeth. *The Collected Prose*. Ed. Robert Giroux. New York: The Noonday Press, 1984.

For entries in **encyclopedias**, **dictionaries**, and **other reference works**, do not include the publisher information in the citation. If the author's name is included, list that first. If not, begin with the article's title.

> "Existentialism." *The American Heritage Encyclopedia*. 3rd ed. 2007.

If **two or more books are by the same author**, a the first listing of the author's name, use three hyphens and a period instead of the author's name. List books alphabetically by title.

> Pound, Ezra. *The A B C of Reading*. New York: New Directions Books, 1970.

> ---. *The Spirit of Romance*. New York: New Directions Books, 1968.

If a book has **no author or editor** given, list and alphabetize by the title of the book.

> *Encyclopedia of Illinois*. New York: Somerset, 2003.

For **translated books**, cite as you would any other book and add "Trans." followed by the translator's name after the title of the book.

> Freud, Sigmund. *Civilization and Its Discontents*. Trans. James Strachey. New York: W.W. Norton & Co., 1961.

For **poems** or **short stories**, treat as if there were a book editor for a chapter in a book.
Bishop, Elizabeth. "Cape Breton." *The Complete Poems 1927–1979*. New York: Noonday Press, 1979. Print.

Cite **dissertations** and **master's theses** as you would a book but include the designation Diss. (or MA/MS thesis) followed by the degree-granting school and the year the degree was awarded. Enclose the title in quotation marks—do not italicize it.

Bile, Jeffrey. "Ecology, Feminism, and a Revised Critical Rhetoric: Toward a Dialectical Partnership." Diss. Ohio University, 2005.

For articles in a magazine, cite by listing the article's author, putting the title of the article in quotation marks, and italicizing the periodical title. Follow with the date and abbreviate the month (except for May, June, and July).

Poniewozik, James. "TV Makes a Too-Close Call." *Time* 20 Nov. 2000: 70–71.

Buchman, Dana. "A Special Education." *Good Housekeeping*. Mar. 2006: 143–148.

Cite a **newspaper article** as you would a magazine article. If there is more than one edition available for that date (as in an early and late edition of a newspaper), identify the edition following the date (e.g., 27 May 2007, early ed.)

Brubaker, Bill. "New Health Center Targets County's Uninsured Patients." *Washington Post* 24 May 2007: LZ01.

For articles in a **scholarly journal**, include author, title of article, title of journal, volume issue, year, and pages.

Bagchi, Alaknanda. "Conflicting Nationalisms: The Voice of the Subaltern in Mahasweta Devi's *Bashai Tudu*." *Tulsa Studies in Women's Literature*. 15.1 (1996): 41–50. Print.

For other reference materials, such as photographs, television shows, e-mail, Web pages, interviews, and surveys, consult the MLA or APA style manuals available in the library or online.

Today, Web pages are common sources of information. Here is some information you should look for and record when searching electronic sources:

- author and/or editor names
- name of the database, or title of project, book, article
- version number and date
- publisher information
- date you found the information
- the electronic address (the URL)

Following is the basic format for an electronic source:

Name of Site. Date of Posting/Revision. Name of institution/organization affiliated with the site (sometimes found in copyright statements). Date you accessed the site, electronic address.

An article in an online scholarly journal should look like this:

Author's name. "Title of article." *Title of journal*. Volume number (year): page numbers (if available, if not, use n. pag.) date of access (day, month, and year) <URL>.

Shehan, Constance L., and Amanda B. Moras. "Deconstructing Laundry: Gendered Technologies and the Reluctant Redesign of Household Labor." *Michigan Family Review* 11 (2006): n. pag. 8 Nov. 2008 http://quod.lib.umich.edu/cgi/t/text/text-idx?c=mfr;cc=mfr; q1=shehan;rgn=main;view=text;idno=4919087.0011.104.

Formatting the References Page(s) of Your Paper Using APA

With the APA style, the sources of the paper are listed alphabetically on a separate page titled "References." Like the MLA Works Cited page(s), entries are listed in alphabetical order according to authors' last names (figure C.5). The section is double-spaced, and the initial line of each entry should be indented about five spaces. (Note: this is the reverse of MLA style, where, for each entry, the first line is on the left margin and subsequent lines are indented.)

Fig C.5 References Page for an APA Formatted Paper References

Campbell, Joseph (1972). *The Hero with a Thousand Faces*.

Princeton: PrincetonUniversity Press.

Frazer, James A. (1981). *The Golden Bough: the Roots of Religion*

and Folklore. New York: Avenel Books.

Friedman, Richard Elliott (1987). *Who Wrote the Bible?* Englewood

Cliffs: Prentice Hall.

Always provide enough information so that readers can locate cited articles. Consult the APA style guide for more information. Remember that a work should not appear on the References page unless it is cited in your paper, and vice versa.

Index

313

Q

"qtd. in" (quoted in), 304
qualifiers, use of, 145
question marks, 306
questions
    in introductions, 103
    multiple, in writing assignment, 158–163
    primary, 132, 134–136, 162–163, 165
quotation marks
    punctuation within, 306
    for quotations, 306
    for titles, 300, 304, 306, 309
    for titles within titles, 301, 306
quotations
    block form of, 305–306
    incorporating, 296
    in introductions, 103
    in writing about literature, 218
    use of, in research papers, 248–249
    in writing assignments, 137–139
quoted in (qtd. in), 304

R

reader-oriented perspective, 114
reasoning, 55–58, 84–87
recursiveness, of writing process, 17, 51
redundancy, 298
Rees, William E., 110–113
reference works, in Works Cited, 308
References Page, 310
relative terms, 265, 284
relevance, 247
repetition, 298
research
    academic essay format with,
      232–236
    in body paragraphs, 107
    methods for doing, 240–243
    organizing, 242–243
    primary, 187
research papers, 231–251
    checklist for revision of, 258–259
    format guidelines, 300–301
    peer review worksheet for, 259–260
response, to another writer's idea,
    136–137, 146, 166–168
results section
    field notebook, 201
    laboratory report, 197
    scientific research paper, 187, 191

reviewer, role of, in peer review workshop,
    115–116, 259
revising process, 17
revision, 113–116
    global, 17
    peer review workshop worksheet for,
      170–172
    research paper checklist for, 258–259
    tools for, 125–126
rhetoric, 4
Rhetoric (Aristotle), 4
rhetorical triangle, 15
Rivera, Diego, 168
A Rose for Emily (Faulkner), 219–225
Rundel, Philip W., 13–14
run-on sentences, 294

S

scholarly journals, in Works Cited, 309
scientific essays, 187–202
    diagram, 191
    formats for, 195–202
    laboratory reports, 196–200
    when to use, 175, 190–195
scientific research papers, 239–240
scope
    of assignment, 139, 143
    burdens of proof and, 87–88
    controlling idea (CI) statement and,
      180–181
    of informative research papers, 237
    of scientific research papers, 239
    in thesis statement, 29–33
Self-Portrait with Thorn and Hummingbird
    (Kahlo), 32
self-evidence and claims, 40–41
semicolons, 294, 295, 306
Sen, Amartya, 139–141
sentence fragments, 293
sentences
    with mixed construction, 292–293
    run-on, 294
    thesis statement, 27–28
    varied, use of, 299
Seven Steps, for drafting a thesis state-
    ment, 132–136
shift left method, 30–32, 41, 43
short stories, in Works Cited, 309
significance, 105
slang, 297

words
  as clues to essay type requirement, 186
  direction, 133–134
  excessive use of, 298
Wordsworth, William, 54
Works Cited, 251, 307–310
  indentation for, 307
  sources, 304
  spacing in, 307
worksheets
  peer review, 127–128, 170–172
  post-draft outline, 126–127
writer
  Aristotle's view of the, 15
  role of, in peer review workshop, 115, 259

writer-oriented perspective, 113–114
writing assignments, 136–146
  comparison and contrast, 152–155
  distinguishing required essay type, 185–186
  multiple part, 158–163, 165–166
  steps for analyzing, 131–136
  types of, 132, 136–146
writing process, 16–17
writing prompts (*See* writing assignments)

X
Xiong, Vicki, 19–21

Y
year of publication, 304, 305
your and *you're*, 290